The New
Answers
Book 2

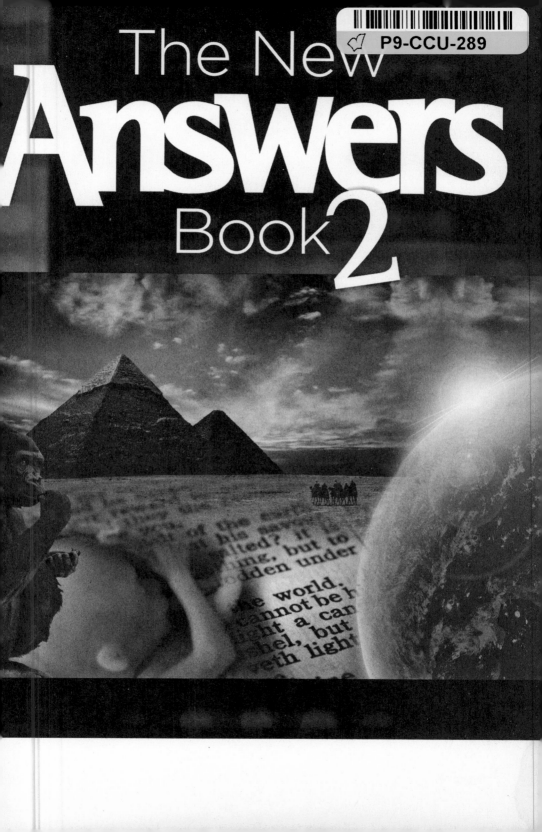

The New Answers Book 2

Book 2

Over 30 Questions on
Creation/Evolution and the Bible

Ken Ham General Editor

First printing: May 2008
Ninth printing: November 2011

ISBN: 978-0-89051-537-2
Library of Congress Number: 2008903202

Unless otherwise noted, the following versions of the Bible were used:
King James Version — introduction, chapters 3, 5, 18, and 20
New King James Version — chapters 4, 13, 14, 17, 19, 22, 25, 28, 29, and conclusion; Scripture taken from the New King James Version. Copyright © 1982 by Thomas Nelson, Inc. Used by permission. All rights reserved.
Modern King James Version — chapters 10, 11, and 12
New International Version — chapter 7

Please consider requesting that a copy of this volume be purchased by your local library system.

Printed in the United States of America

Please visit our website for other great titles:
www.masterbooks.net

For information regarding author interviews,
please contact the publicity department at (870) 438-5288.

Master
Books®
A Division of New Leaf Publishing Group
www.masterbooks.net

ACKNOWLEDGMENTS AND SPECIAL THANKS

We are especially grateful to the following people for lending their expertise in reviewing various aspects of this book:

Dr. Bob Compton (DVM), Dr. David Crandall (former international director of Gospel Literature Service), David Down (Egyptologist, editor-in-chief of the bimonthly magazine *Archaeological Diggings*), Brian Edwards (pastor, apologist, author), Steve Fazekas (theology), Dr. Werner Gitt (engineering; former director and professor at the German Federal Institute of Physics and Technology), Ken Ham (biology, president and CEO of Answers in Genesis-U.S.), Bodie Hodge (engineering, materials), Dave Jolly (biology), Dr. Jason Lisle (astrophysics), Stacia McKeever (biology, psychology), Dr. David Menton (cell biology, retired associate professor of anatomy at Washington University School of Medicine), Dr. Tommy Mitchell (internal medicine), Dr. Terry Mortenson (history of geology), Larry Pierce (chronologist/translator of the *Annals of the World* by James Ussher, and developer of *Online Bible*), Dr. Georgia Purdom (genetics), Dr. Andrew Snelling (geology), Dr. John Whitcomb (theology, president of Whitcomb Ministries), Dr. John Whitmore (geology, associate professor of geology at Cedarville University), Dr. John Reed (geology), David Wright (student of engineering), Gary Vaterlaus (science education).

We are also appreciative of the talents of Dan Lietha, who provided many of the illustrations used in this book. Dan Stelzer did several illustrations as well. All other illustrations that are not AiG images are noted on the illustration, figure, or photograph. Also, thanks to Stacia McKeever for much of the executive editing.

Contents

Why Is the Christian Worldview Collapsing in America?

KEN HAM

B ack in the 16th century, William Tyndale was persecuted, imprisoned, strangled, and his body burned at the stake. Why? Because he worked to translate the Scriptures into English and get copies of the Bible to the average person. Influenced by Luther and others, Tyndale was an integral part of the Reformation that spread God's written Word throughout the world — particularly to the Western world.

At that time, many church leaders believed the Bible should not be in the hands of the common person and that only appointed and scholarly church leaders should tell the public what they should believe. But the spread of God's written Word in the 1500s changed all that as it permeated many nations. It resulted in what we called the "Christian West." However, today we see the Christian influence in our Western world waning — Europe (especially the United Kingdom) is nearly dead spiritually. Right here in America, the Christian worldview is collapsing before our very eyes.

So What Is Happening?

First, let me point out that we need to be like the men of Issachar, who had "understanding of the times" (1 Chronicles 12:32). Today we are seeing an undoing of the Reformation, as society is not honoring some great people of God who were martyred for proclaiming the truths of the Bible.

The Reformation was a movement to call people to the authority of the Word of God. Almost 500 years later, we believe the teaching of millions of years and evolution has been the major tool in this era to undo the work of the Reformation.

To understand the times in which we live, we need to know how this sad transformation has come about — including how people view the Bible:

- The majority of church leaders have adopted the secular religion (i.e., millions of years/evolution) of the age and have compromised God's Word — thus undermining its authority to coming generations.

- Statistics are clear that most people in churches do not study their Bibles as they should. Frankly, we have a very biblically illiterate church today. We also observe church academics of our age beginning to impose a similar philosophy to that seen in Tyndale's time — that it is these learned leaders (most of whom have compromised God's Word) who determine what the public should believe. Increasingly, churchgoers are not like the Bereans who "searched the Scriptures daily to find out whether these things were so" (Acts 17:11).

I want to give you two specific examples of this dramatic change — and I believe you will be quite shocked.

The first is of Dr. James F. McGrath, who holds the Clarence L. Goodwin Chair in New Testament Language and Literature at Butler University in Indianapolis. Recently, Dr. McGrath wrote a blog item[1] concerning AiG's stand on a literal Genesis. First, he quoted another writer:

> Some may excuse Mr. Ham on the ground that he has no theological or biblical training (he has a bachelor's degree in applied science). I am not so inclined for one reason: by assuming the pulpit of churches and declaring he intends to interpret the Bible, he de facto sets himself up as a Bible teacher, and should be held accountable to know not only the relevant facts, but the proper way to exegete and teach a passage of scripture.

---

1. http://blog.echurchwebsites.org.uk/2010/08/03/ken-ham-rachel-held-evans-blogosphere.

If he does not want to give up seven years of his life and tens of thousands of dollars to get training in the Bible, theology, and the ancient languages (the standard degree program for clergy) then that is perfectly understandable. What is not so understandable is his desire to set himself up as a Bible teacher without getting Bible training.

Then Dr. McGrath followed with his own comments about the above statements:

Amen! . . . I think that the best course of action is for those who are well-informed about the Bible to debunk, refute and if necessary "refudiate" the statements of those who have no expertise in any field of scholarship related to the Bible, and yet believe that without any real knowledge of the original languages, historical context, and other relevant factors, their pontifications will do anything but harm the souls of believers and the Christian faith itself.

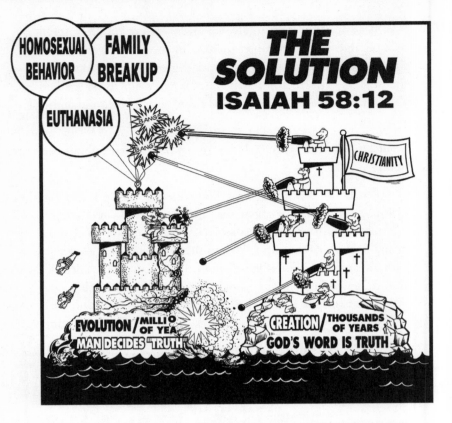

Well, it is true that I personally don't have formal theological training —
but there are those at Answers in Genesis who do (e.g., Dr. Terry Mortenson,
Steve Fazekas, Tim Chaffey, and some of our board members). And we do
have quite a number of other highly qualified theologians whose counsel we
seek to ensure we are accurate in handling God's Word.

By the way, I'm so glad I have not been theologically trained in the way
Dr. McGrath has (and sadly like many who are now being trained in Bible
colleges and seminaries). Otherwise, I might have ended up believing what
he wrote below:

> So why am I a Christian? . . . given that I do not espouse
> Biblical literalism and inerrancy, some might ask whether I am still
> a Christian. . . . I am a Christian in much the same way that I
> am an American . . . the tradition that gave birth to my faith and
> nurtured it is one that has great riches (as well as much else beside.
> . . . Why am I a Christian? Because I prefer to keep the tradition I

have, rather than discarding it with the bathwater and then trying to make something new from scratch.

The second sad example is from Dr. William Dembski, a professor at what is known as a conservative seminary in the South. What he proposes in his book *The End of Christianity* is an undermining of biblical authority, and it's an unfortunate example of the sort of compromise often being taught to our future pastors. Here are a few excerpts from his book:

> For the theodicy I am proposing to be compatible with evolution, God must not merely introduce existing human-like beings from outside the Garden. In addition, when they enter the Garden, God must transform their consciousness so that they become rational moral agents made in God's image.[2]

Also:

> Moreover, once God breathes the breath of life into them, we may assume that the first humans experienced an amnesia of their former animal life: Operating on a higher plane of consciousness once infused with the breath of life, they would transcend the lower plane of animal consciousness on which they had previously operated — though, after the Fall, they might be tempted to resort to that lower consciousness.[3]

Dr. Dembski also states:

> The young-earth solution to reconciling the order of creation with natural history makes good exegetical and theological sense. Indeed, the overwhelming consensus of theologians up through the Reformation held to this view. I myself would adopt it in a heartbeat except that nature seems to present such a strong evidence against it.[4]

By "nature" he is in essence accepting fallible scientists' interpretations of evidence (such as fossils, geologic layers, and so on). His statement concerning "good exegetical and theological sense" is the point exactly! In other

---

2. William A. Dembski, *The End of Christianity* (Nashville, TN: B & H Academic, 2009), p. 159.
3. Ibid., p. 154–155).
4. Ibid., p. 55.

words, we know what the clear teaching of Scripture is — and what the great Reformers knew. But Dembski rejects it.

We would say that Dr. Dembski (who may be a fine Christian man) is taking the belief in billions of years (obtained by man's fallible interpretations of the present in an attempt to connect to the past) as infallible, and in reality making God's Word fallible.

A "Genesis 3 Attack"

This is the "Genesis 3 attack" ("Did God Really Say?") in our era — undoing what the Reformation accomplished. We need a new Reformation to call our Church (and culture) back to the authority of the Word of God. This is why the ministry of Answers in Genesis is so vital today — please pray for us!

Thank you for supporting Answers in Genesis . . . and for helping to bring a new and much-needed Reformation to our church and culture. The battle before us is one about authority: is God's Word the authority, or is it man's words?

We will continue (despite the opposition we receive) to hold compromising church leaders accountable, and stand unashamedly and uncompromisingly on the authority of the Word of God. That's what the Answers in Genesis and Creation Museum outreaches are all about.

1

What Is a Biblical Worldview?

STACIA MCKEEVER & KEN HAM

The history as recorded in the Bible has been attacked by our increasingly secular culture. As a result, recent generations have been brought up to see the Bible as a book that contains many interesting stories and religious teaching, but has no connection to reality.

This limited viewpoint helps explain why there are so many questions about how the Bible can explain dinosaurs, fossils, death, suffering, and many other topics that relate to our real world.

This chapter will outline the major events of the past (and even the future) — the "7 Cs of History" — that are foundational to the Bible's important message and demonstrate how the Bible connects to the real world.

Creation

God created the heavens, the earth, and all that is in them in six normal-length days around 6,000 years ago. His completed *creation* was "very good" (Genesis 1:31), and all the original animals (including dinosaurs) and the first two humans (Adam and Eve) ate only plants (Genesis 1:29–30). Life was perfect and not yet  affected by the Curse — death, violence, disease, sickness, thorns, and fear had no part in the original creation.

After He was finished creating, God "rested" (or stopped) from His work, although He continues to uphold the creation (Colossians 1:17). His creation of all things in six days and resting on the seventh set a pattern for our week, which He designed for us to follow.

The science of "information theory" confirms that first statement of the Bible, "In the beginning God created. . . ." DNA is the molecule of heredity, part of a staggeringly complex system, more information dense than that in the most efficient supercomputer. Since the information in our DNA can only come from a source of greater information (or intelligence), there must have been something other than matter in the beginning. This other source must have no limit to its intelligence; in fact, it must be an ultimate source of intelligence from which all things have come. The Bible tells us there is such a source — God. Since God has no beginning and no end and knows all (Psalm 147:5), it makes sense that God is the source of the information we see all around us! This fits with real science, just as we would expect.[1]

In Genesis, God created things "after their kinds." And this is what we observe today: great variation within different "kinds" (e.g., dogs, cats, elephants, etc.), but not one kind changing into another, as molecules-to-man evolution requires.[2]

Corruption

After God completed His perfect creation, He told Adam that he could eat from any tree in the Garden of Eden (Genesis 2:8) except one — the Tree of the Knowledge of Good and Evil. He warned Adam that death would be the punishment for disobedience (Genesis 2:17). Instead of listening to the command of his Creator,  Adam chose to rebel, eating the fruit from the tree (Genesis 3:6). Because our Holy God must punish sin, He sacrificed animals to make coverings for Adam and Eve, and He sent the first couple from the garden, mercifully denying them access to the Tree of Life so that they would not live forever in their sinful state.

Adam's sin ushered death, sickness, and sorrow into the once-perfect creation (Genesis 3:19; Romans 5:12). God also pronounced a curse on the world (Genesis 3; Romans 8:20–22). As a result, the world that we now live in is a decaying remnant — a *corruption* — of the beautiful, righteous world that Adam and Eve originally called home. We see the results of this corruption all

---

1. For a more in-depth analysis of the complexity of DNA and information theory, see www. AnswersInGenesis.org/go/information_theory.
2. For more information, see www.AnswersInGenesis.org/go/kinds.

around us in the form of carnivorous animals, mutations, sickness, disease, and death.[3] The good news is that, rather than leave His precious handiwork without hope, God graciously promised to one day send a Redeemer who would buy back His people from the curse of sin (Genesis 3:15).

Catastrophe

As the descendants of Adam and Eve married and filled the earth with offspring, their wickedness was great (Genesis 6:5). God judged their sin by sending a global flood to destroy all men, animals, creatures that moved along the ground, and birds of the air (Genesis 6:7). Those God chose to enter the ark — Noah, his family, and land-dwelling representatives of the animal kingdom (including dinosaurs) — were saved from the watery *catastrophe*.

There was plenty of room in the huge vessel for tens of thousands of animals — even dinosaurs (the average dinosaur was only the size of a sheep, and Noah didn't have to take fully grown adults of the large dinosaurs). Noah actually needed only about 16,000 animals on the ark to represent all the distinct kinds of land-dwelling animals.[4]

This earth-covering event has left its mark even today. From the thousands of feet of sedimentary rock found around the world to the billions of dead things buried in rock layers (fossils), the Flood reminds us even today that our righteous God cannot — and will not — tolerate sin, while the ark reminds us that He provides a way of salvation from sin's punishment. The rainbows we experience today remind us of God's promise never again to destroy the earth with water (Genesis 9:13–15). Incidentally, if the Flood were a local event (rather than global in extent), as some claim, then God has repeatedly broken His promise since we continue to experience local flooding even today.[5]

Confusion

After the Flood, God commanded Noah and his family — the only humans left in the world — and the animals to fill the earth (Genesis 8:17). However, the human race once again disobeyed God's command and

---

3. For more information, see www.AnswersInGenesis.org/go/curse.
4. See *Noah's Ark: A Feasibility Study* by John Woodmorappe (Santee, CA: Institute for Creation Research, 1996) for a detailed analysis of the capacity of this huge ship to hold all the residents of the ark.
5. For more information, see www.AnswersInGenesis.org/go/flood.

built a tower, which they hoped would keep them together (Genesis 11:3–4). So, around 100 years after the Flood waters had retreated, God brought a *confusion* (a multiplicity) of languages in place of the common language the people shared, causing them to spread out over the earth. The several different languages created suddenly at Babel (Genesis 10–11) could each subsequently give rise to many more. Languages gradually change; so when a group of people breaks up into several groups that no longer interact, after a few centuries they may each speak a different (but related) language. Today, we have thousands of languages but fewer than 20 language "families."[6]

All the tribes and nations in the world today have descended from these various groups. Despite what you may have been led to believe about our seeming superficial differences, we really are all "one blood" (Acts 17:26) — descendants of Adam and Eve through Noah and his family — and all, therefore, are in need of salvation from sin.

God had created Adam and Eve with the ability to produce children with a variety of different characteristics. This ability was passed on through Noah and his family. As the people scattered, they took with them different amounts of genetic information for certain characteristics — e.g., height, the amount of pigment for hair and skin color (by the way, we all have the same pigment, just more or less of it), and so on.

In fact, the recent Human Genome Project supports this biblical teaching that there is only *one* biological race of humans. As one report says, "It is clear that what is called 'race' . . . reflects just a few continuous traits determined by a tiny fraction of our genes."[7] The basic principles of genetics explain various shades of *one* skin color (not different colors) and how the distinct people groups (e.g., American Indians, Australian Aborigines) came about because of the event at the Tower of Babel. The creation and Flood legends of these peoples, from all around the world, also confirm the Bible's anthropology to be true.

Christ

God's perfect creation was corrupted by Adam when he disobeyed God, ushering sin and death into the world. Because of Adam's disobedience and because we have all sinned personally, we are all deserving of the death penalty and need a Savior (Romans 5:12).

---

6. For more information, see www.AnswersInGenesis.org/go/linguistics.
7. S. Pääbo, "The Human Genome and Our View of Ourselves," *Science* 29, no. 5507 (2001): 1219–1220.

As mentioned before, God did not leave His precious — but corrupted — creation without hope. He promised to one day send Someone who would take away the penalty for sin, which is death (Genesis 3:15; Ezekiel 18:4; Romans 6:23).

God killed at least one animal in the Garden of Eden because of the sin of Adam; subsequently, Adam's descendants sacrificed animals. Such sacrifices could only cover sin — they pointed toward the time when the One whom God would send (Hebrews 9) would make the ultimate sacrifice.

When God gave Moses the Law, people began to see that they could never measure up to God's standard of perfection (Romans 3:20) — if they broke any part of the Law, the result was the same as breaking all of it (James 2:10). They needed Someone to take away their imperfection and present them faultless before God's throne (Romans 5:9; 1 Peter 3:18).

In line with God's purpose and plan for everything, He sent His promised Savior at just the right time (Galatians 4:4). There was a problem, however. All humans are descended from Adam and therefore, all humans are born with sin. God's chosen One had to be perfect, as well as infinite, to take away the infinite penalty for sin.

God solved this "problem" by sending His Son, Jesus *Christ* — completely human and completely God. Think of it: the Creator of the universe (John 1:1–3, 14) became part of His creation so that He might save His people from their sins!

Jesus fulfilled more than 50 prophecies made about Him centuries before, showing He was the One promised over 4,000 years before by His Father (Genesis 3:15). While He spent over 30 years on earth, He never once sinned — He did nothing wrong. He healed many people, fed huge crowds, and taught thousands of listeners about their Creator God and how to be reconciled to Him. He even confirmed the truth of Genesis by explaining that marriage is between one man and one woman (Matthew 19:3–6, quoting Genesis 1:27 and 2:24).

Cross

Jesus is called the "Last Adam" in 1 Corinthians 15:45. While Adam disobeyed God's command not to eat the forbidden fruit, Jesus fulfilled the Creator's purpose that He die for the sin of the world.

The first Adam brought death into the world through his disobedience; the Last Adam brought eternal life with God through His obedience (1 Corinthians 15:21–22).

Because God is perfectly holy, He must punish sin — either the sinner himself or a substitute to bear His wrath. Jesus bore God's wrath for our sin by dying in our place on the Cross (Isaiah 53:6). The Lamb of God (John 1:29; Revelation 5:12) was sacrificed once for all (Hebrews 7:27), so that all those who believe in Him will be saved from the ultimate penalty for sin (eternal separation from God) and will live with Him forever.

Jesus Christ, the Creator of all things (John 1:1–3; Colossians 1:15–16), was not defeated by death. He rose three days after He was crucified, showing that He has power over all things, including death, the "last enemy" (1 Corinthians 15:26). As Paul wrote, "O death, where is your sting? O grave, where is your victory? . . . But thanks be to God who gives us the victory through our Lord Jesus Christ" (1 Corinthians 15:55–57).

When we believe in Christ and understand what He has done for us, we are passed from death into life (John 5:24). The names of those who receive Him are written in the Lamb's Book of Life (Revelation 13:8; 17:8) — when they die, they will go to be with Him forever (John 3:16).

Just as "science" cannot prove that Jesus rose from the dead, it also cannot prove that God created everything in six days. In fact, "science" can't prove any event from history because it is limited in dealings about the past. Historical events are known to be true because of reliable eyewitness accounts. In fact, there are reliable eyewitness accounts that Jesus' tomb was empty after three days and that He later appeared to as many as 500 people at once (1 Corinthians 15:6). Of course, we know that both the Resurrection and creation in six days are true because God, who cannot lie, states in His Word that these things happened.

While the secular history of millions of years isn't true, and evolutionary geology, biology, anthropology, astronomy, etc., do not stand the test of observational science, the Bible's history, from Genesis 1 onward, *is* true; the Bible's geology, biology, anthropology, astronomy, etc., are confirmed by observational science. Therefore, the fact that the Bible's history is true should challenge people to seriously consider the Bible's message of salvation that is based in this history.

Consummation

Death has been around almost as long as humans have. Romans 8 tells us that the whole of creation is suffering because of Adam's sin. As terrible as things are, however, they are not a permanent part of creation.

God, in His great mercy, has promised not to leave His creation in its sinful state. He has promised to do away with the corruption that Adam brought into the world. He has promised to remove, in the future, the curse He placed on His creation (Revelation 22:3) and to make a new heaven and a new earth (2 Peter 3:13). In this new place there will be no death, crying, or pain (Revelation 21:4).

Those who have repented and believed in what Jesus did for them on the Cross can look forward to the consummation of God's kingdom — this new heaven and earth — knowing they will enjoy God forever in a wonderful place. In the future, God will take away the corruption that was introduced in the Garden of Eden, giving us once again a perfect place to live!

A worldview based on a proper understanding of the history of the world, as revealed in the Bible, is what every Christian needs to combat our society's evolutionary propaganda.

2

What's the Best "Proof" of Creation?

KEN HAM

In the ongoing war between creation and evolution, Christians are always looking for the strongest evidence for creation. They are looking for the "magic bullet" that will prove to their evolutionist friends that creation is true and evolution is false. This craving for evidence has led some Christians to be drawn to what we might call "flaky evidence." Over the past several years, some so-called evidence for creation has been shown not to be reliable. Some of these are

- supposed human and dinosaur footprints found together at the Paluxy River in Texas;
- the small accumulation of moon dust found by the Apollo astronauts;
- a boat-like structure in the Ararat region as evidence of Noah's ark;
- a supposed human handprint found in "dinosaur-age rock";
- a dead "plesiosaur" caught near New Zealand.

Most well-meaning, informed creationists would agree in principle that things which are not carefully documented and researched should not be used. But in practice, many of them are very quick to accept the sorts of facts mentioned here, without asking too many questions. They are less cautious than they might otherwise be, because they are so keen to have "our" facts/evidences

to counter "theirs." What they really don't understand, however, is that it's not a matter of "their facts vs. ours." *All* facts are actually interpreted, and *all* scientists actually have the *same* observations — the same data — available to them.

Evidence

Creationists and evolutionists, Christians and non-Christians, all have the same facts. Think about it: we all have the same earth, the same fossil layers, the same animals and plants, the same stars — the facts are all the same.

The difference is in the way we all *interpret* the facts. And why do we interpret facts differently? Because we start with different *presuppositions*; these are things that are assumed to be true without being able to prove them. These then become the basis for other conclusions. *All* reasoning is based on presuppositions (also called *axioms*). This becomes especially relevant when dealing with past events.

Past and Present

We all exist in the present, and the facts all exist in the present. When one is trying to understand how the evidence

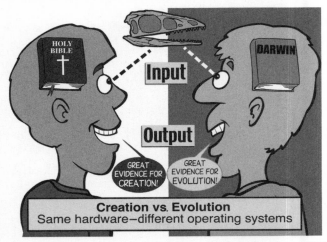

Creation vs. Evolution
Same hardware—different operating systems

came about — Where did the animals come from? How did the fossil layers form? etc. — what we are actually trying to do is to connect the past to the present. However, if we weren't there in the past to observe events, how can we know what happened so that we can explain the present? It would be great to have a time machine so that we could know for sure about past events.

Christians, of course, claim they do have, in a sense, a time machine. They have a book called the Bible, which claims to be the Word of God who has always been there and has revealed to us the major events of the past about which we need to know. On the basis of these events (creation, the Fall, the Flood, Babel, etc.), we have a set of presuppositions to build a way of thinking which enables us to interpret the facts of the present.[1]

Evolutionists have certain beliefs about the past/present that they presuppose (e.g., no God, or at least none who performed acts of special creation), so they build a different way of thinking to interpret the facts of the present.

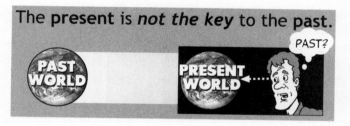

Thus, when Christians and non-Christians argue about the facts, in reality they are arguing about their *interpretations* based on their *presuppositions*.

That's why the argument often turns into something like:

"Can't you see what I'm talking about?"

"No, I can't. Don't you see how wrong you are?"

"No, I'm not wrong. It's obvious that I'm right."

"No, it's not obvious."

And so on.

These two people are arguing about the same facts, but they are looking at the facts through different glasses.

It's not until these two people recognize the argument is really about the presuppositions they have to start with that they will begin to deal with the foundational reasons for their different beliefs. A person will not interpret the facts differently until he or she puts on a different set of glasses — which means to change one's presuppositions.

1. See chapter 1 on "What Is a Biblical Worldview?" for further development of this idea.

A Christian who understands these things can actually put on the evolutionist's glasses (without accepting the presuppositions as true) and understand how he or she looks at facts. However, for a number of reasons, including spiritual ones, a non-Christian usually can't put on the Christian's glasses — unless he or she recognizes the presuppositional nature of the battle and is thus beginning to question his or her own presuppositions.

It is, of course, sometimes possible that just by presenting "evidence" one can convince a person that a particular scientific argument for creation makes sense on "the facts." But usually, if that person then hears a different *interpretation* of the same facts that seems better than the first, that person will swing away from the first argument, thinking he or she has found "stronger facts."

However, if that person had been helped to understand this issue of presuppositions, then he or she would have been better able to recognize this for what it is — a different interpretation based on differing presuppositions (i.e., starting beliefs).

Debate Terms

Often people who don't believe the Bible will say that they aren't interested in hearing about the Bible. They want real proof that there's a God who created. They'll listen to our claims about Christianity, but they want proof *without mentioning the Bible.*

If one agrees to a discussion without using the Bible as these people insist, then we have allowed *them* to set the terms of the debate. In essence these terms are

1. **"Facts" are neutral.** However, there are no such things as "brute facts"; *all* facts are interpreted. Once the Bible is eliminated from the argument, the Christians' presuppositions are gone, leaving them unable to effectively give an alternate interpretation of the facts. Their opponents then have the upper hand as they still have *their* presuppositions.

2. **Truth can/should be determined independently of God.** However, the Bible states: "The fear of the LORD is the beginning of wisdom" (Psalm 111:10); "The fear of the LORD is the beginning of knowledge" (Proverbs 1:7); "But the natural man does not receive the things of the Spirit of God, for they are foolishness to him; neither can he know them, because they are spiritually discerned" (1 Corinthians 2:14).

A Christian cannot divorce the spiritual nature of the battle from the battle itself. A non-Christian is *not* neutral. The Bible makes this very clear: "The one who is not with Me is against Me, and the one who does not gather with Me scatters" (Matthew 12:30); "And this is the condemnation, that the Light has come into the world, and men loved darkness rather than the Light, because their deeds were evil" (John 3:19).

Agreeing to such terms of debate also implicitly accepts the proposition that the Bible's account of the universe's history is irrelevant to understanding that history!

Ultimately, God's Word Convicts

First Peter 3:15 and other passages make it clear we are to use every argument we can to convince people of the truth, and 2 Corinthians 10:4–5 says we are to refute error (as Paul did in his ministry to the Gentiles). Nonetheless, we must never forget Hebrews 4:12: "For the word of God is living and powerful and sharper than any two-edged sword, piercing even to the dividing apart of soul and spirit, and of the joints and marrow, and is a discerner of the thoughts and intents of the heart."

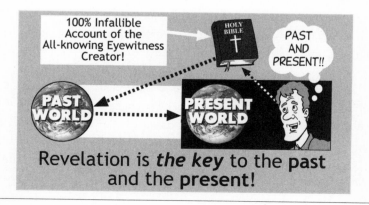

Revelation is *the key* to the past and the present!

Also, Isaiah 55:11 says, "So shall My word be, which goes out of My mouth; it shall not return to Me void, but it shall accomplish what I please, and it shall certainly do what I sent it to do."

Even though our human arguments may be powerful, ultimately it is God's Word that convicts and opens people to the truth. In all of our arguments, we must not divorce what we are saying from the Word that convicts.

Practical Application

When someone says he wants "proof" or "evidence," not the Bible, one might respond as follows:

> You might not believe the Bible, but I do. And I believe it gives me the right basis to understand this universe and correctly interpret the facts around me. I'm going to give you some examples of how building my thinking on the Bible explains the world and is not contradicted by science.

One can, of course, do this with numerous scientific examples, showing, for example, how the issue of sin and judgment is relevant to geology and fossil evidence; how the fall of man, with the subsequent curse on creation, makes sense of the evidence of harmful mutations, violence, and death; or how the original "kinds" of animals gave rise to the wide variety of animals we see today.

Choose a topic and develop it:

> For instance, the Bible states that God made distinct *kinds* of animals and plants. Let me show you what happens when I build my thinking on this presupposition. I will illustrate how processes such as natural selection, genetic drift, etc., can be explained and interpreted. You will see how the science of genetics makes sense based upon the Bible. Evolutionists believe in natural selection — that is real science, as you observe it happening. Well, creationists also believe in natural selection. Evolutionists accept the science of genetics — well, so do creationists.
>
> However, here is the difference: evolutionists believe that, over millions of years, one kind of animal has changed into a totally different kind. However, creationists, based on the Bible's account of origins, believe that God created separate kinds of animals and plants to reproduce their own kind; therefore, one kind will not turn into a totally different kind.

Now this can be tested in the present. The scientific observations support the creationist interpretation that the changes we see are not creating new information. The changes are all within the originally created pool of information of that kind — sorting, shuffling, or degrading it. The creationist account of history, based on the Bible, provides the correct basis to interpret the facts of the present; and real science confirms the interpretation.

After this detailed explanation, continue like this:

Now let me ask you to defend *your* position concerning these matters. Please show me how *your* way of thinking, based on *your* beliefs, makes sense of the same evidence. And I want you to point out where my science and logic are wrong.

In arguing this way, a Christian is

1. using biblical presuppositions to build a way of thinking to interpret the evidence;
2. showing that the Bible and science go hand in hand;
3. challenging the presuppositions of the other person (many are unaware they have these);
4. forcing the debater to logically defend his position consistent with science and his own presuppositions (many will find that they cannot do this), and help this person realize they do have presuppositions that can be challenged;
5. honoring the Word of God that convicts the soul.

If Christians really understood that all facts are actually interpreted on the basis of certain presuppositions, we wouldn't be in the least bit intimidated by the evolutionists' supposed "evidence." We should instead be looking at the evolutionists' (or old-earthers'[2]) *interpretation* of the evidence, and how the same evidence could be interpreted within a biblical framework and confirmed by testable and repeatable science. If more creationists did this, they would be less likely to jump at flaky evidence that seems startling but in reality has been interpreted incorrectly in their rush to find the knockdown, drag-out convincing "evidence" against evolution that they think they desperately need.

The various age-dating methods are also subject to interpretation. All dating methods suffer, in principle, from the same limitations — whether they are used to support a young world or an old world. For instance, the public

---

2. Those who accept millions of years of history.

reads almost daily in newspapers and magazines that scientists have dated a particular rock at billions of years old. Most just accept this. However, creation scientists have learned to ask questions as to how this date was obtained — what method was used and what *assumptions* were accepted to develop this method? These scientists then question those assumptions (questions) to see whether they are valid and to determine whether the rock's age could be interpreted differently. Then the results are published to help people understand that scientists have not proven that the rock is billions of years old and that the facts can be interpreted in a different way to support a young age.

Consider the research from the creationist group Radioisotopes and the Age of The Earth (RATE) concerning the age of zircon crystals in granite.[3] Using one set of assumptions, these crystals could be interpreted to be around 1.5 billion years old, based on the amount of lead produced from the decay of uranium (which also produces helium). However, if one questions these assumptions, one is motivated to test them. Measurements of the rate at which helium is able to "leak out" of these crystals indicate that if they were much older than about 6,000 years, they would have nowhere near the amount of helium still left in them. Hence, the originally applied assumption of a constant decay rate is flawed; one must assume, instead, that there has been acceleration of the decay rate in the past. Using this revised assumption, the same uranium-lead data can now be interpreted to also give an age of fewer than 6,000 years.

Another example involves red blood cells and traces of hemoglobin that have been found in *T. rex* bones, although these should have long decomposed if they were millions of years old. Yet the reaction of the researchers was a perfect illustration of how evolutionary bias can result in trying to explain away hard facts to fit the preconceived framework of millions of years:

> It was exactly like looking at a slice of modern bone. But, of course, I couldn't believe it. I said to the lab technician: "The bones, after all, are 65 million years old. How could blood cells survive that long?"[4]

Whenever you hear a news report that scientists have found another "missing link" or discovered a fossil "millions of years old," try to think about the

---

3. R. Humphreys, "Young Helium Diffusion Age of Zircons Supports Accelerated Nuclear Decay," in Larry Vardiman, Andrew Snelling, and Eugene Chaffin, eds., *Radioisotopes and the Age of the Earth*, vol. 2 (El Cajon, CA: Institute for Creation Research; Chino, Valley, AZ: Creation Research Society, 2005), p. 25–100.

4. *Science* 261 (July 9, 1994): 160; see also, "Scientists Recover *T. rex* Soft Tissue: 70-million-year-old Fossil Yields Preserved Blood Vessels," www.msnbc.msn.com/id/7285683/, March 24, 2005.

right questions that need to be asked to challenge the questions these scientists asked to get their interpretations!

All of this should be a lesson for us to take note of the situation when we read the newspaper — we are reading someone's interpretation of the facts of world history — there very well could be a different way of looking at the same "facts." One can see this in practice on television when comparing a news network that's currently considered fairly liberal (CNN) with one that is more conservative (FOX) — one can often see the same "facts" interpreted differently!

The reason so many Christian professors (and Christian leaders in general) have rejected the literal creation position is that they have blindly accepted the interpretation of facts from the secular world, based on man's fallible presuppositions about history. And they have then tried to reinterpret the Bible accordingly. If only they would start with the presupposition that God's Word is true, they would find that they could then correctly interpret the facts of the present and show overwhelmingly that observational science repeatedly confirms such interpretations.

Don't forget, as Christians we need to always build our thinking on the Word of the One who has the answers to all of the questions that could ever be asked — the infinite Creator God. He has revealed the true history of the universe in His Word to enable us to develop the right way of thinking about the present and thus determine the correct interpretations of the evidence of the present. We should follow Proverbs 1:7 and 9:10, which teach that fear of the Lord is the beginning of true wisdom and knowledge.

The Bottom Line

The bottom line is that it's not a matter of who has the better (or the most) "facts on their side." We need to understand that there are no such things as brute facts — *all* facts are interpreted. The next time evolutionists use what seem to be convincing facts for evolution, try to determine the *presuppositions* they have used to interpret these facts. Then, beginning with the big picture of history from the Bible, look at the same facts through these biblical glasses and interpret them differently. Next, using the real science of the present that an evolutionist also uses, see if that science, when properly understood, confirms (by being consistent with) the interpretation based on the Bible. You will find over and over again that the Bible is confirmed by real science.

But remember that, like Job (42:2–6), we need to understand that compared to God we know next to nothing. We won't have all the answers. However, so many answers have come to light now that a Christian can give a

Secular history   Biblical history

credible defense of the Book of Genesis and show it is the correct foundation for thinking about, and interpreting, every aspect of reality.

Therefore, let's not jump in a blind-faith way at the startling facts we think we need to "prove" creation — trying to counter "their facts" with "our facts." (Jesus himself rose from the dead in the most startling possible demonstration of the truth of God's Word. But many still wouldn't believe — see Luke 16:27–31.) Instead, let's not let apparent facts for evolution intimidate us, but let's understand the right way to think about facts. We can then deal with *the same facts the evolutionists use*, to show they have the wrong framework of interpretation — and that the facts of the real world really do conform to, and confirm, the Bible. In this way we can do battle for a biblical worldview.

Remember, it's no good convincing people to believe in creation, without also leading them to believe and trust in the Creator and Redeemer, Jesus Christ. God honors those who honor His Word. We need to use God-honoring ways of reaching people with the truth of what life is all about.

3

Are Biblical Creationists Divisive?

BODIE HODGE

Biblical creationists[1] are often accused of causing division in the Church. It is claimed that their insistence on accepting Genesis as narrative history introduces dissension by majoring on a "minor" doctrine. However, as will be shown, quite the opposite it true.

Who Is Really Being Divisive?

Far too often, people have the wrong impression about what it means to be divisive. Those who are divisive are those who are against the clear teachings of the Bible. Paul made this clear in his letter to the Christians in Rome.

> Now I urge you, brethren, note those who cause divisions and offenses, contrary to the doctrine which you learned, and avoid them. For those who are such do not serve our Lord Jesus Christ, but their own belly, and by smooth words and flattering speech deceive the hearts of the simple (Romans 16:17–18).

Jude also confirmed that unbiblical beliefs cause divisions:

---

1. Biblical creationists are often termed *young-earth creationists* (YEC). They adopt a "plain" or "straightforward" reading of the Bible; thus Genesis, which is written as historical narrative, is literal history and the days in Genesis 1 are ordinary days. A corollary to this is that the earth is young. See chapter 4, "How Old Is the Earth?" for more information.

But you, beloved, remember the words which were spoken before by the apostles of our Lord Jesus Christ: how they told you that there would be mockers in the last time who would walk according to their own ungodly lusts. These are sensual persons, who cause divisions, not having the Spirit (Jude 1:17–19).

Jude wrote that these divisions are caused by sensual, or worldly minded, beliefs. This should serve as a warning to those who accept man-made ideas that are opposed to the clear teachings of Scripture.

What are some of those clear teachings of Scripture?

- Sin entered the world through one man, and death through sin (Genesis 2:17, 3:17; Romans 5:12).

- Man and animals were originally vegetarian (Genesis 1:29–30).

- The week is composed of seven normal-length days (Genesis 1:1–2:4; Exodus 20:11).

- All people are descendants of Adam and Eve (Genesis 1:26–28, 3:20).

- People began to wear clothing after sin entered the world (Genesis 3:7, 21).

- Thorns and thistles resulted from the curse God placed on His creation after sin entered the world (Genesis 3:18).

- The flood of Noah's day was global in extent (Genesis 6–8).

These are not new doctrines — Paul, the other apostles, and Christ himself accepted these teachings. They (and biblical creationists today) understood that Genesis is a record of actual historical events. As a corollary of this, biblical creationists accept, based on careful study of the Bible, that the earth is thousands of years old (not billions).

The questioning of these teachings by many in the Church began in earnest around two hundred years ago. This was not due to a reexamination of Scripture, but rather because the culture had begun to teach an earth history of "millions of years."[2] The acceptance of the culture's ideas about the past has led to the reinterpretation of Genesis to fit with these man-made ideas. Some

---

2. Dr Terry Mortenson's book *The Great Turning Point* (Green Forest, AR: Master Books, 2004) discusses this in detail.

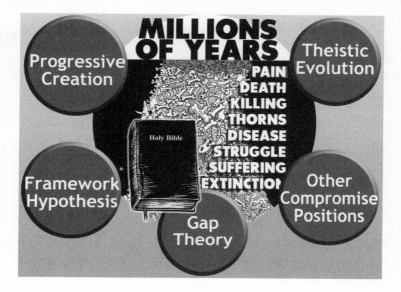

of these reinterpretations are the *framework hypotheses, gap theory, progressive creation*, and *theistic evolution*.

Each of these views attempts to combine the secular/evolutionary view of millions of years with the biblical view of history. In doing so, these views reject one or more of the clear teachings listed above. For example, each view rejects that the Genesis flood was a global event. Whenever one combines a man-made view with the Bible, something has to give. In most cases, this something is the Scripture. When one mixes the Word of God with another belief system, the result is doctrines that deviate from the Bible's clear teachings.

Sadly, these compromising beliefs have infiltrated many churches, Christian colleges, and seminaries. When a biblical creationist teaches people what the Bible plainly says, he is often told by adherents of these compromising views that *he* is being divisive. However, according to Paul, the ones causing division are those who deny the

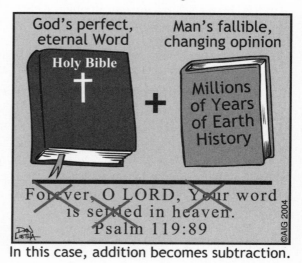

In this case, addition becomes subtraction.

CREATIONWISE

doctrines clearly taught in Scripture. The divisive ones are those who mix the Bible with secular views and refuse to heed the call to return to the clear teachings in the Bible.

Wasn't Jesus Divisive?

Some have claimed, based on the following passages, that Jesus was divisive.

> For from now on five in one house will be *divided*: three against two, and two against three. Father will be *divided* against son and son against father, mother against daughter and daughter against mother, mother-in-law against her daughter-in-law and daughter-in-law against her mother-in-law (Luke 12:52–53; italics added).

> So there was a *division* among the people because of Him (John 7:43; italics added).

> Do not think that I came to bring peace on earth. I did not come to bring peace but a sword. For I have come to "*set a man against his father, a daughter against her mother, and a daughter-in-law against her mother-in-law*"; and "*a man's enemies will be those of his own household.*" He who loves father or mother more than Me is not worthy of Me. And he who loves son or daughter more than Me is not worthy of Me. And he who does not take his cross and follow after Me is not worthy of Me (Matthew 10:34–38; italics in original).

Carefully reread these passages and note that Jesus was not divisive! The *people* were divided because of the message. Jesus' message conformed to the doctrines laid down in the Old Testament; He came to fulfill the Law, not abolish it (Matthew 5:17)! As the perfect God, He was the One who inspired the writings of the Old Testament in the first place. *He* wasn't divisive; rather, those disagreeing with Him were causing divisions. Christ knew that His message would cause division among the people because many wouldn't believe and wouldn't adhere to the doctrines previously established.

The passages in Luke, John, and Matthew teach that the people were divided. There were those who received what Jesus taught (which is what the Scriptures taught, and thus was *not* divisive), and there were those who didn't. The ones who were divisive were those not adhering to what Jesus taught.

How Should I Deal with Those Who Are Divisive?

Paul and Barnabas's message divided the Jews. Some followed the apostle's teachings and others didn't. Remember, those being divisive were the ones opposed to the scriptural teachings.

> Therefore they stayed there a long time, speaking boldly in the Lord, who was bearing witness to the word of His grace, granting signs and wonders to be done by their hands. But the multitude of the city was divided: part sided with the Jews, and part with the apostles. And when a violent attempt was made by both the Gentiles and Jews, with their rulers, to abuse and stone them (Acts 14:3–5).

But notice what happened — those who were divisive found like-minded Gentiles (nonbelievers) to oppose Paul! Did Paul compromise like they did? No. Paul continued teaching the same message.

This is similar to what is happening in today's Church. Many readily adhere to secular millions-of-years teachings over the Bible's teachings. They are opposing the Scriptures. They are being divisive. Biblical creationists will continue to defend the authority of the Bible in all areas, just like Paul did.

Paul instructs us regarding divisive people:

> Reject a divisive man after the first and second admonition, knowing that such a person is warped and sinning, being self-condemned (Titus 3:10–11).

We are to confront the divisive twice or answer them twice. If they refuse to heed the words of correction, we are to have nothing more to do with them. This confirms what Jesus taught to the disciples when they were ministering;

they were to shake the dust from their feet as a testimony against those who refused to listen (Luke 9:5). They weren't to get wrapped up in an argument for extended periods of time but were to continue preaching the truth.

This is an important message for us today. We need to be careful that we don't get caught up in discussions with a divisive person for long periods of time (via e-mail, message boards, letters, phone calls, etc.). Instead, we need seek the millions waiting eagerly to hear the message that the Bible's history is true and the message of the gospel is likewise true.

The harvest is plentiful but the workers are few (Matthew 9:37). And there are fewer still when the harvesters get caught up trying to harvest wheat from a thistle when ten heads of wheat are waiting. Answer a divisive person twice. If that person continues to be divisive, have nothing more to do with him/her. If that person is genuinely willing to learn, continue to answer him/her with gentleness and respect (1 Peter 3:15).

Unity Comes by Uniting around What the Bible Clearly Teaches

Paul, as well as Jesus (John 17:22–23), makes it clear that there shouldn't be divisions but unity.

> Now I plead with you, brethren, by the name of our Lord Jesus Christ, that you all speak the same thing, and that there be no divisions among you, but that you be perfectly joined together in the same mind and in the same judgment (1 Corinthians 1:10).

This unity should not come at the expense of compromising the Scriptures, but should come by adhering to what the Scriptures say. This is why Paul exhorted the Roman Christians to take note of those causing divisions and avoid them (Romans 16:17). In other words, don't learn from those causing divisions (those who have accepted fallible man's ideas), but learn from those who adhere to the doctrines that have been laid down by Scripture.

> See to it that no one takes you captive through hollow and deceptive philosophy, which depends on human tradition and the basic principles of this world rather than on Christ (Colossians 2:8; NIV).

Before Adam and Eve sinned, they were in complete unity with each other and with their Creator. After they sinned, disunity became the norm. Restoring that unity comes at a cost. Christ has paid the price. This is a call for all Christians to return to what the Bible clearly teaches, and obey Christ's Word — starting in Genesis.

The following points provide some practical ways that we can encourage unity among our Christian brethren:

- Pray that the Lord would bring about unity among His people. Pray that He would turn the hearts of His children to the clear teachings in His Word and would keep them from being influenced by fallible man's ideas (Ephesians 4:13).

- Respond to those who are divisive (going against Scripture) twice, with gentleness and respect (1 Peter 3:15). If they are willing to learn, continue to help them. If they continue to be divisive, have nothing more to do with them.

- Avoid those who are openly divisive (going against Scripture). Encourage others to refrain from following their divisive example (Romans 16:17–18).

- Drop any pride of your own (Proverbs 16:18). Read and study the Word of God. Allow it to teach you, and be aware of bringing man-made ideas to it. Learn to love God's Word, and ask the Lord to show you where you are being divisive. No one is perfect, and all are subject to the teachings of the Bible. When we make mistakes, we need to return to the authority of God's Word with humility and a teachable spirit.

4

How Old Is the Earth?

BODIE HODGE

The question of the age of the earth has produced heated discussions on Internet debate boards, TV, radio, in classrooms, and in many churches, Christian colleges, and seminaries. The primary sides are

- Young-earth proponents (biblical age of the earth and universe of about 6,000 years)[1]

- Old-earth proponents (secular age of the earth of about 4.5 billion years and a universe about 14 billion years old)[2]

The difference is immense! Let's give a little history of where these two basic calculations came from and which worldview is more reasonable.

Where Did a Young-earth Worldview Come From?

Simply put, it came from the Bible. Of course, the Bible doesn't say explicitly anywhere, "The earth is 6,000 years old." Good thing it doesn't; otherwise it would be out of date the following year. But we wouldn't expect an all-knowing God to make that kind of a mistake.

---

1. Not all young-earth creationists agree on this age. Some believe that there may be small gaps in the genealogies of Genesis 5 and 11 and put the maximum age of the earth at about 10,000–12,000 years. However, see chapter 5, "Are There Gaps in the Genesis Geologies?"
2. Some of these old-earth proponents accept molecules-to-man biological evolution and so are called theistic evolutionists. Others reject neo-Darwinian evolution but accept the evolutionary timescale for stellar and geological evolution, and hence agree with the evolutionary order of events in history.

God gave us something better. In essence, He gave us a "birth certificate." For example, using a personal birth certificate, a person can calculate how old he is at any point. It is similar with the earth. Genesis 1 says that the earth was created on the first day of creation (Genesis 1:1–5). From there, we can begin to calculate the age of the earth.

Let's do a rough calculation to show how this works. The age of the earth can be estimated by taking the first five days of creation (from earth's creation to Adam), then following the genealogies from Adam to Abraham in Genesis 5 and 11, then adding in the time from Abraham to today.

Adam was created on day 6, so there were five days before him. If we add up the dates from Adam to Abraham, we get about 2,000 years, using the Masoretic Hebrew text of Genesis 5 and 11.[3] Whether Christian or secular, most scholars would agree that Abraham lived about 2,000 B.C. (4,000 years ago).

So a simple calculation is:

$$
\begin{array}{r}
5 \text{ days} \\
+ \sim 2{,}000 \text{ years} \\
+ \sim 4{,}000 \text{ years} \\
\hline
\sim 6{,}000 \text{ years}
\end{array}
$$

At this point, the first five days are negligible. Quite a few people have done this calculation using the Masoretic text (which is what most English translations are based on) and with careful attention to the biblical details, they have arrived at the same time frame of about 6,000 years, or about 4000 B.C. Two of the most popular, and perhaps best, are a recent work by Dr. Floyd Jones[4] and a much earlier book by Archbishop James Ussher[5] (1581–1656). See table 1.

Table 1. Jones and Ussher

Name	Age Calculated	Reference and Date
Archbishop James Ussher	4004 B.C.	*The Annals of the World*, A.D. 1658
Dr. Floyd Nolan Jones	4004 B.C.	*The Chronology of the Old Testament*, A.D. 1993

---

3. Bodie Hodge, "Ancient Patriarchs in Genesis," Answers in Genesis, www.answersingenesis.org/articles/2009/01/20/ancient-patriarchs-in-genesis.
4. Floyd Nolan Jones, *Chronology of the Old Testament* (Green Forest, AR: Master Books, 2005).
5. James Ussher, *The Annals of the World*, transl. Larry and Marion Pierce (Green Forest, AR: Master Books, 2003).

The misconception exists that Ussher and Jones were the only ones to arrive at a date of 4000 B.C.; however, this is not the case at all. Jones[6] lists several chronologists who have undertaken the task of calculating the age of the earth based on the Bible, and their calculations range from 5501 to 3836 B.C. A few are listed in table 2.

Table 2. Chronologists' Calculations According to Dr. Jones

	Chronologist	When Calculated?	Date B.C.
1	Julius Africanus	c. 240	5501
2	George Syncellus	c. 810	5492
3	John Jackson	1752	5426
4	Dr William Hales	c. 1830	5411
5	Eusebius	c. 330	5199
6	Marianus Scotus	c. 1070	4192
7	L. Condomanus	n/a	4141
8	Thomas Lydiat	c. 1600	4103
9	M. Michael Maestlinus	c. 1600	4079
10	J. Ricciolus	n/a	4062
11	Jacob Salianus	c. 1600	4053
12	H. Spondanus	c. 1600	4051
13	Martin Anstey	1913	4042
14	W. Lange	n/a	4041
15	E. Reinholt	n/a	4021
16	J. Cappellus	c. 1600	4005
17	E. Greswell	1830	4004
18	E. Faulstich	1986	4001
19	D. Petavius	c. 1627	3983
20	Frank Klassen	1975	3975
21	Becke	n/a	3974
22	Krentzeim	n/a	3971
23	W. Dolen	2003	3971
24	E. Reusnerus	n/a	3970
25	J. Claverius	n/a	3968
26	C. Longomontanus	c. 1600	3966
27	P. Melanchthon	c. 1550	3964
28	J. Haynlinus	n/a	3963
29	A. Salmeron	d. 1585	3958
30	J. Scaliger	d. 1609	3949
31	M. Beroaldus	c. 1575	3927
32	A. Helwigius	c. 1630	3836

6. Jones, *Chronology of the Old Testament*, p. 26.

As you will likely note from table 2, the dates are not all 4004 B.C. There are several reasons chronologists have different dates,[7] but two primary reasons:

1. Some used the Septuagint or another early translation instead of the Hebrew Masoretic text. The Septuagint is a Greek translation of the Hebrew Old Testament, done about 250 B.C. by about 70 Jewish scholars (hence it is often cited as the LXX, which is the Roman numeral for 70). It is good in most places, but appears to have a number of inaccuracies. For example, one relates to the Genesis chronologies where the LXX indicates that Methuselah would have lived past the Flood, without being on the ark!

2. Several points in the biblical time-line are not straightforward to calculate. They require very careful study of more than one passage. These include exactly how much time the Israelites were in Egypt and what Terah's age was when Abraham was born. (See Jones's and Ussher's books for a detailed discussion of these difficulties.)

The first four in table 2 (bolded) are calculated from the Septuagint, which gives ages for the patriarchs' firstborn much higher than the Masoretic text or the Samarian Pentateuch (a version of the Old Testament from the Jews in Samaria just before Christ). Because of this, the Septuagint adds in extra time. Though the Samarian and Masoretic texts are much closer, they still have a few differences. See table 3.

Using data from table 2 (excluding the Septuagint calculations and including Jones and Ussher), the average date of the creation of the earth is 4045 B.C. This still yields an average of about 6,000 years for the age of the earth.

Extra-biblical Calculations for the Age of the Earth

Cultures throughout the world have kept track of history as well. From a biblical perspective, we would expect the dates given for creation of the earth to align more closely to the biblical date than billions of years.

This is expected since everyone was descended from Noah and scattered from the Tower of Babel. Another expectation is that there should be some discrepancies

7. Others would include gaps in the chronology based on the presences of an extra Cainan in Luke 3:36. But there are good reasons this should be left out. See chapter 5, "Are There Gaps in the Genesis Genealogies?" and chapter 27, "Isn't the Bible Full of Contradictions?"

Table 3. Septuagint, Masoretic, and Samarian Early Patriarchal Ages at the Birth of the Following Son

Name	Masoretic	Samarian Pentateuch	Septuagint
Adam	130	130	230
Seth	105	105	205
Enosh	90	90	190
Cainan	70	70	170
Mahalaleel	65	65	165
Jared	162	62	162
Enoch	65	65	165
Methuselah	187	67	167
Lamech	182	53	188
Noah	500	500	500

about the age of the earth among people as they scattered throughout the world, taking their uninspired records or oral history to different parts of the globe.

Under the entry "creation," *Young's Analytical Concordance of the Bible*[8] lists William Hales's accumulation of dates of creation from many cultures, and in most cases Hales says which authority gave the date. See table 4.

Historian Bill Cooper's research in *After the Flood* provides intriguing dates from several ancient cultures.[9] The first is that of the Anglo-Saxons, whose history has 5,200 years from creation to Christ, according to the Laud and Parker Chronicles. Cooper's research also indicated that Nennius's record of the ancient British history has 5,228 years from creation to Christ. The Irish chronology has a date of about 4000 B.C. for creation, which is surprisingly close to Ussher and Jones! Even the Mayans had a date for the Flood of 3113 B.C.

This meticulous work of many historians should not be ignored. Their dates of only thousands of years are good support for the biblical date of about 6,000 years, but not for billions of years.

The Origin of the Old-earth Worldview

Prior to the 1700s, few believed in an old earth. The approximate 6,000-year age for the earth was challenged only rather recently, beginning in the late 18th

---

8. Robert Young, *Young's Analytical Concordance to the Bible* (Peadoby, MA: Hendrickson, 1996), referring to William Hales, *A New Analysis of Chronology and Geography, History and Prophecy*, vol. 1 (1830), p. 210.
9. Bill Cooper, *After the Flood* (UK: New Wine Press, 1995), p. 122–129.

Table 4. Selected Dates for the Age of the Earth by Various Cultures

Culture	Age, B.C.	Authority listed by Hales
Spain by Alfonso X	6984	Muller
Spain by Alfonso X	6484	Strauchius
India	6204	Gentil
India	6174	Arab records
Babylon	6158	Bailly
Chinese	6157	Bailly
Greece by Diogenes Laertius	6138	Playfair
Egypt	6081	Bailly
Persia	5507	Bailly
Israel/Judea by Josephus	5555	Playfair
Israel/Judea by Josephus	5481	Jackson
Israel/Judea by Josephus	5402	Hales
Israel/Judea by Josephus	4698	University history
India	5369	Megasthenes
Babylon (Talmud)	5344	Petrus Alliacens
Vatican (Catholic using the Septuagint)	5270	N/A
Samaria	4427	Scaliger
German, Holy Roman Empire by Johannes Kepler*	3993	Playfair
German, reformer by Martin Luther*	3961	N/A
Israel/Judea by computation	3760	Strauchius
Israel/Judea by Rabbi Lipman*	3616	University history

* Luther, Kepler, Lipman, and the Jewish computation likely used biblical texts to determine the date.

century. These opponents of the biblical chronology essentially left God out of the picture. Three of the old-earth advocates included Comte de Buffon, who thought the earth was at least 75,000 years old. Pièrre LaPlace imagined an indefinite but very long history. And Jean Lamarck also proposed long ages.[10]

---

10. Terry Mortenson, "The Origin of Old-earth Geology and its Ramifications for Life in the 21st Century," *TJ* 18, no. 1 (2004): 22–26, online at www.answersingenesis.org/tj/v18/i1/oldearth.asp.

However, the idea of millions of years really took hold in geology when men like Abraham Werner, James Hutton, William Smith, Georges Cuvier, and Charles Lyell used their interpretations of geology as the standard, rather than the Bible. Werner estimated the age of the earth at about one million years. Smith and Cuvier believed untold ages were needed for the formation of rock layers. Hutton said he could see no geological evidence of a beginning of the earth; and building on Hutton's thinking, Lyell advocated "millions of years."

From these men and others came the consensus view that the geologic layers were laid down slowly over long periods of time based on the rates at which we see them accumulating today. Hutton said:

> The past history of our globe must be explained by what can be seen to be happening now. . . . No powers are to be employed that are not natural to the globe, no action to be admitted except those of which we know the principle.[11]

This viewpoint is called naturalistic uniformitarianism, and it excludes any major catastrophes such as Noah's flood. Though some, such as Cuvier and Smith, believed in multiple catastrophes separated by long periods of time, the uniformitarian concept became the ruling dogma in geology.

ROCK LAYERS

GOD'S WORD IS TRUTH

MAN DECIDES TRUTH

11. James Hutton, *Theory of the Earth* (Trans. of Roy. Soc. of Edinburgh, 1785); quoted in A. Holmes, *Principles of Physical Geology* (UK: Thomas Nelson & Sons Ltd., 1965), p. 43–44.

Thinking biblically, we can see that the global flood in Genesis 6–8 would wipe away the concept of millions of years, for this Flood would explain massive amounts of fossil layers. Most Christians fail to realize that a global flood could rip up many of the previous rock layers and redeposit them elsewhere, destroying the previous fragile contents. This would destroy any evidence of alleged millions of years anyway. So the rock layers can theoretically represent the evidence of either millions of years or a global flood, but not both. Sadly, by about 1840, even most of the Church had accepted the dogmatic claims of the secular geologists and rejected the global flood and the biblical age of the earth.

After Lyell, in 1899, Lord Kelvin (William Thomson) calculated the age of the earth, based on the cooling rate of a molten sphere, at a maximum of about 20–40 million years (this was revised from his earlier calculation of 100 million years in 1862).[12] With the development of radiometric dating in the early 20th century, the age of the earth expanded radically. In 1913, Arthur Holmes's book, *The Age of the Earth,* gave an age of 1.6 billion years.[13] Since then, the supposed age of the earth has expanded to its present estimate of about 4.5 billion years (and about 14 billion years for the universe).

Table 5. Summary of the Old-earth Proponents for Long Ages

Who?	Age of the Earth	When Was This?
Comte de Buffon	78 thousand years old	1779
Abraham Werner	1 million years	1786
James Hutton	Perhaps eternal, long ages	1795
Pièrre LaPlace	Long ages	1796
Jean Lamarck	Long ages	1809
William Smith	Long ages	1835
Georges Cuvier	Long ages	1812
Charles Lyell	Millions of years	1830–1833
Lord Kelvin	20–100 million years	1862–1899
Arthur Holmes	1.6 billion years	1913
Clair Patterson	4.5 billion years	1956

12. Mark McCartney, "William Thompson: King of Victorian Physics," *Physics World*, December 2002, physicsweb.org/articles/world/15/12/6.

13. Terry Mortenson, "The History of the Development of the Geological Column," in *The Geologic Column,* eds. Michael Oard and John Reed (Chino Valley, AZ: Creation Research Society, 2006).

But there is growing scientific evidence that radiometric dating methods are completely unreliable.[14]

Christians who have felt compelled to accept the millions of years as fact and try to fit them into the Bible need to become aware of this evidence. It confirms that the Bible's history is giving us the true age of the creation.

Today, secular geologists will allow some catastrophic events into their thinking as an explanation for what they see in the rocks. But uniformitarian thinking is still widespread, and secular geologists will seemingly never entertain the idea of the global, catastrophic flood of Noah's day.

The age of the earth debate ultimately comes down to this foundational question: Are we trusting man's imperfect and changing ideas and assumptions about the past? Or are we trusting God's perfectly accurate eyewitness account of the past, including the creation of the world, Noah's global flood, and the age of the earth?

Other Uniformitarian Methods for Dating the Age of the Earth

Radiometric dating was the culminating factor that led to the belief in billions of years for earth history. However, radiometric dating methods are not the only uniformitarian methods. Any radiometric dating model or other uniformitarian dating method can and does have problems, as referenced before. All uniformitarian dating methods require assumptions for extrapolating present-day processes back into the past. The assumptions related to radiometric dating can be seen in these questions:

- Initial amounts?
- Was any parent amount added?
- Was any daughter amount added?
- Was any parent amount removed?
- Was any daughter amount removed?
- Has the rate of decay changed?

If the assumptions are truly accurate, then uniformitarian dates should agree with radiometric dating across the board for the same event. However,

---

14. For articles at the layman's level, see www.answersingenesis.org/home/area/faq/dating.asp. For a technical discussion, see Larry Vardiman, Andrew Snelling, and Eugene Chaffin, eds., *Radioisotopes and the Age of the Earth*, vol. 1 and 2 (El Cajon, CA: Institute for Creation Research; Chino Valley, AZ: Creation Research Society, 2000 and 2005). See also "Half-Life Heresy," *New Scientist*, October, 21 2006, pp. 36–39, abstract online at www.newscientist.com/channel/fundamentals/mg19225741.100-halflife-heresy-accelerating-radioactive-decay.html.

radiometric dates often disagree with one another and with dates obtained from other uniformitarian dating methods for the age of the earth, such as the influx of salts into the ocean, the rate of decay of the earth's magnetic field, and the growth rate of human population.[15]

The late Dr. Henry Morris compiled a list of 68 uniformitarian estimates for the age of the earth by Christian and secular sources.[16] The current accepted age of the earth is about 4.54 billion years based on radiometric dating of a group of meteorites,[17] so keep this in mind when viewing table 6.

Table 6. Uniformitarian Estimates Other than Radiometric Dating Estimates for Earth's Age Compiled by Morris

	0 – 10,000 years	>10,000 – 100,000 years	>100,000 – 1 million years	>1 million – 500 million years	>500 million – 4 billion years	>4 billion – 5 billion years
Number of uniformitarian methods*	23	10	11	23	0	0

* When a range of ages is given, the maximum age was used to be generous to the evolutionists. In one case, the date was uncertain so it was not used in this tally, so the total estimates used were 67. A few on the list had reference to Saturn, the sun, etc., but since biblically the earth is older than these, dates related to them were used.

As you can see from table 6, uniformitarian maximum ages for the earth obtained from other methods are nowhere near the 4.5 billion years estimated by radiometric dating; of the other methods, only two calculated dates were as much as 500 million years.

The results from some radiometric dating methods completely undermine those from the other radiometric methods. One such example is carbon-14 (^{14}C) dating. As long as an organism is alive, it takes in ^{14}C and ^{12}C from the atmosphere; however, when it dies, the carbon intake stops. Since ^{14}C is radioactive (decays into ^{14}N), the amount of ^{14}C in a dead organism gets less and less

15. For many more examples see www.answersingenesis.org/go/young.
16. Henry M. Morris, *The New Defender's Study Bible* (Nashville, TN: World Publishing, 2006), p. 2076–2079.
17. C.C. Patterson, "Age of Meteorites and the Age of the Earth," *Geochemica et Cosmochemica Acta*, 10 (1956): 230–237.

over time. Carbon-14 dates are determined from the measured ratio of radioactive carbon-14 to normal carbon-12 ($^{14}C/^{12}C$). Used on samples that were once alive, such as wood or bone, the measured $^{14}C/^{12}C$ ratio is compared with the ratio in living things today.

Now, ^{14}C has a derived half-life of 5,730 years, so the ^{14}C in organic material supposedly 100,000 years old should all essentially have decayed into nitrogen.[18] Some things, such as wood trapped in lava flows, said to be millions of years old by other radiometric dating methods, still have ^{14}C in them.[19] If the items were really millions of years old, then they shouldn't have any traces of ^{14}C. Coal and diamonds, which are found in or sandwiched between rock layers allegedly millions of years old, have been shown to have ^{14}C ages of only tens of thousands of years.[20] So which date, if any, is correct? The diamonds or coal can't be millions of years old if they have any traces of ^{14}C still in them. This shows that these dating methods are completely unreliable and indicates that the presumed assumptions in the methods are erroneous.

Similar kinds of problems are seen in the case of potassium-argon dating, which has been considered one of the most reliable methods. Dr. Andrew Snelling, a geologist, points out several of these problems with potassium-argon, as seen in table 7.[21]

These and other examples raise a critical question. If radiometric dating fails to give an accurate date on something of which we *do* know the true age, then how can it be trusted to give us the correct age for rocks that had no human observers to record when they formed? If the methods don't work on rocks of known age, it is most unreasonable to trust that they work on rocks of unknown age. It is far more rational to trust the Word of the God who created the world, knows its history perfectly, and has revealed sufficient information in the Bible for us to understand that history and the age of the creation.

---

18. This does not mean that a ^{14}C date of 50,000 or 100,000 would be entirely trustworthy. I am only using this to highlight the mistaken assumptions behind uniformitarian dating methods.
19. Andrew Snelling, "Conflicting 'Ages' of Tertiary Basalt and Contained Fossilized Wood, Crinum, Central Queensland Australia," *Technical Journal* 14, no. 2 (2005): p. 99–122.
20. John Baumgardner, "^{14}C Evidence for a Recent Global Flood and a Young Earth," in *Radioisotopes and the Age of the Earth: Results of a Young-Earth Creationist Research Initiative*, ed. Vardiman *et al.* (Santee, CA: Institute for Creation Research; Chino Valley, AZ: Creation Research Society, 2005), p. 587–630.
21. Andrew Snelling, "Excess Argon: The 'Achilles' Heel' of Potassium-Argon and Argon-Argon Dating of Volcanic Rocks," *Impact*, January 1999, online at www.icr.org/article/436.

Table 7. Potassium-argon (K-Ar) Dates in Error

Volcanic eruption	When the rock formed	Date by (K-Ar) radiometric dating
Mt. Etna basalt, Sicily	122 B.C.	170,000–330,000 years old
Mt. Etna basalt, Sicily	A.D. 1972	210,000–490,000 years old
Mount St. Helens, Washington	A.D. 1986	Up to 2.8 million years old
Hualalai basalt, Hawaii	A.D. 1800–1801	1.32–1.76 million years old
Mt. Ngauruhoe, New Zealand	A.D. 1954	Up to 3.5 million years old
Kilauea Iki basalt, Hawaii	A.D. 1959	1.7–15.3 million years old

Conclusion

When we start our thinking with God's Word, we see that the world is about 6,000 years old. When we rely on man's fallible (and often demonstrably false) dating methods, we can get a confusing range of ages from a few thousand to billions of years, though the vast majority of methods do not give dates even close to billions.

Cultures around the world give an age of the earth that confirms what the Bible teaches. Radiometric dates, on the other hand, have been shown to be wildly in error.

The age of the earth ultimately comes down to a matter of trust — it's a worldview issue. Will you trust what an all-knowing God says on the subject or will you trust imperfect man's assumptions and imaginations about the past that regularly are changing?

Thus says the LORD: "Heaven is My throne, and earth is My footstool. Where is the house that you will build Me? And where is the place of My rest? For all those things My hand has made, and all those things exist," says the LORD. "But on this one will I look: On him who is poor and of a contrite spirit, and who trembles at My word" (Isaiah 66:1–2).

5

Are There Gaps in the Genesis Genealogies?

LARRY PIERCE & KEN HAM

M ost of us love to read portions of Scripture that give accounts of victo- ries, miracles, and drama. We enjoy far less the Scriptures that outline a certain person begat a son or daughter, who in turn begat a son, thus begin- ning a long list of begats. Most people believe the genealogies contain only dull details, but those of us who keep in mind that "every word is given by inspira- tion of God" see that even these so-called dull passages contain vital truth that can be trusted.

Genesis 5 and 11 contain two such genealogies. It may be hard to believe, but Genesis 5 and 11 are actually two of the more controversial chapters in the Bible, even in Christian circles.

Because so many Christians and Christian leaders have accepted the secu- lar dates for the origin of man and the universe, they must work out ways that such dates can somehow be incorporated into the Bible's historical account. In other words, they must convince people that the Bible's genealogical records do not present an unbroken line of chronology. If such an unbroken line exists, then we should be able to calculate dates concerning the creation of man and the universe.

To fit the idea of billions of years into Scripture, many Christian leaders, since the early 19th century, have reinterpreted the days of creation to mean long ages. Biblical creationist literature has meticulously addressed this topic

many times, showing clearly that the word *day*, as used in Genesis 1 for each of the six days of creation, means an ordinary, approximately 24-hour day.[1]

A straightforward addition of the chronogenealogies yields a date for the beginning near 4000 B.C. Chronologists working from the Bible consistently get 2,000 years between Adam and Abraham. Few would dispute that Abraham lived around 2000 B.C. Many Christian leaders, though, claim there are gaps in the Genesis genealogies. One of their arguments is that the word *begat*, as used in the time-line from the first man Adam to Abraham in Genesis 5 and 11, can skip generations. If this argument were true, the date for creation using the biblical time-line of history cannot be worked out.

In a recent debate,[2] a well-known progressive creationist[3] stated that he believed a person could date Adam back 100,000 years from the present. Since most modern scholars place the date of Abraham around 2000 B.C. (Ussher's date for Abraham's birth is 1996 B.C.), the remaining 96,000 years must fit into the Genesis 5 and 11 genealogies, between Adam and Abraham.

---

1. See, for example, www.answersingenesis.org/go/days-of-creation.
2. Ken Ham, Jason Lisle, Hugh Ross, Walt Kaiser, *The Great Debate: Young Earth vs. Old Earth*, DVD (Kentucky: Answers in Genesis, 2006), program 10, bonus 2.
3. Most progressive creationists believe that the six days of creation were actually long periods of time, not 24-hour days.

4004 BC		2348 BC	2242 BC	1996-1821 BC
Creation		Flood	Tower of Babel	Abraham

By accepting these three points (right), we can determine the dates for key events (above) going back to the beginning of time:*

*All are based on the Masoretic text.

1. The word for *day* (Hebrew: *yom*) in Genesis 1 for the days of creation are ordinary days (of approximately 24 hours).
2. The word for *begat* (*yalad*) in the genealogies in Genesis 5 and 11 does not skip any generations.
3. The date of Abraham was 1996 BC.

Now, if we estimate that 40 years equals one generation, which is fairly generous,[4] this means that 2,500 generations are missing from these genealogies. But this makes the genealogies ridiculously meaningless.

Two Keys to Consider

Those who claim that there are gaps in these genealogies need to demonstrate this from the biblical text and not simply say that gaps exist. However, consider the following:

1. Although in the Hebrew way of thinking, the construction "X is the son of Y" does not always mean a literal father/son relationship, additional biographical information in Genesis 5 and 11 strongly supports the view that there are no gaps in these chapters. So we know for certain that the following are literal father/son relationships: Adam/Seth, Seth/Enosh, Lamech/Noah, Noah/Shem, Eber/Peleg, and Terah/Abram. Nothing in these chapters indicates that the "X *begat* Y" means something other than a literal father/son relationship.

2. Nowhere in the Old Testament is the Hebrew word for *begat* (*yalad*) used in any other way than to mean a single-generation (e.g., father/son or mother/daughter) relationship. The Hebrew word *ben* can mean *son* or *grandson*, but the word *yalad* never skips generations.

Six Arguments Refuted

In the recent debate (mentioned previously), various biblical references were given as proofs that the Hebrew word *yalad* does not always point to the

---

4. Jonathan Sarfati, *Refuting Compromise* (Green Forest, AR: Master Books, 2004), p. 295.

very next generation. However, when analyzed carefully, these arguments actually confirm what we are asserting concerning the word *begat*.

Argument 1

Genesis 46:15 says, "These be the sons of Leah, which she bare unto Jacob in Padanaram, with his daughter Dinah: all the souls of his sons and his daughters were thirty and three" (KJV). The word *bare* here is the Hebrew word *yalad*, which is also translated *begat*. It is claimed by some that because there are sons of various wives, grandsons, daughters, etc., in this list of "thirty and three," the word *begat* is referring to all these and can't be interpreted as we assert.

Is Argument 1 Relevant?

A person needs to read the quoted verse carefully to correctly understand its meaning. The *begat* (*bare*) refers to the sons born in Padanaram. Genesis 35:23 lists the six sons born in Padanaram (those whom Leah begat), who are listed as part of the total group of 33 children in Genesis 46:15. Thus, this passage confirms that *begat* points to the generation immediately following — a literal parent/child relationship.

Argument 2

Matthew 1:8 omits Ahaziah, Joash, and Amaziah, going directly from Joram to Uzziah. Matthew 1:11 skips Jehoiakim between Josiah and Jeconiah. These passages prove that the word *begat* skips generations.

Is Argument 2 Relevant?

Here, the Greek word for *begat* is *gennao*, which shows flexibility not found in the Hebrew word and does allow for the possibility that a generation or more may be skipped. The only way we would know that a generation has been skipped is by checking the Hebrew passages. However, it is linguistically deceptive to use the Greek word for *begat* to define the Hebrew word for *begat*. Also, Matthew 1 is intentionally incomplete when reading Matthew 1:1 and Matthew 1:17, merely giving 14 generations between key figures of Abraham, David, and Jesus.

Argument 3

Genesis 46:18, 22, and 25 says, "These are the sons of Zilpah, whom Laban gave to Leah his daughter, and these she bare unto Jacob, even sixteen souls. . . . These are the sons of Rachel, which were born to Jacob: all the souls were fourteen. . . . These are the sons of Bilhah, which Laban gave to Rachel his daughter, and she bare these unto Jacob: all the souls were seven" (KJV). In verse 18, the Hebrew word *yalad* (*begat* or *bore*) implies a grandson, as well as a son; so the word *begat* cannot be used to show a direct relationship.

Is Argument 3 Relevant?

The word *bare* in verse 18 refers to Zilpah's actual sons, referenced in verses 16 (Gad) and 17 (Asher). Note the pattern in this chapter. In verse 15 we are given the total number of Leah's offspring (33), in verse 18 the total of Zilpah's offspring (16), in verse 22 the total of Rachel's offspring (14), and in verse 25 the total of Bilhah's offspring (7). This makes a total of 70. But nowhere is it stated that these four wives physically bore the total number of sons listed for each.

What this passage shows, as stated earlier, is that the Hebrew word for *son* (*ben*) may include grandsons. In the case of Zilpah, her two sons are clearly listed, as well as the children of Gad and Asher. To insist that in this case only (and not the cases of Leah, Rachel, and Bilhah) the summary total given at the end of verse 18 implies that all these were begotten of Zilpah is not justified by the context, and therefore, is not sound hermeneutics. The context makes it very clear that Zilpah had only two sons, and this passage does not show that the Hebrew word *yalad* (*begat* or *bore*) implies a grandson, as well as a son.

Argument 4

An example of where the word *begat* omits generations is 1 Chronicles 7:23–27. It is clear from this passage that there are ten generations from Ephraim to Joshua, whereas Genesis 15:16 says there were only four generations from the time the children of Israel entered Egypt to the time they left. Therefore, the Hebrew word for *begat* does not always mean the next generation.

Is Argument 4 Relevant?

This argument seems logically airtight except for two minor points. The Hebrew word *yalad* for *begat* is not used in the 1 Chronicles passage, and Genesis 15:16 is misquoted. Genesis states that "in the fourth generation" the children of Israel would leave Egypt — not that there would be a maximum of four generations. For this prophecy in Genesis to be fulfilled, some of the fourth generation would be in the exodus from Egypt — and they were. Exodus 6 lists the generations from Levi to Moses, showing that Moses and Aaron were in the fourth generation. Therefore the passage in 1 Chronicles cannot be used to prove that the Hebrew word for *begat* can skip a generation.

It is quite helpful, however, to explain how the Israelites became so numerous during their stay in Egypt. The descendants of Joshua appear to have had a new generation about every 20 years, whereas the descendants of Moses and Aaron had a new generation about every 50 years.

Argument 5

In Luke 3:36, the name Cainan is listed, which is not listed in the Old Testament chronologies.

Is Argument 5 Relevant?

The present copies of the Septuagint (ancient Greek translation of the Old Testament) incorrectly have the name Cainan inserted in the Old Testament genealogies. The great Baptist Hebrew scholar John Gill (c. A.D. 1760), in his exposition on this verse, wrote:

> This Cainan is not mentioned by Moses in Genesis 11:12 nor has he ever appeared in any Hebrew copy of the Old Testament, nor in the Samaritan version, nor in the Targum; nor is he mentioned by Josephus, nor in 1 Chronicles 1:24 where the genealogy is repeated; nor is it in Beza's most ancient Greek copy of Luke: it indeed stands in the present copies of the Septuagint, but was not originally there; and therefore could not be taken by Luke from there, but seems to be owing to some early negligent transcriber of Luke's Gospel, and since put into the Septuagint to give it authority: I say early, because it is in many Greek copies, and in the Vulgate Latin, and all the Oriental versions, even in the Syriac, the oldest of them; but ought not to stand neither in the text, nor in any version: for certain it is, there never was such a Cainan, the son of Arphaxad, for Salah was his son; and with him the next words should be connected.[5]

Since Gill's commentary was written, the oldest manuscript we have of Luke, the *P75*, was found. It dates to the late second century A.D. and does not include Cainan in the genealogy. This verse in Luke should not be used to prove that the genealogies in Genesis have gaps, because it has poor textual authority.

Argument 6

Author and radio host Harold Camping argues for a unique interpretation of the chronologies in Genesis 5 and 11. According to his interpretation, Adam was created in 11,013 B.C. The chronological statements in these two chapters are of the following form.

When X was A years old he begat Y. He lived B years after he begat Y and died at the age of C years. So A + B = C.

---

5. Note on Luke 3:36 in: John Gill, D.D., *An Exposition of the Old and New Testament; The Whole Illustrated with Notes, Taken from the Most Ancient Jewish Writings* (London: printed for Mathews and Leigh, 18 Strand, by W. Clowes, Northumberland-Court, 1809). Edited, revised, and updated by Larry Pierce, 1994–1995 for The Word CD-ROM. See also chapter 27, "Isn't the Bible Full of Contradictions?"

Camping interprets this statement as follows:

> When X was A years old he begat a progenitor of Y. He lived B years after he begat a progenitor of Y and died at age C, which was the same year that Y was born.

Is Argument 6 Relevant?

We must give Mr. Camping credit for originality and ingenuity, for we are not aware of anyone who interpreted these verses as such before him. As proof for this interpretation, Mr. Camping cites Matthew 1:8 that the word *begat* does not mean a father/son relationship. We have already discussed this line of reasoning in argument 2 and refuted it, thus exploding Mr. Camping's argument.

While claiming to honor the text of the Bible, Mr. Camping demonstrates a profound misunderstanding of the Hebrew verb forms for *begat* found in chapter 5 and 11 of Genesis. These verbs use the *hiphil* form of the verb. Most Hebrew verbs use the *qal* form, which corresponds to the active indicative tense in English. *Hiphil* usually expresses the causative action of *qal*.

he eats	he causes to eat
he comes	he causes to come, he brings
he reigned	he made king, he crowned

The *hiphil* has no exact English equivalent and is difficult to capture the meaning in English. Some modern English translations use the word *fathered* instead of the word *begat*, thus removing the ambiguity. To make it absolutely clear, the verb could be translated *X himself fathered Y*, but that is awkward English. It is difficult to father a remote descendant without committing incest! When the Hebrew verb form is honored in English, it precludes the interpretation Mr. Camping places on it. God chose this form to make it absolutely clear that we understand that there are no missing generations in chapters 5 and 11 of Genesis. Any other Hebrew verb form would not have been nearly as emphatic as the *hiphil* form.

In his latest book *Time Has an End*, Mr. Camping sets out a complete chronology for the Bible using his defective understanding of the chronologies in Genesis 5 and 11, which includes the following mistakes.

- Israel's time in Egypt was 430 years.
- The date for the Exodus is wrong.
- The chronology for the time of the judges is confused.

- The chronology of the divided kingdom is partially based on Dr. Edwin Thiele's work *The Mysterious Numbers of the Hebrew Kings*, which contradicts the Bible in many places.

- The end of the world in 2011. (His earlier prediction of 1994 had to be reinterpreted.)

Rather than refute these incorrect ideas, we recommend the *Chronology of the Old Testament* (Master Books, 2005) by Dr. Floyd Jones for a more accurate, biblically based chronology that is devoid of the speculations of Mr. Camping and refutes most of Camping's chronology.

Missing Generations?

Many creationists believe the earth is about 10,000 years old in an attempt to make the biblical record conform to modern archaeological ideas. According to these ideas, Egypt began around 3500 B.C. and Babylon in 4000 B.C. Since these nations speak different languages, their founding must have been after the Tower of Babel, which occurred after the Flood. So some creationists place the Flood around 5000 B.C. and the creation around 10,000 B.C. It is curious that, having rejected the evidence for long ages, these creationists are inadvertently and blindly trusting man's fallible dating methods for archaeological data, which rests on just as flimsy a foundation as does the evidence for long ages.[6]

Assuming these creationists are correct, how many generations are missing from Genesis 5 and 11? We will use the Hebrew text for these calculations; using other versions such as the Septuagint (LXX) makes the matter even more improbable.

According to the Hebrew text, there were 1,656 years between creation and the Flood and 1,556 years between creation and Noah's first son, or 10 generations. Assuming the average generation (from father to son) was 156 years (divide 1,556 by 10), how many extra generations are needed to get 5,000 years from the creation to Noah's first son? Divide 5,000 by 156 and you get about 32 generations. On the average, then, for every generation listed in Genesis 5, two are missing! However, let's examine Genesis 5 more closely:

1. There are no missing generations between Adam and Seth, since Seth is a direct replacement for Abel, whom Cain murdered (Genesis 4:25).

---

6. See Larry Vardiman, Andrew Snelling, and Eguene Chaffin, eds., *Radioisotopes and the Age of the Earth*, vol. 2 (El Cajon, CA: Institute for Creation Research; Chino Valley, AZ: Creation Research Society, 2005).

2. There are no missing generations between Seth and Enosh, since Seth named him (Genesis 4:25).

3. Jude says Enoch was the seventh from Adam (Jude 14), so there are no missing generations between Adam and Enoch.

4. Lamech named Noah, so there are no missing generations there (Genesis 5:29).

5. Some Hebrew scholars believe that the name *Methuselah* means "when he dies it is sent," referring to the Flood. Assuming no gaps in the chronology, Methuselah died the same year the Flood began. Some Jews believed that God gave Noah time to mourn the death of Methuselah, whom they believe died a week before the Flood began (Genesis 7:4). If this is so, then no missing generations can be inserted here. If this were not the case, then this is the only place in Genesis 5 one might attempt to shoehorn the missing 22 generations! Would you trust a chronologist who was so careful to record names and ages yet omit 22 generations in his tabulation in one place? It simply doesn't follow.

As we have seen, careful exegesis of the Bible simply does not allow for an extra 22 generations.

A similar analysis can be done for Genesis 11, which features 10 generations over 355 years, therefore averaging 36 years per generation. Those who hold to a creation occurring in 10,000 B.C. and the Flood happening in 5,000 B.C. have expanded this time period from 355 years to over 2,600 years. Assuming each generation lasts 36 years, then there would be 72 generations, such that for every generation listed, six are missing. If the writer of Genesis was so careless as to omit over 85 percent of the generations in Genesis 11, why did he waste time giving us the information in the first place? What purpose would it serve, since it would be so inaccurate?

These examples show the folly of accepting a creation event as distant as 10,000 B.C. Those who accept even longer ages have a worse problem; they must insert 10 to 100 times as many "missing generations" in Genesis 5 and 11 as those who hold to a creation of about 10,000 B.C. Interestingly, both camps loathe explaining where these missing generations are to be inserted. All they know for sure is that they are missing! Those who hold to the inerrancy of the Scriptures should reject all attempts to make the earth older than the Hebrew text warrants, which is about 4000 B.C.

Conclusion

The Scriptures themselves attest to the fact that the secular dates given for the age of the universe, man's existence on the earth, and so on, are not correct, because they are based on the fallible assumptions of fallible humans. Nothing in observational science contradicts the time-line of history as recorded in the Bible.

But there are two more reasons that these genealogies are vital. First, they are given in Scripture to show clearly that the Bible is real history and that we are all descendants of a real man, Adam; thus all human beings are related.

Second, the Son of God stepped into this history to fulfill the promise of Genesis 3:15, the promise of a Savior. This Savior died and rose again to provide a free gift of salvation to the descendants of Adam — all of whom are sinners and are separated from their Creator.

Without the genealogies, how can it be proven that Jesus is the One who would fulfill this promise? Indeed, perhaps the primary purpose of the genealogies is to show that Jesus fulfilled the promise of God the Father.

We can trust these genealogies because they are a part of the infallible, inerrant Word of God.

6

Can Natural Processes Explain the Origin of Life?

MIKE RIDDLE

When considering how life began, there are only two options. Either life was created by an intelligent source (God) or it began by natural processes. The common perception presented in many textbooks and in the media is that life arose from nonlife in a pool of chemicals about 3.8 billion years ago. The claim by evolutionists is that this formation of life was the result of time, chance, and natural processes. One widely used example of how life could have formed by natural processes is the Miller-Urey experiment, performed in the early 1950s.

Miller's objective was not to create life but to simulate how life's basic building structures (amino acids[1]) might have formed in the early earth. In the experiment, Miller attempted to simulate the early atmosphere of earth by using certain gases, which he thought might produce organic compounds necessary for life. Since the gases he included (water, methane, ammonia, and hydrogen) do not react with each other under natural conditions, he generated electrical currents to simulate some form of energy input (such as lightning) that was needed to drive the chemical reactions. The result was

---

1. The basic building blocks of all living systems are proteins, which consist of only 20 different types of amino acids. The average number of amino acids in a biological protein is over 300. These amino acids must be arranged in a very specific sequence for each protein.

production of amino acids. Many textbooks promote this experiment as the first step in explaining how life could have originated. But there is more to this experiment than what is commonly represented in textbooks.

The Rest of the Story — Some Critical Thinking

When we examine the purpose, assumptions, and results of the Miller experiment, there are three critical thinking questions that can be raised:

1. How much of the experiment was left to chance processes or how much involved intelligent design?
2. How did Miller know what earth's early atmosphere (billions of years ago) was like?
3. Did Miller produce the right type of amino acids used in life?

The Method Used

In the experiment, Miller was attempting to illustrate how life's building blocks (amino acids) could have formed by natural processes. However, throughout the experiment Miller relied on years of intelligent research in chemistry. He purposely chose which gases to include and which to exclude. Next, he had to isolate the biochemicals (amino acids) from the

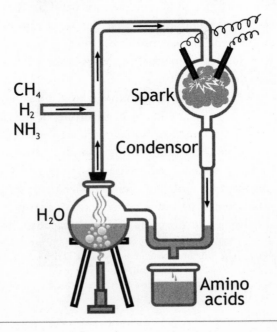

environment he had created them in because it would have destroyed them. No such system would have existed on the so-called primitive earth. It appears Miller used intelligent design throughout the experiment rather than chance processes.

The Starting Ingredients

How did Miller know what the atmosphere was like billions of years ago? Miller assumed that the early earth's atmosphere was very different from today. He based his starting chemical mixture on the assumption that the early earth had a reducing atmosphere (an atmosphere that contains no free oxygen). Why did Miller and many other evolutionists assume there was no free oxygen in earth's early atmosphere? As attested below, it is well known that biological molecules (specifically amino acid bonds) are destroyed in the presence of oxygen, making it impossible for life to evolve.

> Oxygen is a poisonous gas that oxidizes organic and inorganic materials on a planetary surface; it is quite lethal to organisms that have not evolved protection against it.[2]

> In the atmosphere and in the various water basins of the primitive earth, many destructive interactions would have so vastly diminished, if not altogether consumed, essential precursor chemicals, that chemical evolution rates would have been negligible.[3]

Therefore, in order to avoid this problem, evolutionists propose that earth's first atmosphere did not contain any freestanding oxygen. We must ask ourselves, "Is there any evidence to support this claim, or is it based on the assumption that evolution must be true?" As it turns out, the existence of a reducing atmosphere is merely an assumption not supported by the physical evidence. The evidence points to the fact that the earth has always had oxygen in the atmosphere.

> There is no scientific proof that Earth ever had a non-oxygen atmosphere such as evolutionists require. Earth's oldest rocks contain evidence of being formed in an oxygen atmosphere.[4]

2. P. Ward and D. Brownlee, *Rare Earth* (New York: Copernicus, 2000), p. 245.
3. C. Thaxton, W. Bradley, and R. Olsen, *The Mystery of Life's Origin: Reassessing Current Theories* (New York: Philosophical Library, 1984), p. 66.
4. H. Clemmey and N. Badham, "Oxygen in the Atmosphere: An Evaluation of the Geological Evidence," *Geology* 10 (1982): 141.

The only trend in the recent literature is the suggestion of far more oxygen in the early atmosphere than anyone imagined.[5]

If we were to grant the evolutionists' assumption of no oxygen in the original atmosphere, another fatal problem arises. Since the ozone is made of oxygen, it would not exist; and the ultraviolet rays from the sun would destroy any biological molecules. This presents a no-win situation for the evolution model. If there was oxygen, life could not start. If there was no oxygen, life could not start. Michael Denton notes:

> What we have is sort of a "Catch 22" situation. If we have oxygen we have no organic compounds, but if we don't have oxygen we have none either.[6]

Because life could not have originated on land, some evolutionists propose that life started in the oceans. The problem with life starting in the oceans, however, is that as organic molecules formed, the water would have immediately destroyed them through a process called *hydrolysis*. Hydrolysis, which means "water splitting," is the addition of a water molecule between two bonded molecules (two amino acids in this case), which causes them to split apart. Many scientists have noted this problem.

> Besides breaking up polypeptides, hydrolysis would have destroyed many amino acids.[7]

> In general the half-lives of these polymers in contact with water are on the order of days and months — time spans which are surely geologically insignificant.[8]

> Furthermore, water tends to break chains of amino acids apart. If any proteins had formed in the oceans 3.5 billion years ago, they would have quickly disintegrated.[9]

Scientifically, there is no known solution for how life could have chemically evolved on the earth.

---

5. Thaxton, Bradley, and Olsen, *The Mystery of Life's Origin*, p. 80.
6. M. Denton, *Evolution: A Theory in Crisis* (Bethesda, MD: Adler & Adler, 1985), p. 261.
7. *Encyclopedia of Science and Technology*, Vol. 1, 1982: p. 411–412.
8. K. Dose, *The Origin of Life and Evolutionary Biochemistry* (New York: Plenum Press, 1974), p. 69.
9. R. Morris, *The Big Questions* (New York: Times Books/Henry Holt, 2002), p. 167.

On the Other Hand . . .

Because the scientific evidence contradicts the origin of life by natural processes, Miller resorted to unrealistic initial conditions to develop amino acids in his experiment (no oxygen and excessive energy input). However, there is more to the story. Producing amino acids is not the hard part. The difficult part is getting the right type and organization of amino acids. There are over 2,000 types of amino acids, but only 20 are used in life. Furthermore, the atoms that make up each amino acid are assembled in two basic shapes. These are known as *left-handed* and *right-handed*. Compare them to human hands. Each hand has the same components (four fingers and a thumb), yet they are different. The thumb of one hand is on the left, and the thumb of the other is on the right. They are mirror images of each other. Like our hands, amino acids come in two shapes. They are composed of the same atoms (components) but are mirror images of each other, called left-handed amino acids and right-handed amino acids. Objects that have handedness are said to be *chiral* (pronounced "ky-rul"), which is from the Greek for *hand*.

Handedness is an important concept because all amino acids that make up proteins in living things are 100 percent left-handed. Right-handed amino acids are never found in proteins. If a protein were assembled with just one right-handed amino acid, the protein's function would be totally lost. As one PhD chemist has said:

> Many of life's chemicals come in two forms, "left-handed" and "right-handed." Life requires polymers with all building blocks having the same "handedness" (*homochirality*) — proteins have only

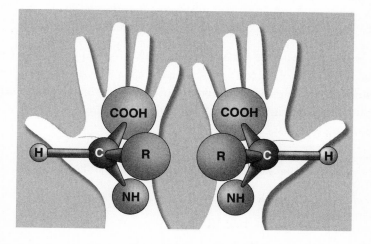

"left-handed" amino acids. . . . But ordinary undirected chemistry, as is the hypothetical primordial soup, would produce equal mixtures of left- and right-handed molecules, called *racemates*.[10]

A basic chemistry textbook admits:

> This is a very puzzling fact. . . . All the proteins that have been investigated, obtained from animals and from plants from higher organisms and from very simple organisms — bacteria, molds, even viruses — are found to have been made of L-amino [left-handed] acids.[11]

The common perception left by many textbooks and journals is that Miller and other scientists were successful in producing the amino acids necessary for life. However, the textbooks and media fail to mention that what they had actually produced was a mixture of left- and right-handed amino acids, which is detrimental to life. The natural tendency is for left- and right-handed amino acids to bond together. Scientists still do not know why biological proteins use only left-handed amino acids.

> The reason for this choice [only left-handed amino acids] is again a mystery, and a subject of continuous dispute.[12]

Jonathan Wells, a developmental biologist, writes:

> So we remain profoundly ignorant of how life originated. Yet the Miller-Urey experiment continues to be used as an icon of evolution, because nothing better has turned up. Instead of being told the truth, we are given the misleading impression that scientists have empirically demonstrated the first step in the origin of life.[13]

Despite the fact that the Miller experiment did not succeed in creating the building blocks of life (only left-handed amino acids), textbooks continue to promote the idea that life could have originated by natural processes. For example, the following statement from a biology textbook misleads students into thinking Miller succeeded:

10. John Ashton, ed., *In Six Days*, (Green Forest, AR: Master Books, 2000), p. 82.
11. Linus Pauling, *General Chemistry*, 3rd ed. (San Francisco, CA: W.H. Freeman & Co., 1970), p. 774.
12. Robert Shapiro, *Origins: A Skeptic's Guide to the Creation of Life on Earth* (New York: Summit Books, 1986), p. 86.
13. J. Wells, *Icons of Evolution* (Washington, DC: Regnery Pub., 2000), p. 24.

By re-creating the early atmosphere (ammonia, water, hydrogen and methane) and passing an electric spark (lightning) through the mixture, Miller and Urey proved that organic matter such as amino acids could have formed spontaneously.[14]

First, note the word *proved*. Miller and Urey proved nothing except that life's building blocks could *not* form in such conditions. Second, the textbook completely ignores other evidence, which shows that the atmosphere always contained oxygen. Third, the textbook ignores the fact that Miller got the wrong type of amino acids — a mixture of left- and right-handed.

The Miller experiment (and all experiments since then) failed to produce even a single biological protein by purely naturalistic processes. Only God could have begun life.

Information

Another important component of life is information. The common factor in all living organisms is the information contained in their cells. Where and how did all this coded information arise? Proteins are amazingly versatile and carry out many biochemical functions, but they are incapable of assembling themselves without the assistance of DNA. The function of DNA is to store information and pass it on (transcribe) to RNA, while the function of RNA is to read, decode, and use the information received from DNA to make proteins. Each of the thousands of genes on a DNA molecule contains instructions necessary to make a specific protein that, in turn, is needed for a specific biological function.

Any hypothesis or model meant to explain how all life evolved from lifeless chemicals into a complex cell consisting of vast amounts of information also has to explain the source of information and how this information was encoded into the genome. All evolutionary explanations are unable to answer this question. Dr. Werner Gitt, former physics professor and director of information processing at the Institute of Physics and Technology in Braunschweig, Germany, and Dr. Lee Spetner both agree that information cannot arise by naturalistic processes:

14. Kenneth Miller and Joseph Levine, *Biology*, 5th ed. (Upper Saddle River, NJ: Pearson Prentice Hall, 2000).

There is no known law of nature, no known process and no known sequence of events which can cause information to originate by itself in matter.[15]

Not even one mutation has been observed that adds a little information to the genome. This surely shows that there are not the millions upon millions of potential mutations the theory [evolution] demands.[16]

The DNA code within all plant and animal cells is vastly more compact than any computer chip ever made. DNA is so compact that a one-square-inch chip of DNA could encode the information in over seven billion Bibles. Since the density and complexity of the genetic code is millions of times greater than man's present technology, we can conclude that the originator of the information must be supremely intelligent.

Two biologists have noted:

DNA is an information code. . . . The overwhelming conclusion is that information does not and cannot arise spontaneously by mechanistic processes. Intelligence is a necessity in the origin of any informational code, including the genetic code, no matter how much time is given.[17]

God, in His Word, tells us that His creation is a witness to himself and that we do not have an excuse for not believing (Romans 1:19–20). The fact that the information encoded in DNA ultimately needs to have come from an infinite source of information testifies to a Creator. And as we saw above, the only known way to link together left-handed amino acids is through purposeful design.

Since no human was present to assemble the first living cell, it is further testimony to an all-wise Creator God.

Given Enough Time . . .

Nobel prize-winning scientist George Wald once wrote:

---

15. W. Gitt, *In the Beginning Was Information* (Green Forest, AR: Master Books, 2006).
16. L. Spetner, *Not by Chance* (New York: Judaica Press, 1997), p. 160.
17. L. Lester and R. Bohlin, *The Natural Limits to Biological Change*, (Dallas, TX: Probe Books, 1989), p. 157.

However improbable we regard this event [evolution], or any of the steps which it involves, given enough time it will almost certainly happen at least once. . . . Time is in fact the hero of the plot. . . . Given so much time, the "impossible" becomes possible, the possible probable, the probable virtually certain. One has only to wait; time itself performs the miracles.[18]

In the case of protein formation, the statement "given enough time" is not valid. When we look at the mathematical probabilities of even a small protein (100 amino acids) assembling by random chance, it is beyond anything that has ever been observed.

What is the probability of ever getting one small protein of 100 left-handed amino acids? (An average protein has at least 300 amino acids in it — all left-handed.) To assemble just 100 left-handed amino acids (far shorter than the average protein) would be the same probability as getting 100 heads in a row when flipping a coin. In order to get 100 heads in a row, we would have to flip a coin 10^{30} times (this is 10 x 10, 30 times). This is such an astounding improbability that there would not be enough time in the whole history of the universe (even according to evolutionary time frames) for this to happen.

The ability of complex structures to form by naturalistic processes is essential for the evolution model to work. However, the complexity of life

18. George Wald, "The Origin of Life," *Scientific American* 191 no. 2 (1954): 48.

appears to preclude this from happening. According to the laws of probability, if the chance of an event occurring is smaller than 1 in 10^{-50}, then the event will never occur (this is equal to 1 divided by 10^{50} and is a very small number).[19]

What have scientists calculated the probability to be of an average-size protein occurring naturally? Walter Bradley, PhD, materials science, and Charles Thaxton, PhD, chemistry,[20] calculated that the probability of amino acids forming into a protein is:

$$4.9 \times 10^{-191}$$

This is well beyond the laws of probability (1×10^{-50}), and a protein is not even close to becoming a complete living cell. Sir Fred Hoyle, PhD, astronomy, and Chandra Wickramasinghe, professor of applied math and astronomy, calculated that the probability of getting a cell by naturalistic processes is:

$$1 \times 10^{-40,000}$$

No matter how large the environment one considers, life cannot have had a random beginning. . . . There are about two thousand enzymes, and the chance of obtaining them all in a random trial is only one part in $(10^{20})^{2000} = 10^{40,000}$, an outrageously small probability that could not be faced even if the whole universe consisted of organic soup.[21]

Conclusion

As we have seen, the scientific evidence confirms that "in the beginning, God created." Life cannot come from nonlife; only God can create life. True science and the Bible will always agree. Whether in biology, astronomy, geology, or any other field of study, we can trust God's Word to be accurate when it speaks about these topics. Let us stand up for the truth of Genesis and take back our culture.

---

19. Probability expert Emile Borel wrote, "Events whose probabilities are extremely small never occur. . . . We may be led to set at 1 to the 50th power the value of negligible probabilities on the cosmic scale." (E. Borel, *Probabilities and Life*, [New York: Dover Publications, 1962], p. 28.)
20. Thaxton, Bradley, and Olsen, *The Mystery of Life's Origin*, p. 80.
21 F. Hoyle and C. Wickramasinghe, *Evolution from Space* (New York: Simon and Schuster, 1984), p. 176.

7

Are Mutations Part of the "Engine" of Evolution?

BODIE HODGE

I n the evolutionary model, mutations are hailed as a dominant mechanism for pond-scum-to-people evolution and provide "proof" that the Bible's history about creation is wrong. But are we to trust the ideas of imperfect, fallible men about how we came into existence, or should we believe the account of a perfect God who was an eyewitness to His creation? Let's look at mutations in more detail and see if they provide the information necessary to support pond-scum-to-people evolution, or if they confirm God's Word in Genesis.

Mutations are primarily permanent changes in the DNA strand. DNA (deoxyribonucleic acid) is the information storage unit for all organisms, including humans, cats, and dogs. In humans, the DNA consists of about three billion base pairs. The DNA is made of two strands and forms a double helix. In sexual reproduction, one set of chromosomes (large segments of DNA) comes from the mother and one set from the father. In asexual reproduction, the DNA is copied whole and then passed along when the organism splits.

The double helix is made up of four types of nitrogen bases called *nucleotides*. These types are guanine, cytosine, adenine, and thymine. They are represented by the letters G, C, A, and T. Each of these base pairs, or "letters," is part of a code that stores information for hair color, height, eye shape, etc. The bases pair up as follows: adenine to thymine and guanine to cytosine.

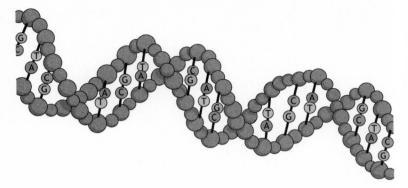

Think of it like Morse code. Morse code is a system in which letters are represented by dashes and dots (if audible, then it is a long sound and short sound). When you combine different dots and dashes, you can spell out letters and words. Here is a copy of Morse code:

A •-	N -•	0 -----
B —•••	O ---	1 •----
C -•-•	P •--•	2 ••---
D -••	Q --•-	3 •••--
E •	R •-•	4 ••••-
F ••-•	S •••	5 •••••
G --•	T -	6 -••••
H ••••	U ••-	7 --•••
I ••	V •••-	8 ---••
J •---	W •--	9 ----•
K -•-	X -••-	Fullstop •-•-•
L •-••	Y -•--	Comma --••--
M --	Z --••	Query ••--••

If someone wanted to call for help using Morse code, for instance, he or she would send the letters SOS (which is the international distress signal). Morse code for SOS is:

S is *dot dot dot* [• • •] or three short sounds.

O is *dash dash dash* [– – –] or three long sounds.

S is *dot dot dot* [• • •] or three short sounds.

Therefore, it would be [• • • – – – • • •], or three short sounds followed by three long sounds, followed by three short sounds.

A mutation would be like changing a dot to a dash in Morse code. If we tried to spell SOS in Morse code, but changed the first dot to a dash, it would accidentally read:

$$[- • • – – – • • •]$$

Dash dot dot is the sequence for D, not S; so it would now read:

D [– • •]
O [– – –]
S [• • •]

So, because of the mistake (mutation), we now read DOS, instead of SOS. If you sent this, no one would think you needed help. This mutation was significant because it did two things to your message:

1. The original word was lost.
2. The intent/meaning was lost.

The DNA strand is similar to, but much more complicated than, Morse code. It uses four letters (G, A, T, C) instead of dashes and dots to make words and phrases. And like Morse code, mutations can affect the DNA strand and cause problems for the organism. These DNA mistakes are called *genetic* mutations.

Theoretically, genetic mutations (that are not static) can cause one of two things:

1. Loss of information[1]
2. Gain of new information

Virtually all observed mutations are in the category of *loss of information*. This is different from loss or gain of *function*. Some mutations can cause an organism to lose genetic information and yet gain some type of function. This is rare but has happened. These types of mutations have a *beneficial* outcome. For example, if a beetle loses the information to make a wing on a windy island, the mutation is beneficial because the beetle doesn't get blown out to

---

1. For a definition of information that is based on the laws of science, see W. Gitt, *In the Beginning Was Information* (Green Forest, AR: Master Books, 2006).

sea and killed. Genetically, the mutation caused a loss of information but was helpful to the beetle. Thus, it was a beneficial outcome.

Besides mutations that cause information loss, in theory there could also be mutations that cause a *gain of new information*. There are only a few alleged cases of such mutations. However, if a mutated DNA strand were built up with a group of base pairs that didn't do anything, this strand wouldn't be useful. Therefore, to be useful to an organism, a mutation that has a gain of new information must also cause a gain of new function.

Types of Genetic Mutations

The DNA strand contains instructions on how to make proteins. Every three "letters" code for a specific amino acid, such as TGC, ATC, GAT, TAG, and CTC. Many amino acids together compose a protein. For simplicity's sake, to illustrate concepts with the DNA strand, we will use examples in English. Here is a segment illustrating DNA in three-letter words:

The car was red. The red car had one key.

The key has one eye and one tip.

Point Mutations

Point mutations are mutations where one letter changes on the DNA sequence. A point mutation in our example could cause "car" in the second sentence to be read "cat":

The car was red. The red **cat** had one key.

The key has one eye and one tip.

With this point mutation, we lost the information for one word (car) as well as changed the meaning of the sentence. We did gain one word (cat), but we lost one word (car) and lost the meaning of one phrase. So the overall result was a loss of information.

But many times, point mutations won't produce another word. Take for instance another point mutation, which changes "car" not to "cat" but to "caa":

The car was red. The red **caa** had one key.

The key has one eye and one tip.

With this point mutation, we lost the information for one word (car) as well as the meaning. We did not gain any new words, and we lost one word and lost the meaning of one phrase. So again, the overall result of this point mutation was a loss of information, but even more so this time.

Point mutations can be very devastating. There is a children's disease called Hutchinson-Gilford progeria syndrome (HGPS), or simply progeria. It was recently linked to a single point mutation. It is a mutation that causes children's skin to age, their head to go bald at a very early age (pre-kindergarten), their bones to develop problems usually associated with the elderly, and their body size to remain very short (about one-half to two-thirds of normal height). Their body parts, including organs, age rapidly, which usually causes death at the average age of 13 years.[2]

Not all point mutations are as devastating, yet they still result in a loss of information. According to biophysicist Lee Spetner, "All point mutations that have been studied on the molecular level turn out to reduce the genetic information and not to increase it."[3]

Inversion Mutations

An inversion mutation is a strand of DNA in a particular segment that reverses itself. An inversion mutation would be like taking the second sentence of our example and spelling it backwards:

The car was red. **Yek eno dah rac der eht.**

The key has one eye and one tip.

With inversion mutations, we can lose quite a bit of information. We lost several words from, and the meaning of, the second sentence. These mutations can cause serious problems to the organism. The bleeding disorder hemophilia A is caused by an inversion in the Factor VIII (F8) gene.

Insertion Mutations

An insertion mutation is a segment of DNA, whether a single base pair or an extensive length, that is inserted into the DNA strand. For this example, let's copy a word from the second sentence and insert it into the third sentence:

The car was red. The red car had one key.

Had the key has one eye and one tip.

2. B. Hodge, "One Tiny Flaw and 50 Years Lost," *Creation* 27(1) (2004): 33.
3. L. Spetner, *Not by Chance* (New York: Judaica Press, 1997), p. 138.

This insertion really didn't help anything. In fact, the insertion is detrimental to the third sentence in that it makes the third sentence meaningless. So this copied word in the third sentence destroyed the combined meanings of the eight words in the third sentence. Insertions generally result in a protein that loses function.[4]

Deletion Mutations

A deletion mutation is a segment of DNA, whether a single base pair or an extensive length, that is deleted from the strand. This will be an obvious loss. In this instance, the second sentence will be deleted.

The car was red. The key has one eye and one tip.

The entire second sentence has been lost. Thus, we have lost its meaning as well as the words that were in the sentence. Some disorders from deletion mutations are facioscapulohumeral muscular dystrophy (FSHD) and spinal muscular atrophy.[5]

Frame Shift Mutations

There are two basic types of frame shift mutations: frame shift due to an insertion and frame shift due to a deletion. These mutations can be caused by an insertion or deletion of one or more letters not divisible by three, which causes an offset in the reading of the "letters" of the DNA.

If a mutation occurs where one or more letters are inserted, then the entire sentence can be off. If a **t** were inserted at the beginning of the second sentence, it would read like this:

The car was red. T<u>t</u>h ere dca rha don eke yth
eke yha son eey ean don eti p.

Four new words were produced (two of them twice): *ere, don, eke* and *son*. These 4 words were not part of the original phrase. However, we lost 14 words. Not only did we lose these words, but we also lost the meaning behind the words. We lost 14 words while gaining only 4 new ones.

Therefore, even though the DNA strand became longer and produced 4 words via a single insertion, it lost 14 other words. The overall effect was a loss of information.

4. DNA Direct website, www.dnadirect.com/resource/genetics_101/GH_DNA_mutations.jsp.
5. Athena Diagnostics website, www.athenadiagnostics.com/site/content/diagnostic_ed/genetics_primer/part_2.asp.

A frame shift mutation can also occur by the deletion of one or more "letters." If the first **t** in the second sentence is deleted, the letters shift to the left, and we get:

The car was red. **Her** edc arh **ado** nek eyt hek

eyh aso **nee yea** ndo **net** ip.

Five new words were produced: *her, ado, nee, yea,* and *net.* However, once again, we lost 14 words. So again, the overall effect was a loss of information, and the DNA strand became smaller due to this mutation.

Frame shift mutations are usually detrimental to the organism by causing the resulting protein to be nonfunctional.

This is just the basics of mutations at a genetic level.[6]

What Does Evolution Teach about Mutations?

Pond-scum-to-people evolution teaches that, over time, by natural causes, nonliving chemicals gave rise to a living cell. Then, this single-celled life form gave rise to more advanced life forms. In essence, over millions of years, increases in information caused by mutations plus natural selection developed all the life forms we see on earth today.

For molecules-to-man evolution to happen, there needs to be a gain in *new* information within the organism's genetic material. For instance, for a single-celled organism, such as an amoeba, to evolve into something like a cow, *new* information (not random base pairs, but complex and ordered DNA) would need to develop over time that would code for ears, lungs, brain, legs, etc.

6. For more on specific mutations and more complex examples, please visit www. answersingenesis.org/go/mutations.

If an amoeba were to make a change like this, the DNA would need to mutate *new* information. (Currently, an amoeba has limited genetic information, such as the information for protoplasm.) This increase of new information would need to continue in order for a heart, kidneys, etc., to develop. If a DNA strand gets larger due to a mutation, but the sequence doesn't code for anything (e.g., it doesn't contain information for working lungs, heart, etc.), then the amount of DNA added is useless and would be more of a hindrance than a help.

There have been a few arguable cases of information-gaining mutations, but for evolution to be true, there would need to be *billions* of them. The fact is, we don't observe this in nature, but rather we see the opposite — organisms losing information. Organisms are changing, but the change is in the wrong direction! How can losses of information add up to a gain?

What Does the Bible Teach?

From a biblical perspective, we know that Adam and Eve had perfect DNA because God declared all that He had made "very good" (Genesis 1:31). This goes for the original animal and plant kinds as well. They originally had perfect DNA strands with no mistakes or mutations.

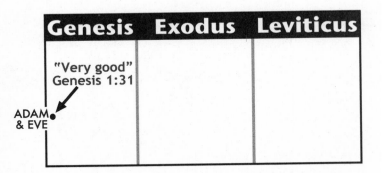

However, when man sinned against God (Genesis 3), God cursed the ground and the animals, and He sentenced man to die (Genesis 2:17; 3:19). At this time, God seemed to withdraw some of His sustaining power to no longer completely uphold everything in a perfect state.

Since then, we would expect mutations to occur and DNA flaws to accumulate. The incredible amount of information that was originally in the DNA has been filtered out, and in many cases lost, due to mutations and natural selection.

Genesis	Exodus	Leviticus
SIN AND THE CURSE ADAM & EVE • Genesis 3		

At the time of Noah's flood, there was a genetic bottleneck where information was lost among many land animals and humans. The only genetic information that survived came from the representatives of the kinds of land-dwelling, air-breathing animals and humans that were on the ark.

Over time, as people increased on the earth, God knew that mutations were rising within the human population and declared that people should no longer intermarry with close relatives (Leviticus 18). Why did He do this? Intermarriage with close relatives results in the possibility of similar genetic mutations appearing in a child due to inheriting a common mutation from both the father and mother. If both parents inherited the same mutated gene from a common ancestor (e.g., a grandparent), this would increase the possibility of both parents passing this mutated gene along to their child.

Marrying someone who is not a close relative reduces the chances that both would have the same mutated gene. If the segment of DNA from the mother had a mutation, it would be masked by the father's unmutated gene. If the segment of DNA from the father had a mutation, it would be masked by the mother's unmutated gene. If the genes from both parents were mutated,

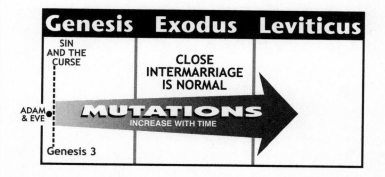

81

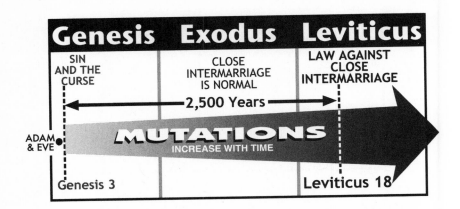

then the mutation would show in the child.[7] Our all-knowing God obviously knew this would happen and gave the command in Leviticus not to marry close relations.

Conclusion

The biblical perspective on change within living things doesn't require that new information be added to the genome as pond-scum-to-people evolution does. In fact, we expect to see the opposite (loss of genetic information) due to the curse in Genesis 3. Biblically, we would expect mutations to produce defects in the genome and would not expect mutations to be adding much, if any, new information.

Observations confirm that mutations overwhelmingly cause a loss of information, not a net gain, as evolution requires.

Mutations, when properly understood, are an excellent example of science confirming the Bible. When one sees the devastating effects of mutations, one can't help but be reminded of the curse in Genesis 3. The accumulation of mutations from generation to generation is due to man's sin. But those who have placed their faith in Christ, our Creator, look forward to a new heaven and earth where there will be no more pain, death, or disease.

7. This is only true for recessive mutations like the one that causes cystic fibrosis. There are some dominant mutations that will appear in the child regardless of having a normal copy of the gene from one parent.

8

Did Humans Really Evolve from Apelike Creatures?

DR. DAVID MENTON

Perhaps the most bitter pill to swallow for any Christian who attempts to "make peace" with Darwin is the presumed ape ancestry of man. Even many Christians who uncritically accept evolution as "God's way of creating" try to somehow elevate the origin of man, or at least his soul, above that of the beasts. Evolutionists attempt to soften the blow by assuring us that man didn't exactly evolve from apes (tailless monkeys) but rather from *apelike* creatures. This is mere semantics, however, as many of the presumed apelike ancestors of man are apes and have scientific names, which include the word *pithecus* (derived from the Greek meaning "ape"). The much-touted "human ancestor" commonly known as "Lucy," for example, has the scientific name *Australopithecus afarensis* (meaning "southern *ape* from the Afar triangle of Ethiopia"). But what does the Bible say about the origin of man, and what exactly is the scientific evidence that evolutionists claim for our ape ancestry?

Biblical Starting Assumptions

God tells us that on the same day He made all animals that walk on the earth (the sixth day), He created man separately in His own image with the intent that man would have dominion over every other living thing on earth (Genesis 1:26–28). From this it is clear that there is no animal that is man's equal, and certainly none his ancestor.

Thus, when God paraded the animals by Adam for him to name, He observed that "for Adam there was not found an help meet for him" (Genesis 2:20). Jesus confirmed this uniqueness of men and women when He declared that marriage is to be between a man and a woman because "from the beginning of the creation God made them male and female" (Mark 10:6). This leaves no room for prehumans or for billions of years of cosmic evolution prior to man's appearance on the earth. Adam chose the very name "Eve" for his wife because he recognized that she would be "the mother of all living" (Genesis 3:20). The apostle Paul stated clearly that man is not an animal: "All flesh is not the same flesh: but there is one kind of flesh of men, another flesh of beasts, another of fishes, and another of birds" (1 Corinthians 15:39).

Evolutionary Starting Assumptions

While Bible-believing Christians begin with the assumption that God's Word is true and that man's ancestry goes back only to a fully human Adam and Eve, evolutionists begin with the assumption that man has, in fact, evolved from apes. No paleoanthropologists (those who study the fossil evidence for man's origin) would dare to seriously raise the question, "*Did* man evolve from apes?" The only permissible question is, "From *which* apes did man evolve?"

Since evolutionists generally do not believe that man evolved from any ape that is now living, they look to fossils of humans and apes to provide them with their desired evidence. Specifically, they look for any anatomical feature that looks "intermediate" (between that of apes and man). Fossil apes having such features are declared to be ancestral to man (or at least collateral relatives) and are called *hominids*. Living apes, on the other hand, are not considered to be hominids, but rather are called *hominoids* because they are only similar to humans but did not evolve into them. Nonetheless, evolutionists are willing to accept mere similarities between the fossilized bones of extinct apes and the bones of living men as "proof" of our ape ancestry.

What Is the Evidence for Human Evolution?

Though many similarities may be cited between living apes and humans, the only historical evidence that could support the ape ancestry of man must come from fossils. Unfortunately, the fossil record of man and apes is very sparse. Approximately 95 percent of all known fossils are marine invertebrates, about 4.7 percent are algae and plants, about 0.2 percent are insects and other invertebrates, and only about 0.1 percent are vertebrates (animals with bones). Finally, only the smallest imaginable fraction of vertebrate fossils consists of primates (humans, apes, monkeys, and lemurs).

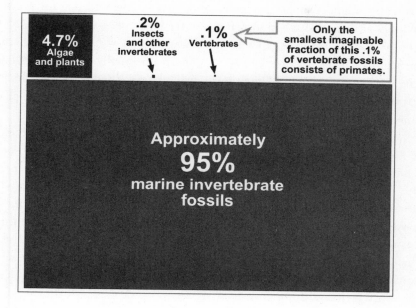

Because of the rarity of fossil hominids, even many of those who specialize in the evolution of man have never actually seen an original hominid fossil, and far fewer have ever had the opportunity to handle or study one. Most scientific papers on human evolution are based on casts of original specimens (or even on published photos, measurements, and descriptions of them). Access to original fossil hominids is strictly limited by those who discovered them and is often confined to a few favored evolutionists who agree with the discoverers' interpretation of the fossil.

Since there is much more prestige in finding an ancestor of man than an ancestor of living apes (or worse yet, merely an extinct ape), there is immense pressure on paleoanthropologists to declare almost any ape fossil to be a "hominid." As a result, the living apes have pretty much been left to find their own ancestors.

Many students in our schools are taught human evolution (often in the social studies class!) by teachers having little knowledge of human anatomy, to say nothing of ape anatomy. But it is useless to consider the fossil evidence for the evolution of man from apes without first understanding the basic anatomical and functional differences between human and ape skeletons.

Jaws and Teeth

Because of their relative hardness, teeth and jaw fragments are the most frequently found primate fossils. Thus, much of the evidence for the ape ancestry of man is based on similarities of teeth and jaws.

In contrast to man, apes tend to have incisor and canine teeth that are relatively larger than their molars. Ape teeth usually have thin enamel (the hardest surface layer of the tooth), while humans generally have thicker enamel. Finally, the jaws tend to be more U-shaped in apes and more parabolic in man.

The problem in declaring a fossil ape to be a human ancestor (i.e., a hominid) on the basis of certain humanlike features of the teeth is that some living apes have these same features and they are not considered to be ancestors of man. Some species of modern baboons, for example, have relatively small canines and incisors and relatively large molars. While most apes do have thin enamel, some apes, such as the orangutans, have relatively thick enamel. Clearly, teeth tell us more about an animal's diet and feeding habits than its supposed evolution. Nonetheless, thick enamel is one of the most commonly cited criteria for declaring an ape fossil to be a hominid.

Artistic imagination has been used to illustrate entire "apemen" from nothing more than a single tooth. In the early 1920s, the "apeman" *Hesperopithecus* (which consisted of a single tooth) was pictured in the *London Illustrated News* complete with the tooth's wife, children, domestic animals, and cave! Experts used this tooth, known as "Nebraska man," as proof for human evolution during the Scopes trial in 1925. In 1927, parts of the skeleton were discovered together with the teeth, and Nebraska man was found to really be an extinct peccary (wild pig)!

Skulls

Skulls are perhaps the most interesting primate fossils because they house the brain and give us an opportunity, with the help of imaginative artists, to look our presumed ancestors in the face. The human skull is easily distinguished from all living apes, though there are, of course, similarities.

The vault of the skull is large in humans because of their relatively large brain compared to apes. Even so, the size of the normal adult human brain varies over nearly a threefold range. These differences in size in the human brain do not correlate with intelligence. Adult apes have brains that are generally smaller than even the smallest of adult human brains, and of course they are not even remotely comparable in intelligence.

Perhaps the best way to distinguish an ape skull from a human skull is to examine it from a side view. From this perspective, the face of the human is nearly vertical, while that of the ape slopes forward from its upper face to its chin.

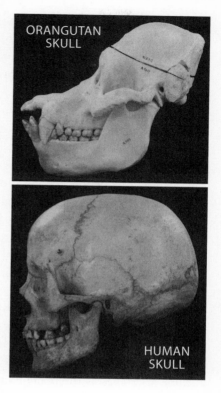

From a side view, the bony socket of the eye (the *orbit*) of an ape is obscured by its broad, flat upper face. Humans, on the other hand, have a more curved upper face and forehead, clearly revealing the orbit of the eye from a side view.

Another distinctive feature of the human skull is the nose bone that our glasses rest on. Apes do not have protruding nasal bones and would have great difficulty wearing glasses.

Leg Bones

The most eagerly sought-after evidence in fossil hominids is any anatomical feature that might suggest *bipedality* (the ability to walk on two legs). Since humans walk on two legs, any evidence of bipedality in fossil apes is considered by evolutionists to be compelling evidence for human ancestry. But we should bear in mind that the way an ape walks on two legs is entirely different from the way man walks on two legs. The distinctive human gait requires the complex integration of many skeletal and muscular features in our hips, legs, and feet. Thus, evolutionists closely examine the hipbones (*pelvis*), thighbones (*femur*), leg bones (*tibia* and *fibula*), and foot bones of fossil apes in an effort to detect any anatomical features that might suggest bipedality.

Evolutionists are particularly interested in the angle at which the femur and the tibia meet at the knee (called the *carrying angle*). Humans are able to keep their weight over their feet while walking because their femurs converge toward the knees, forming a carrying angle of approximately nine degrees with the tibia (in other words, we're sort of knock-kneed). In contrast, chimps and gorillas have widely separated, straight legs with a carrying angle of essentially zero degrees. These animals manage to keep their weight over their feet when walking by swinging their body from side to side in the familiar "ape walk."

Evolutionists assume that fossil apes with a high carrying angle (human-like) were bipedal and thus evolved into man. Certain *australopithecines* (ape-like creatures) are considered to have walked like us and thus to be our ancestors largely because they had a high carrying angle. But high carrying angles are not confined to humans — they are also found on some modern apes that walk gracefully on tree limbs and only clumsily on the ground.

Living apes with a high carrying angle (values comparable to man) include such apes as the orangutan and spider monkey — both adept tree climbers and capable of only an apelike bipedal gait on the ground. The point is that there are *living* tree-dwelling apes and monkeys with some of the same anatomical features that evolutionists consider to be definitive evidence for bipedality, yet none of these animals walks like man and no one suggests they are our ancestors or descendants.

Foot Bones

The human foot is unique and not even close to the appearance or function of the ape foot. The big toe of the human foot is in-line with the foot and does not jut out to the side like an ape's. Human toe bones are relatively straight, rather than curved and grasping like ape toes.

While walking, the heel of the human foot hits the ground first and then the weight distribution spreads from the heel along the outer margin of the foot up to the base of the little toe. From the little toe it spreads inward across the base of the toes and finally pushes off from the big toe. No ape has a foot or push-off like that of a human, and thus, no ape is capable of walking with our distinctive human stride or making human footprints.

Hipbones

The pelvis (hipbones) plays a critically important role in walking, and the characteristic human gait requires a pelvis that is distinctly different from that of the apes. Indeed, one only has to examine the pelvis to determine if an ape has the ability to walk like a man.

The part of the hipbones that we can feel just under our belt is called the iliac blade. Viewed from above, these blades are curved forward like the handles of a steering yolk on an airplane. The iliac blades of the ape, in contrast, project straight out to the side like the handlebars of a scooter. It is simply not possible to walk like a human with an apelike pelvis. On this feature alone one can easily distinguish apes from humans.

Only Three Ways to Make an "Apeman"

Knowing from Scripture that God didn't create any apemen, there are only three ways for the evolutionist to create one:

1 Combine ape fossil bones with human fossil bones and declare the two to be one individual — a real "apeman."
2 Emphasize certain humanlike qualities of fossilized ape bones, and with imagination upgrade apes to be more humanlike.
3 Emphasize certain apelike qualities of fossilized human bones, and with imagination downgrade humans to be more apelike.

These three approaches account for *all* of the attempts by evolutionists to fill the unbridgeable gap between apes and men with fossil apemen.

Combining Men and Apes

The most famous example of an apeman proven to be a combination of ape and human bones is Piltdown man. In 1912, Charles Dawson, a medical doctor and an amateur paleontologist, discovered a mandible (lower jawbone) and part of a skull in a gravel pit near Piltdown, England. The jawbone was apelike, but had teeth that showed wear similar to the human pattern. The skull, on the other hand, was very humanlike. These two specimens were combined to form what was called "Dawn man," which was calculated to be 500,000 years old.

The whole thing turned out to be an elaborate hoax. The skull was indeed human (about 500 years old), while the jaw was that of a modern female orangutan whose teeth had been obviously filed to crudely resemble the human wear pattern. Indeed, the long ape canine tooth was filed down so far that it exposed the pulp chamber, which was then filled in to hide the mischief. It would seem that any competent scientist examining this tooth would have concluded that it was either a hoax or the world's first root canal! The success of this hoax for over 50 years, in spite of the careful scrutiny of the best authorities in the world, led the human evolutionist Sir Solly Zuckerman to declare: "It is doubtful if there is any science at all in the search for man's fossil ancestry."[1]

Making Man out of Apes

Many apemen are merely apes that evolutionists have attempted to upscale to fill the gap between apes and men. These include all the australopithecines, as well as a host of other extinct apes such as *Ardipithecus, Orrorin, Sahelanthropus,* and *Kenyanthropus.* All have obviously ape skulls, ape pelvises, and ape hands and feet. Nevertheless, australopithecines (especially *Australopithecus afarensis*) are often portrayed as having hands and feet identical to modern man; a ramrod-straight, upright posture; and a human gait.

The best-known specimen of *A. afarensis* is the fossil commonly known as "Lucy." A life-like mannequin of "Lucy" in the *Living World* exhibit at the St. Louis Zoo shows a hairy, humanlike female body with human hands and feet but with an obviously apelike head. The three-foot-tall Lucy stands erect in a deeply pensive pose with her right forefinger curled under her chin, her eyes gazing off into the distance as if she were contemplating the mind of Newton.

Few visitors are aware that this is a gross misrepresentation of what is known about the fossil ape *Australopithecus afarensis.* These apes are known

1. S. Zuckerman, *Beyond the Ivory Tower* (London: Weidenfeld & Nicolson, 1970), p. 64.

to be long-armed knuckle-walkers with locking wrists. Both the hands and feet of this creature are clearly apelike. Paleoanthropologists Jack Stern and Randall Sussman[2] have reported that the hands of this species are "surprisingly similar to hands found in the small end of the pygmy chimpanzee–common chimpanzee range." They report that the feet, like the hands, are "long, curved and heavily muscled" much like those of living tree-dwelling primates. The authors conclude that no living primate has such hands and feet "for any purpose other than to meet the demands of full or part-time arboreal (tree-dwelling) life."

Despite evidence to the contrary, evolutionists and museums continue to portray Lucy (*A. afarensis*) with virtually human feet (though some are finally showing the hands with long, curved fingers).

Making Apes out of Man

In an effort to fill the gap between apes and men, certain fossil *men* have been declared to be "apelike" and thus, ancestral to at least "modern" man. You might say this latter effort seeks to make a "monkey" out of man! Human fossils that are claimed to be "apemen" are generally classified under the genus *Homo* (meaning "self"). These include *Homo erectus, Homo heidelbergensis,* and *Homo neanderthalensis.*

The best-known human fossils are of Cro-Magnon man (whose marvelous paintings are found on the walls of caves in France) and Neandertal man. Both are clearly human and have long been classified as *Homo sapiens.* In recent years, however, Neandertal man has been downgraded to a different species — *Homo neanderthalensis.* The story of how Neandertal man was demoted to an apeman provides much insight into the methods of evolutionists.

Neandertal man was first discovered in 1856 by workmen digging in a limestone cave in the Neander valley near Dusseldorf, Germany. The fossil bones were examined by an anatomist (Professor Schaafhausen) who concluded that they were human.

At first, not much attention was given to these finds, but with the publication of Darwin's *Origin of Species* in 1859, the search began for the imagined "apelike ancestors" of man. Darwinians argued that Neandertal man was an apelike creature, while many critical of Darwin (like the great anatomist Rudolph Virchow) argued that Neandertals were human in every respect, though some appeared to be suffering from rickets or arthritis.

---

2. *American Journal of Physical Anthropology* 60 (1983): 279–317.

Over 300 Neandertal specimens have now been found scattered throughout most of the world, including Belgium, China, Central and North Africa, Iraq, the Czech Republic, Hungary, Greece, northwestern Europe, and the Middle East. This group of people was characterized by prominent eyebrow ridges (like modern Australian Aborigines), a low forehead, a long, narrow skull, a protruding upper jaw, and a strong lower jaw with a short chin. They were deep-chested, large-boned individuals with a powerful build. It should be emphasized, however, that none of these features fall outside the range of normal human anatomy. Interestingly, the brain size (based on cranial capacity) of Neandertal man was actually *larger* than average for that of modern man, though this is rarely emphasized.

Most of the misconceptions about Neandertal man resulted from the claims of the Frenchman Marcelin Boule who, in 1908, studied two Neandertal skeletons that were found in France (LeMoustier and La Chapelle-aux-Saints). Boule declared Neandertal men to be anatomically and intellectually inferior brutes who were more closely related to apes than humans. He asserted that they had a slumped posture, a "monkey-like" arrangement of certain spinal vertebrae, and he even claimed that their feet were of a "grasping type" (like those of gorillas and chimpanzees). Boule concluded that Neandertal man could not have walked erectly, but rather must have walked in a clumsy fashion. These highly biased and inaccurate views prevailed and were even expanded by many other evolutionists up to the mid-1950s.

In 1957, the anatomists William Straus and A.J. Cave examined one of the French Neandertals (La Chapelle-aux-Saints) and determined that the individual suffered from severe arthritis (as suggested by Virchow nearly 100 years earlier), which had affected the vertebrae and bent the posture. The jaw also had been affected. These observations are consistent with the Ice Age climate in which Neandertals had lived. They may well have sought shelter in caves, and this, together with poor diet and lack of sunlight, could easily have led to diseases that affect the bones, such as rickets.

In addition to anatomical evidence, there is a growing body of cultural evidence for the fully human status of Neandertals. They buried their dead and had elaborate funeral customs that included arranging the body and covering it with flowers. They made a variety of stone tools and worked with skins and leather. A wood flute was recently discovered among Neandertal remains. There is even evidence that suggests that Neandertals engaged in medical care. Some Neandertal specimens show evidence of survival to old age despite numerous wounds, broken bones, blindness, and disease. This suggests that these individuals were cared for and nurtured by others who showed human compassion.

Still, efforts continue to be made to somehow dehumanize Neandertal man. Many evolutionists now even insist that Neandertal man is not even directly related to modern man because of some differences in a small fragment of DNA! There is, in fact, nothing about Neandertals that is in any way inferior to modern man. One of the world's foremost authorities on Neandertal man, Erik Trinkaus, concludes: "Detailed comparisons of Neandertal skeletal remains with those of modern humans have shown that there is nothing in Neandertal anatomy that conclusively indicates locomotor, manipulative, intellectual, or linguistic abilities inferior to those of modern humans."[3]

Conclusion

Why then are there continued efforts to make apes out of man and man out of apes? In one of the most remarkably frank and candid assessments of the whole subject and the methodology of paleoanthropology, Dr. David Pilbeam (a distinguished professor of anthropology) suggested the following:

> Perhaps generations of students of human evolution, including myself, have been flailing about in the dark; that our data base is too sparse, too slippery, for it to be able to mold our theories. Rather the theories are more statements about us and ideology than about the past. Paleoanthropology reveals more about how humans view themselves than it does about how humans came about. But that is heresy.[4]

Oh, that these heretical words were printed as a warning on every textbook, magazine, newspaper article, and statue that presumes to deal with the bestial origin of man!

No, we are not descended from apes. Rather, God created man as the crown of His creation on day 6. We are a special creation of God, made in His image, to bring Him glory. What a revolution this truth would make if our evolutionized culture truly understood it!

---

3. *Natural History* 87 (1978):10.
4. *American Scientist* 66 (1978):379.

9

Does the Bible Say Anything about Astronomy?

DR. JASON LISLE

The Bible is the history book of the universe. It tells us how the universe began and how it came to be the way it is today.

The Bible is much more than just a history book, however; it was written by inspiration of God. The Lord certainly understands how this universe works; after all, He made it. So His Word, the Bible, gives us the foundation for understanding the universe.

It has been said that the Bible is not a science textbook. This is true, of course, and it's actually a good thing. After all, our science textbooks are based on the ideas of human beings who do not know everything and who often make mistakes. That's why science textbooks change from time to time, as people discover new evidence and realize that they were wrong about certain things.

The Bible, though, never changes because it never needs to. God got it right the first time! The Bible is the infallible Word of God. So when it touches on a particular topic, it's right. When the Bible talks about geology, it's correct. When Scripture addresses biology or anthropology, it's also right.

What does the Bible teach about astronomy? Let's take a look at some of the things the Bible has to say about the universe. We will see that the Bible is absolutely correct when it deals with astronomy.

The Earth Is Round

The Bible indicates that the earth is round. One verse we can look at is Isaiah 40:22, where it mentions the "circle of the earth." From space, the earth always appears as a circle since it is round. This matches perfectly with the Bible.

Another verse to consider is Job 26:10, where it teaches that God has "inscribed" a circle on the surface of the waters at the boundary of light and darkness. This boundary between light and darkness is where evening and morning occur. The boundary is a circle since the earth is round.

The Earth Floats in Space

A very interesting verse to consider is Job 26:7, which states that God "hangs the earth on nothing." This might make you think of God hanging the earth like a Christmas tree ornament, but hanging it on empty space. Although this verse is written in a poetic way, it certainly seems to suggest that the earth floats in space; and indeed the earth does float in space. We now have pictures of the earth taken from space that show it floating in the cosmic void. The earth literally hangs upon nothing, just as the Bible suggests.

- The Hindus believe the earth to be supported on the backs of four elephants, which stand on the shell of a gigantic tortoise floating on the surface of the world's waters.

- The earth of the Vedic priests was set on 12 solid pillars; its upper side was its only habitable side.

- The Altaic people of Northern Siberia affirm that their mighty Ulgen created the earth on the waters and placed under it three great fish to support it.

- The Tartars and many of the other tribes of Eurasia believe the earth to be supported by a great bull.

The Expansion of the Universe

The Bible indicates in several places that the universe has been "stretched out" or expanded. For example, Isaiah 40:22 teaches that God stretches out the heavens like a curtain and spreads them out like a tent to dwell in. This would suggest that the universe has actually increased in size since its creation. God is stretching it out, causing it to expand.

Now, this verse must have seemed very strange when it was first written. The universe certainly doesn't *look* as if it is expanding. After all, if you look at the night sky tonight, it will appear about the same size as it did the previous night, and the night before that.

In fact, secular scientists once believed that the universe was eternal and unchanging. The idea of an expanding universe would have been considered nonsense to most scientists of the past. So it must have been tempting for Christians to reject what the Bible teaches about the expansion of the universe.

I wonder if any Christians tried to "reinterpret" Isaiah 40:22 to read it in an unnatural way so that they wouldn't have to believe in an expanding universe. When the secular world believes one thing and the Bible teaches another, it is always tempting to think that God got the details wrong. But God is never wrong.

Most astronomers today believe that the universe is indeed expanding. In the 1920s, astronomers discovered that virtually all clusters of galaxies appear to be moving away from all other clusters; this indicates that the entire universe is expanding.

You can think of this like points on a balloon. As the balloon is inflated, all the points move farther away from each other. If the entire universe was being stretched out, the galaxies would all be moving away; and that is what they actually appear to be doing.

It is fascinating that the Bible recorded the idea of an expanding universe thousands of years before secular science came to accept the idea.

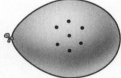

The Age of the Universe

Scripture also addresses the age of the universe. The Bible teaches that the entire universe was created in six days (Exodus 20:11). We know from the genealogies and other events recorded in Scripture that this creation happened about 6,000 years ago.

Yet, this is quite different from what most schools teach. Most secular scientists believe that the universe is many billions of years old, and they usually hold to the big-bang theory. The big bang is a secular speculation about the origin of the universe; it is an alternative to the Bible's teaching. The big bang attempts to explain the origin of the universe without God (see the next chapter, "Does the Big Bang Fit with the Bible?").

People who believe in the big bang usually interpret the evidence according to their already-existing belief in the big bang. In other words, they just assume that the big bang is true; they interpret the evidence to match their beliefs. Of course, the Bible can also be used to interpret the evidence. And since the Bible records the true history of the universe, we see that it makes a lot more sense of the evidence than the big bang does.

Now let's look at some facts about the universe regarding its age. We will see that the evidence is consistent with 6,000 years but doesn't make sense if we hold to the big bang.

Of course, big bang supporters can always reinterpret the evidence by adding extra assumptions. So the following facts are not intended to "prove" that the Bible is right about the age of the universe. The Bible is right in all matters because it is the Word of God. However, when we understand the scientific evidence, we will find that it agrees with what the Bible teaches. The evidence is certainly consistent with a young universe.

Recession of the Moon

The moon is slowly moving away from the earth. As the moon orbits the earth, its gravity pulls on the earth's oceans, which causes tides. The tides actually "pull forward" on the moon, causing the moon to gradually spiral outward. So the moon moves about an inch and a half away from the earth every year. That means that the moon would have been closer to the earth in the past.

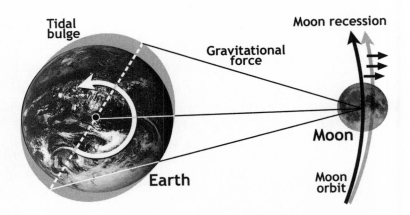

For example, 6,000 years ago, the moon would have been about 800 feet closer to the earth (which is not much of a change, considering the moon is a quarter of a million miles away). So this "spiraling away" of the moon is not a problem over the biblical time scale of 6,000 years. But if the earth and moon were over four billion years old (as evolutionists teach), then we would have big problems. In this case, the moon would have been so close that it would actually have been touching the earth only 1.4 billion years ago. This problem suggests that the moon can't possibly be as old as secular astronomers claim.

Secular astronomers who assume that the big bang is true must use other explanations to get around this. For example, they might assume that the rate at which the moon was receding was actually smaller in the past. But this is an extra assumption needed to make their billions-of-years model work. The simplest explanation is that the moon hasn't been around for that long. The recession of the moon is a problem for a belief in billions of years but is perfectly consistent with a young age.[1]

Magnetic Fields of the Planets

Many of the planets of the solar system have strong magnetic fields. These fields are caused by electrical currents that decay with time. We can even measure this decay of the earth's magnetic field: it gets weaker and weaker every year. If the planets were really billions of years old (as evolutionists believe), then their magnetic fields should be extremely weak by now. Yet they are not. The outer planets of the solar system, in particular, have quite strong magnetic fields. A reasonable explanation for this is that these planets are only a few thousand years old, as the Bible teaches.

Spiral Galaxies

A galaxy is an enormous assembly of stars, interstellar gas, and dust. The galaxy in which we live is called the Milky Way; it has over 100 billion stars. Some galaxies are round or elliptical. Others have an irregular shape, but some of the most beautiful galaxies are spiral in nature, such as our own. Spiral galaxies slowly rotate, but the inner regions of the spiral rotate faster than the outer regions. This means that a spiral galaxy is constantly becoming more and more twisted up as the spiral becomes tighter. After a few hundred million years, the galaxy would be wound so tightly that the spiral structure would no longer be recognizable. According to the big-bang scenario, galaxies are supposed to be many billions of years old. Yet we do see spiral galaxies

---

1. www.answersingenesis.org/home/area/feedback/2006/0811.asp/

— and lots of them. This suggests that they are not nearly as old as the big bang requires. Spiral galaxies are consistent with the biblical age of the universe but are problematic for a belief in billions of years.

Comets

Comets are balls of ice and dirt. Many of them orbit the sun in elliptical paths. They spend most of their time far away from the sun, but occasionally they come very close to it. Every time a comet comes near the sun, some of its icy material is blasted away by the solar radiation. As a result, comets can orbit the sun for only so long (perhaps about 100,000 years at most) before they completely run out of material. Since we still have a lot of comets, this suggests that the solar system is much younger than 100,000 years; this agrees perfectly with the Bible's history.

Yet, secular astronomers believe the solar system is 4.5 billion years old. Since comets can't last that long, secular astronomers must assume that new comets are created to replace those that are gone. So they've invented the idea of an "Oort cloud." This is supposed to be a vast reservoir of icy masses orbiting far away from the sun. The idea is that occasionally an icy mass falls into the inner solar system to become a

"new" comet. It is interesting that there is currently no evidence of an Oort cloud. And there's no reason to believe in one if we accept the creation account in Genesis. Comets are consistent with the fact that the solar system is young.

Supernatural Creation

Aside from age, there are other indications that the universe was supernaturally created as the Bible teaches. These evidences show God's creativity — not a big bang. For example, astronomers have discovered "extrasolar" planets. These are planets that orbit distant stars, not our sun. These planets have not been directly observed. Instead, they have been detected indirectly, usually by the gravitational "tug" they produce on the star they orbit. But the principles being used here are all good "operational science," the kind of testable, repeatable science that can be done in a laboratory. So we have every reason to believe that these are indeed real planets that God created.

These extrasolar planets are actually a problem for big-bang evolutionary models of solar system formation. Secular astronomers had expected that other solar systems would resemble ours, with small planets forming very closely to their star, and large planets (like Jupiter and Saturn) forming farther away. But many of these extrasolar planets are just the opposite; they are large, Jupiter-sized planets orbiting very closely to their star. This is inconsistent with evolutionary models of solar system formation, but it's not a problem for biblical creation. God can create many different varieties of solar systems, and apparently He has done just that.

Conclusion

We have seen that when the Bible addresses the topic of astronomy, it is accurate in every aspect. This shouldn't be surprising, because the Bible, which teaches that the heavens declare the glory and handiwork of God (Psalm 19:1), is the written Word of the Creator. God understands every aspect of the universe He has created, and He never makes mistakes.

In addition, the Word of God provides the correct foundation for understanding the scientific evidence. At the same time, the Bible provides more than just information on the physical universe. It also answers the most profound questions of life. Why are we here? How should we live? What happens when we die? The Word of God even answers the question of why there is death and suffering in the world.[2]

---

2. See www.AnswersInGenesis.org/go/curse.

We can have confidence that what the Bible says about our need for salvation is true, because the Bible has demonstrated itself to be accurate time after time. Showing our children how true science confirms the Bible will help them answer the evolutionary attacks they encounter at schools and in the media.

10

Does the Big Bang Fit with the Bible?

DR. JASON LISLE

T he "big bang" is a story about how the universe came into existence. It proposes that billions of years ago the universe began in a tiny, infinitely hot and dense point called a *singularity*. This singularity supposedly contained not only all the mass and energy that would become everything we see today, but also "space" itself. According to the story, the singularity rapidly expanded, spreading out the energy and space.

It is supposed that over vast periods of time, the energy from the big bang cooled down as the universe expanded. Some of it turned into matter  — hydrogen and helium gas. These gases collapsed to form stars and galaxies of stars. Some of the stars created the heavier elements in their core and then exploded, distributing these elements into space. Some of the heavier elements allegedly began to stick together and formed the earth and other planets.

This story of origins is entirely fiction. But sadly, many people claim to believe the big-bang model. It is particularly distressing that many professing Christians have been taken in by the big bang, perhaps without realizing its atheistic underpinnings. They have chosen to reinterpret the plain teachings of Scripture in an attempt to make it mesh with secular beliefs about origins.

Secular Compromises

There are several reasons why we cannot just add the big bang to the Bible. Ultimately, the big bang is a *secular* story of origins. When first proposed, it was an attempt to explain how the universe could have been created without God. Really, it is an *alternative* to the Bible, so it makes no sense to try to "add" it to the Bible. Let us examine some of the profound differences between the Bible and the secular big-bang view of origins.

The Bible teaches that God created the universe in six days (Genesis 1; Exodus 20:11). It is clear from the context in Genesis that these were days in the ordinary sense (i.e., 24-hour days) since they are bounded by evening and morning and occur in an ordered list (second day, third day, etc.). Conversely, the big bang teaches the universe has evolved over billions of years.

The Bible says that earth was created before the stars and that trees were created before the sun.[1] However, the big-bang view teaches the exact

---

1. The sun and stars were made on day 4 (Genesis 1:14–19). The earth was made on day 1 (Genesis 1:1–5). Trees were made on day 3 (Genesis 1:11–13).

opposite. The Bible tells us that the earth was created as a paradise; the secular model teaches it was created as a molten blob. The big bang and the Bible certainly do not agree about the past.

Many people don't realize that the big bang is a story not only about the past but also about the future. The most popular version of the big bang teaches that the universe will expand forever and eventually run out of usable energy. According to the story, it will remain that way forever in a state that astronomers call "heat death."[2] But the Bible teaches that the world will be judged and remade. Paradise will be restored. The big bang denies this crucial biblical teaching.

Scientific Problems with the Big Bang

The big bang also has a number of scientific problems. Big-bang supporters are forced to accept on "blind faith" a number of notions that are completely *inconsistent* with real observational science. Let's explore some of the inconsistencies between the big-bang story and the real universe.

Missing Monopoles

Most people know something about magnets — like the kind found in a compass or the kind that sticks to a refrigerator. We often say that magnets

2. Despite the name *heat death*, the universe would actually be exceedingly cold.

have two "poles" — a north pole and a south pole. Poles that are alike will repel each other, while opposites attract. A "monopole" is a hypothetical massive particle that is just like a magnet but has only one pole. So a monopole would have either a north pole or a south pole, but not both.

Particle physicists claim that many magnetic monopoles should have been created in the high temperature conditions of the big bang. Since monopoles are stable, they should have lasted to this day. Yet, despite considerable search efforts, monopoles have not been found. Where are the monopoles? The fact that we don't find any monopoles suggests that the universe never was that hot. This indicates that there never was a big bang, but it is perfectly consistent with the Bible's account of creation, since the universe did not start infinitely hot.

The Flatness Problem

Another serious challenge to the big-bang model is called the flatness problem. The expansion rate of the universe appears to be very finely balanced with the force of gravity; this condition is known as flat. If the universe were the accidental by-product of a big bang, it is difficult to imagine how such a fantastic coincidence could occur. Big-bang cosmology cannot explain why the matter density in the universe isn't greater, causing it to collapse upon itself (closed universe), or less, causing the universe to rapidly fly apart (open universe).

The problem is even more severe when we extrapolate into the past. Since any deviation from perfect flatness tends to increase as time moves forward, it logically follows that the universe must have been *even more* precisely balanced in the past than it is today. Thus, at the moment of the big bang, the universe would have been virtually flat to an extremely high precision. This must have been the case (assuming the big bang), despite the fact that the laws of physics allow for an *infinite* range of values. This is a coincidence that stretches

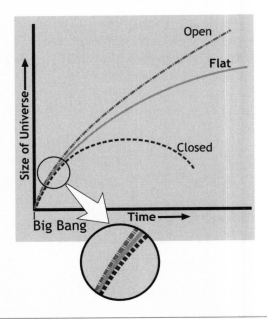

credulity to the breaking point. Of course, in the creation model, "balance" is expected since the Lord has fine-tuned the universe for life.

Inflating the Complexities

Many secular astronomers have come up with an idea called "inflation" in an attempt to address the flatness and monopole problems (as well as other problems not addressed in detail here, such as the horizon problem). Inflation proposes that the universe temporarily went through a period of accelerated expansion. Amazingly, there is no real supporting evidence for inflation; it appears to be nothing more than an unsubstantiated conjecture — much like the big bang itself. Moreover, the inflation idea has difficulties of its own, such as what would start it and how it would stop smoothly. In addition, other problems with the big bang are not solved, even if inflation were true. These are examined below.

Where Is the Antimatter?

Consider the "baryon number problem." Recall that the big bang supposes that matter (hydrogen and helium gas) was created from energy as the universe expanded. However, experimental physics tells us that whenever matter is created from energy, such a reaction also produces *antimatter*. Antimatter has similar properties to matter, except the charges of the particles are reversed. (So whereas a proton has a positive charge, an antiproton has a negative charge.) Any reaction where energy is transformed into matter produces an exactly equal amount of antimatter; there are no known exceptions.

The big bang (which has no matter to begin with, only energy) should have produced exactly equal amounts of matter and antimatter, and that should be what we see today. But we do not. The visible universe is comprised almost entirely of matter — with only trace amounts of antimatter anywhere.

This devastating problem for the big bang is actually consistent with biblical creation; it is a design feature. God created the universe to be essentially matter only — and it's a good thing He did. When matter and antimatter come together, they violently destroy each other. If the universe had equal amounts of matter and antimatter (as the big bang requires), life would not be possible.

Missing Population III Stars

The big-bang model by itself can only account for the existence of the three lightest elements (hydrogen, helium, and trace amounts of lithium).

This leaves about 90 or so of the other naturally occurring elements to be explained. Since the conditions in the big bang are not right to form these heavier elements (as big-bang supporters readily concede), secular astronomers believe that stars have produced the remaining elements by nuclear fusion in the core. This is thought to occur in the final stages of a massive star as it explodes (a supernova). The explosion then distributes the heavier elements into space. Second- and third-generation stars are thus "contaminated" with small amounts of these heavier elements.

If this story were true, then the *first* stars would have been comprised of only the three lightest elements (since these would have been the only elements in existence initially). Some such stars[3] should still be around today since their potential life span is calculated to exceed the (big bang) age of the universe. Such stars would be called "Population III" stars.[4] Amazingly (to those who believe in the big bang), Population III stars have not been found anywhere. All known stars have at least trace amounts of heavy elements in them. It is amazing to think that our galaxy alone is estimated to have over 100 billion stars in it, yet not one star has been discovered that is comprised of *only* the three lightest elements.

The Collapse of the Big Bang

With all the problems listed above, as well as many others too numerous to include, it is not surprising that quite a few secular astronomers are beginning to abandon the big bang. Although it is still the dominant model at present, increasing numbers of physicists and astronomers are realizing that the big bang simply is not a good explanation of how the universe began. In the May 22, 2004, issue of *New Scientist*, there appeared an open letter to the scientific community written primarily by *secular* scientists[5] who challenge the big bang. These scientists pointed out that the copious

---

3. Small (red main sequence) stars do not use up their fuel quickly. These stars theoretically have enough fuel to last significantly longer than the estimated age of the (big bang) universe.
4. If a star has a very small amount of heavy elements, it is called a "Population II" star. Population II stars exist primarily in the central bulge of spiral galaxies, in globular star clusters, and in elliptical galaxies. If a star has a relatively large amount of heavy elements (like the sun), it is called "Population I." These stars exist primarily in the arms of spiral galaxies. The (hypothetical) Population III star would have no heavy elements at all.
5. The alternatives to the big bang that these scientists had suggested are equally unbiblical. These included a steady-state theory and plasma cosmology.

arbitrary assumptions and the lack of successful big-bang predictions challenge the legitimacy of the model. Among other things, they state:

> The big bang today relies on a growing number of hypothetical entities, things that we have never observed — inflation, dark matter and dark energy are the most prominent examples. Without them, there would be a fatal contradiction between the observations made by astronomers and the predictions of the big bang theory. In no other field of physics would this continual recourse to new hypothetical objects be accepted as a way of bridging the gap between theory and observation. It would, at the least, raise serious questions about the validity of the underlying theory.[6]

This statement has since been signed by hundreds of other scientists and professors at various institutions. The big bang seems to be losing considerable popularity. Secular scientists are increasingly rejecting the big bang in favor of other models. If the big bang is abandoned, what will happen to all the Christians who compromised and claimed that the Bible is compatible with the big bang? What will they say? Will they claim that the Bible actually does not teach the big bang, but instead that it teaches the latest secular model? Secular models come and go, but God's Word does not need to be changed because God got it exactly right the first time.

Conclusion

The big bang has many scientific problems. These problems are symptomatic of the underlying incorrect worldview. The big bang erroneously assumes that the universe was *not* supernaturally created, but that it came about by natural processes billions of years ago. However, reality does not line up with this notion. Biblical

6. E. Lerner et al., An open letter to the scientific community, *New Scientist* 182(2448):20, May 22, 2004. Available online at www.cosmologystatement.org.

creation explains the evidence in a more straightforward way without the ubiquitous speculations prevalent in secular models. But ultimately, the best reason to reject the big bang is that it goes against what the Creator of the universe himself has taught: "In the beginning God created the heaven and the earth" (Genesis 1:1).

11

Where Did the Idea of "Millions of Years" Come From?

DR. TERRY MORTENSON

Today, most people in the world, including most people in the Church, take for granted that the earth and universe are millions and millions (even billions) of years old. Our public schools, from kindergarten on up, teach these vast ages, and one is scoffed at if he questions them. But it has not always been that way, and it is important to understand how this change took place and why.

Geology's Early Beginnings

Geology, as a separate field of science with systematic field studies, collection and classification of rocks and fossils, and development of theoretical reconstructions of the historical events that formed those rock layers and fossils, is only about 200 years old. Prior to this, back to ancient Greek times, people had noticed fossils in the rocks. Many believed that the fossils were the remains of former living things turned to stone, and many early Christians (including Tertullian, Chrysostom, and Augustine) attributed them to Noah's flood. But others rejected these ideas and regarded fossils as either jokes of nature, the products of rocks endowed with life in some sense, the creative works of God, or perhaps even the deceptions of Satan. The debate was finally settled when Robert Hooke (1635–1703) confirmed by microscopic analysis of fossil wood that fossils were the mineralized remains of former living creatures.

Prior to 1750, one of the most important geological thinkers was Niels Steensen (1638–1686), or Steno, a Danish anatomist and geologist. He established the principle of *superposition*, namely that sedimentary rock layers are deposited in a successive, essentially horizontal fashion, so that a lower stratum was deposited before the one above it. In his book *Forerunner* (1669), he expressed belief in a roughly 6,000-year-old earth and that fossil-bearing rock strata were deposited by Noah's flood. Over the next century, several authors, including the English geologist John Woodward (1665–1722) and the German geologist Johann Lehmann (1719–1767), wrote books essentially reinforcing that view.

In the latter decades of the 18th century, some French and Italian geologists rejected the biblical account of the Flood and attributed the rock record to natural processes occurring over a long period of time. Several prominent Frenchmen also contributed to the idea of millions of years. The widely respected scientist Comte de Buffon (1707–1788) imagined in his book *Epochs of Nature* (1779) that the earth was once like a hot molten ball that had cooled to reach its present state over about 75,000 years (though his unpublished manuscript says about 3,000,000 years). The astronomer Pierre Laplace (1749–1827) proposed the *nebular hypothesis* in his *Exposition of the System of the Universe* (1796). This theory said that the solar system was once a hot, spinning gas cloud, that over long ages gradually cooled and condensed to form the planets. Jean Lamarck, a specialist in shell creatures, advocated a theory of biological evolution over long ages in his *Philosophy of Zoology* (1809).

Abraham Werner (1749–1817) was a popular mineralogy professor in Germany. He believed that most of the crust of the earth had been precipitated chemically or mechanically by a slowly receding global ocean over the course of about a million years. It was an elegantly simple theory, but Werner failed to take into account the fossils in the rocks. This was a serious mistake, since the fossils tell much about when and how quickly the sediments were deposited and transformed into stone. Many of the greatest geologists of the 19th century were Werner's students, who were impacted by his idea of a very long history for the earth.

In Scotland, James Hutton (1726–1797) was developing a different theory of earth history. He studied medicine at the university. After his studies, he took over the family farm for a while. But he soon discovered his real love: the study of the earth. In 1788 he published a journal article and in 1795 a book, both by the title *Theory of the Earth*. He proposed that the continents were being slowly eroded into the oceans. Those sediments were gradually hardened by the internal heat of the earth and then raised by convulsions to become new landmasses that would later be eroded into the oceans, hardened, and elevated. So in his view, earth history was cyclical, and he stated that he could find no evidence of a beginning in the rock record, making earth history indefinitely long.

Catastrophist — Uniformitarian Debate

Neither Werner nor Hutton paid much attention to the fossils. However, in the early 1800s, Georges Cuvier (1768–1832), the famous French comparative anatomist and vertebrate paleontologist, developed his *catastrophist* theory of earth history. It was expressed most clearly in his *Discourse on the Revolutions of the Surface of the Globe* (1812). Cuvier believed that over the course of long, untold ages of earth history, many catastrophic floods of regional or nearly global extent had destroyed and buried creatures in sediments. All but one of these catastrophes occurred before the creation of man.

William Smith (1769–1839) was a drainage engineer and surveyor who in the course of his work around Great Britain became fascinated with the strata and fossils. Like Cuvier, he had an old-earth catastrophist view of earth history. In three works published from 1815 to 1817, he presented the first geological map of England and Wales and explained an order and relative chronology of the rock formations as defined by certain characteristic (index) fossils. He became known as the "Father of English Stratigraphy" because he developed the method of giving relative dates to the rock layers on the basis of the fossils found in them.

A massive blow to catastrophism came during the years 1830 to 1833, when Charles Lyell (1797–1875), a lawyer and former student of Buckland, published his influen-

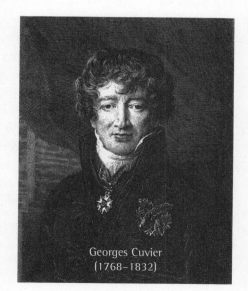

Georges Cuvier
(1768–1832)

Charles Lyell
(1797–1875)

tial three-volume work *Principles of Geology*. Reviving and augmenting the ideas of Hutton, Lyell's *Principles* set forth the principles by which he thought geological interpretations should be made. His theory was a radical *uniformitarianism* in which he insisted that only present-day processes of geological change at *present-day rates of intensity and magnitude* should be used to interpret the rock record of past geological activity. In other words, geological processes of change have been uniform throughout earth history. No continental or global catastrophic floods have ever occurred, insisted Lyell.

Lyell is often given too much credit (or blame) for destroying faith in the Genesis flood and the biblical time scale. But we must realize that many Christians (geologists and theologians) contributed to this undermining of biblical teaching before Lyell's book appeared. Although the catastrophist theory had greatly reduced the geological significance of Noah's flood and expanded earth history well beyond the traditional biblical view, Lyell's work was the final blow for belief in the Flood. By explaining the whole rock record by slow gradual processes, he thereby reduced the Flood to a geological non-event. Catastrophism did not die out immediately, although by the late 1830s only a few catastrophists remained, and they believed Noah's flood was geologically insignificant.

By the end of the 19th century, the age of the earth was considered by all geologists to be in the hundreds of millions of years. Radiometric dating methods began to be developed in 1903, and over the course of the 20th century that age of the earth expanded to 4.5 billion years.

Christian Responses to Old-earth Geology

During the first half of the 19th century, the Church responded in various ways to these old-earth theories of the catastrophists and uniformitarians. A number of writers in Great Britain (and a few in America), who became known as "scriptural geologists," raised biblical, geological, and philosophical arguments against the old-earth theories. Some of them were scientists and some were clergy. Some were both ordained and scientifically well informed, as was common in those days. Many of them were very geologically competent by the standards of their day, both by reading and by their own careful observations of rocks and fossils. They believed that the biblical account of creation and Noah's flood explained the rock record far better than the old-earth theories.[1]

Thomas Chalmers
(1780–1847)

Other Christians in the early 1800s quickly accepted the idea of millions of years and tried to fit all this time into Genesis, even though the uniformitarians and catastrophists were still debating and geology was in its infancy as a science. In 1804, Thomas Chalmers (1780–1847), a young Presbyterian pastor, began to preach that Christians should accept the millions of years; and in an 1814 review of Cuvier's book, he proposed that all the time could fit between Genesis 1:1 and 1:2. By that time, Chalmers was becoming a highly influential evangelical leader and, consequently, this *gap theory* became very popular. In 1823, the respected Anglican theologian George Stanley Faber (1773–1854) began to advocate the *day-age view*, namely that the days of creation were not literal but figurative for long ages.

To accept these geological ages, Christians also had to reinterpret the Flood. In the 1820s, John Fleming (1785–1857), a Presbyterian minister, contended that Noah's flood was so peaceful that it left no lasting geological evidence. John Pye Smith (1774–1851), a Congregational theologian, preferred to see it as a localized inundation in the Mesopotamian valley (modern-day Iraq).

---

1. See T. Mortenson, *The Great Turning Point: The Church's Catastrophic Mistake on Geology—Before Darwin* (Green Forest, AR: Master Books, 2004) for a full discussion of these men and the battle they fought against these developing old-earth theories and Christian compromises.

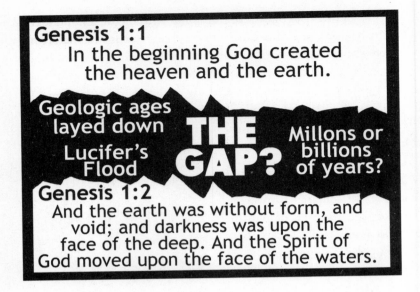

Liberal theology, which by the early 1800s was dominating the Church in Europe, was beginning to make inroads into Britain and North America in the 1820s. The liberals considered Genesis 1–11 to be as historically unreliable and unscientific as the creation and flood myths of the ancient Babylonians, Sumerians, and Egyptians.

In spite of the efforts of the scriptural geologists, these various old-earth reinterpretations of Genesis prevailed, so that by 1845 all the commentaries on Genesis had abandoned the biblical chronology and the global flood; and by the time of Darwin's *Origin of Species* (1859), the young-earth view had essentially disappeared within the Church. From that time onward, most Christian leaders and scholars of the Church accepted the millions of years and insisted that the age of the earth was not important. Many godly men soon accepted evolution as well. Space allows only mention of a few examples.

The Baptist "prince of preachers" Charles Spurgeon (1834–1892) uncritically accepted the old-earth geological theory (though he never explained how to fit the long ages into the Bible). In an 1855 sermon he said:

> Can any man tell me when the beginning was? Years ago we thought the beginning of this world was when Adam came upon it; but we have discovered that thousands of years before that God was preparing chaotic matter to make it a fit abode for

man, putting races of creatures upon it, who might die and leave behind the marks of his handiwork and marvelous skill, before he tried his hand on man.[2]

The great Presbyterian theologian at Princeton Seminary, Charles Hodge (1779–1878), insisted that the age of the earth was not important. He favored the gap theory initially and switched to the day-age view later in life. His compromise contributed to the eventual victory of liberal theology at Princeton about 50 years after his death.[3]

C.I. Scofield put the gap theory in notes on Genesis 1:2 in his Scofield Reference Bible, which was used by millions of Christians around the world. More recently, a respected Old Testament scholar reasoned:

From a superficial reading of Genesis 1, the impression would seem to be that the entire creative process took place in six

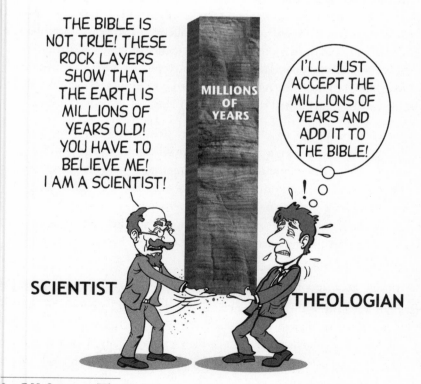

2. C.H. Spurgeon, "Election," *The New Park Street Pulpit* 1 (1990): 318.
3. See J. Pipa and D. Hall, eds., *Did God Create in Six Days?* (Whitehall, WV: Tolle Lege Press, 2005), p. 7–16, for some of the documentation of this sad slide into apostasy.

twenty-four-hour days. If this was the true intent of the Hebrew author . . . this seems to run counter to modern scientific research, which indicates that the planet Earth was created several billion years ago. . . .[4]

Numerous similar statements from Christian scholars and leaders in the last few decades could be quoted to show that their interpretation of Genesis is controlled by the fact that they assume that geologists have proven millions of years. As a result, most seminaries and Christian colleges around the world are compromised.

Compromise Unnecessary

The sad irony of all this compromise is that in the last half century, the truth of Genesis 1–11 has been increasingly vindicated, often unintentionally, by the work of evolutionists. Lyell's uniformitarian *Principles* dominated geology until about the 1970s, when Derek Ager (1923–1993), a prominent British geologist, and others increasingly challenged Lyell's assumptions and argued that much of the rock record shows evidence of rapid catastrophic erosion or sedimentation, drastically reducing the time involved in the formation of many geological deposits. Ager, an atheist to his death (as far as one can tell from his writings), explained the influence of Lyell on geology this way:

> My excuse for this lengthy and amateur digression into history is that I have been trying to show how I think geology got into the hands of the theoreticians [uniformitarians] who were conditioned by the social and political history of their day more than by observations in the field. . . . In other words, we have allowed ourselves to be brain-washed into avoiding any interpretation of the past that involves extreme and what might be termed "catastrophic" processes.[5]

These "neocatastrophist" reinterpretations of the rocks have developed contemporaneously with a resurgence of "Flood geology," a view of earth history very similar to that of the 19th-century scriptural geologists and a key ingredient of young-earth creationism, which was essentially launched into the world by the publication of *The Genesis Flood* (1961) by Drs. John Whitcomb

---

4. G. Archer, *A Survey of Old Testament Introduction* (Chicago, IL: Moody Press, 1985), p. 187.
5. D. Ager, *The Nature of the Stratigraphical Record* (New York: Wiley, 1981), p. 46–47.

and Henry Morris. This movement is now worldwide in scope, and the scientific sophistication of the scientific model is rapidly increasing with time.

Many Christians today are arguing that we need to contend against Darwinism with "intelligent design" arguments and leave Genesis out of the public discussion. But this strategy was tried in the early 19th century with many writings on natural theology, culminating in the famous eight volumes of the 1830s that collectively became known as the *Bridgewater Treatises*. These books were "preaching to the choir" and did nothing to retard the slide in the culture toward atheism and deism. In fact, by compromising on the age of the earth and ignoring Scripture in their defense of Christianity, they actually contributed to the weakening of the Church. The same is happening today.

The renowned atheist evolutionist and Harvard University biologist Ernst Mayr said this:

> The [Darwinian] revolution began when it became obvious that the earth was very ancient rather than having been created only 6,000 years ago. This finding was the snowball that started the whole avalanche.[6]

Mayr was right about the age of the earth (not Darwin's theory) being the beginning of the avalanche of unbelief. He was wrong that the idea of millions of years was a "finding" of scientific research. Rather, it was the fruit of antibiblical philosophical assumptions used to interpret the rocks and fossils. Historical research has shown that Laplace was an open atheist, that Buffon, Lamarck, Werner, and Hutton were deists or atheists, and that Cuvier, William Smith, and Lyell were deists or vague theists. These men (who influenced the thinking of compromised Christians) were NOT unbiased, objective pursuers of truth.

Typical of what Lyell, Buffon, and others wrote is Hutton's statement. He insisted, "The past history of our globe must be explained by what can be seen to be happening now. . . . No powers are to be employed that are not natural to the globe, no action to be admitted except those of which we know the principle."[7] By insisting that geologists must reason only from known, present-day natural processes, he ruled out supernatural creation and the unique global flood, as described in Genesis, before he ever looked at the rocks.

---

6. E. Mayr, "The Nature of the Darwinian Revolution," *Science* 176 (1972): 988.
7. J. Hutton, "Theory of the Earth," Trans. of the Royal Society of Edinburgh, 1788, quoted in A. Holmes, *Principles of Physical Geology* (New York: Ronald Press Co., 1965), p. 43–44.

It is no wonder that Hutton could not see the overwhelming geological evidence confirming the biblical teaching about creation, the Flood, and the age of the earth. And no wonder all the geology students who have been brainwashed with the same presuppositions for the last 200 years haven't been able to see it either. We should not be surprised that most Christian leaders and scholars are ignorant of the evidence. They, too, have been brainwashed, as many young-earth creationists once were also.

Disastrous Consequences of Compromise

The scriptural geologists of the early 19th century opposed old-earth geological theories not only because the theories reflected erroneous scientific reasoning and were contrary to Scripture, but also because they believed that Christian compromise with such theories would eventually have a catastrophic effect on the health of the Church and her witness to a lost world. Henry Cole, an Anglican minister, wrote:

> Many reverend geologists, however, would evince their reverence for the divine Revelation by making a distinction between its *historical* and its *moral* portions; and maintaining, that the latter only is inspired and absolute Truth; but that the former is not so; and therefore is open to any latitude of philosophic and scientific interpretation, modification or denial! According to these impious and infidel modifiers and separators, there is not one third of the Word of God that *is* inspired; for not more, nor perhaps so much, of that Word, is occupied in abstract moral revelation, instruction, and precept. The other two thirds, therefore, are open to any scientific modification and interpretation; or, (if scientifically required), to a total denial! It may however be safely asserted, that whoever professedly, before men, disbelieves the inspiration of any part of Revelation, disbelieves, in the sight of God, its inspiration altogether. . . . What the consequences of such things must be to a revelation-possessing land, time will rapidly and awfully unfold in its opening pages of national skepticism, infidelity, and apostasy, and of God's righteous vengeance on the same![8]

---

8. H. Cole, *Popular Geology Subversive of Divine Revelation* (London: Hatchard and Son, 1834), p. ix–x, 44–45 footnote.

Cole and other opponents of the old-earth theories rightly understood that the historical portions of the Bible (including Genesis 1–11) are foundational to the theological and moral teachings of Scripture. Destroy the credibility of the former and sooner or later you will see rejection of the latter, both inside and outside the Church. If the scriptural geologists were alive today and saw the castle diagram shown below, they would say, "That picture's exactly what we were concerned about!" The history of the once-Christian nations in Europe and North America has confirmed the scriptural geologists' worst fears about the Church and society.

It is time for the Church, especially her leaders and scholars, to stop ignoring the age of the earth and the scientific evidence that increasingly vindicates the Word of God. Christians must repent of their compromise with millions of years and once again believe and preach the literal truth of Genesis 1–11. It is time to take our culture back.

12

What's Wrong
with Progressive Creation?

KEN HAM & DR. TERRY MORTENSON

One result of compromising with our evolutionary culture is the view of creation called the "day-age" theory or "progressive creation." This view, while not a new one, has received wide publicity in the past several years. Much of this publicity is due to the publications and lectures of astronomer Dr. Hugh Ross — probably the world's leading progressive creationist. Dr. Ross's views on how to interpret the Book of Genesis won early endorsements from many well-known Christian leaders, churches, seminaries, and Christian colleges. The teachings of Dr. Ross seemingly allowed Christians to use the term "creationist" but still gave them supposed academic respectability in the eyes of the world by rejecting six literal days of creation and maintaining billions of years. However, after his views became more fully understood, many who had previously embraced progressive creation realized how bankrupt those views are and removed their endorsement.

In this chapter, some of the teachings of progressive creation will be examined in light of Scripture and good science.[1]

---

1. For a more complete analysis, see Tim Chaffey and Jason Lisle, *Old-Earth Creationism on Trial* (Green Forest, AR: Master Books, 2008); Mark Van Bebber and Paul S. Taylor, *Creation and Time: A Report on the Progressive Creation Book by Hugh Ross* (Gilbert, AZ: Eden Publications, 1994); www.answersingenesis.org/go/compromise.

In Summary, Progressive Creation Teaches:

- The big-bang origin of the universe occurred about 13–15 billion years ago.
- The days of creation were overlapping periods of millions and billions of years.
- Over millions of years, God created new species as others kept going extinct.
- The record of nature is just as reliable as the Word of God.
- Death, bloodshed, and disease existed before Adam and Eve.
- Manlike creatures that looked and behaved much like us (and painted on cave walls) existed before Adam and Eve but did not have a spirit that was made in the image of God, and thus had no hope of salvation.
- The Genesis flood was a local event.

The Big Bang Origin of the Universe

Progressive creation teaches that the modern big-bang theory of the origin of the universe is true and has been proven by scientific inquiry and observation. For Hugh Ross and others like him, big-bang cosmology becomes the basis by which the Bible is interpreted. This includes belief that the universe and the earth are billions of years old. Dr. Ross even goes so far as to state that life would not be possible on earth without billions of years of earth history:

> It only works in a cosmos of a hundred-billion trillion stars that's precisely sixteen-billion-years old. This is the narrow window of time in which life is possible.[2]

> Life is only possible when the universe is between 12 and 17 billion years.[3]

This, of course, ignores the fact that God is omnipotent — He could make a fully functional universe ready for life right from the beginning, for with God nothing is impossible (Matthew 19:26).[4]

2. Dallas Theological Seminary chapel service, September 13, 1996.
3. Toccoa Falls Christian College, Staley Lecture Series, March 1997.
4. For an evaluation of the big-bang model, see chapter 10, "Does the Big Bang Fit with the Bible?"

The Days of Creation in Genesis 1

Progressive creationists claim that the days of creation in Genesis 1 represent long periods of time. In fact, Dr. Ross believes day 3 of creation week lasted more than 3 billion years![5] This assertion is made in order to allow for the billions of years that evolutionists claim are represented in the rock layers of earth. This position, however, has problems, both biblically and scientifically.

The text of Genesis 1 clearly states that God supernaturally created all that is in six actual days. If we are prepared to let the words of the text speak to us in accord with the context and their normal definitions, without influence from outside ideas, then the word for "day" in Genesis 1 obviously means an ordinary day of about 24 hours. It is qualified by a number, the phrase "evening and morning," and for day 1, the words "light and darkness."[6]

Dr. James Barr, Regius Professor of Hebrew at Oxford University, who himself does not believe Genesis is true history, admitted the following, as far as the language of Genesis 1 is concerned:

> So far as I know, there is no professor of Hebrew or Old Testament at any world-class university who does not believe that the writer(s) of Gen. 1–11 intended to convey to their readers the ideas that (a) creation took place in a series of six days which were the same as the days of 24 hours we now experience, (b) the figures contained in the Genesis genealogies provided by simple addition a chronology from the beginning of the world up to later stages in the biblical story, (c) Noah's Flood was understood to be world-wide and extinguish all human and animal life except for those in the ark.[7]

Besides the textual problems, progressive creationists have scientific dilemmas as well. They accept modern scientific measurements for the age of the earth, even though these measurements are based on evolutionary, atheistic assumptions. Dr. Ross often speaks of the "facts of nature" and the "facts of science" when referring to the big bang and billions of years. This demonstrates his fundamental misunderstanding of evidence. The scientific "facts" that evolutionists claim as proof of millions of years are really *interpretations* of selected observations that have been made with *antibiblical and usually atheistic, philosophical assumptions.* We all have the same facts: the same living

---

5. Reasons to Believe, "Creation Timeline," www.reasons.org/creation-timeline.
6. See *The New Answers Book 1*, chapter 8 by Ken Ham, for a more detailed defense of literal days in Genesis 1 (Green Forest, AR: Master Books, 2006), p. 88–112.
7. Letter to David C.C. Watson, April 23, 1984.

creatures, the same DNA molecules, the same fossils, the same rock layers, the same Grand Canyon, the same moon, the same planets, the same starlight from distant stars and galaxies, etc. These are the facts; how old they are and how they formed are the *interpretations* of the facts. And what one believes about history will affect how one interprets these facts. History is littered with so-called "scientific facts" that supposedly had proven the Bible wrong, but which were shown years or decades later to be not facts but erroneously interpreted observations because of the antibiblical assumptions used.[8]

The Order of Creation

Progressive Creation

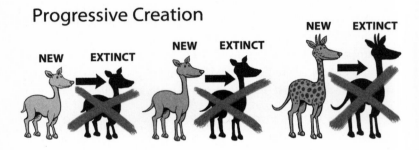

As their name indicates, progressive creationists believe that God progressively created species on earth over billions of years, with new species replacing extinct ones, starting with simple organisms and culminating in the creation of Adam and Eve. They accept the evolutionary order for the development of life on earth, even though this contradicts the order given in the Genesis account of creation.[9] Evolutionary theory holds that the first life forms were marine organisms, while the Bible says that God created land plants first. Reptiles are supposed to have predated birds, while Genesis says that birds came first. Evolutionists believe that land mammals came before whales, while the Bible teaches that God created whales first.

Dr. Davis Young, emeritus geology professor at Calvin College, recognized this dilemma and abandoned the "day-age" theory. Here is part of his explanation as to why he discarded it:

> The biblical text, for example, has vegetation appearing on the third day and animals on the fifth day. Geology, however, had long

---

8. See chapter 2, "What's the Best 'Proof' of Creation?" for more on how our presuppositions influence our interpretations.
9. Dr. Terry Mortenson, "Evolution vs. Creation: The Order of Events Matters!" Answers in Genesis, www.answersingenesis.org/docs2006/0404order.asp.

realized that invertebrate animals were swarming in the seas long before vegetation gained a foothold on the land. . . . Worse yet, the text states that on the fourth day God made the heavenly bodies after the earth was already in existence. Here is a blatant confrontation with science. Astronomy insists that the sun is older than the earth.[10]

The Sixty-seventh Book of the Bible

Dr. Ross has stated that he believes nature to be "just as perfect" as the Bible. Here is the full quote:

> Not everyone has been exposed to the sixty-six books of the Bible, but everyone on planet Earth has been exposed to the sixty-seventh book — the book that God has written upon the heavens for everyone to read.
>
> And the Bible tells us it's impossible for God to lie, so the record of nature must be just as perfect, and reliable and truthful as the sixty-six books of the Bible that is part of the Word of God. . . . And so when astronomers tell us [their attempts to measure distance in space] . . . it's part of the truth that God has revealed to us. It actually encompasses part of the Word of God.[11]

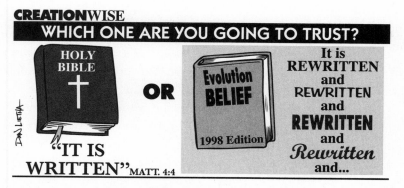

CREATIONWISE

WHICH ONE ARE YOU GOING TO TRUST?

HOLY BIBLE

OR

Evolution BELIEF 1998 Edition

It is REWRITTEN and REWRITTEN and REWRITTEN and *Rewritten* and...

"IT IS WRITTEN" MATT. 4:4

Dr. Ross is right that God cannot lie, and God tells us in Romans 8:22 that "the whole creation groans and labors with birth pangs" because of sin. And not only was the universe cursed, but man himself has been affected by the Fall. So how can sinful, fallible human beings in a sin-cursed universe say that their interpretation of the evidence is as perfect as God's written revelation?

10. D. Young, *The Harmonization of Scripture and Science*, science symposium at Wheaton College, March 23, 1990.
11. Toccoa Falls Christian College, Staley Lecture Series, March 1997.

Scientific assertions must use *fallible* assumptions and *fallen* reasoning — how can this be the Word of God?

The respected systematic theologian Louis Berkhof said:

> Since the entrance of sin into the world, man can gather true knowledge about God from His general revelation only if he studies it in the light of Scripture, in which the elements of God's original self-revelation, which were obscured and perverted by the blight of sin, are republished, corrected, and interpreted. . . . Some are inclined to speak of God's general revelation as a second source; but this is hardly correct in view of the fact that nature can come into consideration here only as interpreted in the light of Scripture.[12]

In other words, Christians should build their thinking on the Bible, not on fallible interruptations of scientific observations about the past.

Death and Disease before Adam

Progressive creationists believe the fossil record was formed from the millions of animals that lived and died before Adam and Eve were created. They accept the idea that there was death, bloodshed, and disease (including cancer) before sin, which goes directly against the teaching of the Bible and dishonors the character of God.

God created a perfect world at the beginning. When He was finished, God stated that His creation was "very good." The Bible makes it clear that man and all the animals were vegetarians before the Fall (Genesis 1:29-30). Plants were given to them for food (plants do not have a *nephesh* [life spirit] as man and animals do and thus eating them would not constitute "death" in the biblical sense[13]).

Concerning the entrance of sin into the world, Dr. Ross writes, "The groaning of creation in anticipation of release from sin has lasted fifteen billion years and affected a hundred billion trillion stars."[14]

However, the Bible teaches something quite different. In the context of human death, the apostle Paul states, "Through one man sin entered the world, and death through sin" (Romans 5:12). It is clear that there was no sin in the world before Adam sinned, and thus no death.

---

12. L. Berkhof, Introductory volume to *Systematic Theology* (Grand Rapids, MI: Wm. B. Eerdmans Publ. Co., 1946), p. 60, 96.
13. See *The New Answers Book 1*, chapter 21 by Andy McIntosh and Bodie Hodge, p. 259–270, for more details.
14. Hugh Ross, "The Physics of Sin," *Facts for Faith*, Issue 8, 2002, www.reasons.org/resources/fff/2002issue08/index.shtml.

God killed the first animal in the Garden and shed blood because of sin. If there were death, bloodshed, disease, and suffering before sin, then the basis for the atonement is *destroyed*. Christ suffered death because death was the penalty for sin. There will be no death or suffering in the perfect "restoration" — so why can't we accept the same in a perfect ("very good") creation before sin?

God must be quite incompetent and cruel to make things in the way that evolution-

ists imagine the universe and earth to have evolved, as most creatures that ever existed died cruel deaths. Progressive creation denigrates the wisdom and goodness of God by suggesting that this was God's method of creation. This view attacks His truthfulness as well. If God really created over the course of billions of years, then He has misled most believers for 4,000 years into believing that He did it in six days.[15]

Spiritless Hominids before Adam

Since evolutionary radiometric dating methods have dated certain humanlike fossils as older than Ross's date for modern humans (approx. 40,000 years), he and other progressive creationists insist that these are fossils of pre-Adamic creatures that had no spirit, and thus no salvation.

Dr. Ross accepts and defends these evolutionary dating methods, so he must redefine all evidence of humans (descendants of Noah) if they are given

15. Dr. Terry Mortenson, "Genesis According to Evolution," *Creation* 26(4) September 2004: 50–51.

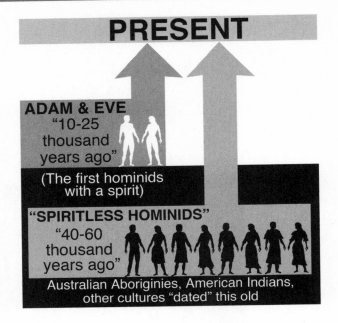

PRESENT

ADAM & EVE
"10-25 thousand years ago"
(The first hominids with a spirit)

"SPIRITLESS HOMINIDS"
"40-60 thousand years ago"
Australian Aboriginies, American Indians, other cultures "dated" this old

evolutionary dates of more than about 40,000 years (e.g., the Neandertal cave sites) as related to spiritless "hominids," which the Bible does not mention. However, these same methods have been used to "date" the Australian Aborigines back at least 60,000 years (some have claimed much older) and fossils of "anatomically modern humans" to over 100,000 years.[16] By Ross's reasoning, none of these (including the Australian Aborigines) could be descendants of Adam and Eve. However, Acts 17:26 says, "And He has made from one blood every nation of men to dwell on all the face of the earth, and has determined their preappointed times and the boundaries of their dwellings" (NKJV). All people on earth are descendants of Adam.

In addition, the fossil record cannot, by its very nature, conclusively reveal if a creature had a spirit or not, since spirits are not fossilized. But there is clear evidence that creatures, which Ross (following the evolutionists) places before Adam, had art and clever technology and that they buried their dead in a way that many of Adam's descendants have.[17] Therefore, we have strong reason to believe that they were fully human and actually descendants of Adam, and that they lived only a few thousand years ago.

16. T. White et al., "Pleistocene *Homo sapiens* from Middle Awash, Ethiopia," *Nature* 423 (\ June 12, 2003): 742–747. Dr. Ross will permit up to 60,000 years, but this is extreme for this position.
17. Marvin Lubelow, *Bones of Contention*, revised and updated (Grand Rapids, MI: Baker Books, 2004).

The Genesis Flood

One important tenet of progressive creation is that the flood of Noah's day was a local flood, limited to the Mesopotamian region. Progressive creationists believe that the rock layers and fossils found around the world are the result of billions of years of evolutionary earth history, rather than from the biblical flood.

Dr. Ross often says that he believes in a "universal" or "worldwide" flood, but in reality he does not believe that the Flood covered the whole earth. He argues that the text of Genesis 7 doesn't really say that the Flood covered the whole earth. But read it for yourself:

19 They [the flood waters] rose greatly on the earth, and *all* the high mountains under the *entire* heavens were covered.

21 *Every* living thing that moved on the earth perished — birds, livestock, wild animals, *all* the creatures that swarm over the earth, and *all* mankind.

22 *Everything* on dry land that had the breath of life in its nostrils died.

23 *Every* living thing on the face of the earth was wiped out; men and animals and the creatures that move along the ground and the birds of the air were wiped from the earth. *Only* Noah was left, and those with him in the ark [emphasis added].

CREATIONWISE

Also, many questions remain for those who teach that the Genesis flood was only local:

- If the Flood was local, why did Noah have to build an ark? He could have walked to the other side of the mountains and missed it.
- If the Flood was local, why did God send the animals to the ark so they could escape death? There would have been other

animals to reproduce that kind if these particular ones had died.

- If the Flood was local, why was the ark big enough to hold all the different kinds of vertebrate land animals? If only Mesopotamian animals were aboard, the ark could have been much smaller.[18]
- If the Flood was local, why would birds have been sent on board? These could simply have winged across to a nearby mountain range.
- If the Flood was local, how could the waters rise to 15 cubits (8 meters) above the mountains (Genesis 7:20)? Water seeks its own level. It couldn't rise to cover the local mountains while leaving the rest of the world untouched.
- If the Flood was local, people who did not happen to be living in the vicinity would not be affected by it. They would have escaped God's judgment on sin. If this had happened, what did Christ mean when He likened the coming judgment of all men to the judgment of "all" men in the days of Noah (Matthew 24:37–39)? A partial judgment in Noah's day means a partial judgment to come.
- If the Flood was local, God would have repeatedly broken His promise never to send such a flood again.

---

18. See John Woodmorappe, *Noah's Ark: A Feasibility Study* (El Cajon, CA: Institute for Creation Research, 1996).

Conclusion

It is true that whether one believes in six literal days does not ultimately affect one's salvation, if one is truly born again. However, we need to stand back and look at the "big picture." In many nations, the Word of God was once widely respected and taken seriously. But once the door of compromise is unlocked and Christian leaders concede that we shouldn't take the Bible as written in Genesis, why should the world take heed of it in *any* area? Because the Church has told the world that one can use man's interpretation of the world (such as billions of years) to reinterpret the Bible, it is seen as an outdated, scientifically incorrect "holy book," not intended to be taken seriously.

As each subsequent generation has pushed this door of compromise open farther and farther, increasingly they are not accepting the morality or salvation of the Bible either. After all, if the history in Genesis is not correct as written, how can one be sure the rest can be taken as written? Jesus said, "If I have told you earthly things and you do not believe, how will you believe if I tell you heavenly things?" (John 3:12; NKJV).

It would not be exaggerating to claim that the majority of Christian leaders and laypeople within the church today do not believe in six literal days. Sadly, being influenced by the world has led to the Church no longer powerfully influencing the world.

The "war of the worldviews" is not ultimately one of young earth versus old earth, or billions of years versus six days, or creation versus evolution — the real battle is the authority of the Word of God versus man's fallible theories.

Belief in a historical Genesis is important because progressive creation and its belief in millions of years (1) contradicts the clear teaching of Scripture, (2) assaults the character of God, (3) severely damages and distorts the Bible's teaching on death, and (4) undermines the gospel by undermining the clear teaching of Genesis, which gives the whole basis for Christ's atonement and our need for a Redeemer. So ultimately, the issue of a literal Genesis is about the authority of the Word of God versus the authority of the words of sinful men.

Why do Christians believe in the bodily resurrection of Jesus Christ? Because of the *words of Scripture* ("according to the Scriptures").

And why should Christians believe in six literal days of creation? Because of the *words of Scripture* ("In six days the Lord made . . .").

The real issue is one of authority — let us unashamedly stand upon God's Word as our sole authority!

13

Is the Intelligent Design Movement Christian?

DR. GEORGIA PURDOM

O ne player in the "war of the worldviews" is the intelligent design movement. ID has gained increasing recognition and publicity over the last several years at both local and national levels. It is especially well known in educational circles, where it has been heralded as an alternative to Darwinism/naturalism.

Intelligent design can be defined as a theory that holds that "certain features" of living things were designed by an "intelligent cause" as opposed to being formed through purely natural means.[1] The ID theory does not name the intelligent cause, and it does not claim that everything is designed, thus allowing for evolution/natural causes to play a role.

The historical roots of the ID movement lie in the natural theology movement of the 18th and 19th centuries. William Paley (1743–1805) reasoned that if one walked across a field and came upon a watch, the assumption would be that there had to be a watchmaker — the complexity and purpose of the watch points to the fact that it is not the result of undirected, unintelligent causes, but the product of a designer.[2] Natural theology sought to support the existence of God through nature (general revelation) apart from the Bible (special revelation), since the Bible was facing much criticism at that time. The scientific

---

1. Discovery Institute Center for Science and Culture, www.discovery.org/csc/topQuestions. php, September 13, 2005.
2. W. Paley, *Paley's Watchmaker*, edited by Bill Cooper (West Sussex, England: New Wine Press, 1997, first published in 1802), p. 29–31.

knowledge of that time was grossly deficient, and it was thought that natural causes were sufficient to bring everything into existence.

In the last 100 years or so, there has been an explosion of knowledge about the complexity of cells, DNA, and microorganisms. Thus, the need for a designer has become even greater. The current ID movement has more than just philosophical arguments for a designer; it uses scientific evidence drawn from biology, chemistry, and physics.

Irreducible Complexity

The ID concept affirms that living things are designed and exhibit *irreducible complexity*. Some examples are the biochemistry of vision and the mammalian blood-clotting pathway. These biological pathways consist of many factors, and *all* the factors are necessary for the pathway to function properly. Thus, evolution (which works via the mechanism of small, gradual steps that keep only that which is immediately functional) could not have formed these pathways. For example, if only three of the blood-clotting factors (there are many factors in the complete pathway) were formed in an organism, blood would not clot, and thus the factors would not be kept because they are not currently useful to the organism. Evolutionary processes do not allow the organism to keep the three factors in the hopes that one day the rest of the blood-clotting factors will form. Evolution is goalless and purposeless; therefore, it does not keep the leftovers.

The question of whether a feature of a living organism displays design can be answered by using what is called an explanatory filter. The filter has three levels of explanation:

1. Necessity — did it have to happen?
2. Chance — did it happen by accident?
3. Design — did an intelligent agent cause it to happen?

This is a very logical, common-sense approach used by individuals every day to deduce cause and effect. For example, consider the scenario of a woman falling:

1. Did she have to fall? No, but she did.
2. Was it an accident?
3. Or was she pushed?

If we apply this explanatory filter to living organisms, a feature must be designed if the first two answers are no.

Let us evaluate the blood-clotting pathway with respect to these three questions:

1. The blood-clotting pathway is compatible with, but not required by, the natural laws of biology and chemistry; so it is not a necessity specified by natural phenomena.
2. It is complex because it is composed of many factors, thus the remote probability that it happened by chance. (Note that complex structures fall into two categories: ordered complexity and specified complexity. A snowflake, although complex structurally, has little information and thus is considered an example of ordered complexity. It is the direct result of natural phenomena rather than intelligent design[3]).
3. The blood-clotting pathway does show design, referred to as specified complexity, because it is complex and has a high amount of information. It is the direct result of an intelligent agent. All the factors must be present and interact with each other in a specified manner in order for the pathway to be functional. Thus, the blood-clotting pathway meets all the requirements for irreducible complexity, and so must be designed.

What the ID Movement Is and Is Not

William Dembski states, "ID is three things: a scientific research program that investigates the effects of intelligent causes; an intellectual movement that challenges Darwinism and its naturalistic legacy; and a way of understanding divine action."[4] The ID theory focuses on what is designed rather than answering the questions of who, when, why, and how. Those within the movement believe this promotes scientific endeavor by looking for function and purpose in those things that are designed, whereas an evolutionary mindset presupposes waste and purposelessness and aborts further scientific thinking. Although it may be a way of understanding divine action outside of a biblical framework, there are some serious implications for the Creator, which we will discuss later.

The ID movement does not speak to the optimality of design because it does not attempt to explain all designs. Remember, only "certain features" are designed, and evolutionary processes are not ruled out. The ID movement also claims not to be religiously motivated. It focuses not on the whom but on the

---

3. See www.intelligentdesign.org/menu/complex/complex3.htm for a more detailed discussion.
4. W. Dembski, "Science and Design," *First Things* 86 (1998): 21–27.

what. This may sound very appealing at first glance. Some biblical creationists believe that the ID movement's tolerance and acceptance of a wide range of beliefs about the supernatural could be useful in reaching a larger audience. Since the movement is very careful not to associate itself with Christianity or any formal religion, some think it will stand a better chance of gaining acceptance as an alternative to Darwinism in the schools, because it does not violate the so-called separation of church and state.

The ID movement does have several positives. The movement has produced many resources, including books and multimedia, that support the biblical creationist viewpoint. It makes clear that Darwinism/naturalism is based on the presupposition that the supernatural does not exist, thus affecting the way one interprets the scientific evidence. ID is based on the presupposition that the supernatural does exist.

ID may serve as a useful tool in *preliminary* discussions about God and creation to gain an audience that might be turned off at the mention of the Bible. However, in further discussions, the Bible as the biblical creationists' foundation should be primary.

However, the central problem with the ID movement is a divorce of the Creator from creation. The Creator and His creation cannot be separated; they reflect on each other. All other problems within the movement stem from this one.

Those within the ID movement claim their science is neutral. However, science is not neutral because it works with hypotheses based on beliefs or presuppositions. It is ironic that ID adherents refuse to see this about their own science, considering that they claim the problem with Darwinism is the presupposition that nothing supernatural exists. All scientists approach their work with presuppositions. The question is whether those beliefs are rooted in man's fallible ideas about the past or rooted in the infallible Word of God, the Bible.

The natural theology movement of the 1800s failed because it did not answer the next logical question: if it is designed, then who designed it? Although most within this movement claimed that design pointed to the God of the Bible, by divorcing general revelation (nature) from special revelation (the Bible), they opened the door to other conclusions. Deism (another movement of the same period) took the idea of excluding the Bible to the extreme and said God can only be known through nature and human reason, and that faith and revelation do not exist.

In today's culture, many are attracted to the ID movement because they can decide for themselves who the creator is — a Great Spirit, Brahman, Allah, God, etc. The current movement does not have unity on the naming of the

Intelligent design

THERE HAS TO BE A "MAKER"

Biblical creation

GOD IS MY "MAKER," AND SAVIOR!

©Answers In Genesis 2005

Romans 1:20   DAN LIETHA

As he spake by the mouth of his holy prophets, which have been since the world began: ... To give knowledge of salvation unto his people by the remission of their sins.   Luke 1:70, 77

creator and focuses more on what is designed. Thus, adherents do not oppose an old age for the earth and allow evolution to play a vital role once the designer formed the basics of life. They fail to understand that a belief in long ages for the earth formed the foundation of Darwinism. If God's Word is not true concerning the age of the earth, then maybe it's not true concerning other events of the creation week, and maybe God was not a necessary part of the equation for life after all.

The ID movement's belief in evolution also allows them to distance themselves from the problem of evil in the natural world. Examples of this include pathogenic microbes, carnivorous animals, disease, and death.

Without the framework of the Bible and the understanding that evil entered the world through man's actions (Genesis 3), God appears sloppy and incompetent, if not downright vicious. People ask why God is unable to prevent evil from thwarting His plans, resulting in such poor design, instead of understanding that because of the Fall there is now a "cursed" design. In addition, because the ID movement does not acknowledge God as Redeemer, there seems to be no final solution for the evil in this world, and by all appearances evil will continue to reign supreme. However, when we trust the Bible, we read that Jesus clearly conquered death by His Resurrection (Romans 6:3–10) and one day death will no longer reign (Revelation 21:4). Again, the Creator and His creation cannot be separated.

The attributes of God are very important when resolving apparent discrepancies in His creation. For example, according to the Bible, the earth is around 6,000 years old. However, starlight can be seen from stars millions of light years away. Also, according to the Bible, God does not lie. Therefore, we must lack some information that would resolve this apparent discrepancy. (Some good research has been done on this issue, and there are several plausible solutions.[5])

Our Creator and Redeemer

Romans 1:20 states that all men know about God through His creation. However, just recognizing that there is a designer is only the first step. Colossians 1:15–20 and 2 Peter 3:3–6 point to the inexorable link between God's role as Creator *and* Redeemer. In Colossians, Paul talks about God as Creator and moves seamlessly to His role as Redeemer. Paul sees creation as a foundation for redemption. In 1 Peter, Peter states that people started disbelieving in the second coming of Christ because they started doubting God's role as Creator.

5. See *The New Answers Book 1*, chapter 19 by Jason Lisle, (Green Forest, AR: Master Books, 2006), p. 245–254.

Again, God's role as Creator becomes foundational to His role as Redeemer. Recognizing a designer is not enough to be saved; submitting to the Redeemer is also necessary. While some might consider ID to be a noble attempt to counter the evolutionary indoctrination of our culture, it falls far short of a thoroughly biblical response.

We must not separate the creation from its Creator; knowledge of God must come through both general revelation (nature) and special revelation (the Bible). The theologian Louis Berkhof said, "Since the entrance of sin into the world, man can gather true knowledge about God from His general revelation only if he studies it in the light of Scripture."[6] It is only then that the *entire* truth about God and what is seen around us can be fully understood and used to help people understand the bad news in Genesis and the good news of Jesus Christ.

For since the creation of the world God's invisible attributes, His eternal power and divine nature, have been clearly seen, being understood through what has been made, so that they are without excuse. Romans 1:20

---

6. L. Berkhof, Introductory volume to *Systematic Theology* (Grand Rapids, MI: Wm. B. Eerdmans Publ. Co., 1946), p. 60.

14

Can Creationists Be "Real" Scientists?

DR. JASON LISLE

Some evolutionists have stated that creationists cannot be real scientists. Several years ago, the National Academy of Sciences published a guidebook entitled *Teaching about Evolution and the Nature of Science*. This guidebook states that biological evolution is "the most important concept in modern biology, a concept essential to understanding key aspects of living things." Famous geneticist Theodosius Dobzhansky stated that "nothing in biology makes sense except in the light of evolution."[1]

But is a belief in particles-to-people evolution really necessary to understand biology and other sciences? Is it even helpful? Have any technological advances been made because of a belief in evolution?

Although evolutionists interpret the evidence in light of their belief in evolution, science works perfectly well without any connection to evolution. Think about it this way: is a belief in molecules-to-man evolution necessary to understand how planets orbit the sun, how telescopes operate, or how plants and animals function? Has any biological or medical research benefited from a belief in evolution? Not at all. In fact, the PhD cell biologist (and creationist) Dr. David Menton has stated, "The fact is that though widely believed, evolution contributes nothing to our understanding of empirical science and thus

1. *The American Biology Teacher* 35:125–129.

plays no essential role in biomedical research or education."[2] And creationists are not the only ones who understand this. Dr. Philip Skell, Emeritus Evan Pugh Professor of Chemistry, Penn State University, wrote:

> I recently asked more than 70 eminent researchers if they would have done their work differently if they had thought Darwin's theory was wrong. The responses were all the same: No.
>
> I also examined the outstanding biodiscoveries of the past century: the discovery of the double helix; the characterization of the ribosome; the mapping of genomes; research on medications and drug reactions; improvements in food production and sanitation; the development of new surgeries; and others. I even queried biologists working in areas where one would expect the Darwinian paradigm to have most benefited research, such as the emergence of resistance to antibiotics and pesticides. Here, as elsewhere, I found that Darwin's theory had provided no discernible guidance, but was brought in, after the breakthroughs, as an interesting narrative gloss. . . . From my conversations with leading researchers it had became [sic] clear that modern experimental biology gains its strength from the availability of new instruments and methodologies, not from an immersion in historical biology.[3]

The rise of technology is not due to a belief in evolution, either. Computers, cellular phones, and DVD players all operate based on the laws of physics, which God created. It is because God created a logical, orderly universe and gave us the ability to reason and to be creative that technology is possible. How can a belief in evolution (that complex biological machines do *not* require an intelligent designer) aid in the development of complex machines, which are clearly intelligently designed? Technology has shown us that sophisticated machines require intelligent designers — not random chance. Science and technology are perfectly consistent with the Bible, but not with evolution.

Differing Assumptions

The main difference between scientists who are creationists and those who are evolutionists is their starting assumptions. Creationists and evolutionists have a different view of history, but the way they do science in the present is the same. Both creationists and evolutionists use observation and experimentation

2. David Menton, "A Testimony to the Power of God's Word," Answers in Genesis, www.answersingenesis.org/docs2003/0612menton_testimony.asp.
3. P. Skell, "Why Do We Invoke Darwin?" *The Scientist* 16:10.

to draw conclusions about nature. This is the nature of observational science. It involves repeatable experimentation and observations in the present. Since observational scientific theories are capable of being tested in the present, creationists and evolutionists are generally in agreement on these models. They agree on the nature of gravity, the composition of stars, the speed of light in a vacuum, the size of the solar system, the principles of electricity, etc. These things can be checked and tested in the present.

But historical events cannot be checked scientifically in the present. This is because we do not have access to the past; it is gone. All that we have is the circumstantial evidence (relics) of past events. Although we can make educated guesses about the past and can make inferences from things like fossils and rocks, we cannot directly test our conclusions because we cannot repeat the past. Furthermore, since creationists and evolutionists have very different views of history, it is not surprising that they reconstruct past events very differently. We all have the same evidence; but in order to draw conclusions about what the evidence means, we use our worldview — our most basic beliefs about the nature of reality. Since they have different starting assumptions, creationists and evolutionists interpret the same evidence to mean very different things.

Ultimately, biblical creationists accept the recorded history of the Bible as their starting point. Evolutionists reject recorded history, and have effectively made up their own pseudohistory, which they use as a starting point for interpreting evidence. Both are using their beliefs about the past to interpret the evidence in the present. When we look at the scientific evidence today, we find that it is very consistent with biblical history and not as consistent with millions of years of evolution. We've seen in this book that the scientific evidence is consistent with biblical creation. We've seen that the geological evidence is consistent with a global flood — not millions of years of gradual deposition. We've seen that the changes in DNA are consistent with the loss of information we would expect as a result of the Curse described in Genesis 3, not the hypothetical gain of massive quantities of genetic information required by molecules-to-man evolution. Real science confirms the Bible.

Real Scientists

It shouldn't be surprising that there have been many *real* scientists who believed in biblical creation. Consider Isaac Newton (1642–1727), who codiscovered calculus, formulated the laws of motion and gravity, computed the nature of planetary orbits, invented the reflecting telescope, and made a number of discoveries in optics. Newton had profound knowledge of, and faith in, the Bible. Carl Linnaeus (1707–1778), the Swedish botanist who developed the

Sir Isaac Newton

double-Latin-name system for taxonomic classification of plants and animals, also believed the Genesis creation account. So also did the Dutch geologist Nicolaus Steno (1631–1686), who developed the basic principles of stratigraphy.

Even in the early 19th century when the idea of millions of years was developed, there were prominent Bible-believing English scientists, such as chemists Andrew Ure (1778–1857) and John Murray (1786?–1851), entomologist William Kirby (1759–1850), and geologist George Young (1777–1848). James Clerk Maxwell (1831–1879) discovered the four fundamental equations that light and all forms of electromagnetic radiation obey. Indeed, Maxwell's equations are what make radio transmissions possible. He was a deep student of Scripture and was firmly opposed to evolution. These and many other great scientists have believed the Bible as the infallible Word of God, and it was their Christian faith that was the driving motivation and intellectual foundation of their excellent scientific work.

CREATIONWISE

Sir Francis Bacon — Established the scientific method

Johannes Kepler — Three laws of planetary motion

Sir Isaac Newton — Co-inventor of calculus

Louis Pasteur — Father of microbiology

James Clerk Maxwell — Laws of electricity and magnetism

Raymond V. Damadian — Inventor of the MRI

BIBLE BELIEVERS CAN'T BE SCIENTISTS!

© AiG 2005

Today there are many other PhD scientists who reject evolution and believe that God created in six days, a few thousand years ago, just as recorded in Scripture. Russ Humphreys, a PhD physicist, has developed (among many other things) a model to compute the present strength of planetary magnetic fields,[4] which enabled him to accurately predict the field strengths of the outer

4. Russell Humphreys, "The Creation of Planetary Magnetic Fields," Creation Research Society, www.creationresearch.org/crsq/articles/21/21_3/21_3.html.

planets. Did a belief in the Bible hinder his research? Not at all. On the contrary, Dr. Humphreys was able to make these predictions precisely because he started from the principles of Scripture. John Baumgardner, a PhD geophysicist and biblical creationist, has a sophisticated computer model of catastrophic plate tectonics, which was reported in the journal *Nature*; the assumptions for this model are based on the global flood recorded in Genesis. Additionally, think of all the people who have benefited from a magnetic resonance imaging (MRI) scan. The MRI scanner was developed by the creationist Dr. Raymond Damadian.[5]

Dr. John Baumgardner

Consider the biblical creationists Georgia Purdom and Andrew Snelling (both authors in this book), who work in molecular genetics and geology, respectively. They certainly understand their fields, and yet are convinced that they do not support evolutionary biology and geology.[6] On the contrary, they confirm biblical creation.

I have a PhD from a secular university and have done extensive research in solar astrophysics. In my PhD research, I made a number of discoveries about the nature of near-surface solar flows, including the detection of a never-before-seen polar alignment of supergranules, as well as patterns indicative of giant overturning cells. Was I hindered in my research by the conviction that the early chapters of Genesis are literally true? No, it's just the reverse. It is because a logical God created and ordered the universe that I, and other creationists, expect to be able to understand aspects of that universe through logic, careful observation, and experimentation.

Clearly, creationists can indeed be real scientists. And this shouldn't be surprising since the very basis for scientific research is biblical creation. This is not to say that noncreationists cannot be scientists. But, in a way, an evolutionist is being inconsistent when he or she does science. The big-bang supporter claims the universe is a random chance event, and yet he or she studies it as if it were logical and orderly. The evolutionist is thus forced to borrow certain creationist principles in order to do science. The universe is logical and orderly

5. Answers in Genesis, "Super-scientist Slams Society's Spiritual Sickness!" www. answersingenesis.org/creation/v16/i3/science.asp.
6. See various articles at www.answersingenesis.org/go/evolution and www.answersingenesis. org/go/geology.

because its Creator is logical and has imposed order on the universe. God created our minds and gave us the ability and curiosity to study the universe. Furthermore, we can trust that the universe will obey the same physics tomorrow as it does today because God is consistent. This is why science is possible. On the other hand, if the universe is just an accidental product of a big bang, why should it be orderly? Why should there be laws of nature if there is no lawgiver? If our brains are the by-products of random chance, why should we trust that their conclusions are accurate? But if our minds have been designed, and if the universe has been constructed by God, as the Bible teaches, then of course we should be able to study nature. Science is possible because the Bible is true.

15

How Should a Christian Respond to "Gay Marriage"?

KEN HAM

Most people have heard of the account of Adam and Eve. According to the first book of the Bible, Genesis, these two people were the first humans from whom all others in the human race descended. Genesis also records the names of three of Adam and Eve's many children — Cain, Abel, and Seth. Christians claim that this account of human history is accurate, because the Bible itself claims that it is the authoritative Word of the Creator God, without error.

To challenge Christians' faith in the Bible as an infallible revelation from God to humans, many skeptics have challenged the Bible's trustworthiness as a historical document by asking questions like, "Where did Cain find his wife?" (Don't worry — this will become highly relevant to the topic of gay marriage shortly!) This question of Cain's wife is one of the most-asked questions about the Christian faith and the Bible's reliability. In short, Genesis 5:4 states that Adam had "other sons and daughters"; thus, originally, brothers had to marry sisters.[1]

---

1. For more information on this topic, see Ken Ham, *The New Answers Book 1*, chapter 6, "Cain's Wife — Who Was She?" (Green Forest, AR: Master Books, 2006), p. 64–76.

An Atheist on a Talk Show

This background is helpful in offering the context of a conversation I had with a caller on a radio talk show. The conversation went something like this:

Caller: "I'm an atheist, and I want to tell you Christians that if you believe Cain married his sister, then that's immoral."

AiG: "If you're an atheist, then that means you don't believe in any personal God, right?"

Caller: "Correct!"

AiG: "Then if you don't believe in God, you don't believe there's such a thing as an absolute authority. Therefore, you believe everyone has a right to their own opinions — to make their own rules about life if they can get away with it, correct?"

Caller: "Yes, you're right."

AiG: "Then, sir, you can't call me immoral; after all, you're an atheist, who doesn't believe in any absolute authority."

AiG: "Do you believe all humans evolved from apelike ancestors?"

Caller: "Yes, I certainly believe evolution is fact."

AiG: "Then, sir, from your perspective on life, if man is just some sort of animal who evolved, and if there's no absolute authority, then marriage is whatever you want to define it to be — if you can get away with it in the culture you live in.

"It could be two men, two women or one man and ten women; in fact, it doesn't even have to be a man with another human — it could be a man with an animal.[2]

"I'm sorry, sir, that you think Christians have a problem. I think it's you who has the problem. Without an absolute authority, marriage, or any other aspect of how to live in society, is determined on the basis of opinion and ultimately could be anything one decides

---

2. See "Man Marries Dog for Luck — Then Dies," www.theage.com.au/
articles/2004/02/04/1075853937098.html?from=storyrhs; and M. Bates, "Marriage in the New Millennium: Love, Honor and Scratch between the Ears," *Oak Lawn (Illinois) Reporter*, April 5, 2001, as referenced at www.freerepublic.com/forum/a3ac9e00d0a87.htm. There are many articles online that discuss the possibility of a man marrying his dog if the sanctity of marriage is not upheld; search for words like *marriage, man,* and *dog.*

— if the culture as a whole will allow you to get away with this. You have the problem, not me."

It was a fascinating — and revealing — exchange.

So the questions, then, that could be posed to this caller and other skeptics are: "Who has the right to determine what is good or bad, or what is morally right or wrong in the culture? Who determines whether marriage as an institution should be adhered to, and if so, what the rules should be?"

The "Pragmatics" Aspect of Opposing Gay Marriage — Some Cautions

Some who defend marriage as a union between one man and one woman claim that it can be shown that cultures that have not adhered to this doctrine have reaped all sorts of problems (whether the spread of diseases or other issues). Thus, they claim, on this basis, it's obvious that marriage should be between one man and one woman only.

Even though such problems as the spread of HIV might be shown to be a sound argument in this issue, ultimately it's not a good basis for stating that one man for one woman must be the rule. It may be a sound argument based on the pragmatics of wanting to maintain a healthy physical body, but why should one or more human beings have the right to dictate to others what they can or can't do in sexual relationships? After all, another person might decide that the relationship between one man and woman in marriage might cause psychological problems and use that as the basis for the argument. So which one is correct?

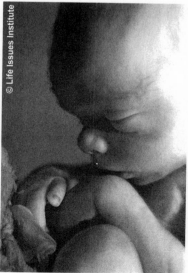

© Life Issues Institute

Say that a person used the argument that research has shown, for example, that the children of gay parents have a higher incidence of depression. Or the argument that since HIV kills people, it is vital that marriage is between a man and a woman. But note how such arguments have also been tried in the case of abortion and *rejected* by the culture.

Let us illustrate. Some researchers claim to have shown a high incidence of depression in people who have had an abortion. The culture, however, has rejected such pragmatic "we shouldn't hurt people" arguments, claiming that it is more important that others have the "right to choose." The argument that abortion kills people is an important one because most people still accept the basic biblical prohibition against taking innocent human life. So we should ensure that people know that the baby is really human. But is it going to be enough in the long term, as even this prohibition cannot be absolute without the Bible?

Allowing the Killing of a Newborn?

A slowly increasing minority of people, like Professor Peter Singer, the Ira W. DeCamp Professor of Bioethics at Princeton University,[3] are quite content to accept the obvious fact that abortion kills human beings, but this does not affect their view of abortion in the slightest. In fact, consistent with the fact that he rejects the Bible and the view that man was made in the image of God, Singer has argued that society should consider having a period after birth in which a baby is still allowed to be killed if socially desirable (e.g., if it has an unacceptable handicap).

Ultimately, it comes down to this: How does a culture determine what is right and what is wrong? If the majority agrees on a set of standards, what happens when that majority is replaced by a different majority?

After all, the majority in power in many of our Western nations once believed abortion was wrong — but now the majority in power doesn't believe this, so the rules have been changed.

The majority in power in many of our Western societies once believed the institution of marriage should be one man for one woman. But this has changed. Many are now allowing "gay marriage." So how long before polygamous or pedophiliac relationships are allowed, which some people are starting to advocate?[4] Who is to say they are wrong, if the majority agrees with them?

Before the Hitler era, nobody would have believed that the majority in a progressive, industrialized Western nation such as Germany could have agreed that it was ethically proper to mass murder the mentally retarded and those with incurable long-term illnesses. Yet the majority of Germans were convinced by their society to see euthanasia as ethically acceptable, even kindhearted.

Some might say that there is no way Western culture would allow pedophilia. Fifty years ago, however, most people probably would not have dreamed

3. www.answersingenesis.org/docs/1186.asp.
4. B. Sorotzkin, "The Denial of Child Abuse: The Rind, *et al.* Controversy," NARTH.com; L. Nicolosi, "The Pedophilia Debate Continues — and DSM Is Changed Again," NARTH.com; and "Russian Region Wants to Allow Men Up to Four Wives," CNN.com, July 21, 1999.

that America or Britain would ever allow gay marriage. Where does one draw the line? And who determines who draws that line? What's the answer?

Does the Church Have the Answer?

The gay marriage issue has been headline news across North America and on other continents. Even the acceptance of gay clergy has been widely noted in both secular and Christian media outlets.

- In November 2003, a part of the Episcopal Church voted to ordain a gay bishop. Thus, the world saw part of the Church now condoning homosexual behavior.[5]
- On March 18, 2004, the Pacific Northwest Conference of the United Methodist Church in America supported a lesbian pastor. Once again, the world looked on as a large denomination legitimized homosexual behavior.[6]

As part of the public debate on the gay marriage issue, many Church leaders have been interviewed on national TV programs and asked to share their position on this topic. While the majority of Church leaders have been speaking against gay unions and have been defending marriage as being between one man and one woman, many of these same Church leaders have not been able to adequately defend their position.

One Christian leader was interviewed on MSNBC-TV and was asked about the gay marriage issue. The interview went something like this:

TV host: "Did Jesus deal directly with the gay marriage issue?"

Christian leader: "No, but then Jesus didn't deal directly with the abortion issue or many other issues. . . ."

This is such a disappointing response. A proper response could have been such a powerful witness — not only to the interviewer but to the potential millions of viewers watching the news program, so people could understand why this Christian leader opposed gay marriage.

The same Christian leader appeared on CNN-TV doing an interview that, in part, went something like the following:

Interviewer: "Why are you against gay marriage?"

---

5. "Episcopal Church Consecrates Openly Gay Bishop," CNN.com, November 3, 2003.
6. Read the church proceedings for and against the Rev. Karen Dammann at www.pnwumc.org/Dammann.htm.

Christian leader: "Because down through the ages, culture after culture has taught that marriage is between a man and a woman."

We believe this kind of answer actually opens the door to gay marriage! How? Because it basically says that marriage is determined by law or opinion.

So, why is it that we don't see many Christian leaders giving the right sorts of answers? I think it's because the majority of them have compromised with the idea of millions of years of history, as well as evolutionary beliefs in astronomy, geology, and so on. As a result, the Bible's authority has been undermined, and it's no longer understood to be the absolute authority.[7]

Gay Marriage — Is Evolution the Cause?

After reading explanations from *Answers in Genesis* such as those above, some critics have concluded that we are saying that belief in millions of years or other evolutionary ideas is the cause of social ills like gay marriage. This is not true at all.

It is accurate to say that the increasing acceptance of homosexual behavior and gay marriage has gone hand in hand with the popularity and acceptance of millions of years and evolutionary ideas. But this does not mean that every person who believes in millions of years/evolution accepts gay marriage or condones homosexual behavior.

But the more people (whether Christian or not) believe in man's ideas concerning the history of the universe, regardless of what God's Word appears to be plainly teaching, the more man's fallible ideas are used as a basis for determining "truth" and overriding the Bible's authority.

People need to understand that homosexual behavior and the gay marriage controversy are ultimately not the problems in our culture, but are the *symptoms* of a much deeper problem. Even though it's obvious from the Bible that homosexual behavior and gay marriage are an abomination (Romans 1 and other passages make this very clear), there is a foundational reason as to why there is an increasing acceptance of these ills in America and societies like it.

> What does the Bible says about homosexual behavior and gay marriage? Study the following verses: Genesis 2:18–25; Leviticus 18:22; Mark 10:6; Romans 1:26–27; 1 Corinthians 6:9–10; 1 Timothy 1:9–10

---

7. For more information on this important point, see chapter 11, "Where Did the Idea of 'Millions of Years' Come From?"

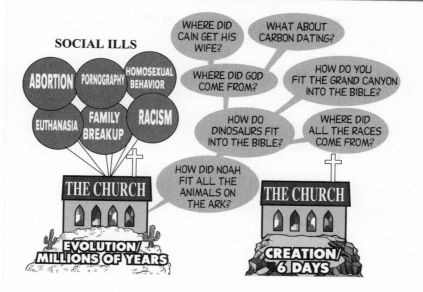

Cultures in the West were once pervaded by a primarily Christian worldview because the majority of people at least respected the Bible as the authority on morality. It needs to be clearly understood that over the past 200 years the Bible's authority has been increasingly undermined, as much of the Church has compromised with the idea of millions of years (this began before Darwin) and has thus begun reinterpreting Genesis. When those outside the Church saw Church leaders rejecting Genesis as literal history, one can understand why they would have quickly lost respect for all of the Bible. If the Church doesn't even believe this Book to be true, then why should the world build its morality on a fallible work that modern science supposedly has shown to be inaccurate in its science and history?

The Bible has lost respect in people's eyes (both within and without the Church) to the extent that the culture as a whole now does not take the Bible's morality seriously at all. The increasing acceptance of homosexual behavior and gay marriage is a symptom of the loss of biblical authority, and is primarily due to the compromise the Church has made with the secular world's teaching on origins.

Mocking the Bible

For example, consider the following. A New Orleans newspaper printed a commentary entitled "In Gay Rights Debate, Genesis Is Losing."[8] The column pointed out (correctly) that God intended marriage to be between one man and

---

8. J. Gill, *Times-Picayune*, New Orleans, Louisiana, March 5, 2004.

one woman. The writer even quoted Genesis 2:24, which declares, "Therefore shall a man leave his father and his mother and shall cleave to his wife and they shall be one flesh."

The author then, mockingly, wrote, "Ah, Genesis. Heaven and earth created in six days, a serpent that talks, and a 600-year-old man building an ark. Just the guide we need to set rational policy."

This secular writer recognized that the literal history of Genesis was the basis for the belief that marriage is one man for one woman. However, by mocking the Genesis account (just as many church leaders effectively do when they reinterpret Genesis 1–11 on the basis of man's fallible ideas), the writer removed the foundations upon which the institution of marriage stands. This opens the door to gay marriage or anything else one might determine about marriage.

Were Homosexuals Created That Way?

Human sexuality is very complex, and the arguments will long rage as to the causes of homosexual behavior. In this fallen world, most behaviors are a complex mix of one's personal choices superimposed on a platform of predisposition. This can come both from one's genetic makeup and one's environment (for example, one's upbringing). Few students of human nature would doubt the proposition that some personalities are much more predisposed to alcoholism and/or wife beating, for instance. But would anyone argue that this would make wife beating acceptable?

The case for a "homosexual gene" has evaporated, but let's say that researchers really were able to identify such a gene. After all, mutations in a cursed, fallen world can cause all sorts of abnormalities and malfunctions. For one thing, that would be a result of the Curse, not creation. And would knowledge of such a gene make right what Scripture clearly says is wrong? Absolute right and wrong exist independent of any secondary causative agencies.

THE TWO PARTS DON'T MAKE ONE

In fact, it is quite possible that a contributing factor to at least some cases of homosexuality is a dysfunctional upbringing right at the time when the child is gaining crucial environmental input regarding his or her own sexual identity. (Notice the importance the Bible places on bringing up children, the family unit, and so on.) But if anything, this highlights one of the huge risks of "married" gay people bringing up adopted children, namely the vulnerability of the children to confused messages about their own sexual identity. To put it simply, if one's environment contributes to homosexuality, gay marriage will tend to increase the likelihood of the next generation being gay.[9]

Gay Marriage – What Is the Answer?

In the Bible in Judges 17:6, we read this statement: "In those days there was no king in Israel; every man did what was right in his own eyes" (NAS95). In other words, when there is no absolute authority to decide right and wrong, everyone has his or her own opinion about what to do.

So how could the Christian leader whose interviews were quoted earlier in this chapter have responded differently? Well, consider this answer:

First of all, Jesus (who created us and therefore owns us and has the authority to determine right and wrong), as the God-man, *did* deal directly with the gay marriage issue, in the Bible's New Testament, in Matthew 19:4–6: "And He answered and said to them, 'Have you not read that He who made them at the beginning "made them male and female," and said, "For this cause a man shall leave father and mother and shall cling to his wife, and the two of them shall be one flesh?" So then, they are no longer two but one flesh. Therefore what God has joined together, let not man separate.' "

He could have continued:

Christ quoted directly from the book of Genesis (and its account of the creation of Adam and Eve as the first man and woman — the first marriage) as literal history, to explain the doctrine of marriage as

9. Two things to note in this section: (1) The idea is already with us that gay "couples" should be freely able to donate their sperm to surrogate mothers or to clone their DNA to perpetuate their own genes. So if there is any genetic basis to homosexuality (i.e., "made that way"), then this too will increase the frequency of homosexuality in future generations. (2) Regarding the capacity of an individual to stop his or her homosexual behavior, we wish to observe that even with what sin has done in this fallen world, the Bible promises that we will not be tested beyond what we can endure (1 Corinthians 10:13) because the power of God is available to all believers.

being one man for one woman. Thus marriage cannot be a man and a man, or a woman and a woman.

Because Genesis is real history (as can be confirmed by observational science, incidentally), Jesus dealt quite directly with the gay marriage issue when he explained the doctrine of marriage.

Not only this, but in John 1 we read: "In the beginning was the Word, and the Word was with God, and the Word was God. The same was in the beginning with God. All things were made by him; and without him was not any thing made that was made" (KJV).

Jesus, the Creator, is the Word. The Bible is the written Word. Every word in the Bible is really the Word of the Creator—Jesus Christ.[10]

Therefore, in Leviticus 18:22, Jesus deals directly with the homosexual issue, and thus the gay marriage issue. This is also true of Romans 1:26–27 and 1 Timothy 1:9–10.

Because Jesus in a real sense wrote all of the Bible, whenever Scripture deals with marriage and/or the homosexual issue, Jesus himself is directly dealing with these issues.

Even in a secular context, the only answer a Christian should offer is this:

The Bible is the Word of our Creator, and Genesis is literal history. Its science and history can be trusted. Therefore, we have an absolute authority that determines marriage.

God made the first man and woman — the first marriage. Thus, marriage can only be a man and a woman because we are accountable to the One who made marriage in the first place.

And don't forget — according to Scripture, one of the primary reasons for marriage is to produce godly offspring.[11] Adam and Eve were told to be fruitful and multiply, but there's no way a gay marriage can fulfill this command!

The battle against gay marriage will ultimately be lost (like the battle against abortion) *unless* the church and the culture return to the absolute authority beginning in Genesis. Then and only then will there be a true foundation for the correct doctrine of marriage — one man for one woman for life.

---

10. See Colossians 1:15–20 as well.
11. Malachi 2:15: "Has not the Lord made them one? In flesh and spirit they are his. And why one? Because he was seeking godly offspring. So guard yourself in your spirit, and do not break faith with the wife of your youth."

16

Did People Like Adam and Noah Really Live Over 900 Years of Age?

DR. DAVID MENTON & DR. GEORGIA PURDOM

"Methuseleh lived 900 years . . . but these stories you're liable to read in the Bible, they ain't necessarily so."[1]

Along with American composer George Gershwin, many people find it difficult to believe that Methuselah lived to be 969 years old. Nevertheless, the Bible teaches quite plainly that the early patriarchs often lived to be nearly 1,000 years old and even had children when they were several hundred years old! Similar claims of long life spans are found in the secular literature of several ancient cultures (including the Babylonians, Greeks, Romans, Indians, and Chinese). But even a life span of nearly 1,000 years is sadly abbreviated when we consider that God initially created us to live *forever*.

According to the Bible, God created the first humans — Adam and Eve — without sin and with the ability to live forever. God gave the first human couple everything they needed for their eternal health and happiness in the Garden of Eden; but He warned them not to eat fruit from the Tree of the Knowledge of Good and Evil or they would die, as indeed would all their descendants after them (Genesis 2:16–17). When Satan's deception prompted

---

1. George Gershwin, "It Ain't Necessarily So," *Porgy & Bess*, 1934.

Eve to disobey this command and then Adam willfully disobeyed, their minds and bodies profoundly changed (Genesis 3). Not only did they become subject to death, but their firstborn child (Cain) became the world's first murderer. Truly, the wages of sin is death, physically and spiritually. It is sobering to think that the Bible would have been only a few pages long — from creation to the fall into sin — were it not for the undeserved love of God who both promised and sent the Messiah to save us from sin and death (Genesis 3:15; Isaiah 25:8; Psalm 49:14–15; 1 John 5:13).

For 1,500 years after creation, men lived such long lives that most were either contemporaries of the first man, Adam, or personally knew someone who was! The ten patriarchs (excluding Enoch) who preceded the Great Flood lived an average of 912 years. Lamech died the youngest at the age of 777, and Methuselah lived to be the oldest at 969. See table 1.

Table 1. Ages of the Patriarchs from Adam to Noah

	Patriarch	Age	Bible Reference
1	Adam	930	Genesis 5:4
2	Seth	912	Genesis 5:8
3	Enosh	905	Genesis 5:11
4	Cainan	910	Genesis 5:14
5	Mahalalel	895	Genesis 5:17
6	Jared	962	Genesis 5:20
7	Enoch	365 (translated)	Genesis 5:23
8	Methuselah	969	Genesis 5:27
9	Lamech	777	Genesis 5:31
10	Noah	950	Genesis 9:29

During the 1,000 years following the Flood, however, the Bible records a progressive decline in the life span of the patriarchs, from Noah who lived to be 950 years old until Abraham at 175 (see figure 1 and table 2). In fact, Moses was unusually old for his time (120 years) because, when he reflected on the brevity of life, he said: "The days of our lives are seventy years; and if by reason of strength they are eighty years, yet their boast is only labor and sorrow; for it is soon cut off, and we fly away" (Psalm 90:10).

Table 2. Ages of the Patriarchs after Noah to Abraham

	Patriarch	Age	Bible Reference
11	Shem	600	Genesis 11:10–11
12	Arphaxad	438	Genesis 11:12–13
13	Shelah	433	Genesis 11:14–15
14	Eber	464	Genesis 11:16–17
15	Peleg	239	Genesis 11:18–19
16	Reu	239	Genesis 11:20–21
17	Serug	230	Genesis 11:22–23
18	Nahor	148	Genesis 11:24–25
19	Terah	205	Genesis 11:32
20	Abraham	175	Genesis 25:7

Extrabiblical evidence to support the long life spans of the people in Genesis is found in the Sumerian King List. This list mentions a flood and gives the length of the reigns of kings before and after a flood. There are many striking parallels between the Sumerian King List and Genesis, such as a flood event, numerical parallels between the pre-Flood biblical patriarchs and the antediluvial kings, and a substantial decrease in life span of people following the flood.[2] One author on this subject concludes, "It is highly unlikely that the biblical account was derived from the Sumerian in view of the differences of the two accounts, and the obvious superiority of the Genesis record both in numerical precision, realism, completion, and moral and spiritual qualities."[3] It is more likely that the Sumerian King List was composed using Genesis for numerical information. Obviously, the Book of Genesis would only be used if the person writing the list believed it to be a true historical account containing accurate information.

Today, man's maximum life span is about 120 years,[4] and our average life expectancy is still only 70–80 years — just as it was when the 90th Psalm was

2. Raul Lopez, "The Antediluvian Patriarchs and the Sumerian King List," *CEN Technical Journal* 12, no. 3 (1998): 347–357.
3. Ibid.
4. It should be noted that Genesis 6:3 does not refer to God mandating a maximum life span for people of 120 years. If this is the case, then the Bible is in error as many people have been recorded as living longer than 120 years. Rather, it refers to the amount of time from when God determined to destroy mankind to when God sent a global flood.

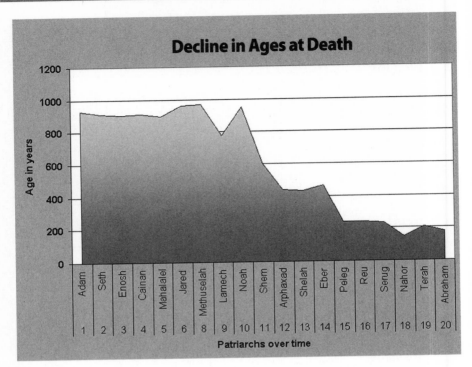

Figure 1

written 3,400 years ago! The precipitous plunge in life spans after the Flood suggests that something changed at the time of the Flood, or shortly thereafter, that was responsible for this decline. A line graph of this decline reveals an exponential curve (see figure 1). An exponential decay rate is often called a "natural" decay rate because it is so often observed in nature. For example, this is the decay curve we see when living organisms are exposed to lethal doses of toxic substances or radiations. Since it is unlikely that people living in pre-Flood times were familiar with exponential decay curves, it is thus unlikely that these dates were fabricated.

The fossil record reveals that prior to the Flood, most of the earth appears to have had a tropical type of environment. Following the Flood, there was clearly an environmental change resulting in an ice age that covered nearly 30 percent of the earth with ice (primarily in the northern latitudes). This, together with other changes following the Flood, could have adversely affected life spans.

Biological Causes of Aging

What exactly causes this process of aging in our body? Although the mechanism of aging (and its prevention) has long been an object of biomedical research, science still has no definitive answer to this question. Around the turn of the century, it was believed that aging didn't directly involve the living cells of our body but rather was an extracellular phenomenon. It was believed that our normal living cells, if properly nourished, could grow and divide indefinitely outside our body. In 1961, this idea was refuted by Leonard Hayflick, who grew human cells outside the body in covered glass dishes containing the necessary nutrients. Hayflick discovered that cells cultured in this way normally died after about 50 cell divisions (*Hayflick's limit*). This suggests that even the individual cells of our body are mortal, apart from any other bodily influence.

Genetic Determinants

Both aging and life span are processes that have genetic determinants that are overlapping and unique. Approximately 20–30 percent of factors affecting life span are thought to be heritable and thus genetic.[5] Life span varies greatly among individuals, indicating that while aging plays a role, other factors are also involved.

Mutations and Genetic Bottlenecks

A mutation is any change in the sequence of DNA.[6] All known mutations cause a loss of information. The rate at which all types of mutations occur per generation has been suggested to be greater than 1,000.[7] We inherit mutations from our parents and also develop mutations of our own; subsequently, we pass a proportion of those on to our children. So it is conceivable in the many generations between Adam and Moses that a large number of mutations would have been present in any given individual.

Genetic bottlenecks (or population bottlenecks) occur when significant proportions of the population dies or proportions become isolated. Such a bottleneck occurred at the time of Noah's flood when the human population was reduced to eight people (Genesis 6–9). Other smaller bottlenecks occurred following the Tower of Babel dispersion (Genesis 11). These events would have resulted in a major reduction of genetic variety.

For every gene there are two or more versions called alleles. This is analogous to the color red (gene) but different shades of red — light and dark (alleles). It is

---

5. T. Perls and D. Terry, "Genetics of Exceptional Longevity," *Experimental Gerontology* 38 (2003): 725–730.
6. See chapter 7, which provides an overview of mutations.
7. J. Sanford, *Genetic Entropy and the Mystery of the Genome* (New York: Ivan Press, 2005), p. 37.

possible for "good" (unmutated) alleles to mask or hide "bad" (mutated) alleles. However, in a smaller population with less allelic variation, this becomes more difficult to accomplish, and thus mutated alleles have a greater effect.

Although Noah lived 950 years, his father, Lamech, lived only 777 years (granted we do not know if he died from old age). In addition, we do not know how long Noah's wife lived, but Noah's son Shem only lived 600 years. Considering that the longest recorded life span of someone born after the Flood was Eber at 464 years, it would appear that both mutations and genetic bottlenecks had severe effects on aging and life span.

Examples of Genetic Determinants Affecting Aging and Life Span

Although many genetic factors are suggested to affect aging and life span, these processes largely remain a mystery. Aging can be thought of as increased susceptibility to internal (i.e., agents that damage DNA) and external (i.e., disease-causing bacteria) stressors because of a decrease in the maintenance, repair, and defensive systems of the body.

For example, DNA repair systems are needed to protect the genome (all our DNA) from mutation. *Xeroderma pigmentosum* (XP) is a genetic disorder caused by a deficient (due to mutations) DNA repair system that normally repairs mutations caused by ultraviolet light. Individuals with this disease must severely limit their exposure to sunlight. Outer surfaces of the body such as skin and lips commonly show signs of premature aging.[8] While this is an extreme example, any mutation that decreases the efficiency of our maintenance, repair, and defensive systems will likely lead to more rapid aging and decreased life span.

Telomeres, long, repetitive sequences of DNA at the ends of human chromosomes, are also thought to play an important role in aging. With each division of the cell, telomeres shorten due to the inability of the enzyme that copies the DNA to go all the way to the end of the chromosome.[9] When telomeres have become too short, the cell stops dividing. This limitation plausibly serves as a quality control mechanism. Older cells will have accumulated many mutations in their DNA, and their continued division may lead to diseases like cancer. Most body cells cannot replicate indefinitely, leading to aging and eventually death. Thus, telomeres are important in determining the life span of cell types that directly affect aging.

---

8. DermNet NZ, "Xeroderma Pigmentosum," www.dermnetnz.org/systemic/xeroderma-pigmentosum.html.
9. P. Monaghan and M. Haussmann, "Do Telomere Dynamics Link Lifestyle and Lifespan?" *TRENDS in Ecology and Evolution* 21 (2006): 47–53.

Job hunting in the days before
Noah's flood.

Genetic determinants of life span or longevity are difficult to pinpoint. Even if the genes are determined to be associated with people who live for many years, their actual role in increasing life span is unknown. Genetic studies of centarians (people who have lived more than 100 years) have produced several possible candidate longevity genes. The gene for apolipoprotein E (APOE), important in the regulation of cholesterol, has certain alleles that are more common among centarians.[10] This is also true for certain alleles of insulin-like growth factor 1 (IGF1), important in cell proliferation and cell death, and superoxide dismutases (SOD), important in the breakdown of agents that damage DNA.[11] Possibly the alleles associated with the centarians more closely reflect the genetic makeup of individuals with a long life span 6,000 years ago. Still, these alleles show the effects of the curse if the highest achievable age today is around 120 years!

10. K. Christensen et al., "The Quest for Genetic Determinants of Human Longevity: Challenges and Insights," *Nature Reviews Genetics* 7 (2006): 436–448.
11. Ibid.

Evolution and the Genetics of Aging and Life Span

Evolution has a difficult time explaining aging and life span. Aging is often viewed as a default. Genes are selected on the basis of how they benefit an individual in their young reproductive years, or the " 'warranty period' [which] is the time required to fulfill the Darwinian purpose of life in terms of successful reproduction for the continuation of generations."[12] However, these same genes may be harmful overall, leading to aging and eventually death.

The problem for evolution is that longevity genes are selected for. To deal with this seeming dichotomy, some evolutionists have suggested that selection of longevity genes serves a purpose in that long-lived individuals can care for more of their descendants, known as the "grandmother effect."[13] The problem is that any theory that is so flexible it can account for everything isn't a very good theory.

Genes associated with aging and life span have been affected as a result of the Fall either directly through mutations or indirectly through genetic bottlenecks. Modern medicine and anti-aging therapies may slow the process of aging and extend our life span, but they will never eradicate the ultimate end — death. Only Jesus Christ, who was victorious over death, can promise eternal life with Him to all who believe (Romans 6:23, 10:9).

Physiological Determinants

In one sense, most of the substance of our body really doesn't continue to get *older* during our life: a great many of our body's parts are constantly repairing and replacing themselves. The epidermal cells that cover the entire surface of our skin, for example, never get older than one month. New cells are continually produced (by cell division) deep in the epidermis, while the older ones continually slough off at the surface. Similarly, the cells lining our intestines completely replace themselves every 4 days; our red blood cells are entirely replaced about every 90 days; and our white blood cells are replaced about every week.

Even cells that never (or rarely) divide, such as cardiac muscle cells and brain cells, turn over molecule by molecule. It is believed that little or nothing in our body is more than about 10 years old. Thus, thanks to cell turnover and replacement, most of the organs in the body of a 90-year-old man are perhaps

---

12. S. Rattan, "Theories of Biological Aging: Genes, Proteins, and Free Radicals," *Free Radical Research* 41 (2006): 1230–1238.
13. W. Browner et al., "The Genetics of Human Longevity," *The American Journal of Medicine* 11 (2004): 851–860.

no older than those of a child. Indeed, you might say our body never actually grows older.

It's rather like the story about "grandpa's ax." It seems a man had an old ax that hung over his fireplace and which he claimed had been passed down in his family for five generations. When asked how old the ax was, he said he wasn't sure because although his great-great-great-great grandfather bought the ax about 300 years ago, he also understood that over the years, the ax had 6 new heads and 12 new handles. Our bodies are something like grandpa's ax in that we too are constantly replacing "heads and handles," and in a sense we never get older.

At this point we might be inclined to ask, why did Methuselah die so *young*? How, indeed, is it even possible for anyone to age and die if the body constantly repairs and replaces its parts? Surely, if our automobile could do this, we would expect it to last forever. Part of the answer may be that certain key parts of our body *fail* to repair or replace themselves. Our critically important heart muscle cells, for example, fail to multiply, repair, or replace themselves after birth (although, like all muscle cells, they can increase in size). This is why any disruption in the blood supply to the heart muscle during a heart attack leads to permanent death of that part of the heart. The nerve cells of our brain — including those of our eye and inner ear — also fail to multiply or repair themselves. From the time of our birth to the end of our life, we lose thousands of nerve cells a minute from our central nervous system, and we can never replace them. As we get older, this causes a progressive loss of our ability to hear, see, smell, taste, and . . . ahh . . . something else, but I just can't remember it!

The important point is that science offers no hope for eternal life, or even for the significant lengthening of life. It has been estimated that if complete cures, or preventions, were found for the three major killers (cancer, stroke, and coronary artery disease), the maximum life span of man would still not increase (although more people would approach this maximum). And such long-lived people would still become progressively weaker with age, as critical components of their body continue to deteriorate.

We may conclude that God's Word, not science, has the complete solution to the problem of aging and death. The solution has been "revealed by the appearing of our Savior Jesus Christ, who has abolished death and brought life and immortality to light through the gospel" (2 Timothy 1:10).

17

Why 66?

BRIAN H. EDWARDS

How can we be sure that we have the correct 66 books in our Bible? The Bible is a unique volume. It is composed of 66 books by 40 different writers over 1,500 years. But what makes it unique is that it has one consistent storyline running all the way through, and it has just one ultimate author — God. The story is about God's plan to rescue men and women from the devastating results of the Fall, a plan that was conceived in eternity, revealed through the prophets, and carried out by the Son of God, Jesus Christ.

Each writer of the Bible books wrote in his own language and style, using his own mind, and in some cases research, yet each was so overruled by the Holy Spirit that error was not allowed to creep into his work. For this reason, the Bible is understood by Christians to be a book without error.[1]

This collection of 66 books is known as the "canon" of Scripture. That word comes from the Hebrew *kaneh* (a rod), and the Greek *kanon* (a reed). Among other things, the words referred equally to the measuring rod of the carpenter and the ruler of the scribe. It became a common word for anything that was the measure by which others were to be judged (see Galatians 6:16,

---

1. For a more full discussion of the inspiration of the Bible, see Brian Edwards, *Nothing But the Truth* (Darlington, UK: Evangelical Press, 2006), p.116–143. In this, the following definition can be found: "The Holy Spirit moved men to write. He allowed them to use their own style, culture, gifts and character, to use the results of their own study and research, to write of their own experiences and to express what was in their mind. At the same time, the Holy Spirit did not allow error to influence their writings; he overruled in the expression of thought and in the choice of words. Thus they recorded accurately all that God wanted them to say and exactly how he wanted them to say it, in their own character, style and language."

The New Answers Book 2

for example). After the apostles, church leaders used it to refer to the body of Christian doctrine accepted by the churches. Clement and Origen of Alexandria, in the third century, were possibly the first to employ the word to refer to the Scriptures (the Old Testament).[2] From then on, it became more common in Christian use with reference to a collection of books that are fixed in their number, divine in their origin, and universal in their authority.

In the earliest centuries, there was little *debate* among Christians over which books belonged in the Bible; certainly by the time of the church leader Athanasius in the fourth century, the number of books had long been fixed. He set out the books of the New Testament just as we know them and added:

> These are the fountains of salvation, that whoever thirsts may be satisfied by the eloquence which is in them. In them alone is set forth the doctrine of piety. Let no one add to them, nor take anything from them.[3]

Today, however, there are attempts to undermine the clear witness of history; a host of publications, from the novel to the (supposedly) academic challenge the long-held convictions of Christians and the clear evidence of the past. Dan Brown in *The Da Vinci Code* claimed, "More than eighty gospels were considered for the New Testament, and yet only relatively few were chosen for inclusion — Matthew, Mark, Luke and John among them."[4] Richard Dawkins, professor of popular science at Oxford, England, has made similar comments.[5]

So, what is the evidence for our collection of 66 books? How certain can we be that these are the correct books to make up our Bible — no more and no less?

The Canon of the Old Testament

The Jews had a clearly defined body of Scriptures that collectively could be summarized as the Torah, or Law. This was fixed early in the life of Israel, and there was no doubt as to which books belonged and which did not. They did

2. Clement of Alexandria, *The Miscellanies* bk. VI.15. He comments, "The ecclesiastical rule (canon) is the concord and harmony of the Law and the Prophets." B.F. Westcott, referring to Origen's commentary on Matthew 28, wrote: "No one should use for the proof of doctrine books not included among the canonized Scriptures." (*The Canon of the New Testament During the First Four Centuries* [Cambridge: Macmillan & Co.,1855], p. 548).
3. From the Festal Epistle of Athanasius XXXIX. Translated in *Nicene and Post-Nicene Fathers*, vol. IV., p. 551–552.
4. Dan Brown, *The Da Vinci Code* (London: Bantam Press, 2003), p. 231.
5. Richard Dawkins, *The God Delusion* (London: Bantam Press, 2006), p. 237.

not order them in the same way as our Old Testament, but the same books were there. *The Law* was the first five books, known as the Pentateuch, which means "five rolls" — referring to the parchment scrolls on which they were normally written. *The Prophets* consisted of the Former Prophets (unusually for us these included Joshua, Judges, Samuel, and Kings) and the Latter Prophets (Isaiah, Jeremiah which included Lamentations, and the 12 smaller prophetic books). *The Writings* gathered up the rest. The total amounted generally to 24 books because many books, such as 1 and 2 Samuel and Ezra and Nehemiah, were counted as one.

When was the canon of the Old Testament settled? The simple response is that if we accept the reasonable position that each of the books was written at the time of its history — the first five at the time of Moses, the historical records close to the period they record, the psalms of David during his lifetime, and the prophets written at the time they were given — then the successive stages of acceptance into the canon of Scripture is not hard to fix. Certainly, the Jews generally held this view.

There is a lot of internal evidence that the books of the Old Testament were written close to the time they record. For example, in 2 Chronicles 10:19, we have a record from the time of Rehoboam that "Israel has been in rebellion against the house of David to this day." Clearly, therefore, that must have been recorded prior to 721 B.C., when the Assyrians finally crushed Israel and the cream of the population was taken away into captivity — or at the very latest before 588 B.C., when Jerusalem suffered the same fate. We know also that the words of the prophets were written down in their own lifetime; Jeremiah had a secretary called Baruch for this very purpose (Jeremiah 36:4).

Josephus, the Jewish historian writing around A.D. 90, clearly stated in his defense of Judaism that, unlike the Greeks, the Jews did not have many books:

> For we have not an innumerable multitude of books among us, disagreeing from and contradicting one another [as the Greeks have] but only twenty-two books, which contain the records of all the past times; which are justly believed to be divine.[6]

The Council of Jamnia

Between A.D. 90 and 100, a group of Jewish scholars met at Jamnia in Israel to consider matters relating to the Hebrew Scriptures. It has been suggested that the canon of the Jewish Scriptures was agreed here; the reality is

---

6. Josephus, *Against Apion*, trans. William Whiston (London: Ward, Lock & Co.), bk. 1, ch. 8. His 22 books consisted of exactly the same as our 39 for the reasons given in the text.

that there is no contemporary record of the deliberations at Jamnia and our knowledge is therefore left to the comments of later rabbis. The idea that there was no clear canon of the Hebrew Scriptures before A.D. 100 is not only in conflict with the testimony of Josephus and others, but has also been seriously challenged more recently. It is now generally accepted that Jamnia was not a council nor did it pronounce on the Jewish canon; rather it was an assembly that examined and discussed the Hebrew Scriptures. The purpose of Jamnia was not to decide which books should be included among the sacred writings, but to examine those that were already accepted.[7]

The Apocrypha and the Septuagint

There is a cluster of about 14 books, known as the Apocrypha, which were written some time between the close of the Old Testament (after 400 B.C.) and the beginning of the New. They were never considered as part of the Hebrew Scriptures, and the Jews themselves clearly ruled them out by the confession that there was, throughout that period, no voice of the prophets in the land.[8] They looked forward to a day when "a faithful prophet" should appear.[9]

The Old Testament had been translated into Greek during the third century B.C., and this translation is known as the Septuagint, a word meaning 70, after the supposedly 70 men involved in the translation. It was the Greek Septuagint that the disciples of Jesus frequently used since Greek was the common language of the day.

Whether or not the Septuagint also contained the Apocrypha is impossible to say for certain, since although the earliest copies of the Septuagint available today do include the Apocrypha — placed at the end — these are dated in the fifth century and therefore cannot be relied upon to tell us what was common half a millennium earlier. Significantly, neither Jesus nor any of the apostles ever quoted from the Apocrypha, even though they were obviously using the Greek Septuagint. Josephus was familiar with the Septuagint and made use of it, but he never considered the Apocrypha part of the Scriptures.[10]

---

7. This is a widespread view. See for example R. Beckwith, *The Old Testament Canon of the New Testament Church* (London: SPCK, 1985), p. 276. Also, A. Bentzen, *Introduction to the Old Testament*, vol. 1 (Copenhagen: G.E.C. Gad, 1948), p. 31; Bruce Metzger, *The Canon of the New Testament* (Oxford: Oxford University Press, 1987), p. 110; John Wenham, *Christ and the Bible* (London: Tyndale Press, 1972), p.138–139.

8. The Apocrypha. 1 Maccabees 9:27 at the time of revolt against Syrian occupation in the mid second century B.C. by Judas Maccabeas: "There was a great affliction in Israel, the like whereof was not since the time that a prophet was not seen among them."

9. The Apocrypha. 1 Maccabees 14:41.

10. It should be noted that the Roman Catholic and Eastern Orthodox churches do accept some of the Apocryphal books as Scripture because they support, for example, praying for the dead.

The Dead Sea Scrolls

The collection of scrolls that has become available since the discovery of the first texts in 1947 near Wadi Qumran, close by the Dead Sea, does not provide scholars with a definitive list of Old Testament books, but even if it did, it would not necessarily tell us what mainstream orthodox Judaism believed. After all, the Samaritans used only their own version of the Pentateuch, but they did not represent mainstream Judaism.

What can be said for certain, however, is that all Old Testament books are represented among the Qumran collection with the exception of Esther, and they are quoted frequently as Scripture. Nothing else, certainly not the Apocrypha, is given the same status.

In spite of suggestions by critical scholars to the contrary, there is no evidence, not even from the Dead Sea Scrolls, that there were other books contending for a place within the Old Testament canon.

For the Jews, therefore, Scripture as a revelation from God through the prophets ended around 450 B.C. with the close of the book of Malachi. This was the Bible of Jesus and His disciples, and it was precisely the same in content as our Old Testament.

The New Testament scholar John Wenham concludes: "There is no reason to doubt that the canon of the Old Testament is substantially Ezra's canon, just as the Pentateuch was substantially Moses' canon."[11]

Jesus, His Disciples, and the Early Church Leaders

For their part, the Christian community both in the days of Jesus and in the centuries following had no doubt that there was a body of books that made up the records of the old covenant. Since there are literally hundreds of direct quotations or clear allusions to Old Testament passages by Jesus and the apostles, it is evident what the early Christians thought of the Hebrew Scriptures. The New Testament writers rarely quote from other books and never with the same authority. The Apocrypha is entirely absent in their writing.

While it is true that some of the early church leaders quoted from the Apocrypha — though very rarely compared to their use of the Old Testament books — there is no evidence that they recognized these books as equal to the Old Testament.[12]

The conviction that there was a canon of old covenant books that could not be added to or subtracted from doubtless led the early Christians to expect

11. John Wenham, *Christ and the Bible* (London: Tyndale Press, 1972), p.134.
12. This is a point made firmly by John Wenham in *Christ and the Bible*, p. 146–147.

the same divine order for the story of Jesus, the record of the early church, and the letters of the apostles.

The Canon of the New Testament

The earliest available list of New Testament books is known as the Muratorian Canon and is dated around A.D. 150. It includes the four Gospels, Acts, thirteen letters of Paul, Jude, two (perhaps all three) letters of John, and the Revelation of John. It claims that these were accepted by the "universal church." This leaves out 1 and 2 Peter, James, and Hebrews. However, 1 Peter was widely accepted by this time and may be an oversight by the compiler (or the later copyist). No other books are present except the Wisdom of Solomon, but this must be an error since that book belongs in the Apocrypha and no one ever added it to the New Testament!

By A.D. 240, Origen from Alexandria was using all our 27 books as "Scripture," and no others, and referred to them as the "New Testament."[13] He believed them to be "inspired by the Spirit."[14] But it was not until A.D. 367 that Athanasius, also from Alexandria, provided us with an actual *list* of New Testament books identical with ours.[15]

However, long before we have that list, the evidence shows that the 27 books, and only those, were widely accepted as Scripture.

Why Did It Take So Long?

The New Testament was not all neatly printed and bound by the Macedonian Pub. Co. at Thessalonica shortly after Paul's death and sent out by the pallet load into all the bookstores and kiosks of the Roman Empire. Here are six reasons why it took time for the books of the New Testament to be gathered together.

---

13. *Origen De Principiis (Concerning Principles)*, pref. 4. He used the title "New Testament" six times in *De Principiis*.
14. *Origen De Principiis*, pref. 4, ch. 3:1.
15. From the Festal Epistle of Athanasius XXXIX. Translated in *Nicene and Post-Nicene Fathers*, vol. IV. p. 551–552. This is what he wrote: "As the heretics are quoting apocryphal writings, an evil which was rife even as early as when St. Luke wrote his gospel, therefore I have thought good to set forth clearly what books have been received by us through tradition as belonging to the Canon, and which we believe to be divine. [Then follows the books of the Old Testament with the unusual addition of the Epistle of Baruch.] Of the New Testament these are the books . . . [then follows the 27 books of our New Testament, and no more]. These are the fountains of salvation, that whoever thirsts, may be satisfied by the eloquence which is in them. In them alone is set forth the doctrine of piety. Let no one add to them, nor take anything from them."

1. The originals were scattered across the whole empire. The Roman Empire reached from Britain to Persia, and it would have taken time for any church even to learn about all the letters Paul had written, let alone gather copies of them.

2. No scroll could easily contain more than one or two books. It would be impossible to fit more than one Gospel onto a scroll, and even when codices (books) were used, the entire New Testament would be extremely bulky and very expensive to produce. It was therefore far more convenient for New Testament books to be copied singly or in small groups.

3. The first-century Christians expected the immediate return of Christ. Because of this, they didn't plan for the long-term future of the Church.

4. No one church or leader bossed all the others. There were strong and respected leaders among the churches, but Christianity had no supreme bishop who dictated to all the others which books belonged to the canon and which did not.

5. The early leaders assumed the authority of the Gospels and the apostles. It was considered sufficient to quote the Gospels and apostles, since their authority was self-evident. They did not need a list — inconvenient for us, but not significant for them.

6. Only when the heretics attacked the truth was the importance of a canon appreciated. It was not until the mid-second century that the Gnostics and others began writing their own *pseudepigrapha* (false writing); this prompted orthodox leaders to become alert to the need for stating which books had been recognized across the churches.

In the light of all this, the marvel is not how long it took before the majority of the churches acknowledged a completed canon of the New Testament, but how soon after their writing each book was accepted as authoritative.

Facts about the New Testament Canon

- There were only ever the four Gospels used by the churches for the life and ministry of Jesus. Other pseudo-gospels were written but these were immediately rejected by the churches across the empire as spurious.

- The Acts of the Apostles and 13 letters of Paul were all accepted without question or hesitation from the earliest records.

- Apart from James, Jude, 2 and 3 John, 2 Peter, Hebrews, and Revelation, all other New Testament books had been universally accepted by A.D. 180. Only a few churches hesitated over these seven.

- Well before the close of the first century, Clement of Rome quoted from or referred to more than half the New Testament and claimed that Paul wrote "in the Spirit" and that his letters were "Scriptures."

- Polycarp, who was martyred in A.D. 155, quoted from 16 NT books and referred to them as "Sacred Scriptures."

- Irenaeus of Lyons, one of the most able defenders of the faith, around A.D. 180 quoted over 1,000 passages from all but four or five New Testament books, and called them "the Scriptures" given by the Holy Spirit.

- Tertullian of Carthage, around A.D. 200, was the first serious expositor and used almost all the NT books. They were equated with the Old Testament, and he referred to "the majesty of our Scriptures." He clearly possessed a canon almost, if not wholly, identical to ours.

- By A.D. 240, Origen of Alexandria was using all our 27 books, and only those, as Scripture alongside the Old Testament books.

And these are just examples of many of the church leaders at this time.

What Made a Book "Scripture"?

At first, the churches had no need to define what made a book special and equal to the Old Testament Scriptures. If the letter came from Paul or Peter, that was sufficient. However, it was not long before others began writing additional letters and gospels either to fill the gaps or to propagate their own ideas. Some tests became necessary, and during the first 200 years, five tests were used at various times.

1. Apostolic — does it come from an apostle?

The first Christians asked, "Was it written by an apostle or under the direction of an apostle?" They expected this just as the Jews had expected theirs to be underwritten by the prophets. Paul was insistent that his readers should be reassured that the letters they received actually came from his pen (e.g., 2 Thessalonians 3:17).

2. Authentic — does it have the ring of truth?

The authoritative voice of the prophets, "This is what the Lord says," is matched by the apostles' claim to write not the words of men but the words of God (1 Thessalonians 2:13). It was the internal witness of the texts themselves that was strong evidence of canonicity.

3. Ancient — has it been used from the earliest times?

Most of the false writings were rejected simply because they were too new to be apostolic. Early in the fourth century, Athanasius listed the New Testament canon as we know it today and claimed that these were the books "received by us through tradition as belonging to the Canon."[16]

4. Accepted — are most of the churches using it?

Since, as we have seen, it took time for letters to circulate among the churches, it is all the more significant that 23 of the 27 books were almost universally accepted well before the middle of the second century.

When tradition carries the weight of the overwhelming majority of churches throughout the widely scattered Christian communities across the vast Roman Empire, with no one church controlling the beliefs of all the others, it has to be taken seriously.

5. Accurate — does it conform to the orthodox teaching of the churches?

There was widespread agreement among the churches across the empire as to the content of the Christian message. Irenaeus asked the question whether a particular writing was consistent with what the churches taught.[17] This is what ruled out so much of the heretical material immediately.

Providence

Our final appeal is not to man, not even to the early church leaders, but to God, who by His Holy Spirit has put His seal upon the New Testament. By

---

16. Athanasius, *Festal Epistle* XXXIX.
17. Irenaeus, *Against Heresies*, bk. III, ch. 3:3. "This is most abundant proof that there is one and the same vivifying faith, which has been preserved in the Church from the apostles until now, and handed down in truth."

their spiritual content and by the claim of their human writers, the 27 books of our New Testament form part of the "God breathed" Scripture. It is perfectly correct to allow this divine intervention to guard the process by which eventually all the canonical books — and no others — were accepted. The idea of the final canon being an accident, and that any number of books could have ended up in the Bible, ignores the evident unity and provable accuracy of the whole collection of 27 books.

Bruce Metzger expressed it well: "There are, in fact, no historical data that prevent one from acquiescing in the conviction held by the Church Universal that, despite the very human factors . . . in the production, preservation, and collection of the books of the New Testament, the whole process can also be rightly characterized as the result of divine overruling."[18]

A belief in the authority and inerrancy of Scripture is bound to a belief in the divine preservation of the canon. The God who "breathed out" (2 Timothy 3:16) His word into the minds of the writers ensured that those books, and no others, formed part of the completed canon of the Bible.

18. Metzger, *The Canon of the New Testament*, p. 285.

18

What Was the Christmas Star?

DR. JASON LISLE

The apostle Matthew records that the birth of Jesus was accompanied by an extraordinary celestial event: a star that led the magi[1] (the "wise men") to Jesus. This star "went before them, till it came and stood over where the young child was" (Matthew 2:9). What was this star? And how did it lead the magi to the Lord? There have been many speculations.

Common Explanations

The star mentioned in Matthew is not necessarily what we normally think of as a star. That is, it was not necessarily an enormous mass of hydrogen and helium gas powered by nuclear fusion. The Greek word translated *star* is *aster* (αστηρ), which is where we get the word *astronomy*. In the biblical conception of the word, a star is any luminous point of light in our night sky. This would certainly include our modern definition of a star, but it would also include the planets, supernovae, comets, or anything else that resembles a point of light. But which of these explanations best describes the Christmas star?

A supernova (an exploding star) fits the popular Christmas card conception of the star. When a star in our galaxy explodes, it shines very brightly for

---

1. Magi (pronounced mā'jī') were scholars of the ancient world, possibly a class of Zoroastrian priests from Media or Persia. It is commonly assumed that three magi came on the journey to visit Christ since they brought three gifts. However, the Bible does not actually give the number of magi.

several months. These beautiful events are quite rare and outshine all the other stars in the galaxy. It seems fitting that such a spectacular event would announce the birth of the King of kings — the God-man who would outshine all others. However, a supernova does not fit the biblical text. The Christmas star must not have been so obvious, for it went unnoticed by Israel's King Herod (Matthew 2:7). He had to ask the magi when the star had appeared, but everyone would have seen a bright supernova.

Nor could the Christmas star have been a bright comet. Like a supernova, everyone would have noticed a comet. Comets were often considered to be omens of change in the ancient world. Herod would not have needed to ask the magi when a comet had appeared. Moreover, neither a comet nor a supernova moves in such a way as to come and stand over a location on earth as the Christmas star did (Matthew 2:9). Perhaps the Christmas star was something more subtle: a sign that would amaze the magi but would not be noticed by Herod.

A Conjunction?

This leads us to the theory that the Christmas star was a *conjunction* of planets. A conjunction is when a planet passes closely by a star or by another planet. Such an event would have been very meaningful to the magi, who were knowledgeable of ancient astronomy, but would likely have gone unnoticed by others. There were several interesting conjunctions around the time of Christ's birth. Two of these were triple conjunctions; this is when a planet passes a star (or another planet), then backs up, passes it again, then reverses direction and passes the star/planet a third time. Such events are quite rare.

Nonetheless, there was a triple conjunction of Jupiter and Saturn beginning in the year 7 B.C. Also, there was a triple conjunction of Jupiter and the bright star Regulus beginning in the year 3 B.C. Of course, we do not know the exact year of Christ's birth, but both of these events are close to the estimated time. Advocates of such conjunction theories point out that the planets and stars involved had important religious significance in the ancient world. Jupiter was often considered the king of the gods, and Regulus was considered the "king star." Did such a conjunction announce the birth of the King of kings? However, the Bible describes the Christmas star as a single star — not a conjunction of two or more stars. Neither of the above conjunctions was close enough to appear as a single star.

But there was one (and *only* one) extraordinary conjunction around the time of Christ's birth that could be called a "star." In the year 2 B.C., Jupiter and Venus moved so close to each other that they briefly appeared to merge into a single bright star. Such an event is extremely rare and may have been perceived as highly significant to the magi. Although this event would have been really spectacular, it does not fully match the description of the Christmas star. A careful reading of the biblical text indicates that the magi saw the star on at least two occasions: when they arrived at Jerusalem (Matthew 2:2) and after meeting with Herod (Matthew 2:9). But the merging of Jupiter and Venus happened only once — on the evening of June 17.

Although each of the above events is truly spectacular and may have been fitting to announce the birth of the King of kings, none of them seems to fully satisfy the details of the straightforward reading of Matthew 2. None of the above speculations fully explain how the star "went ahead of" the magi nor how it "stood over where the child was." Indeed, no known natural phenomenon would be able to stand over Bethlehem since all natural stars continually move due to the rotation of the earth.[2] They appear to rise in the east and set in the west, or circle around the celestial poles. However, the Bible does not say that this star was a *natural* phenomenon.

Natural Law

Of course, God can use natural law to accomplish His will. In fact, the laws of nature are really just descriptions of the way that God normally upholds the universe and accomplishes His will. But God is not bound by natural law; He is free to act in other ways if He so chooses. The Bible records a number of occasions where God has acted in a seemingly unusual way to accomplish an extraordinary purpose.

The Virgin Birth itself was a supernatural event; it cannot be explained within the context of known natural laws. For that matter, God has previously used apparently supernatural signs in the heavens as a guide. In Exodus 13:21, we find that God guided the Israelites by a cloud by day and a pillar of fire by night. It should not be surprising that a supernatural sign in the heavens would accompany the birth of the Son of God. The star that led the magi seems to be one of those incredible acts of God — specially designed and created for a unique purpose.[3] Let us examine what this star did according to Matthew 2.

---

2. The star that moves the least is the North Star because it is almost directly in line with the earth's North Pole. However, this would not have been the case at the time of Christ's birth, due to a celestial phenomenon called "precession." There was no "North Star" during Christ's earthly ministry.

3. Although this star seems to break all the rules, it is perhaps even more amazing that essentially all the other stars do not. The fact that all the stars in our night sky obey orderly logical laws of nature is consistent with biblical creation and inconsistent with secular notions. For more information on the laws of nature, see www.answersingenesis.org/articles/am/v1/n2/god-natural-law.

Purpose of the Star

First, the star alerted the magi to the birth of Christ, prompting them to make the long trek to Jerusalem. These magi were "from the East," according to verse 1; they are generally thought to be from Persia, which is east of Jerusalem. If so, they may have had some knowledge of the Scriptures since the prophet Daniel had also lived in that region centuries earlier. Perhaps the magi were expecting a new star to announce the birth of Christ from reading Numbers 24:17, which describes a star coming from Jacob and a King ("Scepter")[4] from Israel.[5]

Curiously, the magi seem to have been the only ones who saw the star — or at least the only ones who understood its meaning. Recall that King Herod had to ask the magi when the star had appeared (Matthew 2:7). If the magi alone saw the star, this further supports the notion that the Christmas star was a supernatural manifestation from God rather than a common star, which would have been visible to all. The fact that the magi referred to it as "His star" further supports the unique nature of the star.[6]

The position of the star when the magi first saw it is disputed. The Bible says that they "saw His star in the east" (Matthew 2:2). Does this mean that the *star* was in the eastward heavens when they first saw it, or does it mean that the *magi* were "in the East" (i.e., Persia) when they saw the star?[7] If the star was in the East, why did the magi travel west? Recall that the Bible does not say that the star guided the magi to Jerusalem (though it may have); we only know for certain that it went before them on the journey from Jerusalem to the house of Christ. It is possible that the star initially acted only as a sign, rather than as a guide. The magi may have headed to Jerusalem only because this would have seemed a logical place to begin their search for the King of the Jews.

But there is another interesting possibility. The Greek phrase translated *in the East* (εν ανατολη) can also be translated *at its rising*. The expression can be used to refer to the east since all normal stars rise in the east (due to earth's rotation). But the Christmas star may have been a supernatural exception — rising

---

4. This verse makes use of synecdoche — the part represents the whole. In this case, the scepter represents a scepter bearer (i.e., a king). This is clear from the synonymous parallelism (see the next note).
5. This verse is written in synonymous parallelism, which is a form of Hebrew poetry in which a statement is made followed by a very similar statement with the same basic meaning. "A star shall come forth from Jacob, and a Scepter shall rise from Israel." Both statements poetically indicate the coming of a future king (Christ). Star and Scepter (bearer) both indicate a king, and Israel and Jacob are two names for the same person who is the ancestor of the coming king.
6. Granted, all stars were created by God and therefore belong to Him. But the Christmas star is specially designated as "His" (Christ's), suggesting its unusual nature.
7. The latter view is indicated by John Gill in his commentary.

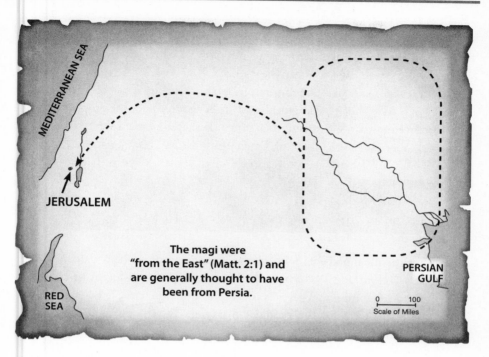

MEDITERRANEAN SEA

JERUSALEM

The magi were
"from the East" (Matt. 2:1) and
are generally thought to have
been from Persia.

PERSIAN GULF

RED SEA

0   100
Scale of Miles

in the *west* over Bethlehem (which from the distance of Persia would have been indistinguishable from Jerusalem). The wise men would have recognized such a unique rising. Perhaps they took it as a sign that the prophecy of Numbers 24:17 was fulfilled since the star quite literally rose from Israel.

Clearing Up Misconceptions

Contrary to what is commonly believed, the magi did not arrive at the manger on the night of Christ's birth; rather, they found the young Jesus and His mother living in a house (Matthew 2:11). This could have been nearly two years after Christ's birth, since Herod — afraid that his own position as king was threatened — tried to have Jesus eliminated by killing all male children under the age of two (Matthew 2:16).

It seems that the star was not visible at the time the magi reached Jerusalem but then reappeared when they began their (much shorter) journey from Jerusalem to the Bethlehem region, approximately 6 miles (10 km) away. This view is supported by the fact that first, the magi had to ask King Herod where the King of the Jews was born, which means the star wasn't guiding them at that time (Matthew 2:2). And second, they rejoiced exceedingly when they saw the star (again) as they began their journey to Bethlehem (Matthew 2:10).

This chart uses computer modeling to depict the night sky of Jerusalem as it probably appeared some 2,000 years ago. The Bethlehem star is shown in the southern sky as it may have appeared when the magi were journeying to Bethlehem.

After the magi had met with Herod, the star went on before them to the Bethlehem region[8] and stood over the location of Jesus. It seems to have led them to the very house that Jesus was in — not just the city. The magi already knew that Christ was in the Bethlehem region. This they had learned from Herod, who had learned it from the priests and scribes (Matthew 2:4–5, 8). For a normal star, it would be impossible to determine which house is directly beneath it. The star over Christ may have been relatively near the surface of earth (an "atmospheric" manifestation of God's power) so that the magi could discern the precise location of the Child.

Whatever the exact mechanism, the fact that the star led the magi to Christ is evidence that God uniquely designed the star for a very special purpose. God can use extraordinary means for extraordinary purposes. Certainly the birth of our Lord was deserving of honor in the heavens. It is fitting that God used a celestial object to announce the birth of Christ since "the heavens declare the glory of God" (Psalm 19:1).

---

8. Although we know Christ was born in the town of Bethlehem, there is no reason to suppose that He remained there for the entire time of the magi's journey. We know that Christ's family brought Him to the Temple in Jerusalem after the days of purification (Luke 2:22); it is possible that they went directly to Nazareth after that (Luke 2:39) and then returned to Bethlehem sometime later. The wise men apparently did meet Christ in the Bethlehem region, however. We know this because as soon as they departed, God warned Joseph (Matthew 2:13) that Herod was about to kill all the male children in Bethlehem and its environs (Matthew 2:16), necessitating the escape to Egypt.

19

Is Jesus God?

DR. RON RHODES

s Jesus really God? There are many cults and false religions today that deny it. The Jehovah's Witnesses, for example, believe Jesus was created by the Father billions of years ago as the Archangel Michael and is hence a "lesser god" than the Father. The Mormons say Jesus was born as the first and greatest spirit child of the Heavenly Father and heavenly mother, and was the spirit-brother of Lucifer. New Agers claim Jesus was an enlightened master. Unitarian Universalists say Jesus was just a good moral teacher. What is the truth about Jesus Christ? We turn to the Scriptures for the answer.

Jesus Truly Is God

There are numerous evidences for the absolute deity of Jesus Christ in the Bible. The following is a summary of the more important evidences.

Jesus Has the Names of God

Jesus Christ possesses divine names — names that can *only* be used of God. For example:

Jesus is Yahweh. Yahweh is a very common Hebrew name for God in the Old Testament, occurring over 5,300 times. It is translated LORD (all capitals) in many English translations of the Bible.

We first learn of this name in Exodus 3, where Moses asked God by what name He should be called. God replied to him, "I AM WHO I AM. . . .Thus you shall say to the children of Israel, 'I AM has sent me to you' " (verse 14). *Yahweh* is basically a shortened form of "I AM WHO I AM" (verse 15). The name conveys the idea of eternal self-existence. Yahweh never came into being at a point in time for He has always existed.

Jesus implicitly ascribed this divine name to himself during a confrontation He had with a group of hostile Jews. He said, "I say to you, before Abraham was, I AM" (John 8:58). Jesus deliberately contrasted the created origin of Abraham — whom the Jews venerated — with His own eternal, uncreated nature as God.

Jesus is Kurios. The New Testament Greek equivalent of the Old Testament Hebrew name Yahweh is *Kurios*. Used of God, *Kurios* carries the idea of a sovereign being who exercises absolute authority. The word is translated *Lord* in English translations of the Bible.

To an early Christian accustomed to reading the Old Testament, the word *Lord*, when used of Jesus, would point to His identification with the God of the Old Testament (*Yahweh*). Hence, the affirmation that "Jesus is Lord" (*Kurios*) in the New Testament constitutes a clear affirmation that Jesus is Yahweh, as is the case in passages like Romans 10:9, 1 Corinthians 12:3, and Philippians 2:5–11.

Jesus is Elohim. Elohim is a Hebrew name that is used of God 2,570 times in the Old Testament. The name literally means "strong one," and its plural ending (*im* in Hebrew) indicates fullness of power. Elohim is portrayed in the Old Testament as the powerful and sovereign governor of the universe, ruling over the affairs of humankind.

Jesus is recognized as both Yahweh *and* Elohim in the prophecy in Isaiah 40:3: "Prepare the way of the LORD [*Yahweh*]; make straight in the desert a highway for our God [*Elohim*]." This verse was written in reference to John the Baptist preparing for the coming of Christ (as confirmed in John 1:23) and represents one of the strongest affirmations of Christ's deity in the Old Testament. In Isaiah 9:6, we likewise read a prophecy of Christ with a singular variant (*El*) of *Elohim*: "And His name will be called Wonderful, Counselor, Mighty God [*El*], Everlasting Father, Prince of Peace."

Jesus is Theos. The New Testament Greek word for God, *Theos*, is the corresponding parallel to the Old Testament Hebrew term *Elohim*. A well-known example of Christ being addressed as God (*Theos*) is found in the story of "doubting Thomas" in John 20. In this passage, Thomas witnesses the resurrected Christ and worshipfully responds: "My Lord and my God [*Theos*]" (John 20:28).

Jesus is called *Theos* throughout the rest of the New Testament. For example, when a jailer asked Paul and Silas how to be saved, they responded: "Believe on the Lord Jesus, and you will be saved, you and your household" (Acts 16:31).

After the jailer believed and became saved, he "rejoiced, having believed in God [*Theos*] with all his household" (verse 34). Believing *in Christ* and believing *in God* are seen as identical acts.

Jesus Possesses the Attributes of God

Jesus possesses attributes that belong only to God.

Jesus is eternal. John 1:1 affirms: "In the beginning was the Word, and the Word was with God, and the Word was God." The word *was* in this verse is an imperfect tense, indicating continuous, ongoing existence. When the time-space universe came into being, Christ already existed (Hebrews 1:8–11).

Jesus is self-existent. As the Creator of all things (John 1:3; Colossians 1:16; Hebrews 1:2), Christ himself must be *un*created. Colossians 1:17 tells us that Christ is "before all things, and in Him all things consist."

Jesus is everywhere-present. Christ promised His disciples, "Where two or three are gathered together in My name, I am there in the midst of them" (Matthew 18:20). Since people all over the world gather in Christ's name, the only way He could be present with them all is if He is truly omnipresent (see Matthew 28:20; Ephesians 1:23, 4:10; Colossians 3:11).

Jesus is all-knowing. Jesus knew where the fish were in the water (Luke 5:4, 6; John 21:6–11), and He knew just which fish contained the coin (Matthew 17:27). He knew the future (John 11:11, 18:4), specific details that would be encountered (Matthew 21:2–4), and knew from a distance that Lazarus had died (John 11:14). He also knows the Father as the Father knows Him (Matthew 11:27; John 7:29, 8:55, 10:15, 17:25).

Jesus is all-powerful. Christ created the entire universe (John 1:3; Colossians 1:16; Hebrews 1:2) and sustains the universe by His own power (Colossians 1:17; Hebrews 1:3). During His earthly ministry, He exercised power over nature (Luke 8:25), physical diseases (Mark 1:29–31), demonic spirits (Mark 1:32–34), and even death (John 11:1–44).

Jesus is sovereign. Christ presently sits at the right hand of God the Father, "angels and authorities and powers having been made subject to Him" (1 Peter 3:22). When Christ comes again in glory, He will be adorned with a majestic robe, and on the thigh section of the robe will be the words, "KING OF KINGS AND LORD OF LORDS" (Revelation 19:16).

Jesus is sinless. Jesus challenged Jewish leaders: "Which of you convicts Me of sin?" (John 8:46). The apostle Paul referred to Jesus as "Him who knew no sin" (2 Corinthians 5:21). Jesus is one who "loved righteousness and hated lawlessness" (Hebrews 1:9), was "without sin" (Hebrews 4:15), and was "holy, harmless, [and] undefiled" (Hebrews 7:26).

Jesus Possesses the Authority of God

Jesus always spoke in His own divine authority. He never said, "Thus saith the Lord" as did the prophets; He always said, "Verily, verily, I say unto you. . . ." He never retracted anything He said, never guessed or spoke with uncertainty, never made revisions, never contradicted himself, and never apologized for what He said. He even asserted, "Heaven and earth will pass away, but My words will by no means pass away" (Mark 13:31), hence elevating His words directly to the realm of heaven.

Jesus Performs the Works of God

Jesus' deity is also proved by His miracles. His miracles are often called "signs" in the New Testament. Signs always *signify* something — in this case, that *Jesus is the divine Messiah*.

Some of Jesus' more notable miracles include turning water into wine (John 2:7–8); walking on the sea (Matthew 14:25; Mark 6:48; John 6:19); calming a stormy sea (Matthew 8:26; Mark 4:39; Luke 8:24); feeding 5,000 men and their families (Matthew 14:19; Mark 6:41; Luke 9:16; John 6:11); raising Lazarus from the dead (John 11:43–44); and causing the disciples to catch a great number of fish (Luke 5:5–6).

Jesus Is Worshiped as God

Jesus was worshiped on many occasions in the New Testament. He accepted worship from Thomas (John 20:28), the angels (Hebrews 1:6), some wise men (Matthew 2:11), a leper (Matthew 8:2), a ruler (Matthew 9:18), a blind man (John 9:38), an anonymous woman (Matthew 15:25), Mary Magdalene (Matthew 28:9), and the disciples (Matthew 28:17).

Scripture is emphatic that only God can be worshiped (Exodus 34:14; Deuteronomy 6:13; Matthew 4:10). In view of this, the fact that both humans and angels worshiped Jesus on numerous occasions shows He is God.

Old Testament Parallels Prove Jesus Is God

A comparison of the Old and New Testaments provides powerful testimony to Jesus's identity as God. For example, a study of the Old Testament indicates that it is *only* God who saves. In Isaiah 43:11, God asserts: "I, even I, am the LORD, and besides Me there is no savior." This verse indicates that (1) a claim to be Savior is, in itself, a claim to deity; and (2) there is only one Savior — the Lord God. It is thus highly revealing of Christ's divine nature that the New Testament refers to Jesus as "our great God and Savior" (Titus 2:13).

Likewise, God asserted in Isaiah 44:24: "I *am* the LORD, who makes all things, who stretches out the heavens *all alone*, who spreads abroad the earth by *Myself*" (emphasis added). The fact that God *alone* "makes all things" (Isaiah 44:24) — and the *accompanying* fact that Christ is claimed to be the Creator of "all things" (John 1:3; Colossians 1:16; Hebrews 1:2) — proves that Christ is truly God.

Preincarnate Appearances of Christ

Many theologians believe that appearances of the "angel of the Lord" (or, more literally, "angel of Yahweh") in Old Testament times were preincarnate appearances of Jesus Christ. (The word *preincarnate* means "before becoming a human being.") There are a number of evidences for this view:

1. The angel of Yahweh appeared to Moses in the burning bush and *claimed to be God* (Exodus 3:6).

2. Yet, the angel of Yahweh was *sent* into the world *by* Yahweh (Judges 13:8–9), just as Jesus was sent into the world in New Testament times by the Father (John 3:17).

3. The angel of Yahweh prayed *to* Yahweh on behalf of the people of God (Zechariah 1:12), just as Jesus prays to the Father for the people of God today (Hebrews 7:25; 1 John 2:1–2).

4. It would seem that appearances of this "angel" could not be the Father or the Holy Spirit. After all, the Father is One "whom no one has seen or can see" (1 Timothy 6:16, NIV; see also John 1:18, 5:37). Moreover, the Holy Spirit cannot be physically seen (John 14:17). That leaves only Jesus.

5. The angel of Yahweh and Jesus engaged in amazingly similar ministries — such as delivering the enslaved (Exodus 3; Galatians 1:4; 1 Thessalonians 1:10; 2 Timothy 4:18; Hebrews 2:14–15) and comforting the downcast (Genesis 16:7–13; 1 Kings 19:4–8; Matthew 14:14, 15:32–39).

These evidences suggest that appearances of the angel of Yahweh in Old Testament times were preincarnate appearances of Christ. Assuming this is correct, the word "angel" is used of Christ in these verses in accordance with its Hebrew root, which means "messenger, one who is sent, envoy." Christ, as the angel of Yahweh, was acting on behalf of the Father, just as He did in New Testament times.

The Biblical Basis for the Trinity

The deity of Christ is intimately connected to the doctrine of the Trinity. This doctrine affirms that there is only one God and that in the unity of the one godhead there are three coequal and coeternal persons — the Father, the Son, and the Holy Spirit. Let us briefly consider the evidence for this doctrine.

There Is One God

In the course of God's self-disclosure to humankind, He revealed His nature in progressive stages. First, God revealed that He is the *only true God*. This was a necessary starting point for God's self-revelation. Throughout history, Israel was surrounded by pagan nations deeply engulfed in the belief that there are many gods. Through the prophets, God communicated to Israel that there is only one true God (Deuteronomy 6:4, 32:39; Psalm 86:10; Isaiah 44:6). Even at this early juncture, however, we find preliminary indications of the Trinity (Genesis 1:26, 11:7; Isaiah 6:8, 48:16). God's oneness is also emphasized in the New Testament (Romans 3:29–30; 1 Corinthians 8:4; Galatians 3:20; 1 Thessalonians 1:9; 1 Timothy 1:17, 2:5; James 2:19; Jude 25).

The Father Is God

As history unfolded, God progressively revealed more about himself. It eventually became clear that while there is only one God, there are three distinct persons within the one godhead, each individually recognized as God (Matthew 28:19).

The Father, for example, is explicitly called God (John 6:27; Romans 1:7; Galatians 1:1; 1 Peter 1:2). He is also portrayed as having all the attributes of deity — such as being everywhere-present (Matthew 19:26), all-knowing (Romans 11:33), all-powerful (1 Peter 1:5), holy (Revelation 15:4), and eternal (Psalm 90:2).

The Son Is God

Jesus is also explicitly called "God" in Scripture (Titus 2:13; Hebrews 1:8). And He, too, has all the attributes of deity — including being everywhere-present (Matthew 28:20), all-knowing (Matthew 9:4), all-powerful (Matthew 28:18), holy (Acts 3:14), and eternal (Revelation 1:8, 17).

The Holy Spirit Is God

The Holy Spirit is also recognized as God (Acts 5:3–4). He, too, possesses the attributes of deity, including being everywhere-present (Psalm 139:7–9), all-knowing (1 Corinthians 2:10–11), all-powerful (Romans 15:19), holy (John 16:7–14), and eternal (Hebrews 9:14).

Three-in-Oneness in the Godhead

Scripture also indicates there is three-in-oneness in the godhead. In Matthew 28:19, the resurrected Jesus instructed the disciples, "Go therefore and make disciples of all the nations, baptizing them in the name of the Father and of the Son and of the Holy Spirit" (Matthew 28:19). The word *name* is singular in the Greek, thereby indicating God's oneness. However, the definite articles in front of Father, Son, and Holy Spirit (in the original Greek) indicate they are distinct personalities, even though there is just one God.

These distinct personalities relate to each other. The Father and Son, for example, *know* each other (Matthew 11:27), *love* each other (John 3:35), and *speak* to each other (John 11:41–42). The Holy Spirit *descended upon* Jesus at His baptism (Luke 3:22), is called *another* comforter (John 14:16), was *sent* by the Father and Jesus (John 15:26), and seeks to *glorify* Jesus (John 16:13–14).

An Analogy

A helpful analogy of the Trinity is that God is like a triangle that is one figure yet has three different sides (or corners) at the same time. So there is a simultaneous *threeness* and *oneness*. Of course, no analogy is perfect since in every analogy there is a similarity and a difference. For example, water can exist simultaneously in three different states as ice, water, and steam; that is, as a solid, liquid, and a gas at pressure of 4 Torr and temperature of 273K. One substance but three totally different personalities.

Answering Objections

Cults and false religions often raise objections against both the deity of Christ and the doctrine of the Trinity. In what follows, key objections will be briefly summarized and answered.

Jesus Is the Son of God

Some claim that because Jesus is the Son of God, He must be a lesser God than God the Father. Among the ancients, however, an important meaning of *Son of* is "one who has the same nature as." Jesus, as the Son of God, has the very *nature of God* (John 5:18, 10:30, 19:7). He is thus not a lesser God.

The Father Is "Greater" Than Jesus

Some cults argue that because Jesus said the Father is "greater" than Him (John 14:28), this must mean Jesus is a lesser God. Biblically, however, Jesus is equal with the Father in His divine nature (John 10:30). He was *positionally* lower than the Father from the standpoint of His becoming a servant by taking on human likeness (Philippians 2:6–11). Positionally, then, the Father was "greater" than Jesus.

Jesus Is the Firstborn

Some cults argue that because Jesus is the "firstborn of creation" (Colossians 1:15), He is a created being and hence cannot be truly God. Biblically, however, Christ was not created but is the Creator (Colossians 1:16; John 1:3). The term *firstborn*, defined biblically, means Christ is "first in rank" and "preeminent" over the creation He brought into being.

Jesus Is Not All-Knowing

Some cults argue that because Jesus said no one knows the day or hour of His return except the Father (Mark 13:32), Jesus must not be all-knowing, and hence He must not be truly God. In response, Jesus in the Gospels sometimes spoke from the perspective of His divinity and at other times from the perspective of His humanity. In Mark 13:32, Jesus was speaking from the limited perspective of His humanity (see Philippians 2:5–11). Had he been speaking from His divinity, He would not have said He did not know the day or hour. Other verses show that Christ, *as God*, knows all things (Matthew 17:27; Luke 5:4–6; John 2:25, 16:30, 21:17).

Jesus Prayed

Some cults argue that because Jesus prayed to the Father, He could not truly be God. Biblically, however, it was in His humanity that Christ prayed to the Father. Since Christ came as a man — and since one of the proper duties of man is to worship, pray to, and adore God — it was perfectly proper for Jesus to address the Father in prayer. Positionally speaking as a man, as a Jew, and as our High Priest — "in all things He had to be made like His brethren" (Hebrews 2:17) — Jesus could pray to the Father. But this in no way detracts from His intrinsic deity.

The Trinity Is Illogical

Some cults claim the Trinity is illogical ("three in one"). In response, the Trinity may be *beyond* reason, but it is not *against* reason. The Trinity does not entail three gods in one God, or three persons in one person. Such claims would be nonsensical. There is nothing contradictory, however, in affirming three persons in one God (or three *whos* in one *what*).

The Trinity Is Pagan

Some cults have claimed the doctrine of the Trinity is rooted in ancient paganism in Babylon and Assyria. In response, the Babylonians and Assyrians believed in triads of gods who headed up a pantheon of many other gods. These triads constituted three separate gods (polytheism), which is utterly different from the doctrine of the Trinity that maintains that there is only one God (monotheism) with three persons within the one godhead.

Our God Is an Awesome God

We have seen that Jesus must be viewed as God by virtue of the facts that He has the *names* of God, the *attributes* of God, and the *authority* of God; He does the *works* of God; and He is *worshiped* as God. We have also seen persuasive scriptural evidences for the doctrine of the Trinity. *Our triune God is an awesome God!*

20

Information:
Evidence for a Creator?

MIKE RIDDLE

T he battle of the ages began when Satan deceived himself into thinking he could overthrow the sovereign rule of God. Since then, Satan has opposed God and has become known as the adversary or great deceiver. Two opposing kingdoms are in conflict. The kingdom of Satan attacked the kingdom of God with the goal of destroying it. Both God and Satan have a purpose for history; but since God is God, and Satan is His created creature, God's purpose is the ultimate one.

With the birth of the Church, Satan had a new enemy to contend with. The Church's preaching of the gospel poses a serious threat to his kingdom. Every time the gospel is preached to nonbelievers, Satan is in danger of them believing it and leaving his kingdom. Thus, in order to prevent losing members in his kingdom, Satan must attack the Church and its message. Throughout the history of the Church, Satan has used various tactics from physical persecution to deceiving the Church into believing wrong ideas and compromising God's Word. Satan has launched these attacks from both outside and inside the Church. People have burned the Bible, banned it, changed it, or considered it irrelevant, especially in this modern scientific age. One of Satan's major strategies against the church has been and is the philosophy of *materialism*.

Materialism is the assumption that all that exists is mass and energy (matter); there are no supernatural forces, nothing exists that is nonmaterial, and no God. Materialism is the foundational presupposition for atheism, humanism, and evolutionism.

The Cosmos is all that is or ever was or ever will be.[1]

We atheists . . . try to find some basis of rational thinking on which we can base our actions and our beliefs, and we have it. . . . We accept the technical philosophy of materialism. *It is a valid philosophy which cannot be discredited.* Essentially, materialism's philosophy holds that nothing exists but natural phenomena. . . . There are no supernatural forces, no supernatural entities such as gods, or heavens, or hells, or life after death (emphasis added).[2]

The challenge by materialists is that the Church cannot defend against the philosophy of materialism. The materialists do not believe the Church can demonstrate the existence of God. Further, they know that if materialism is true, then evolution must also be true. But what if the assumption of materialism is false? What if it could be shown through empirical science that the universe consists of more than just mass and energy?

Good News

For Darwinian (molecules-to-man) evolution to actually work, new genetic information is required each step of the way. In order for a fish to grow legs, new information must be encoded into the DNA. For a reptile to grow feathers, new information must be encoded into the DNA. For an apelike creature to evolve into a human, new information must be encoded into the DNA. This new information must add to or replace old information with new instructions to grow legs, or feathers, or human characteristics. But what is information and where does it come from?

Follow me in this illustration: Imagine for a moment that it is your mother's birthday and you want to wish her a happy birthday, but you are stuck in an area without power. You know your friend a couple of miles away has power and knows Morse code. So you build a fire and begin using smoke signals to spell out Morse code for your friend to call your brother to have him send an e-mail on your behalf to your mother for her birthday.

Information went from you to the smoke signals directly to your friend's eyes and from your friend's mouth through sound waves to the phone receiver then through electronic signals in the phone to your brother and back into sound waves for your brother to hear it. Then the information went through

1. Carl Sagan, *Cosmos* (New York: Random House, 1980), p. 4.
2. Madalyn O'Hair, *What on Earth Is an Atheist!* (Austin, TX: American Atheist Press, 1972), p. 39–40.

his fingers and was transferred into code on the computer and again through electronic means to your mother who received the information on her computer screen as an understandable concept — *Happy Birthday*. Nothing material actually transferred from you to your mother, but information did, which shows that everything isn't material.

This is the good news! Why is this good news? Because the foundation for materialism (atheism, humanism, evolution) is that the universe consists of only two entities[3]: mass and energy. Therefore, if a third entity can be shown to exist, then materialism and all philosophies based on it must also be false. Information is this third fundamental entity.

What Is Information?

There are several definitions of information currently in use; however, each of these definitions are generally too broad. For example, one definition of information includes symbols with or without meaning, and another includes everything in its definition of information. Imagine sending random symbols as smoke signals to your friend — would *Happy Birthday* ever get sent to your mother on her birthday? Imagine sending a bunch of smoke signal dots in the air to your friend — would *Happy Birthday* ever get sent to your mother?

In July 2006, a team of scientists representing various scientific disciplines met to evaluate a definition of information proposed by information scientist Dr. Werner Gitt,[4] which is precise and corresponds very well to human languages and machine languages. The team proposed that this definition be called Universal Definition of Information (UDI) and agreed that there are four essential attributes that define it:

1. **Code** (syntax): Information within all communications systems contains a code. A code contains a set of symbols and rules for using letters, words, phrases, or symbols to represent something else. One reason for coding is to enable communication. Examples of codes would be the English alphabet,

---

3. Entity: The state of having existence; something with distinct and independent existence.
4. Team members included Werner Gitt, PhD, engineering/information; Jason Lisle, PhD, astrophysics; John Sanford, PhD, genetics; Bob Compton, PhD, physiology, DVM; Georgia Purdom, PhD, molecular genetics; Royal Truman, PhD, chemistry; Kevin Anderson, PhD, microbiology; John Oller, PhD, linguistics; Andy McIntosh, PhD, combustion theory/thermodynamics; Mike Riddle, BS, mathematics/ MA, education; Dave Mateer, BS, mathematics and computer science.

words, and syntax; hieroglyphics; or codes used in computers (for example, C, Fortran, or Cobol).

2. **Meaning** (semantics): Meaning enables communication by representing real objects or concepts with specific symbols, words, or phrases. For example, the word *chair* is not the physical chair but represents it. Likewise, the name "Bob" is not the physical person but represents the real person. When words are associated with real objects or concepts, it gives the word meaning.

   For example, *aichr* and *Bbo* do not have meaning because they do not represent any real object or concept. However, if in the future one of these character strings were to represent a real object or concept, it would have meaning. Prior to the computer Internet age, the word *blog* had no meaning; today it is associated with a web page that serves as a personal log (derived from *web log*) of thoughts or activities. It can also mean a discussion community about personal issues. Another new word with meaning is *simplistic*. New words are continually being designated with meaning.

3. **Expected Action** (pragmatics): Expected action conveys an implicit or explicit request or command to perform a given task. For example, in the statement, "Go to the grocery store and buy some chocolate chips," the expected action is that someone will go to the store. This does not mean the action will actually happen, but it is expected to happen.

4. **Intended Purpose** (apobetics): Intended purpose is the anticipated goal that can be achieved by the performance of the expected action(s). For example, in the statement, "Go to the grocery store and buy some chocolate chips," the intended purpose might be to bake and eat chocolate chip cookies.

These four essential attributes specify the definition domain for information. A definition of information (Universal Definition of Information) was formulated by using these four attributes:

An encoded, symbolically represented message conveying expected action and intended purpose.

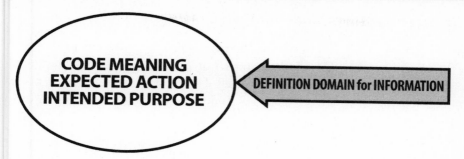

Encoded	Code
Symbolically represented message	Meaning
Expected action	Action
Intended purpose	Purpose

Anything not containing *all four* attributes is not considered information by this Universal Definition of Information (UDI).

Examples of entities that do contain Information [UDI]:

- The Bible
- Newspaper
- Hieroglyphics
- Sheet music
- Mathematical formulas

Examples of entities that do *not* contain Information [UDI] (one or more of the attributes are missing):

- **A physical star:** Lacks a code and lacks meaning because it does not represent something else; it is the physical object that the word *star* represents.

- **A physical snowflake:** Lacks a code and lacks meaning because it does not represent something else; it is the physical object.

- **Random sequence of letters:** Has a symbol set, but lacks rules for words or grammar (no code). Since it is random, it has no meaning to any sequence of letters.

- **A physical piano:** Lacks meaning because it does not represent something else; it is the physical object.

Investigating Information [UDI] Scientifically

The lowest level of operational science begins with ideas originated and formulated by man. These include models, hypotheses, theories, assumptions, speculations, etc. This is the lowest level of scientific certainty because man's understanding of reality is incomplete, faulty, and constantly changing. A very large gap exists between this level of science and the highest level. This highest level contains scientific laws.

Scientific laws are precise statements formulated from discoveries made through observations and experiments that have been repeatedly verified and never contradicted. There are scientific laws about matter (Newton's law of gravity, laws of thermodynamics, laws of electricity, and laws of magnetism). There is Pasteur's law about life (law of biogenesis). Each of these laws is universal with no known exceptions. Scientific evidence that supports or refutes a scientific concept determines its level of certainty.

The information team evaluated scientific laws about information formulated by Dr. Werner Gitt that determine the nature and origin of information [UDI].

Fundamental Law 1 (FL1)
A purely material entity, such as physicochemical processes, cannot create a nonmaterial entity. (Something material cannot create something nonmaterial.)

Physical entities include mass and energy (matter). Examples of something that is not material (nonmaterial entity) include thought, spirit, and volition (will).

Fundamental Law 2 (FL2)
Information is a nonmaterial fundamental entity and *not* a property of matter.

The information recorded on a CD is nonmaterial. If you weigh a modern blank CD, fill it with information, and weigh it again, the two weights will be the same. Likewise, erasing the information on the CD has no effect on the weight.

The same information can be transmitted on a CD, a book, a whiteboard, or using smoke signals. This means the information is independent of the material source. A material object is required to store information, but the information is not part of the material object. Much like people in an airplane are being stored and transferred in the plane, they are not part of the physical plane.

The first law of thermodynamics makes it clear that mass and energy (matter) can neither be created nor destroyed. All mass and energy in the universe is being conserved (the total sum is constant). However, someone can write a new complicated formula on a whiteboard and then erase the formula. This is a case of creating and destroying information.

White Board
New Math Formula

Since the first law of thermodynamics states that mass and energy (matter) cannot be created or destroyed, and information (UDI) can be created and destroyed, information (UDI) must be nonmaterial.

The genetic information system is the software of life and, like the symbols in a computer, is purely symbolic and independent of its environment. Of course, the genetic message, when expressed as a sequence of symbols, is nonmaterial but must be recorded in matter and energy.[5]

Indeed, Einstein pointed to the nature and origin of symbolic information as one of the profound questions about the world as we know it. He could identify no means by which matter could bestow meaning to symbols. The clear implication is that symbolic information, or language, represents a category of reality distinct from matter and energy.[6]

5. Hubert Yockey, *Information Theory, Evolution, and the Origin of Life* (New York: Cambridge University Press, 2005), p. 7.
6. John Baumgardner, "Highlights of the Los Alamos Origins Debate," www.globalflood.org.

First Law of Information (LI1)

Information cannot originate in statistical processes. (Chance plus time cannot create information no matter how many chances or how much time is available.)

There is no known law of nature, no known process, and no known sequence of events which can cause information to originate by itself in matter.[7]

Second Law of Information (LI2)

Information can only originate from an intelligent sender

Corollary 1[8]

All codes result from an intentional choice and agreement between sender and recipient.

THE SOURCE of INFORMATION

This is not the source . . .   **Author: Ken Ham**

We observe daily a continual input of new information (UDI) from an intelligent source (human beings). At present, on earth, the only new information we have detected being created is from human beings. Careful examination of other systems will determine if there are any other intelligent sources of new UDI.

---

7. Werner Gitt, *In the Beginning Was Information* (Green Forest, AR: Master Books, 1997), p. 106.
8. A corollary is a logical inference that follows directly from the proof of another proposition.

> **Corollary 2**
> Any given chain of information can be traced backward to an intelligent source.

For two people to effectively communicate, there must be some agreement on the language or code that is used.

Law of Matter about Machines (LM1)
When information (UDI) is utilized in a material domain, it always requires a machine.

Definition of a machine: A machine is a material device that uses energy to perform a specific task.

> **Corollary 1 to LM1**
> Information is required for the design and construction of machines.

What does this mean? Both information (UDI) and matter are necessary for the development of a machine. It is the information that determines and directs the assembly of the material system into the necessary configuration, thereby creating a machine. This means that tracing backward to the manufacture and design of any machine capable of performing useful work will lead to the discovery or necessity of information and ultimately to its intelligent source.

Testing UDI Universally (Living Systems)

Does the code in all living systems (DNA) exhibit all four attributes of Universal Definition of Information (UDI)?

Since all living systems contain DNA and DNA information contains all four attributes, it meets the UDI definition of information. Furthermore, the capacity and density of the information encoded in DNA surpasses anything mankind has accomplished.

> There is no information system designed by man that can even begin to compare to it [DNA].[9]

---

9. John Sanford, *Genetic Entropy and the Mystery of the Genome* (Lima, NY: Elim Publishing, 2005), p. 1.

Code	The decoded portion of DNA contains 4 letters (ATCG) that make up three-letter words (codon). These codons are arranged linearly in a various sequence (syntax).
Meaning	Each three-letter word represents 1 of the 20 specific amino acids used in life. The sequence (syntax) of the DNA words designates the specific sequence of the amino acids in protein formation.
Expected Action	Cellular proteins are biomachines essential for construction, function, maintenance, and reproduction of the entire organism
Intended Purpose	Existence of life

MORE COMPACT

The information encoded in DNA is billions of times more compact than a modern PC hard drive.

How long would it take using naturalistic processes to type out such a code?

A billion universes each populated by billions of typing monkeys could not type out a single gene of this genome.[10]

But a purposeful, all-knowing, all-powerful Creator could create complex codes in less than a day.

> Ah Lord God! behold, thou hast made the heaven and the earth by thy great power and stretched out arm, and there is nothing too hard for thee (Jeremiah 32:17).

The information team agreed upon a precise definition of information (UDI) that is consistent with the information found in human natural languages and in machine languages. Additionally, scientific laws that govern the UDI definition domain were established. It was agreed that the information encoded within the DNA belongs to the UDI domain.

---

10. Johnjoe McFadden, *Quantum Evolution* (New York: W.W. Norton & Company, 2002), p. 84.

Seven Conclusions

If we apply these laws governing UDI to DNA information, we can make logically sound arguments (conclusions).

1. Since the DNA code of all life forms is clearly within the UDI definition domain of information, **we conclude there must be a sender** (LI 1, 2).

2. Since the density and complexity of the DNA encoded information is billions of times greater than man's present technology, **we conclude the sender must be supremely intelligent** (LI 2, plus corollaries).

3. Since the sender must have
   - encoded (stored) the information into the DNA molecules
   - constructed the molecular biomachines required for the encoding, decoding, and synthesizing processes
   - designed all the features for the original life forms

   we conclude the sender must be purposeful and supremely powerful (LM 1, plus corollary).

4. Since information is a nonmaterial fundamental entity and cannot originate from purely material quantities, **we conclude the sender must have a nonmaterial component (Spirit). God is Spirit** (FL1, 2; LI 2, plus corollaries)!

5. Since information is a nonmaterial fundamental entity and cannot originate from purely material quantities, and since information also originates from man, **we conclude man's nature must have a nonmaterial component (spirit). Man has a spirit** (FL 1, 2; LI 2, plus corollaries)!

6. Since information is nonmaterial and the third fundamental entity, **we conclude that the assumption "the universe is composed solely of mass and energy" is false** (FL 1, 2).

   The philosophy of materialism is false!

7. Since all theories of chemical and biological evolution require that information must originate solely from mass and energy alone (no sender), **we conclude all theories of**

chemical and biological evolution are false (Fl 1, 2; LI 1, 2, plus corollaries).

The evolution of life is false!

Therefore, the scientific laws governing the UDI domain have

- Refuted the presupposition of atheism, humanism, and the like, including the theories of chemical and biological evolution.

- Confirmed the existence of an eternal, all-knowing, all-powerful being (God).

Summary

The importance of information to the creation/evolution debate is founded in the presuppositions of each model. The presupposition of the evolutionary model is materialism, which is the idea that everything in the universe is solely comprised of matter (mass and energy). From this foundational assumption, evolutionists logically conclude that cosmic evolution, chemical evolution, and biological evolution are all true. The presupposition of materialism has been shown scientifically to be false.

The presupposition of the Bible is that there is a God who created the universe, the earth, and all organisms living on earth. This has been shown to be consistent with scientific discoveries that there is a nonmaterial third fundamental entity called information that originates only from an intelligent source. The universe consists of more than just mass and energy, and the information found within the DNA system of all life originated from an all-knowing, all-powerful Creator God.

The Challenge

Anyone who disagrees with these laws and conclusions must falsify them by demonstrating the initial origin of information from purely material sources. This challenge has never been scientifically achieved.

21

Is Evolution a Religion?

DR. TOMMY MITCHELL & DR. A.J. MONTY WHITE

W e are sure that many people will find the question posed as the title of this chapter a little strange. Surely, evolution is about the origin and development of life forms on earth — what has this got to do with religion? Evolution is science, isn't it? And we are told that it has got to be separate from religious belief — at least in the classroom! Well, let's see if evolution fits the bill as a true science as opposed to a religious belief. In order to do so, we must define some terms.

What Is Science?

Creationists are often accused of being unscientific or pseudoscientific, while at the same time those who promote evolution assume the mantle of "real scientist." But what is science anyway? According to *The American Heritage Dictionary*, science is "the observation, identification, description, experimental investigation, and theoretical explanation of phenomena."[1] Or put more simply, science involves observing things in the real world and trying to explain how they work. The key word here is *observation*.

You see, creationists do, indeed, believe in real "observational science," sometimes called "operational science." We enjoy the benefits of observational science every day. Whether flying in an airplane, having our illness cured by the wonders of modern medicine, or writing this book on a space-age laptop computer, we are benefiting from the technology that applies genuine observational

---

1. *The American Heritage Dictionary of the English Language*, 1996, s.v. "Science."

OBSERVATIONAL SCIENCE

© 2006 Answers in Genesis

science to real-world needs. These triumphs of science exist in the present and can therefore be the subjects of examination and investigation.

Another type of science is known as "historical science," sometimes called "origins science." Historical science is the process of using the methods of science in the present to determine what happened in the past. Since the physical world exists in the present, all the evidence a scientist has available to examine the physical world also exists in the present. The scientist has no method to examine directly the past, thus he must make *assumptions* in order to come to conclusions. However, assumptions are unproven, and generally unprovable, beliefs. Assumptions are no more than untestable guesses.

Things that happened in the past are just that, past. They cannot be observed or tested in the present. They cannot be repeated or verified in the present. Then, you ask, how do we *know* so much about the past?

Understanding the Past

Perhaps an example here would help illustrate this issue. If you were to ask a roomful of people, "Do you think George Washington was a real person?" what would you expect the response to be? Of course, everyone would say that he or she believed George Washington actually existed.

Now ask this question: "Can you give me a way to prove his existence scientifically, that is, by some experimental procedure?" The usual responses are "Test his DNA," or "Dig up his bones." But actually, these methods won't work. First of all, DNA testing would only work if you already had a valid sample of his DNA to use as a comparison. If you dug up his bones, you still could not prove they were his. In order to make any conclusions, you would have to make some assumptions based on things you could not actually test.

George Washington

Well then, if there is no scientific method to prove he lived, how do we know George Washington existed? It's easy! We have abundant historical documentation of his life. These documents were held to be valid by the people who lived in that day and are not disputed. Thus, we have reliable evidence that he actually walked the earth. (Whether or not he actually chopped down a cherry tree is still a matter of debate!)

What Does This Have to Do with Evolution?

Molecules-to-man evolution is based on the premise that, through mutation and natural selection, organisms have, over the past three billion or so years, become more complex. These organisms have then progressed into an ever-increasing array of creatures until, ultimately, humans arrived on the scene.

When asked if anyone has ever seen one type of creature change into another, the answer is always no. Confronted with this, the evolutionists will usually counter that it happens *too slowly to be seen*. The claim is that it takes millions of years for these painfully slow processes to occur. Well then, if the process is too slow to be seen, how do we know it happened at all? After all, no one was there to observe all these organisms slowly changing into more complex forms. Also, there is no way in the present to test or repeat what happened in the past. Any conclusions about things that are not testable in the present must be based on improvable assumptions about the untestable past.

Ernst Mayr, who is considered by many to be one of the 20th century's most influential evolutionists, put it this way:

> Evolutionary biology, in contrast with physics and chemistry, is an *historical science* — the evolutionist attempts to explain events and processes that have already taken place. Laws and experiments are *inappropriate techniques* for the explication of such events and processes. Instead one *constructs a historical narrative*, consisting of a tentative reconstruction of the particular scenario that led to the events one is trying to explain[2] (emphasis added).

He then amazingly concludes, "No educated person any longer questions the validity of the so-called theory of evolution, which we know now to be *a simple fact*"[3] (emphasis added).

So-called Evidence for Evolution

What is so obvious in our world that Mayr can call goo-to-you evolution "a simple fact," which according to him no educated person would question? There are many supposed evidences for evolution. We will now consider two of these supposed evidences here and will examine them in the light of observational, rather than historical, science.

Evolutionists often claim that the theory of evolution has nothing to do with origin of life. They argue that evolution only deals with issues of the changes in organisms over time. They contend that life has progressed through purely naturalistic means, without any supernatural intervention. However, if they argue that life progresses by purely naturalistic mechanisms, then they must also delineate a natural process by which life came into being.

One supposed evidence for evolution is that life began spontaneously in the earth's vast oceans approximately three billion years ago.[4] Textbooks, magazines, and television documentaries constantly bombard us with this so-called fact. Just what is the evidence for the evolution of life from nonliving molecules? There

---

2. Ernst Mayr, "Darwin's Influence on Modern Thought," *Scientific American*, July 2000, p. 80.
3. Ibid., p. 83.
4. For the sake of this discussion, we will not consider the proposal made by some who claim that primitive life was brought to earth by aliens in the distant past.

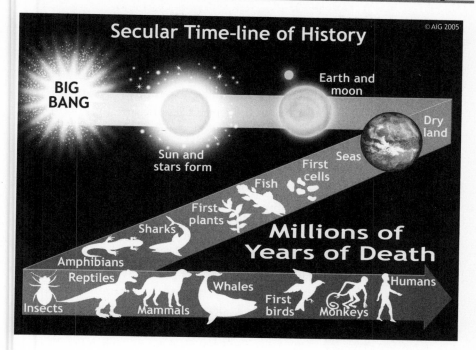

Secular Time-line of History

© AiG 2005

BIG BANG

Earth and moon

Dry land

Sun and stars form

Seas

First cells

Fish

First plants

Sharks

Millions of Years of Death

Amphibians

Reptiles

Whales

First birds

Humans

Insects

Mammals

Monkeys

isn't any! There is no method to determine what the earth's "ancient atmosphere" was like or the composition of the oceans at that time.[5] No one was there to test or examine that environment. No one can say with certainty what the chemical makeup of the primordial oceans was. So how can it be claimed that simple proteins and nucleic acids arose spontaneously?

Based on our knowledge of these molecules using observational science in the present, it is difficult to imagine these processes happening by naturalistic processes. No scientific observation has ever shown how these complex molecules could arise spontaneously, let alone evolve simultaneously and assemble themselves in such a way as to become alive. One prominent evolutionist, Leslie Orgel, notes, "And so, at first glance, one might have to conclude that life could never, in fact, have originated by chemical means."[6]

One of the primary evidences used to support the theory of evolution is the fossil record. Evolutionists have long proposed that the fossilized remains of dead organisms, both plant and animal, found in the rock layers prove that life has evolved on the earth over millions of years. Using observational science, how

5. The authors accept the biblical view of history, not the millions-of-years view. They do not accept the evolutionary time scale; this is presented here merely for the sake of this discussion.

6. Leslie E. Orgel, "The Origin of Life on Earth," *Scientific American*, October 1994, p. 78.

can this conclusion be reached? There are only the fossils themselves to examine. These fossils only exist in the present. There is no method to determine directly what happened to these creatures; neither to determine how they died, nor how they were buried in the sediment, nor how long it took for them to fossilize. Although it is possible to make up a story to explain the fossil record, this contrived story does not meet the criteria for true scientific investigation. A story about the past cannot be scientifically tested in the present.

The creationist looking at the fossil record reaches a far different conclusion from the evolutionist. To the creationist, the fossils in the rocks represent the result of a global cataclysm with massive sedimentation rapidly burying millions upon millions of creatures. This catastrophic event would account not only for the fossil record but also for the rock layers themselves. (Deposition of sediment in layers would have resulted from sorting in the turbulent Flood and post-Flood waters.) So which viewpoint is correct? Neither the creationist's nor the evolutionist's explanation can be tested in the present.

But in this regard the creationist does have evidence. Evidence is found in a book called the Bible. The Bible claims to be the Word of God. It is a record of what God did and when He did it. In the Bible we learn how life began — God created it. The Bible helps us understand the fossil record — much of it is the result of a worldwide flood as described in Genesis 6–8. Like the historical documents that establish George Washington existed, we have a reliable historical document called the Bible to give us answers about our origin and about our world.

An evolutionist has no historical documentation for his viewpoint. He relies on the assumptions of historical science for support. Herein lies a fundamental misunderstanding of the purpose and potential of science. Scientific inquiry properly involves the investigation of processes that are observable, testable, and repeatable. The origin and development of life on earth cannot be observed, tested, or repeated because it happened in the past.

So, is evolution observable science? No, evolution falls under the realm of historical science; it is a belief system about the past. How can an evolutionist believe these things without rigorous scientific proof? The answer is that he *wants to*. Evolutionists are quite sincere in their beliefs, but ultimately these beliefs are based on their view that the world originated by itself through totally naturalistic processes. There is a term for this type of belief system — that term is *religion*. Religion is "a cause, a principle, or an activity pursued with zeal or conscientious devotion."[7] It should be pointed out that religion does not necessarily involve the concept of God.

Perhaps a few observations from some of the world's leading evolutionists will now put the question posed in the title of this chapter into perspective.

Evolution as a Religion

Dr. Michael Ruse, from the Department of Philosophy at the University of Guelph in Ontario, is a philosopher of science, particularly of the evolutionary sciences. He is the author of several books on Darwinism and evolutionary theory and in an article in the *National Post* he wrote:[8]

> Evolution is promoted by its practitioners as more than mere science. Evolution is promulgated as an ideology, a secular religion — a full-fledged alternative to Christianity, with meaning and morality. . . . Evolution is a religion. This was true of evolution in the beginning, and it is true of evolution still today.

This is an incredible admission: the study of the origin and development of life-forms on earth is not "mere science," but "a secular religion."

However, this is also the view of William Provine, the Charles A. Alexander Professor of Biological Sciences at the Department of Ecology and Evolutionary Biology at Cornell University. Writing in *Origins Research,* he tells us, "Let me summarize my views on what modern evolutionary biology tells us loud and clear."[9] Now you would expect this leading professor of biology to say that modern evolutionary biology tells us something about the origin of life or something about natural selection or something about the origin of species or something about genetics. But, no! According to this leading evolutionary biologist, modern evolutionary biology tells us loud and clear that:

> There are no gods, no purposes, no goal-directed forces of any kind. There is no life after death. When I die, I am absolutely certain that I am going to be dead. That's the end for me. There is no ultimate foundation for ethics, no ultimate meaning to life, and no free will for humans, either.[10]

---

7. *The American Heritage Dictionary of the English Language.* 1996, s.v., "Religion."
8. Michael Ruse, "Saving Darwinism from the Darwinians," *National Post*, May 13, 2000, p. B-3.
9. William B Provine, *Origins Research* 16, no. 1 (1994): 9.
10. Ibid.

It is obvious that these two influential biologists in the United States believe that evolution *is* a religion — a religion of atheism where there are no end products and where evolution reigns supreme.

Religion of Atheism

Writing a superb article about the rise of the Darwinian fundamentalism in *The Spectator*, the journalist Paul Johnson sums up the belief system of atheistic evolutionists with great insightfulness.

> Nature does not distinguish between a range of mountains, like the Alps, or a stone or a clever scientist like Professor Dawkins, because it is sightless, senseless and mindless, being a mere process operating according to rules which have not been designed but simply are.[11]

Although Paul Johnson uses the word *nature*, he actually is referring to evolution. By this he means chance random processes honed by natural selection over eons of time. This is the process by which *everything* has been created, according to the evolutionists. The *everything* can be an inanimate object like a range of mountains, or it can be incredibly complex creatures like you and the authors of this book.

This belief in molecules-to-man evolution can and does cause people to become atheists as admitted by leading atheist Dr. Richard Dawkins, the Charles Simonyi Professor of the Public Understanding of Science at Oxford University. In answer to the question "Is atheism the logical extension of believing evolution?" Dawkins replied, "My personal feeling is that understanding evolution led me to atheism."[12]

Evolution Contrasted with Christianity

The only true real religion is Christianity, and this can be used as *the* template to explain what a religion is. A religion will therefore give an explanation for

- *A holy book* — Christianity teaches that the Bible is the Word of God and that this book teaches us what to believe concerning God and what God requires of us. The holy book of the evolutionists is Darwin's *Origin of Species*. The evolutionists

---

11. Paul Johnson, "Where the Darwinian Fundamentalists Are Leading Us," *The Spectator*, April 23, 2005, p. 32.
12. Laura Sheahen and Dr. Richard Dawkins, "The Problem with God: Interview with Richard Dawkins," www.beliefnet.com/story/178/story_17889.html.

believe that this book gives an explanation for the origin and development of life on earth[13] without the need of any God or supernatural agent.

- *The origin of everything* — Christianity teaches that in the beginning God created everything (that is, the entire universe with all its stars and planets, all plant life and all animal and human life) out of nothing over a period of six literal days. In comparison, evolution teaches that in the beginning nothing exploded and gradually evolved over billions of years into the universe that we see today.

- *The origin of death and suffering* — Christianity teaches that when God created everything, it was perfect. As a result of the sin of the first man, Adam, death, disease, and suffering entered the scene of time. Evolution does not recognize the word *sin* but teaches that fish-to-philosopher evolution can only proceed via death. Hence death, disease, and suffering are the necessary driving forces of evolution; from this concept, we get the phrase *survival of the fittest*.

- *The reason why humans are here* — Christianity teaches that humans are the pinnacle of God's creation and that they were made in God's image and likeness. In contrast, amoeba-to-architect evolution teaches that humans have evolved from some apelike ancestor, which in turn evolved from another sort of animal.

- *The future of humans* — Christianity teaches that one day the Lord Jesus Christ will return to this earth and that He will create a new heavens and earth where those people who trusted Him as their Lord and Savior in this life will live with God forever. Evolution, on the other hand, teaches that humans are not the end product of evolution; evolution will continue and humans will either become extinct or evolve into some other species of creature that will definitely not be human.

- *The future of the universe* — Christianity teaches that the present universe will be burned up by God, and He will then

---

13. I (MW) once knew a professor of biology who told me that he believed that Darwin's writings were inspired and that he read from the *Origin of Species* for at least 20 minutes every night before retiring to bed!

create a new heavens and earth. Evolution, on the other hand, teaches that one day the universe will reach what is called a *heat death*, although it is in effect a *cold* death, for the temperature of the universe will be just a fraction of a degree above absolute zero. This will happen when all the energy that is available to do work will have been used up, and then nothing will happen — the universe will just "be." The time period for the universe to reach this state is almost unimaginable. It is thought that it will take about a thousand billion years for all the stars to use up all their fuel and fizzle out. By then, of course, there will be no life in the universe; every single life-form, including humans, will have become extinct billions of years previously. There will still be, however, occasional flashes of starlight in the dark universe as very large stars collapse in on themselves to form black holes. For the next 10^{122} (that is the figure 1 followed by 122 zeros!) years, this so-called Hawking radiation will be the only thing happening in the universe. Then, when all the black holes have evaporated, there will be darkness for 10^{26} years, during which time the universe will simply "be" and nothing will happen.

Evolution — an Attractive Religion

At first sight, believing in evolution may not seem an attractive proposition. However, what makes it attractive is that there is no God to whom you have to give an account of your actions. This is borne out by the following quote from an atheist:

> We no longer feel ourselves to be guests in someone else's home and therefore obliged to make our behavior conform with a set of pre-existing cosmic rules. It is our creation now. We make the rules. We establish the parameters of reality. We create the world, and because we do, we no longer feel beholden to outside forces. We no longer have to justify our behavior, for we are now the architects of the universe. We are responsible to nothing outside ourselves, for we are the kingdom, the power, and the glory forever and ever. [14]

Evolution therefore leads to the teaching that you can do as you please. You can live your life just to please yourself. Many people today live such a life.

14. Jeremy Rifkin, *Algeny* (New York: Viking Press, 1983), p. 244.

They have abandoned the faith of their forefathers and have embraced the doctrines of evolution with its atheism. No wonder we are living in a "me, me, me" hedonistic society where everything that you do is to try to please and bring pleasure to yourself. This is more than "selfish ambition"; it is totally decadent and is in total contrast to what Christianity teaches about what our ambition should be — our chief end is to glorify God (not oneself) and to enjoy Him (not oneself) forever.

22

Is the Bible Enough?

PAUL TAYLOR

For so many people today, it would appear that the Bible is not enough. This is the case even (or perhaps especially) among people who have not actually read it. Witness the current popularity of those who would add extra books to the canon of Scripture. Or witness the claims that certain ancient documents are supposedly *more reliable* than the books of the Bible but were kept out of the canon because of petty jealousies.

The last few years have seen the publication of books such as *Holy Grail, Holy Blood*; *The Da Vinci Code*; and *The Gospel of Judas*. What such works proclaim, along with myriad TV documentaries, is that our Bible is suspect, allegedly having been compiled some three centuries after Christ by the winners of an intense theological/political debate. Are such claims true? Are there really other books that should be viewed as Scripture?

Other chapters in this book lay to rest the myth that the Bible was compiled three centuries after Christ. It is the purpose of this chapter to show that the books that allegedly "didn't quite make it" are not inspired and have no merit compared with the books that are part of the canon of Scripture.

Canon

We have become quite used to the word *canon* these days. The word is frequently used of a body of literature. For example, one can refer to the complete works of Shakespeare as the *Shakespearian* canon. More bizarrely, I recently read a discussion about whether certain novels about *Doctor Who* could be considered to be part of the *Doctor Who* canon. Strangely, this last usage was closer to the correct use of the word *canon*, as applied to Scripture. The argument went that the novels introduced concepts and ideas that were later contradicted or not found to be in harmony with events reported in the recent revised TV series. Presumably, the writer of the article felt that these *Doctor Who* novels were not following an accepted rule or pattern.

The word *canon*, in the context of literature, comes from a Greek word meaning "rule." We see the word used in Galatians 6:16.

> And as many as walk according to this rule, peace and mercy be upon them, and upon the Israel of God.

The Strong's number[1] for the word *rule* is 2583 and catalogues the Greek word from which we derive the word *canon*. The word is not referring to a law, but rather a way of doing things — a pattern of behavior. In the context of biblical literature, the word implies that the Bible is self-authenticating — that it is not merely complete, but that it is also internally self-consistent.

Another chapter in this book deals with the subject of alleged discrepancies in the Bible. In that chapter, we see that it is possible to interpret different passages of the Bible as if they contradict each other, but that if one approaches the Bible acknowledging that it is internally self-consistent, then the alleged discrepancies all easily disappear. That is why the apostle Peter describes the people who twist Scripture in this way as "untaught and unstable" (2 Peter 3:16). In our present study, we will see that the extrabiblical writings — and the so-called missing gospels — do not pass the test of self-consistency with the rest of Scripture and are therefore easy to dismiss as not being part of the consistent whole pattern of the Bible — the *canon*.

Apocrypha

The existence in the English language of names such as Toby (from Tobit) and Judith testify to the fact that the so-called Apocrypha was once influential in English society. The word *apocrypha* comes from the Greek word meaning "hidden." However, it popularly refers to a group of books considered by the Roman Catholic Church as part of the Old Testament.

---

1. Dr. James Strong (1822–1894) published his *Exhaustive Concordance of the Bible* in 1890. One invaluable feature of the work was that he assigned numbers to root words from the original Hebrew or Greek. These numbers have frequently been used by other Bible concordances and, more recently, by Bible software. The numbers enable students of the Bible to recognize where the same original words have been used, even if they do not know Hebrew or Greek.

Traditionally, Protestant churches have dismissed the apocryphal books. For example, Article VI of the Church of England's Thirty-Nine Articles lists first the canonical books of the Old Testament, and then lists the apocryphal books prefaced with this warning:

> And the other Books (as Hierome saith) the Church doth read for example of life and instruction of manners; but yet doth it not apply them to establish any doctrine; such are these following:
>
> The Third Book of Esdras, The rest of the Book of Esther, The Fourth Book of Esdras, The Book of Wisdom, The Book of Tobias, Jesus the Son of Sirach, The Book of Judith, Baruch the Prophet, The Song of the Three Children, The Prayer of Manasses, The Story of Susanna, The First Book of Maccabees, Of Bel and the Dragon, The Second Book of Maccabees.

The Hierome referred to in the Articles is Jerome. Jerome lived c. 347 to c. 420. He translated the Bible into Latin — the well-known *Vulgate* or common version. Originally, he used the Septuagint as the source of his Old Testament translation. The Septuagint (usually abbreviated to LXX) is a translation of the Old Testament into Greek. Many LXX manuscripts contain the apocryphal books. However, Jerome later revised the Vulgate, going back to Hebrew manuscripts for the Old Testament. It was at this point that he expressed dissatisfaction with the apocrypha, making the comment the Church of England used in its Articles above.

This illustrates that it was not merely a Protestant Reformation decision to remove the Apocrypha. In fact, the Apocrypha was never originally part of the OT canon and was added later. Interestingly, the apocryphal books themselves do not actually claim to be canonical. For example, in 1 Maccabees 9:27, the writer states: "So there was a great affliction in Israel, unlike anything since the time *a prophet had ceased to be seen among them*" (emphasis mine). Moreover, New Testament writers do not quote from apocryphal books, even though they are prepared to quote from other extrabiblical books (e.g., Paul quoted from Greek poets in Acts 17, and Jude quoted from the *Book of Enoch*).

The apocryphal books fail the internal self-consistency test. For example, 2 Maccabees 12:42 contains this exhortation to pray for the dead.

> And they turned to prayer, beseeching that the sin which had been committed [by the dead] might be wholly blotted out (Revised Oxford Apocrypha).

This sentiment is contrary to what is found in the rest of Scripture, both Old and New Testaments, such as Deuteronomy 18:11 and Hebrews 9:27. Similarly, inconsistencies and inaccuracies can be found between other apocryphal books and the correct canon of Scripture.

Da Vinci Decoded

Much of the modern preoccupation with extrabiblical writings has come from the publication of Dan Brown's novel *The Da Vinci Code*, and the earlier "serious" treatise on the subject, *Holy Blood, Holy Grail* by Richard Leigh and Michael Baigent. These, and other sensational books and TV documentaries, tend to focus on opposing biblical truth by stating the following:

- Jesus did not die on the cross.
- Jesus married, or had a close and sexual relationship with, Mary Magdalene.
- Mary Magdalene was supposed to be the leader of the new "church," but misogynist disciples usurped her position.
- These "truths" have been kept secret from the general public over the centuries and are known only to special initiates.

The "initiates" who have this secret knowledge are reputed to be found in many of the traditional "secret" organizations, such as Freemasons or the Knights Templar. At the heart of the so-called secret knowledge are the various doctrines and practices collectively known as *Gnosticism*. Before one even notes the way in which Gnosticism diverges from biblical truth, it is worth reflecting that the Bible makes claim that it should be understood mostly by plain reading. Gnostics, on the other hand, always have codes or secret knowledge required to interpret what God has said. Perhaps it was Gnostics that the apostle Paul had in mind when he warned Timothy thus:

> O Timothy! Guard what was committed to your trust, avoiding the profane and idle babblings and contradictions of what is falsely called knowledge — by professing it some have strayed concerning the faith. Grace be with you (1 Timothy 6:20–21).

The Strong's number for *knowledge* in this passage is 1108 and indicates the Greek word *gnosis*, meaning *knowledge*. In the Authorized Version, the word is translated as *science*. Certainly, Paul's criticism of the requirement for special knowledge is pertinent even if he didn't actually have the people we know as Gnostics in mind.

In his book *The Missing Gospels*, Darrell Bock shows that the documents and people labeled as *Gnostic* in fact hold to quite a wide variety of views and doctrines. There are, however, some common traits:

> An essential aspect of Gnosticism was its view of deity, namely, the distinction between and relationship of the transcendent God to the Creator God. This is important because this view of God produced the orthodox reaction against those texts.[2]

Bock observes five characteristics by which Gnostic writings differ from the Bible:

1. Dualism. Gnostics see a distinction between the transcendent God and the Creator God.

2. Cosmogony. This leads to a different view of the universe. Gnostics see an eternal battle between good and evil and do not view God as necessarily being more powerful than the devil.

3. Soteriology. Gnosticism's mode of salvation is by gaining the higher levels of secret knowledge.

4. Eschatology. In common with their view that matter is suspect, Gnostics are not usually looking forward to a bodily resurrection.

5. Cult. Gnostic groups perform various rituals. One of those described in *The Da Vinci Code* involved one of the characters taking part in a naked dance in the forest.

Bock goes on to place the rise of Gnosticism as clearly later than the writing of biblical texts, though there may be reference to Gnostic principles in the passage quoted above. Bock shows Gnosticism to be an unbiblical aberration, rather than being able to live up to the claim that it is the correct teaching of Christ — and that all the other scholars down the centuries have it wrong.

Are These Books Really Scripture?

Brian Edwards has produced a useful little summary of Gnostic ideas as presented in *The Da Vinci Code*.[3] Some of his thoughts are further summarized in the following.

2. Darrell Bock, *The Missing Gospels* (Nashville, TN: Thomas Nelson, 2006), p. 21.
3. Brian Edwards, *Da Vinci: A Broken Code* (Leominster, UK: Day One Publications, 2006).

The *Gospel of Thomas* does not contain a life story. Instead, it is a collection of 114 alleged sayings of Jesus. Some of these are contrary to the rest of Scripture. Not one serious scholar believes that the document was written by the apostle Thomas.

The *Gospel of Philip* contains a lot of Gnostic teaching. Some of the teachings are obscure, in a mystical kind of way.

> Light and darkness, life and death, right and left, are brothers of one another. They are inseparable. Because of this neither are the good good, nor evil evil, nor is life life nor death death.

Other teachings are aberrant, such as the idea that God made a mistake in creation.

> For he who created it wanted to create it imperishable and immortal. He fell short of attaining his desire.

The teaching given here is that the world is imperfect because God made a mistake. The Bible makes clear that God did indeed make the world perfect, but it is imperfect today because of our sin. In other words, by this teaching, Gnosticism is seeking to remove the responsibility from the human race and hand it to God.

The *Gospel of Mary* purports to be by Mary Magdalene. It certainly attempts to boost her position. It is an article of faith in Dan Brown's novel that Mary Magdalene was actually Jesus's chosen successor and wife — and father of his child.

> Peter said to Mary, "Sister we know that the Savior loved you more than the rest of woman. Tell us the words of the Savior which you remember, which you know, but we do not, nor have we heard them." Mary answered and said, "What is hidden from you I will proclaim to you."

The legends put forward in the books by Brown and Baigent and Leigh are not new. The legend is that, after the crucifixion, Mary fled, as she was pregnant with Jesus's son. She eventually arrived in what is today called France. The Merovingian dynasty claimed to be descended from her, as did Joan of Arc, as did the Stuart dynasty in Scotland and England. They claim that the Holy Grail was actually Mary's womb, and now represents the so-called holy bloodline of descendants of Jesus.

One thinks immediately of Isaiah 53, where the prophet makes clear that the Messiah, the Suffering Servant, will have no descendants.

He was taken from prison and from judgment, and who will declare His generation? For He was cut off from the land of the living; for the transgressions of My people He was stricken (Isaiah 53:8).

The only people who can really have any claim of "descent" from Jesus are those of us who are saved by repentance and faith in Him.

When You make His soul an offering for sin, He shall see His seed, He shall prolong His days, and the pleasure of the LORD shall prosper in His hand. He shall see the labor of His soul, and be satisfied. By His knowledge My righteous Servant shall justify many, for He shall bear their iniquities (Isaiah 53:10–11).

The concept of a married Jesus runs counter to the whole theme of the Bible. Passages in both Old and New Testaments compare our relationship with the Savior as individuals, but more specifically as the Church to a marriage. See, for example, Song of Songs, Psalm 45, and Revelation 19. If Jesus had a real, earthly wife, then this analogy would be inappropriate.

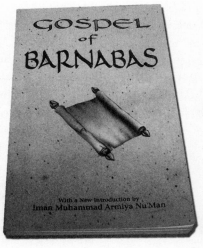

In the *Gospel of Barnabas*, it is claimed that Judas took on the appearance of Jesus and was mistakenly crucified in Jesus's place. The gospel also claims that Jesus told His mother and disciples that He had not been crucified.

It is noteworthy that the *Gospel of Barnabas* claims that the Messiah was to be descended, not from Isaac, but from Ishmael. The document is therefore much quoted by Muslims wanting to prove Islam to be the true faith. It has since been found that it was written in medieval times long after Christ.[4]

The *Gospel of Judas*, an extraordinary document written by Gnostics, claims that Jesus taught one message to 11 of His disciples, but a special, true, secret message to Judas. As part of the secret plan, Jesus persuaded Judas to "betray" Him, thus taking on the highest service for Jesus. This rehabilitation of Judas is remarkable, but as with other Gnostic

---

4. Answering Islam, "The Gospel of Barnabas," www.answering-islam.org/Nehls/Answer/barnabas.html.

writings, the authenticity of authorship is dubious, plus it still suffers from being entirely contrary to what is taught in actual biblical books.

Other Publications

The *Book of Enoch* falls into a different category from the pseudipigraphal or apocryphal works listed above. Although it is an intertestamental book, it is not part of the official Apocrypha. No books from the official Apocrypha are quoted in the New Testament, but there is a quote from the *Book of Enoch*; Jude quotes a prophecy of Enoch (see verses 14–15), taken from Enoch 1:9. It should be noted that the inclusion of such a quotation in a canonical work does not qualify the rest of the *Book of Enoch* to be part of the canon of Scripture. A similar example is that Paul quotes Greek poets in his address at Mars Hill in Athens (Acts 17). Clearly, the inclusion of this particular prophecy of Enoch proves this individual prophecy to be inspired, but it is not possible therefore to assume inspiration of any of the rest of the book.

A similar claim of authority is sometimes made for the *Book of Jasher*. This book is mentioned in the Bible twice. It is referred to in Joshua 10:13 and again in 2 Samuel 1:18. The title literally means "the book of the upright one." This book is, however, lost, and this loss would itself seem to underline that it is not an inspired, canonical book. Once again, the mention in the Bible of extrabiblical literature does not in itself add any authenticity to that literature. Numerous manuscripts have been published claiming to be the actual *Book of Jasher*. The most well known of these was published by the Church of Jesus Christ of Latter Day Saints. Another example of their literature is discussed below.

The popular name for the Latter Day Saints' Church is *Mormonism*. This name derives from their main "holy" book, the *Book of Mormon*. Many Christians have written detailed criticism of this work, so this paragraph can do no more than scratch the surface.[5] Suffice it to say that there are many reasons why the *Book of Mormon* cannot be accepted as genuine Scripture. The teenaged "prophet" Joseph Smith supposedly translated it

---

5. I would personally recommend J. Ankerberg and J. Weldon, *Behind the Mask of Mormonism* (Eugene, OR: Harvest House, 1996).

from gold plates. These plates have conveniently vanished. It is remarkable, therefore, that some passages of this book quote word for word not just from the Bible, but from a specific translation of the Bible — the KJV. If the book were genuinely inspired, one might expect it to include the same material. But for the wording to be identical to a specific English translation, when the OT was in Hebrew and the *Book of Mormon* supposedly in some other language, is beyond coincidence — for example, compare Isaiah 53:5 from the KJV with Mosiah 14:5. Even the (noninspired) verse divisions are identical, proving that the *Book of Mormon*, far from translating God's words from gold plates, is, in fact, just made up while using direct copies from books such as the KJV Bible.

The Watchtower Bible and Tract Society, or Jehovah's Witnesses, have published a number of magazines (*Watchtower, Awake,* etc.) and books, without which, they claim, it is impossible to interpret the Bible correctly. Although they claim to believe only the Bible, in practice, their religion has added to God's words. Not only that, but it has changed God's Word to suit its own ends. For example, their *New World Translation* of the Bible famously renders John 1:1 as, "In the beginning was the Word, and the Word was with God and the Word was *a god*" (emphasis mine). This use of the term *a god* is in contradiction to all accepted translations, and indeed is contrary to the rabbinical concept of the *Mamre* (or Word of God), to which John, under inspiration, was alluding. As with Mormon literature above, there is a great deal more to be said on the subject of Watchtower literature.[6]

Conclusion

From Edwards and Bock we have seen that the Gnostic documents are of dubious authenticity, not having been written by the authors claimed for them. Secondly, we have seen that their teaching fails the internal self-consistency test, as the documents contain teaching that is counter to what is taught in the accepted canon of Scripture.

---

6. For more information, see Ron Rhodes, *Reasoning from the Scriptures with the Jehovah's Witnesses* (Eugene, OR: Harvest House Publishers, 1993).

At Answers in Genesis, we understand that the Bible is under severe attack in today's world. Most of that attack seems to be centered on the Book of Genesis, but this is not an exclusive attack. What better way to undermine our belief in Scripture than to produce extra books, outside of the Bible, claiming that their omission from the Bible was merely due to fourth-century politics.

Neither the Old Testament Apocrypha nor the so-called missing gospels have any right to be treated as Scripture. Their authorship is dubious, their quotability negligible, and their agreement with the rest of Scripture nonexistent. Moreover, the argument about the listing of the canon not occurring until the third or fourth centuries is fallacious. As early as A.D. 90, verses from New Testament books were being quoted and referred to as Scripture.

The reader can be sure to have confidence in God's Word. It is all true — all 66 books of the accepted canon. For those who would disbelieve parts of the Bible, there is a warning. For those who would like to study all these other possible ways to God, the same warning applies:

> Every word of God is pure; He is a shield to those who put their trust in Him. Do not add to His words, lest He rebuke you, and you be found a liar (Proverbs 30:5–6).

23

Aren't Millions of Years Required for Geological Processes?

DR. JOHN WHITMORE

Geology became established as a science in the middle to late 1700s. While some early geologists viewed the fossil-bearing rock layers as products of the Genesis flood, one of the common ways in which most early geologists interpreted the earth was to look at present rates and processes and assume these rates and processes had acted over millions of years to produce the rocks they saw. For example, they might observe a river carrying sand to the ocean. They could measure how fast the sand was accumulating in the ocean and then apply these rates to a sandstone, roughly calculating how long it took sandstone to form.

Similar ideas could be applied to rates of erosion to determine how long it might take a canyon to form or a mountain range to be leveled. This type of thinking became known as *uniformitarianism* (the present is the key to the past) and was promoted by early geologists like James Hutton and Charles Lyell.

These early geologists were very influential in shaping the thinking of later biologists. For example, Charles Darwin, a good friend of Lyell, applied slow and gradual uniformitarian processes to biology and developed the theory of naturalistic evolution, which he published in the *Origin of Species* in 1859. Together, these early geologists and biologists used uniformitarian theory as an atheistic explanation of the earth's rocks and biology, adding millions of years

Figure 1. Layered sedimentary rocks from the Grand Canyon, Arizona. Photo by John Whitmore.

to earth history. The earlier biblical ideas of creation, catastrophism, and short ages were put aside in favor of slow and gradual processes and evolution over millions of years.

This chapter will document that geological processes that are usually assumed to be slow and gradual can happen quickly. It will document that millions of years are not required to explain the earth's rocks, as Hutton, Lyell, Darwin, and so many others have assumed.

Rapid Lithification of Sedimentary Rock

Long periods of time are not required to harden rock. Sedimentary rock generally consists of sediment (mud, sand, or gravel) that has been turned into rock. Sedimentary rocks include sandstones, shales, and limestones. Sedimentary rock is usually formed under water and is easy to recognize because of its many layers. A familiar example would be the layered rocks of the Grand Canyon (figure 1).

Layers in sedimentary rocks can be seen at small scales too, like the finely laminated beds from the Green River Formation in Wyoming (figure 2). When sediment turns into rock, or becomes hard, we say the sediment has become *lith-ified*. Lithification occurs during sediment compaction (which drives out water) and cementation, or gluing together of the sedimentary grains. The process of lithification is not time dependent, but rather dependent upon whether the rock becomes compacted or not and whether a source of cement is present (usually a mineral like quartz or calcite). If these conditions are met, sediment can be turned rapidly into rock.

Many examples of rock forming rapidly have been reported in the creationist literature: a clock (figure 3), a sparkplug, and keys have all been found in

Figure 2. Finely laminated sedimentary layers from the Green River Formation, Wyoming. The U.S. penny is for scale (1.9 cm diameter). The dark oblong-shaped objects between the laminations are fish coprolites (feces). As many as ten laminations per mm can occur in these rocks. Photo by John Whitmore.

Figure 3. Remains of a clock encased in sedimentary rock. It was found on a beach along the coast of Washington state by Dolores Testerman.

cemented sedimentary rock. Also a hat and a bag of flour[1] have been found petrified. Examples of bolts, anchors, and bricks found in beach rock have also been reported.[2] All of these examples show that sediment and other materials can be hardened within a relatively short time span. In many of these examples, rock probably formed as microbes (microscopic bacteria and other small organisms) precipitated calcite cement, which in turn bound sediments together and/or filled pore

1. Tas Walker, "Petrified Flour," *Creation*, December 2000, p. 17.
2. K.A. Rasmussen, I.G. Macintyre, L. Prufert, and V.V. Romanovsky, "Late Quaternary Coastal Microbialites and Beachrocks of Lake Issyk-Kul, Kyrgyzstan; Geologic, Hydrographic, and Climatic Significance," *Geological Society of America Abstracts with Programs* 28, no. 7 (1996): 304.

spaces. Examples of rapid lithification of this type include limestones that have been cemented together on the ocean floor.[3]

Rapid Formation of Thin, Delicate Rock Layers

Thin, delicate rock layers don't necessarily represent quiet, docile sedimentary processes; thin layers of rock can be formed catastrophically. On May 18, 1980, Mount St. Helens violently erupted. It was one of the most well-studied and scientifically documented volcanic eruptions in earth history, both by conventional scientists[4] and creationists.[5]

The volcano remained geologically active during the months and years following the 1980 eruption. Fresh lava is still oozing out of the volcano today. During the violent eruptions of the volcano, pyroclastic material (hot volcanic ash and rock) was thrown from the volcano with hurricane force velocity. One of the most fascinating discoveries following the eruption was that some of these pyroclastic deposits, those that contained fine volcanic ash particles, were thinly laminated.[6] When geologists see thin layers like this (figure 4), they usually assume that slow, delicate processes formed the layers (like mud settling to a lake bottom). However, in this case, the layers were formed during a catastrophic volcanic eruption.

Figure 4. Finely laminated beds produced during a violent pyroclastic flow from Mount St. Helens on June 12, 1980. Photo by Steve Austin, copyright 1989, Institute for Creation Research; used by permission.

---

3. J.A.M. Kenter, P.G. Della, and P.M. Harris, "Steep Microbial Boundstone-dominated Platform Margins; Examples and Implications," *Sedimentary Geology* 178, no. 1-2 (2005): 5–30.

4. For example, see P.W. Lipman and D.R. Mullineaux, eds., *The 1980 Eruptions of Mount St. Helens, Washington*, U.S. Geological Survey Professional Paper 1250 (Washington, D.C.: United States Government Printing Office, 1981).

5. S.A. Austin, ed., *Grand Canyon: Monument to Catastrophe* (Santee, CA: Institute for Creation Research, 1994), p. 284; H.G. Coffin, "Erect Floating Stumps in Spirit Lake, Washington," *Geology* 11 (1983): 298–299.

6. S.A. Austin, "Mt. St. Helens and Catastrophism," *Impact*, July 1986, online at www.icr.org/article/261/. Laminations are thin layers of sediment, usually a few millimeters or less.

Other types of thin, delicate rock layers can also form quickly too. Fossil fish are very abundant in the thin, laminated mudstones of the Green River Formation of Wyoming (figure 2). After death, fish rot very quickly. Scales and flesh can slough off within a matter of days, and fish can completely disappear within a week or two.[7] In order for the Green River fish to be preserved as well as they are, it would have been necessary for a thin layer of calcite mud to cover the fish immediately after death (figure 5).

These thin layers of mud are what make up the thin, laminated layers of the Green River Formation. If a fish is

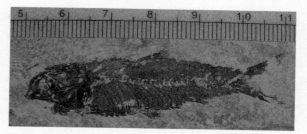

Figure 5. A well-preserved fish *(Knightia)* from the Green River Formation, Wyoming. In order for fish to be preserved like this, before major decay ensues, the fish must be buried within days of death. Scale in cm. Photo by John Whitmore.

Figure 6. A fish *(Diplomystus)* that decayed for several days before burial, Green River Formation, Wyoming. Note the sloughed scales. Burial a few days after death, by a thin layer of calcite mud, arrested the decay and prevented the fish from complete destruction. Scale in cm. Photo by John Whitmore.

not covered immediately, but several days after its death, scales will slough off and scatter around the fish carcass (figure 6). Because many of the layers in the Green River Formation contain well-preserved fish, we can conclude that many of layers were formed within a day or two. A study of fish coprolites (feces) also concluded that the thin layers must have formed quickly.[8] The Green River Formation was probably made in a post-Flood lake setting where sediments were accumulating rapidly.[9] These few examples of thin layers being made quickly

7. J.H. Whitmore, "Experimental Fish Taphonomy with a Comparison to Fossil Fishes," (PhD diss., Loma Linda, CA: Loma Linda University, 2003).
8. D.A. Woolley, "Fish Preservation, Fish Coprolites and the Green River Formation," *TJ* 15, no. 1 (2001): 105–111.
9. J.H. Whitmore, "The Green River Formation: A Large Post-Flood Lake System," *Journal of Creation* 20, no. 1 (2006): 55–63.

does not mean that all thinly laminated rock layers have formed quickly; it shows that some thinly laminated layers can form quickly.

Rapid Erosion

Erosion can happen catastrophically, at scales that are difficult for us to imagine. When standing along the edge of a canyon and seeing a river in the bottom, one is inclined to imagine that the very river in the bottom of the gorge has cut the canyon over long periods of time. However, geologists are realizing that many canyons have been cut by processes other than rivers that currently occupy canyons.

Massive erosion during catastrophic flooding occurs by several processes. This includes abrasion,[10] hydraulic action,[11] and cavitation.[12] The "Little Grand Canyon" of the Toutle River was cut by a mudflow on March 19, 1982, that originated from the crater of Mount St. Helens. The abrasive mudflow cut through rockslide and pumice deposits from the 1980 eruptions. Parts of the new canyon system are up to 140 feet deep.

Engineer's Canyon was also cut by the mudflow and is 100 feet deep. There is a small stream in the bottom of Engineer's Canyon (figure 7). One would be inclined to think that this stream was responsible for cutting the canyon over long periods of time if one did not know the canyon was cut catastrophically by a mudflow. In this case, the canyon is responsible for the stream; the stream is *not* responsible for the canyon.

Other large canyons and valleys are known to have been cut catastrophically as well. One of the most famous examples is the formation of the Channeled

---

10. Abrasion is wearing away of bedrock by particles that are being carried in the water or along the stream bottom. As rocks and sand are being carried along, they grind away the bedrock on the stream bottom. The process is similar to smoothing a piece of wood with sandpaper.

11. Hydraulic action is erosion of bedrock by the shee r force or energy of the water. Water moving at great speeds can work its way into cracks and force rocks apart, can slam boulders against a cliff face, causing rocks to crumble, and can pluck large pieces of bedrock from the stream bottom.

12. Cavitation is erosion by exceedingly rapidly moving water that creates vacuum bubbles as it flows across imperfections or depressions in a bedrock surface. As the vacuum bubbles implode (collapse violently in on themselves), they can destroy the bedrock below them, acting like sledgehammer blows. Cavitation has been known to quickly deteriorate bedrock, cement, and even steel. For example, rapidly rotating submarine propellers can create vacuum bubbles that destroy the propeller and the rudder behind it, removing large chunks of steel. A concrete spillway tunnel was damaged by cavitation in the Glen Canyon Dam in 1983. Cavitation produced a 32- x 40- x 150-foot hole in the bottom of a 40-foot diameter, 3-foot thick, steel-reinforced concrete spillway (Austin, *Grand Canyon: Monument to Catastrophe*, p. 104–107).

Figure 7. Engineer's Canyon, Mount St. Helens, Washington. The canyon was cut by a mudflow originating from the crater of the volcano on March 19, 1982. The cliff on the left is about 100 feet high. Note the small stream in the bottom of the canyon. In this case, *the stream did not form the canyon,* the canyon came first and *is responsible for the stream* being there! Photo by Steve Austin, copyright 1989, Institute for Creation Research; used by permission.

Scabland[13] of eastern Washington state. The catastrophic explanation of the enigmatic topography is now well accepted, but when it was first proposed in the 1920s by J Harland Bretz,[14] it was radical. The idea was not well accepted until nearly 50 years later, in 1969.

Bretz was trying to explain a whole series of deep, abandoned canyons (cut in hard, basaltic bedrock), dry waterfalls, deep plunge pools, hanging valleys, large stream ripples, gravel bars, and large exotic boulders. The Scabland formed as a glacier blocked the Clark Fork River in Idaho during the Ice Age. The glacially dammed river caused water to back up and form a huge lake (Lake Missoula) in western Montana, in places 2,000 feet deep!

---

13. The Scablands are a whole series of deep, abandoned canyons, hundreds of feet deep, cut into hard, basaltic bedrock.
14. See the following papers by JH. Bretz all in the *Journal of Geology,* "The Channeled Scablands of the Columbia Plateau," 31 (1923): 617–649; "Alternative Hypothesis for Channeled Scabland I," 36 (1928): 193–223; "Alternative Hypothesis for Channeled Scabland II," 36 (1928): 312–341; "The Lake Missoula Floods and the Channeled Scabland," 77 (1969): 505–543.

Figure 8. Dry Falls, near Coulee City, Washington. This is part of Grand Coulee, a canyon that is 50 miles long and as much as 900 feet deep, cut during the catastrophic Missoula Flood. The flood water poured over the lip of this 350-foot escarpment in the center of the photo, at five times the width of Niagara Falls. The lakes are filled plunge pools (300 feet deep) cut by water cascading over the cliff. Photo by John Whitmore.

Eventually, the ice dam burst, releasing water equivalent in volume to Lakes Erie and Ontario combined. The water rushed through Idaho and into eastern Washington, carving the Scabland topography. Hard basaltic bedrock was rapidly cut by abrasion, hydraulic action, and cavitation (figure 8). As the water drained into the Pacific Ocean, it created a delta more than 200 mi^2 in size. It took Lake Missoula about two weeks to drain. It has been estimated that at peak volume, the flood represented about 15 times the combined flow of all the rivers in the world![15] Catastrophic floods of this magnitude were unthinkable at the height of uniformitarian geology in the early 1900s. Today, they are becoming more widely accepted as explanations of large parts of the earth's topography.[16]

The origin of the Grand Canyon has been a topic of much speculation. Conventional geologists have not reached any consensus on its origin. Dr. Steve Austin, of the Institute for Creation Research, published in 1994 that the Grand Canyon was cut by a catastrophic flood that originated from post-Flood lakes ponded behind the Kaibab Upwarp.[17] In 2000, a symposium was

15. An excellent creationist summary on the formation of the Channeled Scabland region can be found in M.J. Oard, "Evidence for Only One Gigantic Lake Missoula Flood," *Proceedings of the Fifth International Conference on Creationism*, ed. R.L. Ivey Jr. (Pittsburgh, PA: Creation Science Fellowship, 2003), p. 219–231.

16. For example, see I.P. Martini, V.R. Baker, and G. Garzen, eds., *Flood and Megaflood Processes and Deposits: Recent and Ancient Examples*, Special Publication 32, International Association of Sedimentologists (Oxford: Blackwell Science, 2002).

17. Austin, *Grand Canyon: Monument to Catastrophe*, p. 83–110. Whitmore and Austin discussed and independently originated this idea in 1985, while Whitmore was a graduate student at ICR. The first person to originate this idea may have been E. Blackwelder in 1934 (GSA Bulletin, v. 45, p. 551–566).

convened in Grand Canyon National Park to discuss the canyon's origin. One paper[18] was published that was similar to Austin's idea, although the authors gave him no credit. Evidence in favor of the lake failure hypothesis for the catastrophic carving of the Grand Canyon is growing.

Recent work from the Anza Borrego Desert of California also supports this theory.[19] Austin believes that several lakes ponded behind the Kaibab Upwarp, containing a volume of about 3,000 mi^3 of water, about three times the volume of Lake Michigan,[20] or about six times the volume of Lake Missoula. Austin proposed that the lakes drained because the limestones of the Kaibab Upwarp, which held back the ponded water and developed caves (through solution by carbonic acid), catastrophically piping the water out of the lakes, cutting the canyon.

Rapid Fossil Formation[21]

When an organism is turned into stone (i.e., fossilized), the process usually must happen rapidly, or the organism will be lost to decay. *Taphonomy* is a relatively new branch of geology that studies everything that happens from the death of an organism to its inclusion in the fossil record. Many experiments have been performed to see what happens to all types of animal carcasses in all types of settings including marine, freshwater, and terrestrial settings.

The goal of many of these experiments is to make actualistic taphonomic observations so the fossil record can be better understood. One common theme throughout many of these experiments is rapid disintegration of soft animal tissue. In the absence of scavengers, bacteria and other microbes can rapidly digest animal carcasses in nearly all types of environments. For example, I have documented that fish can completely disintegrate in time frames from days to weeks in both natural and laboratory settings under all types of variable

18. N. Meek and J. Douglass, "Lake Overflow: An Alternative Hypothesis for Grand Canyon Incision and Development of the Colorado River" in *Colorado River Origin and Evolution*, eds. R.A. Young and E.E. Spamer, Proceedings of a Symposium held at Grand Canyon National Park in June 2000 (Grand Canyon, AZ: Grand Canyon Association, 2001), p. 199–204.
19. R.J. Dorsey, A. Fluette, K. McDougall, B.A. Housen, S.U. Janecke, G J. Axen and C.R. Shirvell, "Chronology of Miocene-Pliocene Deposits at Split Mountain Gorge, Southern California: A Record of Regional Tectonics and Colorado River Evolution," *Geology* 35, no. 1 (2007): 57–60.
20. Austin, *Grand Canyon Monument to Catastrophe*, p. 104.
21. An expanded version of this section can be found in Whitmore, "Fossil Preservation," in *Rock Solid Answers: Responses to Popular Objections to Flood Geology*, eds. M.J. Oard and J.K. Reed (Green Forest, AR: Master Books, in press).

conditions (temperature, depth, oxygen levels, salinity, and species).[22] The taphonomic literature has shown this is generally true for many other types of organisms as well.[23]

Simply put, in order for an animal carcass to be turned into a fossil, it must be sequestered from decay very soon after death. The most common way for this to happen is via deep rapid burial so the organism can be protected from scavengers that may churn through the sediment in search of nutrients. Many fossil deposits around the world are considered to be *Lagerstätten* deposits (like the Green River Formation), or deposits that contain abundant fossils with exceptional preservation. It is widely recognized that most of these deposits were formed by catastrophic, rapid burial of animal carcasses.[24]

Common experience tells us that soft tissues disappear quickly if something doesn't happen to prevent their decay. However, what about the hard parts of organisms, like clam or snail shells? Shouldn't they be able to last almost indefinitely without being buried? Numerous experiments have been completed, watching what happens to shells on the ocean floor over time.[25] Not surprisingly, these experiments have shown that thick, durable shells last longer than thin, fragile shells.

If the fossil record has accumulated by slow gradual processes, like those that are occurring in today's oceans, then the fossil record should be biased toward thick, durable shells and against thin, fragile shells. This was exactly the hypothesis that a recent paper tested.[26] The authors used the online Paleobiology Data Base, consisting of extensive fossil data from all over the world and throughout geologic time. Contrary to their expectations, they found thin, fragile material is just as likely to be found in the fossil record as thick, durable material. A reasonable interpretation of this finding (which the authors did not consider) is that much of the fossil record was produced catastrophically! This finding supports the hypothesis that much of the record was produced rapidly, during the Flood.

---

22. See reference 11.
23. For good reviews of the literature see S.M. Kidwell and K.W. Flessa, "The Quality of the Fossil Record: Populations, Species, and Communities," *Annual Reviews of Ecology and Systematics* 26 (1995): 269–299; or P.A. Allison and D.E.G. Briggs, eds., *Taphonomy: Releasing the Data Locked in the Fossil Record* (New York: Plenum Press, 1991).
24. C.E. Brett and A. Seilacher, "Fossil Lagerstätten: A Taphonomic Consequence of Event Stratification," in *Cycles and Events in Stratigraphy*, eds. G. Einsele, W. Ricken, and A. Seilacher (Berlin: Springer-Verlag, 1991), p. 283–297.
25. See reference 27.
26. A.K. Behrensmeyer, F.T. Fursich, R.A. Gastaldo, S.M. Kidwell, M.A. Kosnik, M. Kowalewski, R.E. Plotnick, R.R. Rogers, and J. Alroy, "Are the Most Durable Shelly Taxa also the Most Common in the Marine Fossil Record?" *Paleobiology* 31 (2005): 607–623.

Rapid Coal Formation

Coal does not take long periods of time to form. Coal forms from peat, which is highly degraded wood and plant material. Peat looks much like coffee grounds or peat moss. During the Flood, large quantities of peat were likely produced and buried as a result of pre-Flood vegetation being ripped up and destroyed.

The extensive coal beds we find throughout the world may have also been the result of pre-Flood floating forests that were destroyed and buried.[27] Coal has been produced experimentally in the laboratory from wood and peat.[28] Most of these experiments have used reasonable geologic conditions of temperature (212–390°F, 100–200° C) and pressure (to simulate depth of burial). These experiments have succeeded in producing coal in just weeks of time. It appears time is probably not a significant factor in coal formation. The most important factors appear to be the quality of the organic material (peat), heat, and pressure (depth of burial).

Rapid Formation of Salt Deposits

Salt deposits can form in other places and in other ways besides large salt lakes that evaporate over long periods of time (like the Great Salt Lake in Utah or the Dead Sea in Israel). Geologists have traditionally interpreted thick salt deposits as *evaporites*. In other words, they picture a large basin of seawater (like the Mediterranean Sea) being enclosed and sealed off from the surrounding ocean. The confined salt water evaporates, forming a thick deposit of salt on the bottom of the basin.

Conventional scientists have recognized that this model is fraught with many paradoxes and unresolved problems.[29] Recently, a new theory of salt formation

27. K.P. Wise, "The Pre-Flood Floating Forest: A Study in Paleontological Pattern Recognition," in *Proceedings of the Fifth International Conference on Creationism*, ed. R.L. Ivey Jr. (Pittsburgh, PA: Creation Science Fellowship, 2003), p. 371–381.
28. Many experiments in "artificial coalification" have been carried out. A few examples are: W.H. Orem, S.G. Neuzil, H.E. Lerch and C.B. Cecil, "Experimental Early-stage Coalification of a Peat Sample and a Peatified Wood Sample from Indonesia," *Organic Geochemistry* 24, no. 2 (1996): 111–125; A.D. Cohen and A.M. Bailey, "Petrographic Changes Induced by Artificial Coalification of Peat: Comparison of Two Planar Facies (Rhizophora and Cladium) from the Everglades-mangrove Complex of Florida and a Domed Facies (Cyrilla) from the Okefenokee Swamp of Georgia," *International Journal of Coal Geology* 34 (1997): 163–194; S. Yao, C. Xue, W. Hu, J. Cao, C. Zhang, "A Comparative Study of Experimental Maturation of Peat, Brown Coal and Subbituminous Coal: Implications for Coalification," *International Journal of Coal Geology* 66 (2006): 108–118.
29. J.K. Warren, *Evaporites: Their Evolution and Economics* (Oxford: Blackwell Science, 1999).

has been proposed that overcomes some of these difficulties.[30] This theory points out that salt is not very soluble[31] at high temperatures and pressures. These situations are common near deep-sea hydrothermal vents. The authors cite examples from the Red Sea and Lake Asale (Ethiopia) where these situations exist and are associated with abundant salts. Several times throughout the paper, the authors cite that rapid deposition of the salt with accompanying rapid sedimentation rates are necessary conditions for the salt to be preserved. If the salt is not rapidly covered, it will dissolve back into the seawater when the conditions change.

Rapid Coral Reef Formation[32]

Under certain conditions, coral reefs can grow rapidly. Modern coral reefs are often small accumulations of corals, coralline algae, and other organisms that secrete calcium carbonate (calcite, the main ingredient of limestone) exoskeletons. However, some can be massive and thick, like the Great Barrier Reef (thickness of 180 feet [55 m])[33] off the coast of Australia or Eniwetok Atoll[34] (thickness of 4,590 feet [1,400 m])[35] in the Marshall Islands of the Pacific. Some have argued that because of the slow growth rate of corals, large reefs need tens of thousands of years to grow.[36] Corals, which build coral reefs, have been reported to grow as much as 4 to 17 inches (99–432 mm) per year.[37]

Large coral accumulations have been found on sunken World War II ships after only several decades.[38] *Acropora* colonies have reached 23–31 inches (60–80

30. M. Hovland, H.G. Rueslåtten, H.K. Johnsen, B. Kvamme and T. Kuznetsova, "Salt Formation Associated with Sub-surface Boiling and Supercritical Water," *Marine and Petroleum Geology* 23 (2006): 855–869.
31. If something is not very soluble, it means that it can't dissolve easily, or it will come out of solution easily and form a solid precipitate.
32. An expanded version of this section can be found in: Whitmore, "Modern and Ancient Reefs," in *Rock Solid Answers: Responses to Popular Objections to Flood Geology*, eds. M.J. Oard and J.K. Reed (Green Forest, AR: Master Books, in press).
33. P. Read and A. Snelling, "How Old Is Australia's Great Barrier Reef?" *Creation Ex Nihilo*, November 1985, p. 6–9.
34. An atoll is a circular reef with a central lagoon that rises from the deep ocean floor, not the continental shelf like the Great Barrier Reef of Australia. It has been documented that most atolls sit on volcanic pedestals.
35. H.S. Ladd and S.O. Schlanger, "Drilling Operations on Eniwetok Atoll," *U.S. Geological Survey Professional Paper* 260-Y (1960): 863–903.
36. D.E. Wonderly, *God's Time-Records in Ancient Sediments* (Hatfield, PA: Interdisciplinary Biblical Research Institute, 1977, reprinted in 1999 with minor corrections).
37. A.A. Roth, *Origins*, (Hagerstown, MD: Review and Herald Publishing Association, 1998), p. 237.
38. S.A. Earle, "Life Springs from Death in Truk Lagoon," *National Geographic* 149, no. 5 (1976): 578–603.

cm) in diameter in just 4.5 years in some experimental rehabilitation studies.[39] At the highest known growth rates, the Eniwetok Atoll (the thickest known reef at 4,590 feet [1,400 m]) would have taken about 3,240 years to rise from the ocean floor. However, *coral growth rate* is not equal to *reef growth rate*; it is usually much less. Reef growth is a balance between constructive and destructive processes and has proved particularly difficult to measure. Reefs are constructed by coral growth and sediment, which settles and becomes cemented between reef organisms.

Modern reefs are destroyed by a number of processes, including active bioeroders (parrotfish, sea urchins), chemical dissolution, boring organisms (sponges, clams, and various worms), tsunamis, and storm waves. Reef growth occurs by the addition of mass, particularly from corals. Reef volume increases as living animals and their dead remains become cemented together with sediments to form the reef. Reef growth slows or even stops as the reef reaches sea level, because the reef organisms need to be submerged in water. Hence, the growth rate of a reef is slower than that of fast-growing corals.

So how might a thick reef, like the Eniwetok Atoll, have grown from the ocean floor since the time of the Flood? The Eniwetok Atoll is not made completely of corals that have grown on top of each other. Drilling operations into the atoll have shown that a significant amount of the material (up to 70 percent of the bore hole) was "soft, fine, white chalky limestone,"[40] *not* well-cemented reef limestone. It may be significant that this atoll, along with many of the other atolls in the western Pacific, ultimately rise from volcanic pedestals. It is known that heat coming from these volcanoes draws cold, nutrient-rich water into the cavernous atoll framework and circulates it upward, through the atoll via convection. This process is called geothermal endo-upwellling[41] and helps provide nutrients to the reef organisms near sea level.

Here is a possible scenario of how the Eniwetok Atoll may have become so thick in the few thousand years since the Flood (figure 9). The reef began as a volcanic platform. Carbonates (limestones) began to accumulate on the platform as the result of bacteria and other organisms that can precipitate calcite, especially in volcanically warmed water. This produced much of the "soft, fine,

39. H.E. Fox, "Rapid Coral Growth on Reef Rehabilitation Treatments in Komodo National Park, Indonesia," *Coral Reefs* 24 (2005): 263.

40. See reference 38.

41. F. Rougerie and J.A. Fagerstrom, "Cretaceous History of Pacific Basin Guyot Reefs: A Reappraisal Based on Geothermal Endo-upwelling," *Palaeogeography, Palaeoclimatology, Palaeoecology* 112 (1994): 239–260; A.H. Saller and R.B. Koepnick, "Eocene to Early Miocene Growth of Eniwetok Atoll: Insight from Strontium-isotope Data," *Geological Society of America Bulletin* 102, no. 3 (1990): 381–390.

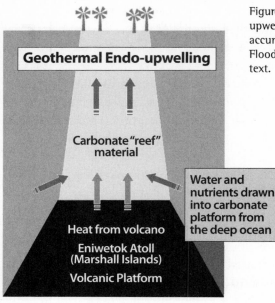

Figure 9. How geothermal endo-upwelling might explain thick "reef" accumulations since the time of the Flood. The process is explained in the text.

chalky limestone" found within the reef. Carbonate-producing organisms (like corals) were brought to the platform as small larval forms, transported by ocean currents. This explains the occasional occurrence of various corals and mollusks found within the deeper parts of the drill core. The volcanic heat source allowed the carbonate mound to grow, deep below sea level, and the process of geothermal endo-upwelling to begin. The combination of nutrient supply and heat may have allowed the carbonate mound to grow much faster than observed coral reef growth rates today. As the carbonate mound approached sea level, shallow water reef corals were permanently established and thrived as a result of the upwelling process.

Concluding Remarks

Many modern geologists realize that most rocks contain evidence of rapid accumulation. However, the idea that the earth is millions of years old is still a common belief. So if the time is not within the rocks, where is it? Many believe the time is within the "cracks" or "hiatuses" between the rocks (see figure 10). Derek Ager, who was not friendly toward creationist ideas, explained it like this: "The history of any one part of the earth, like the life of a soldier, consists of long periods of boredom and short periods of terror."[42] He viewed most of the physical rock record as accumulating quickly (i.e., "the short periods of terror") and the breaks in between rock layers representing long periods of time (i.e., "the long periods of boredom"). In other words, the "breaks" or "cracks" are

---

42. D.V. Ager, *The Nature of the Stratigraphical Record*, 2nd edition, (London: MacMillan Press, 1981), p. 106–107.

Figure 10. Today, conventional geologists still believe that the earth is millions of years old. However, they believe that individual rock layers may represent short periods of time, or "events." So where do they put all of the time? The time is placed in between the layers (at the arrows). Each event (A, B, C, D, E) represents a short period of time, but each arrow represents a long period of time, or "hiatus." During the hiatus, either perfectly flat erosion levels the surface before the next event (removing accumulated deposits), or nondeposition occurs over millions of years.

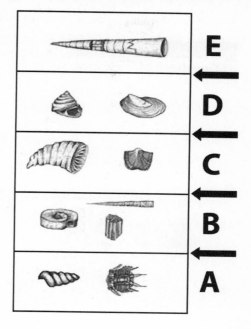

where most of the time is placed. The belief then is that these surfaces represent either long periods of nondeposition or surfaces of perfectly flat erosion. But both of these propositions have problems. For example, if a surface is exposed for long periods of time, why don't organisms churning through the mud extensively disturb the sediments below the surface? In observational studies, it is estimated that bottom-dwelling organisms can rework the annual sediment accumulation several times over![43]

This chapter has only examined a few processes in geology that are assumed to take long periods of time. There are many more issues that could be addressed. Today, ideas of uniformitarianism are fading quickly in geology. In fact, many conventional geologists would like to abandon the idea of uniformitarianism altogether, although they are careful not to advocate biblical catastrophism.[44]

Conventional geologists are recognizing that catastrophic processes can form many parts of the geologic record, and this is being widely reported in the literature.[45] The eventual nemesis will be time. Time will continue to be placed

---

43. D.C. Rhoads, "Rates of Sediment Reworking by Yoldia limatula in Buzzards Bay, Massachusetts, and Long Island Sound," *Journal of Sedimentary Petrology* 33, no. 3 (1963): 723–727.

44. K.J. Hsü, "Actualistic Catastrophism," *Sedimentology* 30 (1983): 3–9; P.D. Krynine, "Uniformitarianism Is a Dangerous Doctrine," *Journal of Sedimentary Petrology* 26, no. 2 (1956): 184; J.H. Shea, "Twelve Fallacies of Uniformitarianism," *Geology* 10 (1982): 455–460.

45. W.A. Berggren and J.A. Van Couvering, eds., *Catastrophes and Earth History; the New Uniformitarianism* (Princeton, NJ: Princeton University Press, 1984). This book is a

in between the rocks, not because there is evidence for it, but that is the only place left for it.[46] Conventional geological paradigms demand long periods of time be accounted for, whether there is evidence for it or not.

collection of 18 essays. Note especially the essays by S.J. Gould (chapter 1) and D.V. Ager (chapter 4).

46. One example of an attempt to place time in between rock layers is carbonate hardgrounds. These are hardened cement-like surfaces that occur on the ocean floor. It is often claimed these surfaces occur in the rock record, too, and represent surfaces where long periods of time passed. Creationists have recently begun to address hardgrounds at a classic site in Ohio: J. Woodmorappe, and J.H. Whitmore, "Field Study of Purported Hardgrounds of the Cincinnatian," *TJ* 18, no. 3 (2004): 82–92, 2004; J. Woodmorappe, "Hardgrounds and the Flood: The Need for a Re-evaluation," *Journal of Creation* 20, no. 3 (2006): 104–110.

24

Doesn't Egyptian Chronology Prove That the Bible Is Unreliable?

DR. ELIZABETH MITCHELL

Egyptology, originally expected to support the history recorded in the Old Testament, has produced a chronology that contradicts the Bible. This so-called traditional Egyptian chronology would have the pyramids predate the flood of Noah's day; such cannot be the case, for pyramids could never withstand a worldwide flood. And when traditional Egyptian chronology is used to evaluate archaeological findings, landmark events such as the mass exodus of Hebrew people from Egypt appear to have left no evidence. Such discrepancies between traditional Egyptian chronology and the Bible are used to attack the Bible's historical accuracy. Instead of simply assuming the accuracy of traditional Egyptian chronology and modifying the Bible, people should carefully examine traditional chronology to see if it is as reliable as some claim it to be.

Traditional Egyptian Chronology

Though traditional Egyptian chronology dominates modern understanding of ancient history, traditional chronology is inconsistent with the Bible. When there is a discrepancy between traditional chronology and the Bible's chronology, scholars usually ignore the Bible. Though many claim that traditional chronology is indisputable, a close look at this chronology reveals its shaky foundation. Dr. Rene Grognard of the University of Sydney says, "It is important to show the weaknesses or errors in our understanding of a theory in order to leave our minds free to think of a more acceptable alternative."[1] Before exploring an acceptable alternative to traditional Egyptian chronology, this chapter will show some of the errors it is built on.

Traditional Egyptian chronology is built on Manetho's history and the Sothic theory. In the third century B.C., Manetho compiled a list of pharaohs and the lengths of their reigns. The Sothic cycle theory assigns familiar calendar dates to those reigns. However, both Manetho's history and the Sothic theory have flaws that make them an unreliable foundation for chronology.

Manetho's History

Ptolomy II commissioned a priest named Manetho to compile a history of Egypt. Traditional Egyptian chronology bases its outlines of Egyptian dynasties on Manetho's history (see chart). However, Manetho's writings are unsuitable for establishing a reliable Egyptian chronology because Manetho's history:

- was never intended to be a chronological account of Egyptian history,
- is inconsistent with contemporary Egyptian sources.

Traditional Egyptian Chronology (simplified overview)[2]		
Old Kingdom	Dynasties 1–6	2920–2770 B.C.
Great Pyramids of Giza	4th Dynasty	2600–2500 B.C.
First Intermediate Period	Dynasties 7–11	2150–1986 B.C.
Middle Kingdom	Dynasties 12–13	1986–1759 B.C.
Second Intermediate Period	Dynasties 14–17	1759–1525 B.C.
New Kingdom	Dynasties 18–20	1525–1069 B.C.
Third Intermediate Period	Dynasties 21–25	1069–664 B.C.
Late Period (Persian)	Dynasties 26–31	664–332 B.C.
Alexander the Great		332–323 B.C.
Ptolemaic Period		323–30 B.C.
Roman Period		began 30 B.C.

1. D. Mackey, "Sothic Star Dating: The Sothic Star Theory of the Egyptian Calendar," abridged thesis, Sydney, Australia, 1995; available at www.specialtyinterests.net/sothic_star.html.
2. D. Rohl, *Pharaohs and Kings: A Biblical Quest* (New York: Crown Publishers, 1995), p. 24. Dynasties are grouped in sets called Old Kingdom, Middle Kingdom, and New Kingdom. After each set is an Intermediate Period whose history is less clear. Duration of dynasties comes from Manetho. Dates come from various interpretations of the Sothic cycle. Note: Meyer, Breasted, and many others give even earlier dates.

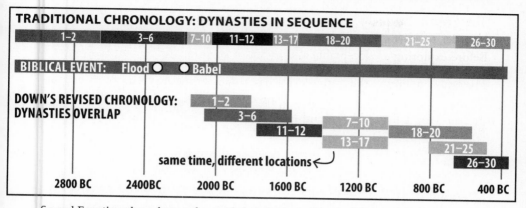

Several Egyptian pharaohs may have ruled at the same time in different regions of the land, as archaeologist David Down suggests in his revised chronology.

Manetho, whose writings only survive as a partially preserved "garbled abridgement,"[3] did not intend for his history to be a chronological account of Egyptian history. Like everyone else in the ancient world, Manetho measured time in regnal years ("in the fifth year of King So-and-So"). Eusebius, the fourth-century historian who quoted Manetho extensively, did not believe that Manetho intended for his regnal years to be added up consecutively. Eusebius says, "Several Egyptian kings ruled at the same time. . . . It was not a succession of kings occupying the throne one after the other, but several kings reigning at the same time in different regions."[4] Because Manetho's history lists the reigns of kings who ruled simultaneously, historians should not add the years of the kings' reigns together as if the kings ruled one after another.

Manetho's history is also inconsistent with contemporary Egyptian sources. Professor J. H. Breasted, author of *History of Egypt,* calls Manetho's history "a late, careless and uncritical compilation, which can be proven wrong from the contemporary monuments in the vast majority of cases, where such documents have survived."[5] Manetho's interpretation of each variation in spelling as a different king creates numerous nonexistent generations. Because Manetho's history contradicts actual Egyptian records from the time of the pharaohs, historians should not consider Manetho's history authoritative.

---

3. A. Gardiner, *Egypt of the Pharaohs* (Oxford: Oxford University Press, 1961), p. 46, quoted in D. Mackey's thesis. Manetho is quoted by Josephus, Eusebius, Africanus, and Syncellus.
4. J. Ashton and D. Down, *Unwrapping the Pharaohs* (Green Forest, AR: Master Books, 2006), p. 73.
5. D. Mackey, "Sothic Star Dating."

The Sothic Cycle

Eduard Meyer created the Sothic cycle in 1904 to give Egypt a unified calendar[6] that aligns Egyptian regnal years with modern historians' B.C. dates. Historians combine the Sothic cycle dates with Manetho's history to get traditional Egyptian dates. Meyer proposed that the Egyptian calendar, having no leap year, fell steadily behind until it corrected itself during the year of the "rising of Sothis." The theory says the Egyptians knew that 1,460 years were necessary for the calendar to correct itself because the annual sunrise appearance of the star Sirius corresponded to the first day of Egypt's flood season only once every 1,460 years.[7] Sothic theory claims that the Egyptian calendar was correct only once every 1,460 years (like a broken watch that is correct twice a day) and that the Egyptians dated important events from this Great Sothic Year. In reality, there is no evidence for this Sothic cycle in ancient Egypt.

The Sothic cycle is not reliable because it

- is based on contradictory starting points,
- has little historical support.

Meyer had to depend on later non-Egyptian writers to establish a starting point for his calculations, and those sources are contradictory. Censorinius, a third-century Roman writer, and Theon, a fourth-century Alexandrian astronomer, give different starting points. According to Censorinius, the Great Sothic Year occurred in A.D. 140, but according to Theon, it occurred in 26 B.C. Meyer subtracted multiples of 1,460 years from A.D. 140 and proposed 4240 B.C. as a totally certain date for the establishment of Egypt's civil calendar.[8]

The Sothic cycle finds little historical support. History gives no hint that the Egyptians regularly dated important events from the rising of Sothis. The second-century astronomer Claudius Ptolemy never mentions the rising of Sothis.[9] Furthermore, whenever Egyptian writings mention the rising of Sothis in connection with a regnal year, the pharaoh is unnamed,[10] or the reference is ambiguous.[11] For these reasons, many Egyptologists have consistently rejected Sothic-cycle-based chronology.

6. D. Mackey, "Fall of the Sothic Theory: Egyptian Chronology Revisited," *TJ* 17 no. 3 (2003): 70–73, available at www.answersingenesis.org/tj/v17/i3/sothic_theory.asp.
7. Rohl, *Pharaohs and Kings: A Biblical Quest,* p. 129–130.
8. Mackey, "Fall of the Sothic Theory: Egyptian Chronology Revisited."
9. Ibid.
10. Ibid.
11. Rohl, *Pharaohs and Kings: A Biblical Quest,* p. 134–135. The famous Ebers Papyrus allegedly confirms a 1517 B.C. date for the ninth year of Amenhotep I. However, this document refers to a *monthly* rising of Sothis, an astronomical impossibility.

Discrepancies

Whenever two chronologies disagree, at least one must be wrong. Traditional Egyptian chronology disputes the Hebrew chronology recorded in the Bible as well as secular data from neighboring nations. As Damien Mackey summarized in his thesis:

> The value of any one nation's absolute chronology must ultimately depend on its ability to *integrate with all known data from other regions as well.* It would be useless to establish a complete system of chronology that can exist only in isolation, but that cannot stand up to scrutiny by comparison with other systems. For the Sothic scheme [of Egyptian chronology] to be valid — just as for Mesopotamian, Palestinian, Greek or Anatolian chronologies to be valid — *it is necessary for each period of Egyptian history to be capable of perfect alignment with any relevant period of history of one or another ancient nation.* This is most especially true in the case of Egyptian history because . . . *the historians of other nations tend to look to Egyptian chronology as the rule according to which they estimate and adjust their own chronologies*[12] (emphasis added).

Biblical Discrepancies

Traditional dates for Egyptian pyramids predate Noah's flood (see chart). Since the pyramids could not have survived a global flood, some people question the reliability of the Bible's chronology. Others use the traditional dates for the pyramids to support the idea that Noah's flood was a local flood that did not affect Egypt.[13] The pyramids do not come with labels declaring their dates, and the traditional dates used for them create an irreconcilable discrepancy with the Bible.

Bible Time-line (B.C.)				
4004	2348	1491	586	4
Creation	Noah's flood	Exodus	Temple destroyed	Christ's birth

Traditional Egyptian Dates (B.C.)		
3150[14] to 2920	2600 to 2500	1290
Zoser's pyramid	Great Pyramid	Exodus

---

12. D. Mackey, "Sothic Star Dating: The Sothic Star Theory of the Egyptian Calendar," abridged thesis, Sydney, Australia, 1995.
13. The inconsistency of the local flood idea with both science and the rest of the Bible is discussed in chapter 10 of *The New Answers Book 1* (Green Forest, AR: Master Books, 2006).
14. Earlier date comes from W. Durant, *Our Oriental Heritage* (New York: Simon and Schuster, 1954), p. 147.

Traditional dates for the Old Testament stories involving Egypt remain unconfirmed by archaeology and actually contradict Scripture. The characters of the Bible stories left no archaeological evidence of their existence in the times traditionally assigned to them. Bible-believing Egyptologists assigned these dates in error. The early Egyptologists, hoping to find the Bible confirmed in Egypt, contributed to the errors in traditional chronology by incorrectly applying the Bible in two instances. They incorrectly:

- assumed that Ramses the Great was the pharaoh of the oppression,
- identified Shoshenq as Shishak of the Bible.

The first error assigned an Exodus date inconsistent with the rest of Scripture. The second error provided support for the excessive antiquity of traditional dating. Both errors caused scholars to assign inconsistent, unsupported dates to the Bible accounts.

Scholars routinely disregard the biblical date for the Exodus.[15] As Gleason Archer says, "But notwithstanding . . . consistent testimony of Scripture to the 1445 date (or an approximation thereof), the preponderance of scholarly opinion today is in favor of a considerably later date, the most favored one at present being 1290 B.C., or about ten years after Ramses II began to reign."[16] The traditional date for Ramses II "the Great," a 19th dynasty king, is nearly two centuries after the Exodus. Because Exodus 1:11 says that the Hebrew slaves built the city Ramses, early Egyptologists assumed that Ramses II was the pharaoh who oppressed the Israelites. On that basis, most scholars assign Ramses' traditional date to the Exodus and ignore the Bible's testimony.

The name *Ramses* should not restrict the oppression to the 19th dynasty because this name is not unique to the 19th dynasty. *Ramses,* which means "son of Ra — the sun god," was a name commonly used to honor pharaohs. For instance, Ahmose, the founder of the 18th dynasty, was also called Ramses, as was a later 18th dynasty king, Amenhotep III.[17] Archaeology of the 18th and 19th dynasties shows no evidence of enslaved Israelites because the Hebrews

---

15. Conservative Bible scholars calculate the Exodus to have occurred sometime between 1491–1445 B.C. Solomon began to build the temple in the fourth year of his reign, in the 480th year after the Exodus from Egypt, according to I Kings 6:1. Accepted dates for the beginning of Solomon's reign, as calculated from the lengths of the reigns of Old Testament kings, range from 1015 to 970 B.C. From this data, the Exodus occurred around 1491 to 1445 B.C. The dates are confirmed by additional Scriptures. See Dr. Jones's *Chronology of the Old Testament* for a full discussion.
16. G. Archer, *A Survey of Old Testament Introduction* (Chicago, IL: Moody Press, 1994), p. 241.
17. F.N. Jones, *Chronology of the Old Testament* (Green Forest, AR: Master Books, 2004), p. 50–51.

had left Egypt centuries before. Scholars should neither assume that Ramses II was the pharaoh of the oppression nor assign his date to the Exodus.

Jean Champollion,[18] the father of Egyptology, unwittingly gave support to biblically inconsistent chronology when he erroneously identified pharaoh Shoshenq as the Shishak of the Bible. Champollion found an inscription about Shoshenq, founder of the 22nd dynasty, at the temple of Karnak. Because the names sound similar, Champollion assumed that Shoshenq was the Shishak who plundered Jerusalem in the fifth year of King Rehoboam.[19] Using the biblical date for Rehoboam as a starting point, chronologists used Manetho's list to outline the next three centuries of Egyptian history.

The two problems with Shoshenq's identification involve military strategy and phonics. According to the inscriptions, Shoshenq attacked the northern part of Israel, not Rehoboam's Jerusalem or Judah. During Rehoboam's time, Jeroboam ruled the northern kingdom. Jeroboam was Shishak's ally.[20] If Shoshenq were Shishak, then Shoshenq attacked his ally and ignored his enemy. Furthermore, the phonetics of these two pharaohs' names only sound similar in their transliterated forms, not in the original languages.[21] Because of this faulty identification of Shoshenq with Shishak, Egyptologists ignore the rest of the biblical facts relating to the geography and characters involved. Because the dates constructed from this biblical misinterpretation actually coincide with the traditional dating of the third intermediate period, many Bible scholars trust the traditional chronology even when it disputes the Old Testament.

Secular Discrepancies

Traditional Egyptian chronology disputes not only biblical chronology but also information from nonbiblical sources. Egypt's traditional dates clash with secular data in at least two areas:

- The Hittite connection with Assyrian chronology
- Carbon dating

The Hittites built a powerful empire based in Asia Minor, but scholars have to depend on dates from other ancient nations to determine Hittite chronology. *Synchronisms* are events shared by two cultures, and Egypt shares many

---

18. Jean Champollion translated the famous Rosetta stone, unlocking the secret of Egyptian hieroglyphics.
19. Rohl, *Pharaohs and Kings: A Biblical Quest*, p. 120–121. See 1 Kings 14:25.
20. Rohl, *Pharaohs and Kings: A Biblical Quest*, p. 122–127 and 1 Kings 11:40. Jeroboam had fled to Shishak during Solomon's lifetime.
21. Ashton and Down, *Unwrapping the Pharaohs*, p. 185.

synchronisms with the Hittites. Therefore, Egypt's erroneous dates have been assigned to the Hittites. For instance, the traditional date of 1353 B.C. for pharaoh Akhenaten's accession[22] to the throne is assigned to Hittite king Supiluliumas because Supiluliumas sent to a letter of congratulations to Akhenaten.[23] The date 1275 B.C. for the battle of Kadesh,[24] at which both Ramses II and Hittite king Muwatalli II claimed victory, comes from the traditional dates for Ramses the Great. (His dates derive from Sothic theory and Manetho's history.) Finally, when Ramses III recorded his traditionally dated 1180 B.C.[25] victory over sea people, he said that the sea people had already annihilated the Hittites. According to these Egyptian dates, the Hittites became extinct about 1200 B.C. (see chart).

Traditional Time-line (B.C.)				
3150[26]	2600	1290	1275	1200
Zoser's Pyramid	Great Pyramid	Exodus	Kadesh	Hittites extinct

The Egyptian version of Hittite chronology falls apart, however, when compared to more recent Assyrian archaeological discoveries. Assyrian inscriptions record wars with the Hittites during the eighth and ninth centuries B.C., centuries after the Hittites supposedly ceased to exist. These inscriptions describe wars during the reigns of Assyrian kings Shalmaneser III and Sennacherib and even name the same Hittite kings as the Egyptian records[27] (see chart). The Assyrian time-line is consistent with well-established dates such as Nebuchadnezzar's conquest of Jerusalem. Traditional Egyptian dates must be wrong.

Problems Time-line (B.C.)				
2600	2348	1275	1200	800s–700s
(trad.)	(bib.)	(trad.)	(trad.)	(Assyr.)
Great Pyramid	flood	Kadesh	Hittites extinct	Hittite/Assyrian wars

Acceptance of the biblical account of Hittite history could have prevented the incorrect dating of the Hittites even before the discovery of the Assyrian monumental inscriptions. According to 2 Kings 7:6, during Elisha's lifetime the

22. Rohl, *Pharaohs and Kings: A Biblical Quest*, p. 20.
23. Ashton and Down, *Unwrapping the Pharaohs*, p. 75.
24. *Anatolia: Cauldron of Cultures* (Alexandria, VA: Time-Life Books, 1995), p. 64.
25. Ibid, p. 69.
26. W. Durant, *Our Oriental Heritage* (New York: Simon and Schuster, 1954), p. 147.
27. Ashton and Down, *Unwrapping the Pharaohs*, p. 75–76.

Hittites were as formidable as Egypt. One explorer, Irish missionary William Wright, correctly evaluated the hieroglyphics he found in Asia Minor because he accepted the Bible's history. In 1872, despite scholarship that insisted the Hittites and the Bible were unhistorical, Wright believed that the inscriptions he had found "would show that a great people, called Hittites in the Bible, but never referred to in classic history, had once formed a mighty empire in that region."[28]

Carbon dating[29] also disputes traditional chronology. According to the *Cambridge Encyclopedia on Archaeology*:

> When the radiocarbon method was first tested, good agreement was found between radiocarbon dates and historical dates for samples of known age. . . . As measurements became more precise, however, it gradually became apparent that there were systematic discrepancies between the dates that were being obtained and those that could be expected from historical evidence [i.e., the traditional dates]. These differences were most marked in the period before about the mid-first millennium B.C., in which *radiocarbon dates appear too recent, by up to several hundred years, by comparison with historical dates.* Dates for the earliest comparative material available, reeds used as bonding between mud brick courses of tombs of Egyptians Dynasty I, about 3,100 B.C., *appeared to be as much as 600 years, or about 12% too young*[30] (emphasis added).

Just as carbon dating is more consistent with a young earth than most people realize, carbon dating is consistent with a much younger Egyptian civilization than traditional chronology claims.

Revised Chronologies

In *Centuries of Darkness,* Peter James calls traditional chronology a "gigantic academic blunder."[31] David Rohl writes, "The only real solution to the archaeological problems which have been created is to pull down the whole structure and start again, reconstructing from the foundations upward."[32] Revised chronology reflects the relationships between ancient nations more accurately

---

28. *Anatolia*, p. 41.
29. Carbon dating is discussed in chapter 7 of *The New Answers Book 1* (Green Forest, AR: Master Books, 2006).
30. D. Downs, "The Chronology of Egypt and Israel," from *Diggings*, available at www.biblicalstudies.qldwide.net.au/chronology_of_egypt_and_israel.html.
31. P. James, *Centuries of Darkness*, 320, quoted in Ashton and Down, *Unwrapping the Pharaohs*, p. 184.
32. Rohl, *Pharaohs and Kings: A Biblical Quest*, p. 9.

and reveals "remarkable agreement between the histories of Egypt and Israel."[33] Revised chronology bolsters the Christian's trust in the Bible and equips him with answers for a skeptical world.

Efforts to assign familiar dates to events of antiquity require a starting point, a known date. Four starting points provide secure anchors for the chronology of the Middle East. By counting both backward and forward from these four dates, the chronologist can assign familiar dates from creation to Christ[34] and combine the annals of the ancient nations to build a consistent chronology. These four anchor points are summarized on the "Starting Points" chart.

Starting Points				
664 B.C.	621 B.C.	605 B.C.	586 B.C.	A.D. 26
Thebes sacked	Lunar eclipse	Battle of Carchemish	Temple destroyed	15th year of Tiberias
Taharka Dies	Nabopolassar's 5th year	Nebuchadnezzar's 1st year (*sole rex*)	Nebuchadnezzar's 19th year	Christ's 30th year

Space does not permit analysis of all the revised chronologies. A number of scholars, including Peter James, David Rohl, D.A. Courville, and David Down, have produced fine work in this area. Some begin with the Bible, while others begin with starting points such as the battle of Thebes. The Christian should only accept revised chronology that is consistent with the Bible. New evidence may someday shed new light on the identity of a pharaoh, but nothing should ever rock the Christian's faith in the trustworthiness of God's Word.

David Down, in *Unwrapping the Pharaohs*, has synthesized the work of many experts into a cohesive narrative consistent with the Bible. He points out many synchronisms between the histories of Israel and Egypt, providing a highly plausible identification for many of the characters in the Old Testament. Furthermore, his work is consistent with the history of surrounding nations and allows the Hittites to slip into their proper niche in the context of their Assyrian and Egyptian neighbors.

---

33. Down, "The Chronology of Egypt and Israel."
34. Jones, *Chronology of the Old Testament*, p. 23, 123, and 309. Claudius Ptolemy documented a lunar eclipse that occurred on April 15, 621 B.C. (Gregorian calendar), during the fifth year of Nabopolassar, Nebuchadnezzar's father. Counting forward gives the 605 B.C. and 586 B.C. dates. Ashurbanipal's sacking of Thebes in 664 B.C. comes from several independent ancient sources. (See Rohl, *Pharaohs and Kings: A Biblical Quest*, p. 119.) Contemporary Roman writers confirm the Tiberius date. (See Jones, *Chronology of the Old Testament*, p. 218.)

The Revision Compared to the Absolute Authority — the Bible

Synchronisms between Old Testament characters and Egypt include the following:

- Pre-Dynastic and Old Kingdom
  Mizraim, Abram

- Middle Kingdom
  Joseph, Moses

- New Kingdom
  Solomon, Rehoboam, Asa, Ahab

- Third Intermediate and Late Periods
  Hezekiah, Josiah, Jeremiah

Predynastic Egypt and Old Kingdom — the Post-Flood World

Most histories begin with the unsubstantiated notion that primitive people slowly developed civilization from rudimentary beginnings. Archaeology around the world has instead revealed advanced ancient technology without discernible periods of evolution.[35] This sudden appearance of cultures possessing advanced technology approximately 4,000 years ago is consistent with the Bible's account of the Flood, the proliferation of intelligent people on the plains of Shinar, and their subsequent scattering from the Tower of Babel.[36]

1. Mizraim's Family

Each group leaving Babel took with it whatever skills its members possessed.

Mizraim, Noah's grandson, founded Egypt around 2188 B.C., a date consistent with both biblical and secular records.[37] The Egyptians, the Sumerians, and the Mayans all retained the technology to build pyramids. Imhotep designed Egypt's first pyramid for third dynasty pharaoh Zoser. The Great Pyramid of

---

35. D. Chittick, *Puzzle of Ancient Man* (Newberg, OR: Creation Compass, 2006), p. 8–15.
36. Archbishop Ussher calculated the date for the Tower of Babel 2242 B.C. from Genesis and from Manetho's statement that the confusion occurred in the fifth year of Peleg's life. L. Pierce, "In the Days of Peleg," *Creation* 22 no. 1 (1999): p. 46–49, available at www.answersingenesis.org/creation/v22/i1/peleg.asp.
37. Ibid. The 12th-century historian Constantinus Manasses wrote that Egypt endured for 1,663 years. Egypt lost her independence around 526 B.C. with the Persian conquest. Hence, 2188 B.C. is a reasonable date for Egypt's founding and is consistent with a 2242 B.C. date for the Tower of Babel.

Giza, built for pharaoh Khufu of the fourth dynasty, is "the largest and most accurately constructed building in the world."[38] This pyramid required advanced optical, surveying, mathematical, and construction techniques, an impressive leap beyond the technology demonstrated in earlier pyramids.

2. Abram and Khufu's Pyramid

Abram's visit to Egypt may explain Egypt's sudden advance. Abram grew up in the advanced but idolatrous culture of Ur about three centuries after the Flood. Josephus wrote that Abram "communicated to them arithmetic, and delivered to them the science of astronomy; for before Abram came into Egypt they were unacquainted with those parts of learning; for that science came from the Chaldeans into Egypt."[39] Based on Josephus's statement, Abram's visit to Egypt may well have occurred during the fourth dynasty.

Middle Kingdom – Joseph and Moses

In contrast to the lack of evidence for an Israelite population in Egypt during the New Kingdom of Ramses' time, there is significant evidence of the Israelite presence during the Middle Kingdom. The 12th and 13th dynasties provide the backdrop for the stories of Joseph, the oppression of the Israelites, Moses, and the Exodus. The biblical dates for these events can provide dates for these dynasties (see chart).

1. Joseph as Vizier

Sesostris I of the 12th dynasty had a powerful vizier named Mentuhotep. Mentuhotep held the office of chief treasurer and wielded authority "like the declaration of the king's power."[40] "Mentuhotep . . . appears as the alter ego of the king. When he arrived, the great personages bowed down before him at the outer door of the royal palace."[41]

Compare Mentuhotep to Joseph in Genesis 41:40, 43. Furthermore, Ameni, a provincial governor under Sesostris I, had the following inscribed on his tomb: "No one was unhappy in my days, not even in the years of famine, for I had tilled all the fields of the Nome of Mah, up to its southern and northern frontiers. Thus I prolonged the life of its inhabitants and preserved the food which it produced."[42]

---

38. Ibid, p. 106.
39. Josephus, *The Works of Josephus: New Updated Edition*, book 1, chapter 8, as translated by William Whiston (Peabody, MA: Hendrickson Publishers, 1987), p. 39.
40. Ashton and Down, *Unwrapping the Pharaohs*, p. 83, quoting from James Henry Breasted's *History of Egypt*.
41. Ibid, quoting from Emille Brugsch's *Egypt Under the Pharaohs*.
42. Ibid, p. 83–84.

Ameni sounds like a man with the inside track on the agricultural forecast! Ameni's employer, vizier Mentuhotep, may have been Jacob's son Joseph.

2. Israelite Slavery

The late 12th dynasty reveals evidence for Israelite slavery. Sesostris III, the fifth king of the 12th dynasty, built cities in the delta including Bubastis, Qantir, and Ramses. The building material of choice in the Middle Kingdom was no longer stones but rather bricks composed of mud and straw.[43] A large Semitic slave population lived in the villages of Kahun and Gurob during the latter half of the 12th dynasty. On one papyrus slave list, 48 of the 77 legible names are typical of a "Semitic group from the northwest,"[44] many listed beside the Egyptian name assigned by the owner.[45] The presence of Semitic slaves in Egypt during this time is consistent with the biblical account of the oppression of the Israelites.

3. Moses' Adoption

Traditional chronology has tried to fit Moses into the 18th or 19th dynasty where there is no evidence of Semitic slavery on a large scale, but Moses' unusual adoption does fit into the late 12th dynasty. Amenemhet III, the dynasty's sixth king, had two daughters but no sons. Josephus describes a childless daughter of pharaoh finding a child in the river and telling her father, "As I have received him [Moses] from the bounty of the river, in a wonderful manner, I thought proper to adopt him for my son and the heir of thy kingdom."[46] Amenemhet III's daughter Sobekneferu was childless and eventually ruled briefly as pharaoh herself, making Sobekneferu a likely candidate for Moses' foster mother.[47]

4. Testimony of the Dead

Examinations of cemeteries at Tell ed-Daba and Kahun, areas with high Semitic slave populations, have been particularly supportive of the biblical narrative. Graves at ed-Daba reveal that 65 percent of the dead were infants.[48] This extraordinarily high figure is consistent with the slaughter of Israelite infants ordered by Pharaoh. Also consistent with the prescribed slaughter are "wooden boxes . . . discovered underneath the floors of many houses at

43. Ibid, p. 79.
44. Ibid, p. 92, quoting from Dr. Rosalie David's *The Pyramid Builders of Ancient Egypt*.
45. Rohl, *Pharaohs and Kings: A Biblical Quest*, p. 275–276.
46. W. Whiston, transl., book 2, chapter 9, section 7, *The Works of Josephus* (Peabody, MA: Hendrickson Publishers, 1987), p. 68.
47. Ashton and Down, *Unwrapping the Pharaohs*, p. 92.
48. Rohl, *Pharaohs and Kings: A Biblical Quest*, p. 271.

Kahun. They contained babies, sometimes buried two or three to a box, and aged only a few months at death."[49]

Examination of graves in a more recent section, datable to the late 13th dynasty, reveals shallow mass graves without the customary grave goods. These disorganized, crowded burials suggest the need for rapid burial of large numbers of people.[50] The death of the firstborn in the tenth plague would have created just such a situation.

5. The Exodus

In the 13th dynasty, during the reign of Neferhotep I, the Semitic slaves suddenly departed from Tel ed-Daba[51] and Kahun.

> Completion of the king's pyramid was not the reason why Kahun's inhabitants eventually deserted [Kahun], abandoning their tools and other possessions in the shops and houses. . . . The quantity, range, and type of articles of everyday use which were left behind suggest that the departure was sudden and unpremeditated.[52]

Furthermore, Neferhotep I's mummy has never been found, and his son Wahneferhotep did not ever reign, Neferhotep being succeeded by his brother Sobkhotpe IV.[53] The sudden departure of the Semitic slave population fits the biblical account of the Hebrew slaves' sudden exodus from Egypt after the tenth plague. The pharaoh's mummy is missing because he died in the Red Sea with his army when he pursued the slaves, and his son never ruled because he died in the tenth plague.

6. The Hyksos

Just a few years after the Exodus, the 13th dynasty ended, and the Second Intermediate Period, the time of Hyksos rule, began. The Hyksos have puzzled scholars, and everyone has a pet theory as to the Hyksos's identity. Manetho reported:

> Men of ignoble birth out of the eastern parts . . . had boldness enough to make an expedition into our country and with ease subdue

---

49. D. Down, "Searching for Moses," *TJ* 15 no. 1 (2001): 53-57, available at www.answersingenesis.org/tj/v15/i1/moses.asp.

50. Rohl, *Pharaohs and Kings: A Biblical Quest*, p. 279.

51. Ibid., reporting findings by Professor Manfred Bietak of Austrian Institute for Egyptology.

52. Ashton and Down, *Unwrapping the Pharaohs*, p. 100, quoting Dr. Rosalie David's *The Pyramid Builders of Ancient Egypt*.

53. Ibid., p. 103.

it by force, yet *without our hazarding a battle with them. . . .* This whole nation was styled Hycsos[54] (emphasis added).

Manetho places this conquest at the end of the 13th dynasty.[55]

Since no evidence of chariots had been found in pre-Hyksos Egypt, tradition has held that the Hyksos were able to defeat Egypt because they possessed chariots. Therefore, since Exodus 14 describes Pharaoh's pursuit with chariots, many have thought that the Exodus occurred after the Hyksos conquest. However, discoveries in recent years have confirmed the use of horses and chariots in the 12th and the 13th dynasties, prior to the Hyksos invasion. For example, an engraving from the 13th dynasty shows Khonsuemmwaset, a pharaoh's son and army commander, with a pair of gloves, the symbol for charioteer, under his seat.[56]

The drowning of the Egyptian army in the Red Sea explains the conquest of the powerful nation of Egypt without a battle. Some have hypothesized that the Hyksos were Amalekites.[57] Whoever the Hyksos were, they ruled Egypt from Avaris in the delta as the 15th and 16th dynasties, while their puppets in the 17th dynasty ruled from Thebes nearly 500 miles to the south. The 17th dynasty overthrew the Hyksos[58] and began the New Kingdom.

New Kingdom — Israel's Early Monarchy

1. David and Tahpenes's Husband

During David's reign, a young Edomite named Hadad found refuge in Pharaoh's house and married Queen Tahpenes's sister.[59] Hadad and the queen's sister had a son named Genubath. Genubath eventually became king of Edom. Records of the 18th dynasty's founder, Ahmose, refer to a name that resembles Tahpenes.[60] Later in the 18th dynasty, Thutmosis III received tribute from the land of Genubatye.[61]

---

54. Ibid.,, p. 102, quoting Josephus.
55. Rohl, *Pharaohs and Kings: A Biblical Quest,* p. 280–281.
56. Rohl, *Pharaohs and Kings: A Biblical Quest,* p. 285.
57. Ashton and Down, *Unwrapping the Pharaohs,* p. 103, referencing Courville's *The Exodus Problem and Its Ramifications.*
58. Ashton and Down, *Unwrapping the Pharaohs,* p. 106. Rebellion arose after the Hyksos king picked a fight with the Theban king Seqenenre by claiming the hippopotamus noise from the new canal in Thebes was keeping him awake at night.
59. 1 Kings 11:15–20
60. Phonetic similarity is certainly no guarantee of identity, as the case of Shishak's misidentification has shown. However, the occurrence of both of these names in the time sequence consistent with the times of David's and Solomon's reigns is at least a strong suggestion of synchronism.
61. "Contemporary Personalities and Affairs of the Early Israelite and 18th Dynasty Egyptian Kings," from The California Institute for Ancient Studies, www.specialtyinterests.net/solsen. html.

2. Solomon and the Egyptian Princess

Thutmosis I of the 18th dynasty had two daughters, Hatshepsut and Nefrubity. Nefrubity dropped out of the Egyptian records and may have been the Egyptian princess that Solomon married to seal his 1 Kings 3:1 treaty with Egypt.[62]

3. Queen of Sheba and Hatshepsut

Another mysterious Bible character emerges from the 18th dynasty. The female pharaoh Hatshepsut's trip to the land of Punt is famous, but the identity of Punt has remained a mystery despite engravings commemorating the treasures she brought home. First Kings 10 says the queen of Sheba visited Solomon, giving and receiving great gifts. Josephus identified this queen of Sheba as "queen of Egypt and Ethiopia."[63] In Matthew 12:42 the Lord Jesus refers to the queen of Sheba as "the queen of the south." "The south" is a biblical designation for Egypt.[64] Thus, Hatshepsut was probably the queen of Sheba.

4. Rehoboam and Shishak

When Thutmosis III became pharaoh, he conquered much of Palestine, ultimately taking away the treasures in Rehoboam's Jerusalem without a battle. He listed these treasures on the wall of the temple at Karnak. His list mirrors the Bible's account from 1 Kings 6:32, 10:17, and 14:25–26, including the 300 gold shields and doors overlaid with gold.[65] Thutmosis III was Shishak.

5. Asa and Zerah the Ethiopian

Asa, Rehoboam's grandson, had an encounter with Egypt. Second Chronicles 14 describes God's miraculous defense against an overwhelming attack by Zerah the Ethiopian. Ethiopia (Kush) refers to southern Egypt or Sudan. The 18th dynasty's headquarters was in southern Egypt, so this reference likely refers to another 18th dynasty pharaoh, possibly Amenhotep II.[66]

6. Ahab and Akhenaton

Late in the 18th dynasty, one of Egypt's most famous families set the stage for both biblical and Hittite synchronisms. Clay tablets found in Akhenaton's archives at Tel el-Amarna in 1887 included 60 letters from the king of Sumur, likely the Egyptian name for *Samaria*. The city of Samaria, according to 1 Kings 22:26, had a governor named Amon (an Egyptian name). The Amarna letters

62. Ashton and Down, *Unwrapping the Pharaohs*, p. 111. See 1 Kings 3:1.
63. Ibid., p. 121.
64. Daniel 11:5 and 8–9.
65. Ashton and Down, *Unwrapping the Pharaohs*, p. 126–128.
66. Ibid., p. 134.

call this governor Aman-appa and describe a severe famine that is consistent with the famine in the days of Ahab and Elijah.[67]

7. The Hittites and Tutankhamen

Akhenaton's son, the famous King Tutankhamen, died young, leaving no heir and a widowed queen called Ankhesenamen. According to the *Deeds of Suppiluliuma as told by his son Mursili II* in the Hittite archives, Tut's widow wrote to the powerful Hittite king Supililiumas, pleading, "Give me one son of yours . . . he would become my husband. . . . In Egypt he will be king"[68] Had Supililiumas's son Zannanza survived his trip to Egypt, the balance of power would have shifted against Assyria in favor of a Hittite-Egyptian coalition. Zannanza was assassinated, and Tut's general, Harmheb, assumed power. Upon Harmheb's death, his vizier, Ramses I the Great, took the throne as the first pharaoh of the 19th dynasty.

The dates for Ramses the Great's reign[69] and his battle of Kadesh with the Hittites are uncertain, because historians have no biblical parallels and no way to assess the preceding dynasty's duration. The rest of the revised chronology shifts the 19th dynasty dates three to five centuries later than the traditional dates. Ramses III, of the 20th dynasty, reported the annihilation of the Hittites during his reign. Revised chronology allows the Hittites to still exist at the time the Assyrians claimed to be at war with them.

8. "Israel Is Laid Waste"

The real 19th dynasty was concerned with the power of Assyria, not the plagues of Moses. Merneptah, the son of Ramses the Great, recorded the change in the region's power structure by listing many places Assyria had seized. His monument states, "Israel is laid waste, his seed is not."[70] This inscription not only places the latter part of the 19th dynasty in the 8th century B.C.; it also documents that Israel was an actual nation by the time of the 19th dynasty.

Third Intermediate and Late Periods — Judah's Late Monarchy and Captivity

The Third Intermediate Period contains dynasties 21–25, but some of these dynasties were concurrent, not sequential as assumed in the traditional

67. Ibid., p. 154.
68. G. Johnson, "Queen Ankhesenamen and the Hittite Prince," 1999, available at www.guardians.net/egypt/georgejohnson/queenankhesenamen.htm.
69. Rohl, *Pharaohs and Kings: A Biblical Quest,* places him in 900s B.C. (p. 175); Down, *Unwrapping the Pharaohs,* in 700s B.C. (p. 209) depending on uncertain 18th dynasty co-regencies.
70. Ashton and Down, *Unwrapping the Pharaohs,* p. 178.

chronology. In fact, the Royal Cache at Luxor contained a labeled 21st dynasty mummy wrapped in 22nd dynasty linen![71] The linen label names Sheshonq, the same pharaoh earlier mistaken for Shishak.

1. Hezekiah and Taharka

The biblical synchronism in this period involves Hezekiah. The imminent arrival of Assyria's enemy Taharka,[72] the last pharaoh of the 25th dynasty, helped Hezekiah by putting Sennacherib to flight in 709 B.C. Taharka later rebelled against the Assyrian domination of Egypt, dying in 664 B.C. when Ashurbanipal sacked Thebes.[73]

2. Josiah and Necho

After Ninevah's destruction, Pharaoh Necho II of the 26th dynasty marched to Carchemish, where the Assyrian remnant was making its last stand. On the way, according to 2 Chronicles 35, Necho killed Judah's king Josiah at Megiddo. Returning from his 605 B.C. defeat at Carchemish, Necho took Jehoahaz as a hostage and placed Jehoiakim on the throne of Judah.

3. Jeremiah and Hophra

One final biblical synchronism occurs in connection with the fate of 26th dynasty pharaoh, Hophra. Following a coup, Hophra fled to Babylon. There, he acquired an army and returned to reclaim his throne. Jeremiah predicted his defeat, and the prophecy recorded in Jeremiah 44:30 was fulfilled.

Table of Biblical and Egyptian Synchronisms[74]

Date B.C.	Bible	Egyptians	Dynasty
4004	Adam		
2348	Noah's flood		
post-Babel	Mizraim		
late 1900s	Abraham	Khufu	4
1706	Joseph; Jacob to Egypt	Sesostris I	12
1635	Joseph dies		
after 1635	enslavement	Sesostris III	12
1571	Moses born	Amenemhet III	12

71. Rohl, *Pharaohs and Kings: A Biblical Quest*, pp. 75–76.
72. 2 Kings 19:9, referred to as Tirhakah king of Ethiopia.
73. Rohl, *Pharaohs and Kings: A Biblical Quest*, p. 22.
74. Dates for biblical events are from Dr. Floyd-Nolen Jones's *Chronology of the Old Testament*, chosen for its careful analysis and internal consistency with regard to Scripture.

1491	Exodus	Neferhotep I	13
	Judges	Hyksos	15-17
late 1000s	David (1 Kings 11:19)	Ahmosis or Amenhotep I	18
1012	Solomon starts temple	Thutmosis I	18
	Queen of Sheba	Hatshepsut	18
971	Rehoboam; Shishak invades	Thutmosis III	18
late 900s	Asa; Zerah the Ethiopian	Amenhotep II	18
late 900s	Ahab; Elijah	Akhenaton	18
uncertain		Raamses II	19
722	Assyria destroys Israel	Merneptah	19
709	Hezekiah; Assyrian invasion	Taharka	25
664	Manasseh	Taharka dies	25
609	Josiah dies	Necho	26
605		Necho; Carchemish	26
589	Jeremiah	Hophra	26
586	Temple destroyed		
525		Cambyses of Persia	

Conclusion

Isaiah warned against going down to Egypt for help (Isaiah 31:1). This phrase has come to symbolize a warning not to go to the world for truth. God determines truth. Historians examine fragmentary clues and fill in the gaps based on their presuppositions. Those presuppositions may be biblical or traditional. Accepting traditional Egyptian chronology necessitates rejection of biblical truth. Accepting biblical chronology allows a reconstruction of ancient chronology on a foundation of truth. Viewing the evidence from a biblical framework makes the histories of Egypt and the Old Testament fit together like two sides of a zipper.

Since the original publication of this chapter, Isaac Newton's work on revised chronologies has become available in English. *Newton's Revised History of Ancient Kingdoms* makes available much additional information and insight about the history of ancient Egypt as well as the history of other ancient kingdoms. For further studies of revised chronologies, because the Bible is the ultimate standard, I suggest consulting Dr. Floyd Jones' book *The Chronology of the Old Testament*.

25

What about Satan and the Origin of Evil?

BODIE HODGE

C hristians are often asked questions about Satan: Who is he? Was he created? When was he created?

These and similar questions are valid questions to ask. To answer them, we
need to carefully consider what the Bible says, since it is the only completely
reliable source of information about Satan. The Bible doesn't give much information about Satan or the angels, but it does give enough to answer some of
these questions.

God's Word is infallible and the absolute authority, and we need to be
leery of conclusions drawn from sources outside the Bible, such as man's ideas
or traditions. Let's consider what the Bible says related to these questions.

Who Is Satan and Was He Always Called Satan?

The first use of the name *Satan* is found in 1 Chronicles 21:1; chronologically, Job, which was written much earlier, surpasses this. *Satan* is found
throughout Job 1 and 2. Satan literally means "adversary" in Hebrew.

Another name appears in the Old Testament in the King James Version:

> How art thou fallen from heaven, O Lucifer, son of the morn-
> ing! How art thou cut down to the ground, which didst weaken the
> nations! (Isaiah 14:12; KJV).

This is the only passage that uses the name *Lucifer* to refer to Satan. This name doesn't come from Hebrew but Latin. Perhaps this translation into English was influenced by the Latin Vulgate, which uses this name. In Latin, *Lucifer* means "light bringer."

The Hebrew is *heylel* and means "light bearer," "shining one," or "morning star." Many modern translations translate this as *star of the morning* or *morning star*. In this passage, *heylel* refers to the king of Babylon and Satan figuratively. Of course, Jesus lays claim to this title in Revelation 22:16. Though the passage in Revelation is in Greek while the passage in Isaiah is Hebrew, both are translated similarly.

Some believe that Lucifer was a heavenly or angelic name that was taken from Satan when he rebelled. The Bible doesn't explicitly state this, though Satan is nowhere else referred to as Lucifer but instead is called other names like the devil, Satan, etc. This tradition may hold some truth, although the idea seems to miss that this verse is referring to him *during* and *after* his fall — not before. Since other scriptural passages refer to him as Satan, Lucifer wasn't necessarily his pre-Fall name any more than Satan would be.

Even though Satan is first mentioned by name in Job, previous historical accounts record his actions (see Genesis 3, when Satan influenced the serpent, and Genesis 4 where Cain belonged to him [1 John 3:12]).

In the New Testament, other names reveal more about Satan's current nature. *Devil* (*diabolos*) means "false accuser, Satan, slanderer" in Greek and is the word from which the English word *diabolical* is formed. Satan is called a dragon in Revelation 12:9 and 20:2, as well as the "evil one" in several places. Revelation 12:9 calls him "that ancient serpent" or "serpent of old," and Matthew 4:3 calls him the "tempter." Other names for Satan include *Abaddon* (destruction), *Apollyon* (destroyer, Revelation 9:11), *Beelzebub* or *Beelzebul* (Matthew 12:27) and *Belial* (2 Corinthians 6:15). Satan is also referred to as the god of this world/age (2 Corinthians 4:4), prince of this world (John 12:31), and father of lies (John 8:44).

Was Satan Originally a Fallen Angel from Heaven?

Satan is mentioned in conjunction with angels (Matthew 25:41; Revelation 12:9) and the "sons of God" (Job 1:6, 2:1), which many believe to be angels. Although no Bible verse actually states that he was originally an angel, he is called a cherub in Ezekiel 28:16. The meaning of *cherub* is uncertain, though it is usually thought of as an angelic or heavenly being. (Ezekiel 28 is discussed in more detail later.)

In 2 Corinthians 11:14, we find that Satan masquerades as an angel of light — another allusion to his angel-like status:

And no wonder! For Satan himself transforms himself into an angel of light.

Although it is possible that Satan was an angel, it may be better to say that he was originally a "heavenly host" (which would include angels), since we know that he came from heaven, but don't know with certainty that he was an actual angel. Recall Isaiah 14:12:

How you are fallen from heaven, O Lucifer, son of the morning! How you are cut down to the ground, you who weakened the nations!

When Satan, the great dragon in Revelation (12:9), fell, it appears that he took a third of the heavenly host with him (a "third of the stars" were taken to earth with him by his tail, Revelation 12:4). We know that angels who fell have nothing good to look forward to:

Then He will also say to those on the left hand, "Depart from Me, you cursed, into the everlasting fire prepared for the devil and his angels" (Matthew 25:41).

For if God did not spare the angels who sinned, but cast them down to hell and delivered them into chains of darkness, to be reserved for judgment (2 Peter 2:4).

What these passages *don't* say is who and where the angels and Satan were originally.

And it grew up to the host of heaven; and it cast down some of the host and some of the stars to the ground, and trampled them (Daniel 8:10).

Daniel is speaking of heavenly hosts and angels, which were often spoken of as stars or luminaries (see Judges 5:20; Daniel 8:10; Jude 13; Revelation 1:20). It is unlikely that this passage refers to physical stars, as such would destroy the earth. The Hebrew word for stars (*kowkab*) also includes planets, meteors, and comets. Were these stars comets and meteors? Likely not, since the context refers to heavenly beings, which would be trampled on. This is further confirmation that Satan (and perhaps some other heavenly host) and his angels sinned and fell.

Another key passage to this is Ezekiel 28:15–17 (discussed in more detail later). The passage indicates that Satan was indeed perfect before his fall. He was in heaven and was cast to the earth.

Were the Heaven of Heavens, Satan, and His Angels Created?

The Bible doesn't give an *exact* time of Satan's creation or of his fall but does give some clues. Paul says in Colossians that *God/Christ created all things*:

> For by Him all things were created that are in heaven and that are on earth, visible and invisible, whether thrones or dominions or principalities or powers. All things were created through Him and for Him (Colossians 1:16).

So logically, Satan was created, as was the "heaven of heavens." We already found that Satan was originally in heaven prior to his fall. So the question becomes, when was the heaven of heavens created? The Bible uses the word *heaven* in several ways. The first mention is Genesis 1:1:

> In the beginning God created the heavens and the earth.

The Hebrew word for *heavens* is plural (dual form): *shamayim,* dual of an unused singular *shameh.* The word itself means "heaven, heavens, sky, visible heavens, abode of stars, universe, atmosphere," and "the abode of God." The context helps determine the meaning of a particular word; *heavens* is properly plural, and many Bible scholars and translators have rightly translated it as such.

Therefore, it seems safe to assume that the "heaven of heavens" was created along with the physical heavens (the space-time continuum, i.e., the physical universe, where the stars, sun, and moon would abide after they were created on day 4) during creation week.

The definition of the Greek word for *heaven(s)* (*ouranos*) is similar: "the vaulted expanse of the sky with all things visible in it; the universe, the world; the aerial heavens or sky, the region where the clouds and the tempests gather, and where thunder and lightning are produced; the sidereal or starry heavens; the region above the sidereal heavens, the seat of order of things eternal and consummately perfect where God dwells and other heavenly beings."

By usage, this could include the heaven of heavens. However, other biblical passages also help to answer whether the heaven of heavens was created.

> You alone are the LORD; You have made heaven, the heaven of heavens, with all their host, the earth and everything on it, the seas and all that is in them, and You preserve them all. The host of heaven worships You (Nehemiah 9:6).

A clear distinction is made between at least two heavens — the physical heavens and the heaven of heavens. The physical heavens include the expanse made on day 2, the place where the stars were placed on day 4, and the atmosphere (birds are referred to as "of the air" and "of the heavens," e.g., 1 Kings 14:11; Job 12:7; Psalm 104:12). The heaven of heavens is the residing place of the heavenly host, angels, and so on. This would seem to be the third heaven, which Paul mentions:

> I know a man in Christ who fourteen years ago — whether in the body I do not know, or whether out of the body I do not know, God knows — such a one was caught up to the third heaven (2 Corinthians 12:2).

The passage in Nehemiah indicates that God made the heavens; they are not infinite as God is. So the question now becomes, when?

Since the heaven of heavens is referred to with the earth, seas, and physical heaven, we can safely assume that they were all created during the same time frame — during creation week. The creation of the heaven of heavens did not take place on day 7, as God rested on that day from all of His work of creating. So it must have happened sometime during the six prior days.

> Then God saw everything that He had made, and indeed it was very good. So the evening and the morning were the sixth day. Thus the heavens and the earth, and all the host of them, were finished (Genesis 1:31–2:1).

Everything that God made, whether on earth, sky, seas, or heaven, was "very good." Did this include the heaven of heavens and Satan and the angels? Absolutely! Satan is spoken to in Ezekiel 28:15:

> You were perfect in your ways from the day you were created, till iniquity was found in you.

This passage says that Satan was blameless, hence he was *very good* originally. It would make sense then that the heaven of heavens was also a recipient of this blessed saying, since Satan was. In fact, this is what we would expect from an all-good God: a very good creation. Deuteronomy 32:4 says every work of God is perfect. So the heaven of heavens, Satan, and the angels were originally very good.

Ezekiel 28:15 says "from the *day*" (emphasis added) Satan was created. Obviously, then, Satan had a beginning; he is not infinite as God is. Thus, Satan has some sort of binding to time. Other Scriptures also reveal the relationship between Satan and time.

For this reason, rejoice, O heavens and you who dwell in them. Woe to the earth and the sea, because the devil has come down to you, having great wrath, knowing that *he has only a short time* (Revelation 12:12; NASB, emphasis added).

When the devil had finished every temptation, he departed from Him until an *opportune time* (Luke 4:13; NASB, emphasis added).

As a created being with a beginning, Satan is bound by time. He is not omnipresent as God is, nor is he omniscient. God has declared the end from the beginning (Isaiah 46:10); Satan cannot.

We can be certain that Satan, the heaven of heavens, and all that is in them had a beginning.

When Were the Angels and Satan Created?

The Bible doesn't give the exact timing of the creation of Satan and the angels; however, we can make several deductions from Scripture concerning the timing. Let's begin by examining Ezekiel 28:11–19:

11 Moreover the word of the LORD came to me, saying,

12 "Son of man, take up a lamentation for the king of Tyre, and say to him, 'Thus says the Lord GOD: "You were the seal of perfection, full of wisdom and perfect in beauty.

13 You were in Eden, the garden of God; every precious stone was your covering: the sardius, topaz, and diamond, beryl, onyx, and jasper, sapphire, turquoise, and emerald with gold. The workmanship of your timbrels and pipes was prepared for you on the day you were created.

14 You were the anointed cherub who covers; I established you; you were on the holy mountain of God; you walked back and forth in the midst of fiery stones.

15 You were perfect in your ways from the day you were created, till iniquity was found in you.

16 By the abundance of your trading you became filled with violence within, and you sinned; therefore I cast you as a profane thing out of the mountain of God; and I destroyed you, O covering cherub, from the midst of the fiery stones.

17 Your heart was lifted up because of your beauty; you corrupted your wisdom for the sake of your splendor; I cast you to the ground, I laid you before kings, that they might gaze at you.

18 You defiled your sanctuaries by the multitude of your iniquities, by the iniquity of your trading; therefore I brought fire from your midst; it devoured you, and I turned you to ashes upon the earth in the sight of all who saw you.

19 All who knew you among the peoples are astonished at you; you have become a horror, and shall be no more forever." ' "

In the sections prior to this, the word of the Lord was to Tyre itself (Ezekiel 27:2) and to the ruler of Tyre (Ezekiel 28:2). Beginning in Ezekiel 28:11, a lament (expression of grief or mourning for past events) is expressed to the king of Tyre; or more specifically, to the one *influencing* the king of Tyre. Note well that the king of Tyre was never a model of perfection (verse 12), nor was he on the mount of God (verse 14), nor was he in the Garden of Eden (verse 13; note that the Flood has destroyed the Garden of Eden several hundred years prior to this time period).

God easily sees Satan's influence and speaks directly to him. Elsewhere the Lord spoke to the serpent in Genesis 3: Genesis 3:14 is said to the serpent; Genesis 3:15 is said to Satan who influenced the serpent. Jesus rebuked Peter and then spoke to Satan (Mark 8:33). In Isaiah 14, the passage speaks to the king of Babylon and some parts to Satan, who was influencing him.

In the Ezekiel passage we note that Satan was originally perfect (blameless) from the *day* he was created until he sinned (wickedness was found in him). Thus, we can deduce that Satan was created during creation week; since he was blameless, he was under God's "very good" proclamation (Genesis 1:31) at the end of day 6.

In Job 38:4–7, God spoke to Job:

Where were you when I laid the foundations of the earth? Tell Me, if you have understanding. Who determined its measurements? Surely you know! Or who stretched the line upon it? To what were its foundations fastened? Or who laid its cornerstone, when the morning stars sang together, and all the sons of God shouted for joy?

Although a poetic passage, it may tell us that some of God's creative work was eyewitnessed by angels and that morning stars sang. Are morning stars symbolic of heavenly host or other angelic beings? It is possible — recall stars are often equated with angelic or heavenly beings, and most commentators suggest this refers to angels.

If so, the creation of the angels was prior to day 3 during creation week. From Genesis 1, God created the foundations of the earth on either day 1 (earth created) or day 3 (land and water separated). The logical inference is that the angels were created on either day 1 or at least by day 3.

If not, then the physical stars (created on day 4) were present while the angels shouted for joy. If this was the case, then morning stars and angels did their singing and shouting after the stars were created.

It seems most likely that *morning stars* symbolize heavenly host. Satan, a heavenly host, was called a morning star; therefore, Satan and the angels were created sometime prior to day 3 (or early on day 3), possibly on day 1.

When Did Satan Fall?

Satan sinned when pride overtook him and he fell from perfection (Ezekiel 28:15–17). When was this? The Bible doesn't give an exact answer either, but deductions can again be made from the Scriptures.

> How you are fallen from heaven, O Lucifer, son of the morning! How you are cut down to the ground, you who weakened the nations! For you have said in your heart: "I will ascend into heaven, I will exalt my throne above the stars of God; I will also sit on the mount of the congregation on the farthest sides of the north; I will ascend above the heights of the clouds, I will be like the Most High" (Isaiah 14:12–14).

When he sinned, he was cast from heaven (Isaiah 14:12). This must have been after day 6 of creation week because God pronounced everything very good (Genesis 1:31). Otherwise, God would have pronounced Satan's rebellion very good; yet throughout Scripture, God is absolute that sin is detestable in His eyes.

God sanctified the seventh day. It seems unlikely that God would have sanctified a day in which a great rebellion occurred. In Genesis 1:28, God commanded Adam and Eve to be fruitful and multiply. Had they waited very long to have sexual relations, they would have been sinning against God by not being fruitful. So, it couldn't have been long after day 7 that Satan tempted the woman through the serpent.

Archbishop Ussher, the great 17th-century Bible scholar, placed Satan's fall on the tenth day of the first year, which is the Day of Atonement. The Day of Atonement seems to reflect back to the first sacrifice when God made coverings for Adam and Eve from the coats of animal skins (Genesis 3:21). It may be that the generations to come (from Abel to Noah to Abraham to the Israelites) followed this pattern of sacrificing for sins on the Day of Atonement.

Regardless, the fall of Satan would likely have been soon after day 7.

How Could Satan, Who Was Created Good, Become Evil?

The answer to this question delves deep into the "sovereignty of God vs. man's responsibility" debate over which the Church has battled for ages.

From what we can tell from studying the Bible, Satan was the first to sin. He sinned before the woman sinned, and before Adam sinned. Some claim that we sin because Satan enters us and causes us to sin, but the Bible doesn't teach this. We sin whether Satan enters us or not. Satan was influencing the serpent when the woman sinned and when Adam sinned; they sinned on their own accord without being able to claim, "Satan made me do it."

But what causes this initial sin; why did Satan sin in the first place?

> Let no one say when he is tempted, "I am tempted by God"; for God cannot be tempted by evil, nor does He Himself tempt anyone. But each one is tempted when he is drawn away by his own desires and enticed. Then, when desire has conceived, it gives birth to sin; and sin, when it is full-grown, brings forth death (James 1:13–15).

Death is the punishment for sin. Sin originates in desire — one's own desire. James (1:14) hints that evil comes from one's own desire. It was by Satan's own desire that his pride in his own beauty and abilities overtook him.

In the "very good" original creation, it seems likely that Satan and mankind had the power of contrite choice.[1] In the Garden of Eden, the woman was convinced by her own *desire* (the tree was *desirable* to make one wise — Genesis 3:6). Satan had not entered her; she was enticed by her own desire.

God is not the author of sin; our desires are. God did not trick or deceive Satan into becoming full of pride. God hates pride (Proverbs 8:13), and it would not be in His character to cause one to become prideful. Nor was He the one who deceived Eve. Deception and lies go hand in hand (Psalm 78:36; Proverbs 12:17), yet God does not lie or deceive (Titus 1:2; Hebrews 6:18).

Note that since Satan's *own desires* caused his pride, the blame for evil's entrance into creation cannot be God's. To clarify, this doesn't mean God was unaware this would happen, but God permitted it to happen. God is sovereign and acted justly by casting Satan out of heaven after he rebelled against the Creator.

Therefore, when God incarnate came to destroy evil and the work of the devil (1 John 3:8), it was truly an act of love, not a gimmick to correct what He "messed up." He was glorified in His plan for redemption.

---

1. Whether mankind had this power after the Fall is not the topic of discussion in this section.

Some have asked why God didn't send Satan to hell instead of casting him to earth, assuming this would have prevented death, suffering, or curses for mankind. But God is love, and this shows that God was patient with him as God is patient with us. Perhaps Satan would have had a possibility of salvation had he not continued in his rebellion and sealed his fate, although Genesis 3:15 revealed that Satan's head would be crushed (after his continued sin and deception of the woman).

A related question is: was Satan required for man to sin? Satan's temptation of the woman instigated her to look at the fruit of the tree of the knowledge of good and evil, but it was she who *desired* it and sinned. Can we really say with certainty that on another day, without Satan, the woman and/or Adam would not have desired the fruit and sinned? However, in the words of Aslan, the lion in C.S. Lewis's *Chronicles of Narnia*, "There are no what-ifs."

In reality, we suffer death and the Curse because Adam sinned (Genesis 3) and we sinned in Adam (Hebrews 7:9–10), and we continue to sin (Romans 5:12). Adam did his part, but we must take responsibility for our part in committing high treason against the Creator of the universe. It is faulty to think that death and suffering are the result of Satan's rebellion. Man had dominion over the world, not Satan. When Satan rebelled, the world wasn't cursed; when Adam sinned, the ground was cursed, death entered the world, and so on. This is why we needed a last Adam (1 Corinthians 15:45), not a last Eve or a last Satan. This is why Christ came. The good news is that for those in Christ, the punishment for sin (death) will have no sting (1 Corinthians 15:55).

Why Would God, Who Is Not Evil, Allow Evil to Continue to Exist?

As with the other questions in this chapter, great theologians have struggled over how to effectively answer this. Paul, in his book to the Christians in Rome, offers some insight into the overarching perspective that we should have:

> And we know that all things work together for good to those who love God, to those who are the called according to His purpose (Romans 8:28).

All things, including the evil in this world, have a purpose. God is glorified through the plan of salvation that He worked out from the beginning. From the first Adam to the Last Adam, God planned a glorious way to redeem a people for himself through the promise of a Savior who would conquer both sin and death.

Jesus was glorified when He conquered Satan, sin, and death through His death and resurrection (see John 7:39, 11:4, 12:16, 12:23; 1 Peter 1:21; Acts 3:13). Both God the Son and God the Father were glorified through the Resurrection (see John 11:4, 13:31–32). Everything that happens is for the glory of God, even when we can't see how God can be glorified from our limited perspective.

Those who have received the gift of eternal life look forward to the time when we join God in heaven — a place there will be no evil (Revelation 21:27). This 6,000-year-old cursed world is only a blip compared to eternity. This relatively brief time on earth is all the time that evil will be permitted.

What Will Become of Satan?

Satan's days are numbered, and he will be condemned eternally.

> Therefore rejoice, O heavens, and you who dwell in them! Woe to the inhabitants of the earth and the sea! For the devil has come down to you, having great wrath, because he knows that he has a short time (Revelation 12:12).

> And he cast him into the bottomless pit, and shut him up, and set a seal on him, so that he should deceive the nations no more till the thousand years were finished. But after these things he must be released for a little while (Revelation 20:3).

We should have no fear of Satan or his minions, since God has power over him and has already decreed what his outcome will be — a second death — an eternal punishment called hell.

> Then He will also say to those on the left hand, "Depart from Me, you cursed, into the everlasting fire prepared for the devil and his angels" (Matthew 25:41).

> The devil, who deceived them, was cast into the lake of fire and brimstone where the beast and the false prophet are. And they will be tormented day and night forever and ever (Revelation 20:10).

> Then Death and Hades were cast into the lake of fire. This is the second death (Revelation 20:14).

Some people may claim that they want to "rule with Satan in hell," rather than go to heaven with and enjoy the infinite goodness of God. Sadly, these people fail to realize that Satan has *no* power in hell, nor will they. Satan is not the "ruler" in hell but a captive just as they will be if they don't receive the free gift of eternal life by repenting of their sins and believing in the finished work of Jesus Christ on the cross.

We trust those reading this book will realize that the only way of salvation is found through a personal relationship with Jesus Christ. God has provided a way of salvation, a right relationship with Him, and a means of forgiveness; have you received Christ as your Savior?

26

Why Is the Scopes Trial Significant?

BY KEN HAM & DR. DAVID MENTON

In recent years, removing the Ten Commandments from public spaces has been big news. In fact, Christian morality on the whole seems to be rapidly declining in America and the western hemisphere: abortion is on the rise, divorce rates are climbing, gay marriage issues are increasing. But did you know there is a connection between these events and the 1925 Scopes trial?

In 2003, news reports featured many people demonstrating in front of the Alabama court building after the decision to remove the Ten Commandments monument as a public display. Some were lying prostrate on the ground, crying out to the Lord to stop this from happening. But how many of these people really understood the foundational nature of this battle?

If we asked the demonstrators, "Do you believe in millions of years for the age of the earth — and what about the days of creation in Genesis 1?" — well, our long experience in creation ministry indicates that the answer would most likely be something like "What? They're taking the Ten Commandments out — why are you asking me irrelevant questions?"

Or if asked, "Where did Cain get his wife?" they might say, "Can't you see what's happening? They're taking the Ten Commandments out of a courthouse — don't waste my time asking a question that has nothing to do with this!"

In fact, these questions do relate to the real reason the culture is acting this way. During the Scopes trial similar questions were asked; the answers given still resonate today. Let us explain.

The Scopes Trial

The Scopes trial[1] took place during a hot July in 1925 in the little town of Dayton, nestled in the Cumberland Mountains of Tennessee. In a time when modern court trials can drag on for months or even years, it is amazing to consider that the Scopes trial lasted only 12 days (July 10–21) — including the selection of the jury!

The leadership of the American Civil Liberties Union (ACLU) in New York City initiated the Scopes trial. The ACLU became alarmed over "anti-evolution" bills that were being introduced in the legislatures of 20 states in the early 1920s. These bills were all very similar and forbade public schools to teach the evolution of man but generally ignored the evolution of anything else.

The ACLU hoped that a test case might overthrow these bills or at least make them unenforceable. They chose to pursue their case in Tennessee, where the state legislature had unanimously passed the Butler Act. This act declared that it shall be "unlawful for any teacher in any of the Universities, Normals, and all other public schools of the state which are supported in whole or in part by the public school funds of the State, to teach any theory that denies the story of the Divine Creation of man as taught in the Bible, and to teach instead that man has descended from a lower order of animals."

The ACLU placed advertisements in Tennessee newspapers that read in part: "We are looking for a Tennessee teacher who is willing to accept our services in testing this law in the courts." George Rappleyea, a mine operator in Dayton, read the ACLU ad in a Chattanooga newspaper and decided that he would like to see such a trial held in Dayton. Rappleyea's interest was neither scientific nor educational, but rather he hoped that hosting the trial would bring national attention to the town of Dayton and encourage investments in his mining operations.

John Scopes

Rappleyea approached a young friend named John Scopes who had taught math and coached the football team for one year at the local Rhea County high school. Scopes had no background in science and had little interest or understanding of evolution. Indeed, the only qualification Scopes had as a science teacher was that he filled in for an ill biology teacher the last two weeks of the school year. Nonetheless, Rappleyea talked a reluctant Scopes into participating in the ACLU's test case.

---

1. Many believe the movie *Inherit the Wind* to be a factual account of the Scope trial. It's not. To find out how the real trial differs from the Hollywood version portrayed in the movie, visit www.answersingenesis.org/creation/v19/i1/scopes.asp.

Although Scopes never taught evolution during his two weeks as a biology teacher, and thus really didn't violate the Butler Act, it was considered sufficient that the class textbook, Hunter's *Civic Biology*, did cover the evolution of man. For example, the Hunter textbook speculated that in his early history, "Man must have been little better than one of the lower animals" and concluded, "At the present time there exist upon the earth five races or varieties of man . . . the highest type of all, the Caucasians, represented by the civilized white inhabitants of Europe and America." Sadly, this sort of blatant racism in the name of evolution was enthusiastically endorsed by most of the academic world as well as by many Christian groups.

John Scopes

After the ACLU agreed to accept John Scopes for their test case and pay all expenses, he was arrested for teaching the evolution of man and immediately released on a $1,000 bond. The Dayton lawyer who served the warrant for Scopes' arrest was Sue Hicks (the subject of the Johnny Cash hit song "A Boy Named Sue," by the way). It was also Hicks who came up with the idea of calling upon the popular Christian lawyer/politician William Jennings Bryan to serve as head of the prosecution of John Scopes. When the ACLU chose the famous criminal lawyer and outspoken atheist/agnostic Clarence Darrow to head the defense team for John Scopes, a high visibility trial was virtually guaranteed.

William Jennings Bryan

Bryan had been the leader of the Democratic Party for 25 years and had run three times unsuccessfully for president of the United States. While considered a conservative Christian, his political views were very liberal for his time; indeed even the archliberal Clarence Darrow supported him in his first two attempts for the presidency. Bryan served as secretary of state under President Woodrow Wilson.

Bryan was well informed about the creation/evolution controversy and regularly corresponded with scientists of his time, such as Henry Fairfield Osborn, on the evidence for and against evolution. While Bryan was a staunch

William Jennings Bryan

creationist and a strong critic of biological evolution, he accepted geological evolution and an old age for the earth. In his autobiography, *The Memoirs of William Jennings Bryan*, Bryan said that his objectives in the Scopes trial were to "establish the right of taxpayers to control what is taught in their schools" and to "draw a line between teaching evolution as a fact and teaching it as a theory."

Clarence Darrow

Clarence Darrow was an immensely successful criminal lawyer who specialized in defending unpopular people and radical causes, often winning seemingly impossible cases. His agnostic convictions led him to believe that man's actions were ultimately just the result of body chemistry, and that concepts of good and evil were essentially meaningless. In his autobiography, *The Story of My Life*, Darrow explained his purpose for participating in the Scopes trial: "My object and my only object, was to focus the attention of the country on the program of Mr. Bryan and the other Fundamentalists in America."

Clarence Darrow

The Trial

Technically, the only legal issue in the Scopes trial was: did John Scopes violate the Butler Act by teaching that man descended from a lower order of animals? For both Bryan and Darrow, however, the real issue wasn't Scopes's guilt or innocence, but rather should evolution be taught as fact in the public schools? Darrow had hoped to have a number of evolutionist scientists testify in the court to the "fact" of evolution, but this wasn't permitted by the judge because the evidence for evolution was technically not at issue in the trial, and Darrow refused to allow his evolutionists to be cross-examined by the prosecution. As a result, most of the testimony by the scientists at the trial was written and filed into record — none was heard by the jury.

Anyone taking the time to read the transcript of the Scopes trial (*The World's Most Famous Court Trial*, Bryan College) will note that Darrow and his defense team of lawyers knew little about evolution and failed in their efforts to establish why it was necessary to teach evolution in the classroom. They lamely attempted to justify its reality and importance by equating evolution with human embryology.

For example, the development of the embryo from a single cell (the fertilized egg) was often cited as evidence that all life came (evolved?) from a single cell. Even the evolutionary expert Dr. Maynard Metcalf of Johns Hopkins University confused evolution with human embryonic development and the aging process!

Much of Darrow's effort at the trial amounted to a caustic diatribe against the Bible and Christianity. His anti-Christian hostility was so intense that there was fear on the part of liberal theologians and organizations that supported his evolutionary views that he might turn popular opinion against them. Darrow even turned his anger and hostility against Judge John T. Raulston by repeatedly interrupting and insulting him, for which he was cited for contempt of court.

After a self-serving apology from Darrow, Judge Raulston forgave Darrow for his contempt with these words: "The Man that I believe came into the world to save man from sin, the Man that died on the cross that man might be redeemed, taught that it was godly to forgive and were it not for the forgiving nature of himself I would fear for man. The Savior died on the Cross pleading with God for the men who crucified Him. I believe in that Christ. I believe in these principles. I accept Col. Darrow's apology." It's difficult to imagine a judge saying such a thing in our "enlightened" day, but not difficult to imagine what would happen to one who did.

Bryan Takes the Witness Stand

On the seventh day of the trial, Darrow challenged Bryan to take the witness stand as an expert on the Bible. Going against the advice of his co-counsel, Bryan foolishly agreed to this outrageous and unprecedented arrangement, with the agreement that Darrow would in turn take his turn at the witness stand to be questioned on his agnostic and evolutionary views.

In his questioning, Darrow sarcastically and often inaccurately recounted several miracles of the Old Testament such as Eve and the serpent, Jonah and the whale, Joshua's long day, Noah's flood, confusion of tongues at the Tower of Babel, and biblical inspiration. Darrow ridiculed Bryan for his belief and defense of these miracles, but Bryan steadfastly stuck with the clear words of Scripture, forcing Darrow to openly deny the Word of God.

Then came the turning point. Darrow raised the matter of a six-day creation. Bryan denied that the Bible says God created everything in six ordinary days of approximately 24 hours. When Darrow asked, "Does the statement 'the morning and the evening were the first day,' and 'the morning and the evening were the second day' mean anything to you?" Bryan replied, "I do not see that there is any necessity for constructing the words, 'the evening and the morning,' as meaning necessarily a 24-hour day."

When Darrow asked, "Creation might have been going on for a very long time?" Bryan replied, "It might have continued for millions of years." With the help of Bryan's compromise on the days of creation, Darrow achieved his goal of making the Bible subject to reinterpretation consistent with the ever-changing scientific and philosophical speculations of man.

The Significance

At the time of the trial, some probably thought, *What have the age of the earth, the days of creation, and Cain's wife got to do with this trial?* But actually, Darrow understood the connection — the same connection that these questions have to the Ten Commandments controversy (and general loss of Christian morality) today.

While in the witness box, Bryan, who stood for Christianity, couldn't answer the question about Cain's wife, and admitted he didn't believe in six literal creation days but accepted the millions of years for the earth's age.

That's when Darrow knew he had won, because he had managed to get the Christian to admit, in front of a worldwide audience, that he couldn't defend the Bible's history (e.g., Cain's wife), and didn't take the Bible as written (the days of creation), and instead accepted the world's teaching (millions of years). Thus, Bryan (unwittingly) had undermined biblical authority and paved the way for secular philosophy to pervade the culture and education system.

Sadly, most Christians today have, like Bryan, accepted the world's teaching and rejected the plain words of the Bible regarding history. Thus, they have helped the world teach generations of children that the Bible cannot be trusted in Genesis. After years of such indoctrination, a generation has now arisen that is also (logically) rejecting the morality based on the Bible. Today, with, for example, the removal of the Ten Commandments from public places, we are seeing the increasing elimination of the Christian foundational structure in the nation.

This is a major reason why the influence of Christianity has been so weakened in our Western world — the Church is giving the message that we need to trust in man's theories — not the Word of God. The answer isn't to merely protest such removals — or to simply protest other anti-Christian actions (e.g., abortion, euthanasia, gay marriage) — but to teach people *why* they can believe the Bible is true in every area it touches on. We need to provide Bible-based answers to the questions the world asks about the Christian faith (Who was Cain's wife? Isn't the earth millions of years old? Weren't the days in Genesis 1 long periods of time?). As we do this, people will begin to see that they can trust the Bible when it speaks of "earthly" things, and thus, when it speaks of "heavenly" things (salvation, absolute moral standards, etc.), as Jesus teaches in John 3:12.

27

Isn't the Bible Full of Contradictions?

PAUL F. TAYLOR

Christian talk radio show in America frequently broadcasts an advertisement for a product. In this ad, a young lady explains her take on Scripture: "The Bible was written a long time ago, and there wasn't a lot of knowledge back then. I think that if you read between the lines, it kinda contradicts itself." The show's host replies, "Oh no, it doesn't!" but nevertheless her view is a common view among many people.

Some years ago, I was participating in an Internet forum discussion on this topic. Another participant kept insisting that the Bible couldn't be true because it contradicts itself. Eventually, I challenged him to post two or three contradictions, and I would answer them for him. He posted over 40 alleged contradictions. I spent four hours researching each one of those points and then posted a reply to every single one. Within 30 seconds, he had replied that my answers were nonsense. Obviously, he had not read my answers. He was not interested in the answers. He already had an *a priori* commitment to believing the Bible was false and full of contradictions. It is instructive to note that after a quick Google search, I discovered that his list of supposed Bible contradictions had been copied and pasted directly from a website.

This anecdote shows that, for many people, the belief that the Bible contains contradictions and inaccuracies is an excuse for not believing. Many such people have not actually read the Bible for themselves. Still fewer have analyzed any of the alleged contradictions. It has been my experience that, after a little research, all the alleged contradictions and inaccuracies are explainable.

If you, the reader, are prepared to look at these answers with an open mind, then you will discover that the excuse of supposed inaccuracies does not hold water. If, however, you have already convinced yourself that such an old book as the Bible just has to contain errors, then you may as well skip this chapter. Like my Internet forum opponent, nothing (apart from the work of the Holy Spirit) is going to convince you that the Bible is 100 percent reliable — especially not the facts!

On Giants' Shoulders

In attempting to explain some of the Bible's alleged errors, I am standing on the shoulders of giants. I will not be able to address every alleged error for reason of space; others have done the job before me. In my opinion, chief among these is John W. Haley, who wrote the definitive work on the subject, *Alleged Discrepancies of the Bible*.[1] Haley tackles a comprehensive list of alleged discrepancies under the headings "doctrinal," "ethical," and "historical." This chapter uses a similar thematic approach because it will be possible to examine only a representative sample of alleged discrepancies. Readers are referred to Haley's work for a more exhaustive analysis of the subject.

Law of Noncontradiction

One of our own presuppositions could be labeled as the "law of non-contradiction." This stems directly from the belief that the Bible is the inspired, inerrant, and authoritative word of God. Although the 66 books of the Bible were written by diverse human authors in differing styles over a long period of time, it is our contention that the Bible really has only one author — God. The law of noncontradiction has been defined by theologian James Montgomery Boice as follows: "If the Bible is truly from God, and if God is a God of truth

---

1. For explanations of more supposed contradictions, see www.answersingenesis.org/go/contradictions; John W. Haley, *Alleged Discrepancies of the Bible* (Grand Rapids, MI: Baker, 1988). The book was originally published in 1874.

(as He is), then . . . if two parts seem to be in opposition or in contradiction to each other, our interpretation of one or both of these parts must be in error."[2] Wayne Grudem makes the same point thus:

> When the psalmist says, "The sum of your word is truth; and every one of your righteous ordinances endures for ever" (Ps 119:160), he implies that God's words are not only true individually but also viewed together as a whole. Viewed collectively, their "sum" is also "truth." Ultimately, there is no internal contradiction either in Scripture or in God's own thoughts.[3]

Boice proceeds to describe two people who are attempting to understand why we no longer perform animal sacrifices. One sees the issue as consistent with the evolution of religion. Another emphasizes the biblical concept of Jesus' ultimate and perfect fulfilment and completion of the sacrificial system. Boice says:

> The only difference is that one approaches Scripture looking for contradiction and development. The other approaches Scripture as if God has written it and therefore looks for unity, allowing one passage to throw light on another.[4]

Our presupposition that the Bible will not contain error is justified by the Bible itself. In Titus 1:2, Paul refers to God "who cannot lie," and the writer to the Hebrews, in 6:17–18, shows that by His counsel and His oath "it is impossible for God to lie." However, if a Bible student is determined to find error in the Bible, he will find it. It is a self-fulfilling prophecy. Yet, the error is not really there.

Inerrancy Only for Original Manuscripts

Historical evangelical statements of faith claim inerrancy for the Scriptures for the original manuscripts. Apparently, this is a problem for some and leads to claims of inconsistency. The argument goes that there have

2. James M. Boice, *Foundations of the Christian Faith* (Downers Grove, IL: InterVarsity Press, 1986), p. 91.
3. Wayne Grudem, *Systematic Theology* (Grand Rapids, MI: Zondervan, 1994), p. 35.
4. Boice, *Foundations of the Christian Faith*, p. 93.

been many translators and copyists since the Bible times and that these translators and copyists must have made errors. Therefore, it is said, we cannot trust current translations of the Bible to be accurate. Boice asks if an appeal to an inerrant Bible is meaningless.

> It would be if two things were true: (1) if the number of apparent errors remained constant as one moved back through the copies toward the original writing and (2) if believers in infallibility appealed to an original that differed substantially from the best manuscript copies in existence. But neither is the case.[5]

In fact, recent discoveries of biblical texts show that the Bible is substantially the same as when it was written. What few discrepancies might still remain are due to mistranslations or misunderstandings. These issues are all known to biblical scholars and are easily explained.

Presuppositional Discrepancies

A number of alleged Bible discrepancies could be described as *presuppositional discrepancies*. What I mean by the term is that there are a number of alleged discrepancies that are only discrepancies because of the presuppositions of the one making the allegations. Many such alleged discrepancies involve scientific argument and are covered in detail in other literature, including elsewhere in this book. Such discrepancies disappear immediately if the reader decides to interpret them in the light of a belief in the truth of the Bible.

> *The Bible says the world is only 6,000 years old and was created in six days, but science has proved that the earth is millions of years old.*

This sort of alleged discrepancy is very common. The supposed inaccuracy of the early chapters of Genesis is very often used as a reason to state that the whole Bible is not true. Many articles on the Answers in Genesis website (www.answersingenesis.org) and in *Answers* magazine tackle such issues, so it is not relevant to repeat the arguments again here. Readers are referred to the chapter "Did Jesus Say He Created in Six Literal Days?" in the *New Answers Book 1*[6] or to my detailed analysis in the *Six Days of Genesis*.[7]

Answers in Genesis endeavors show that a belief in the truth of Scripture from the very first verse is a reasonable and rational position to take. Once that

5. Boice, *Foundations of the Christian Faith*, p. 75.
6. Ken Ham, ed., *The New Answers Book 1* (Green Forest, AR: Master Books, 2007).
7. Paul F. Taylor, *The Six Days of Genesis* (Green Forest, AR: Master Books, 2007).

point is understood, many of these pseudoscientific objections to Scripture fade away.

Let us briefly comment on another such presuppositional discrepancy.

Genesis 6–8 suggest that the whole world was once covered by water. There is no evidence for this.

Detailed answers to this allegation can, once again, be found in much of our literature. For example, see the relevant chapter in *The New Answers Book 1*.[8]

It cannot be emphasized too strongly that creationists and evolutionists do not have different scientific evidence. We have the same scientific evidence; the *interpretation* of this evidence is different.

Thus, if one starts from the assumption that the fossil record was laid down over millions of years before human beings evolved, then the fossils do not provide evidence for the Flood. However, if one starts with the presupposition that the Bible's account is true, then we see the fossil record itself as evidence for a worldwide flood and there is no evidence of millions of years! As Ken Ham has often said, "If there really was a worldwide flood, what would you expect to see? Billions of dead things, buried in rock layers laid down by water all over the earth." This is exactly what we see.

Incorrect Context

Strongly related to the presuppositional discrepancies are the supposed errors caused by taking verses out of context. For example, a passage in the Bible states, "There is no God." However, the meaning of the phrase is very clear when we read the context: "The fool has said in his heart, 'There is no God.'" (Psalm 14:1). The words "There is no God" are consequently found on the lips of someone the Bible describes as a *fool*.[9]

This discrepancy might seem trivial, but there are more sophisticated examples of the same problem. These often arise by comparing two separate passages, which are referring to slightly different circumstances. For example, consider the following:

Ecclesiastes says that we are upright, while Psalms says that we are sinners.

8. Ham, *The New Answers Book 1*, Ken Ham and Tim Lovett, "Was There Really a Noah's Ark & Flood?" p. 125–140.
9. Unless otherwise stated, Bible passages quoted in this chapter are from the New King James Version (NKJV). Other translations are indicated by standard letters, such as KJV (King James Version), NIV (New International Version), and Tyndale (William Tyndale's translation).

The verses to which this statement alludes are these:

> God made man upright (Ecclesiastes 7:29).
> Behold, I was brought forth in iniquity (Psalm 51:5).

Looking at the contexts of both verses removes the discrepancy. In Ecclesiastes 7:29, the writer is talking about Adam and Eve, stating that we were *originally* created upright. In Psalm 51, David is speaking of his personal situation as a sinner, especially in the light of his sinful adultery with Bathsheba and his causing the death of Uriah. Thus, there is no contradiction between these passages.

Translational Errors

A common allegation against the Bible is that it is likely to have been mistranslated. When one actually analyzes possible mistranslations, however, it is found that there are actually very few real mistranslations. All of these have been studied and documented and can be found in Haley's book. As we have a number of good English translations today, it is often helpful to compare a couple of these. Once this comparison has been made, many of the so-called translational errors disappear.

> *There are two creation accounts: Genesis 1 and 2 give different accounts. In chapter 1, man and woman are created at the same time after the creation of the animals. In chapter 2, the animals are created after people.*

This apparent contradiction is best illustrated by looking at Genesis 2:19.

> Out of the ground the LORD God formed every beast of the field and every bird of the air, and brought them to Adam to see what he would call them (NKJV).

The language appears to suggest that God made the animals after making Adam and then He brought the animals to Adam. However, in Genesis 1, we have an account of God creating animals *and then* creating men and women.

The difficulty with Genesis 2:19 lies with the use of the word *formed*. The same style is read in the KJV.

> And out of the ground the LORD God formed every beast of the field, and every fowl of the air; and brought them unto Adam to see what he would call them.

The NIV has a subtly different rendition.

> Now the LORD God had formed out of the ground all the beasts of the field and all the birds of the air. He brought them to the man to see what he would name them.

The NIV suggests a different way of viewing the first two chapters of Genesis. Genesis 2 does not suggest a chronology. That is why the NIV suggests using the style "the LORD God *had formed* out of the ground all the beasts of the fields." Therefore, the animals being brought to Adam had already been made and were not being brought to him immediately after their creation. Interestingly, Tyndale agrees with the NIV — and Tyndale's translation predates the KJV.

> The Lord God had made of the earth all manner of beasts of the field and all manner fowls of the air.

Tyndale and the NIV are correct on this verse because the verb in the sentence can be translated as *pluperfect* rather than *perfect*. The pluperfect tense can be considered as the past of the past — that is to say, in a narration set in the past, the event to which the narration refers is already further in the past. Once the pluperfect is taken into account, the perceived contradiction completely disappears.

In the Book of Leviticus, bats are described as birds.

The passage to which the allegation refers is Leviticus 11:13–20.

13 And these you shall regard as an abomination among the birds; they shall not be eaten, they are an abomination: the eagle, the vulture, the buzzard,

14 the kite, and the falcon after its kind;

15 every raven after its kind,

16 the ostrich, the short–eared owl, the sea gull, and the hawk after its kind;

17 the little owl, the fisher owl, and the screech owl;

18 the white owl, the jackdaw, and the carrion vulture;

19 the stork, the heron after its kind, the hoopoe, and the bat.

20 All flying insects that creep on all fours shall be an abomination to you (NKJV).

13 And these are they which ye shall have in abomination among the **fowls**; they shall not be eaten, they are an abomination: the eagle, and the ossifrage, and the ospray,

14 And the vulture, and the kite after his kind;

15 Every raven after his kind;

16 And the owl, and the night hawk, and the cuckow, and the hawk after his kind,

17 And the little owl, and the cormorant, and the great owl,

18 And the swan, and the pelican, and the gier eagle,

19 And the stork, the heron after her kind, and the lapwing, and the bat.

20 All **fowls** that creep, going upon all four, shall be an abomination unto you (KJV).

Bible critics point out that, in their view, the writer of Leviticus is ignorant. He must have thought bats were birds, whereas we now classify them as mammals. Many Bible critics might also go on to discuss the supposed evolutionary origin of bats and birds.

A look at the KJV sheds some light on what the passage actually means. The KJV uses the word *fowls* instead of *birds*. Today, we would not see a significant difference, but notice that the KJV also describes insects as *fowls* in verse 20. The actual Hebrew word is *owph* (Strong's 05775). Although *bird* is usually a good translation of *owph*, it more accurately means *has a wing*. It is therefore completely in order for the word to be used of birds, flying insects, and bats. It could presumably also be used of the pteradons and other flying reptiles.

This translation of *owph* is supported by noting its use in Genesis 1:20.

Then God said, "Let the waters abound with an abundance of living creatures, and let birds fly above the earth across the face of the firmament of the heavens" (NKJV).

How could the young Samuel have been sleeping in the Temple when the Temple was not built until much later?

There are two allegations referred to 1 Samuel 3:3. The verse is quoted below from the KJV, the NIV, and the NKJV.

And ere the lamp of God went out in the temple of the Lord, where the ark of God was, and Samuel was laid down to sleep (KJV).

The lamp of God had not yet gone out, and Samuel was lying down in the temple of the Lord, where the ark of God was (NIV).

And before the lamp of God went out in the tabernacle of the Lord where the ark of God was, and while Samuel was lying down (NKJV).

The translation used by the NKJV gives a clue as to where the first misunderstanding comes from. The Hebrew word is *hēkāl*. This word is used of the temple, but the word is literally a large building or edifice. Commentators[10] have suggested that before the building of the temple the word was often applied to the sacred tabernacle. Therefore, it is perfectly possible for Samuel to have been asleep in this tabernacle. This alleged discrepancy is not so much a mistranslation as a misunderstanding.

The other alleged discrepancy with this verse is that Samuel was sleeping in the sacred portion of this tabernacle, the holy of holies, where the ark of God was. The NKJV gets it correct by pointing out that light went out where the holy of holies was while Samuel was lying down, not that he was lying down in this very holy place. This shows the difficulty of translating Hebrew into English when not careful. This brings us to our next section, where we find alleged discrepancies due to use of language.

Use of Language

Some alleged discrepancies occur because of the way that language has changed. It is interesting that while Hebrew has changed very little over the

---

10. See, for example, Haley, *Alleged Discrepancies of the Bible*, p. 396.

centuries, English is a language undergoing constant major change. The study of how English has altered is fascinating, though outside the scope of this chapter. As an aside, we can easily see how different strands of English have developed in different ways. The best example of this is the divergence between British and American English — a source of tremendous scope for misunderstanding, one-upmanship, and humor (or is it humour?).

Many of the biblical misunderstandings caused by change of language are found in the KJV, which was first translated in 1611. The English language has changed much since 1611, on both sides of the Atlantic. For example, we know that few people today refer to each other as *thee* and *thou,* except some of the older generation in the counties of Lancashire and Yorkshire in Northern England. The KJV uses this terminology to address God, and we can mistakenly think that this is a term of respect. In fact, the use of *thou* is much more specific. It is used to refer to a close friend or relative. In a society that uses the word *thou,* it would never be used in reference to someone to whom one was being especially polite. For example, in his youth my Lancastrian father would refer to his school friends as *thee* but to his teacher as *you.* Therefore, to refer to God as *thou,* while certainly not being disrespectful, implies a degree of intimacy usually associated with families or close friends.

Genesis 1 must contain a gap, because God commanded people to "replenish" the earth. You cannot replenish something, unless it was once previously full.

Genesis 1:28 contains the following command: "Be fruitful, and multiply, and replenish the earth, and subdue it" (KJV). Most other translations use the word *fill* rather than *replenish*. In fact, the Tyndale Bible, which predates the KJV, uses the word *fill*. So did the translators of the KJV get it wrong?

On the contrary. The word *replenish* was a very suitable word to choose in 1611 because at that time the word meant *to fill completely*, refuting any alleged gap. It therefore carries a slightly stronger emphasis than simply the word *fill*, and the Hebrew word has this emphasis. The word *replenish* did not imply doing something again as many words beginning with *re* do. Its etymology is common with the word *replete*, which still today carries no connotation of a repeated action. However, over the centuries the meaning of *replenish* has altered, so that if we now, for example, suggest replenishing the stock cupboard, we are suggesting that we refill a cupboard, which is now less full than it once was.

There are many other examples of misunderstandings caused by these changes in the English language. None of these misunderstandings were caused by errors on the part of the KJV translators. In fact, they chose the best English words at the time. The problems are caused simply because of the way that English has changed.

Another example of this is to ask why the Psalmist seems to be trying to prevent God from doing something in Psalm 88.

> But unto thee have I cried, O LORD; and in the morning shall my prayer *prevent* thee (Psalm 88:13, KJV, emphasis mine).

The NKJV renders the same verse as follows:

> But to You I have cried out, O LORD, And in the morning my prayer *comes before* You (Psalm 88:13, NKJV, emphasis mine).

Which translation is correct? The answer is that they both are. In 1611, the word *prevent* meant *to come before*. Compare the French verb *venir* (to come) with *prevenir* (to come before). However, in the following centuries, the word *prevent* has altered its meaning in English.

Some problems with use of language exist because of the sort of idioms used in the original languages, which would have been familiar to the original readers but sometimes pass us by. For example:

> *Moses says insects have four legs, whereas we know they have six.*

I have come across this alleged discrepancy frequently. I sometimes wonder if those using this allegation have really thought it through. Do they honestly believe that Moses was so thick that he couldn't count the legs on an insect correctly?

The passage concerned is Leviticus 11:20–23.

> All flying insects that creep on all fours shall be an abomination to you. Yet these you may eat of every flying insect that creeps on all fours: those which have jointed legs above their feet with which to leap on the earth. These you may eat: the locust after its kind, the destroying locust after its kind, the cricket after its kind, and the grasshopper after its kind (NKJV).

In fact, we use the phrase *on all fours* in a similar manner to Hebrew. The phrase is colloquial. It is referring to the actions of the creature (i.e., walking around) rather than being a complete inventory of the creature's feet. Also, when the Bible is referring to locusts and similar insects, it is actually being very precise. Such insects do indeed have four legs with which to "creep" and another two legs with which to "leap," which Moses points out (*those which have jointed legs above their feet with which to leap*). Once again, we find that the allegation of biblical discrepancy does not show up under the light of common sense.

If Jesus was to be in the grave three days and nights, how do we fit those between Good Friday and Easter Sunday?

There are several solutions to this problem. Some have suggested that a special Sabbath might have occurred, so that Jesus was actually crucified on a Thursday. However, a solution, which seems to me to be more convincing, is that Jesus was indeed crucified on a Friday but that the Jewish method of counting days was not the same as ours.

In Esther 4:16, we find Esther exhorting Mordecai to persuade the Jews to fast. "Neither eat nor drink for three days, night or day" (NKJV). This was clearly in preparation for her highly risky attempt to see the king. Yet just two verses later, in Esther 5:1, we read: "Now it happened on the third day that Esther put on her royal robes and stood in the inner court of the king's palace." If three days and nights were counted in the same way as we count them today, then Esther could not have seen the king until the fourth day. This is completely analogous to the situation with Jesus's crucifixion and resurrection.

> For as Jonah was three days and three nights in the belly of the great fish, so will the Son of Man be three days and three nights in the heart of the earth (Matthew 12:40; NKJV).

Now after the Sabbath, as the first day of the week began to dawn, Mary Magdalene and the other Mary came to see the tomb (Matthew 28:1; NKJV).

Then, as they were afraid and bowed their faces to the earth, they said to them, "Why do you seek the living among the dead? He is not here, but is risen! Remember how He spoke to you when He was still in Galilee, saying, 'The Son of Man must be delivered into the hands of sinful men, and be crucified, and the third day rise again'" (Luke 24:5–7; NKJV).

If the three days and nights were counted the way we count them, then Jesus would have to rise on the fourth day. But, by comparing these passages, we can see that in the minds of people in Bible times, "the third day" *is equivalent to* "after three days."

In fact, the way they counted was this: part of a day would be counted as one day. The following table, reproduced from the Christian Apologetics and Research Ministry (CARM) website, shows how the counting works.[11]

Day One		Day Two		Day Three	
FRI starts at sundown on Thursday	**FRI** ends at sundown	**SAT** starts at sundown on Friday	**SAT** ends at sundown	**SUN** starts at sundown on Saturday	**SUN** ends at sundown
Night	Day	Night	Day	Night	Day
Crucifixion		Sabbath		Resurrection	

This table indicates that Jesus died on Good Friday; that was day one. In total, day one includes the day and the previous night, even though Jesus died in the day. So, although only part of Friday was left, that was the first day and night to be counted. Saturday was day two. Jesus rose in the morning of the Sunday. That was day three. Thus, by Jewish counting, we have three days and nights, yet Jesus rose on the third day.

It should not be a surprise to us that a different culture used a different method of counting days. As soon as we adopt this method of counting, all the supposed biblical problems with counting the days disappear.

---

11. Christian Apologetics and Research Ministry, "How Long Was Jesus Dead in the Tomb?" www.carm.org/diff/Matt12_40.htm.

Copyist Error

It does not undermine our belief in the inerrancy of Scripture to suppose that there may be a small number of copyist errors. With a little logical analysis, this sort of error is not too difficult to spot.

There must be an error in Luke 3:36. The genealogy gives an extra Cainan not found in similar genealogies, such as Genesis 11:12.

Expositor Dr. John Gill gives ample reasons why this was a copyist error.[12] Gill says:

This Cainan is not mentioned by Moses in #Ge 11:12 nor has he ever appeared in any Hebrew copy of the Old Testament, nor in the Samaritan version, nor in the Targum; nor is he mentioned by Josephus, nor in #1Ch 1:24 where the genealogy is repeated; nor is it in Beza's most ancient Greek copy of Luke: it indeed stands in the present copies of the Septuagint, but was not originally there; and therefore could not be taken by Luke from thence, but seems to be owing to some early negligent transcriber of Luke's Gospel, and since put into the Septuagint to give it authority: I say "early," because it is in many Greek copies, and in the Vulgate Latin, and all the Oriental versions, even in the Syriac, the oldest of them; but ought not to stand neither in the text, nor in any version: for certain it is, there never was such a Cainan, the son of Arphaxad, for Salah was his son; and with him the next words should be connected.

If the first Cainan was not present in the original, then the Greek may have read in a manner similar to the following. Remember that NT Greek had no spaces, punctuation, or lower case letters.

ΤΟΥΣΑΡΟΥΧΤΟΥΡΑΓΑΥΤΟΥΦΑΛΕΓΤΟΥΕΒΕΡΤΟΥΣΑΛΑ
ΤΟΥΑΡΦΑΞΑΔΤΟΥΣΗΜΤΟΥΝΩΕΤΟΥΛΑΜΕΧ
ΤΟΥΜΑΘΟΥΣΑΛΑΤΟΥΕΝΩΧΤΟΥΙΑΡΕΔΤΟΥΜΑΛΕΛΕΗΛΤΟΥΚΑΙΝΑΝ
ΤΟΥΕΝΩΣΤΟΥΣΗΘΤΟΥΑΛΑΜΤΟΥΘΕΟΥ

12. Note on Luke 3:36, in: John Gill, D.D., *An Exposition of the Old and New Testament; The Whole Illustrated with Notes, Taken from the Most Ancient Jewish Writings* (London: printed for Mathews and Leigh, 18 Strand, by W. Clowes, Northumberland-Court, 1809), edited, revised, and updated by Larry Pierce, 1994–1995 for The Word CD-ROM. Available online at eword.gospelcom.net/comments/luke/gill/luke3.htm. See also chapter 5, "Are There Gaps in the Genesis Genealogies?"

If an early copyist glanced at the third line, while copying the first line, it is conceivable that the phrase TOYKAINAN (son of Cainan) may have been copied there.

ΤΟΥΣΑΡΟΥΧΤΟΥΡΑΓΑΥΤΟΥΦΑΛΕΓΤΟΥΕΒΕΡΤΟΥΣΑΛΑΤΟΥΚΑΙΝΑΝ
ΤΟΥΑΡΦΑΞΑΔΤΟΥΣΗΜΤΟΥΝΩΕΤΟΥΛΑΜΕΧ
ΤΟΥΜΑΘΟΥΣΑΛΑΤΟΥΕΝΩΧΤΟΥΙΑΡΕΔΤΟΥΜΑΛΕΛΕΗΛΤΟΥΚΑΙΝΑΝ
ΤΟΥΕΝΩΣΤΟΥΣΗΘΤΟΥΑΛΑΜΤΟΥΘΕΟΥ

There is some circumstantial evidence for this theory. The Septuagint (LXX) is a Greek translation of the Old Testament said to be translated by about 72 rabbis. Early copies of LXX do not have the extra Cainan in Genesis 11, but later copies postdating Luke's gospel do have the extra Cainan.

It might seem odd to suggest that there could be a copyist error in our translations of the Bible. What is even more remarkable to me, however, is that such possible copyist errors are so extremely rare. Paradoxically, the possible existence of such an error merely reinforces how God has preserved His Word through the centuries.

Conclusion

This chapter has discussed only some of the many alleged Bible contradictions and discrepancies. However, the methods of disposing of the supposed discrepancies used here can also be used on other alleged errors. There is one matter on which the reader should be very confident — the supposed Bible errors are well known to Bible scholars and have all been addressed and found not to be errors after all. In every case, there is a logical explanation for the supposed error. The Bible is a book we can trust — no, more than that — it is the *only* book we can fully trust.

28

Was the Dispersion at Babel a Real Event?

BODIE HODGE

W hen did the events at the Tower of Babel happen? What did the tower look like? Are there any records of Noah's descendants found throughout the world after they left Babel? What about different languages? Are Noah and his sons found in any ancient genealogies? In this chapter, we'll examine the fascinating answers to questions about what happened on the plain of Shinar. For background to this chapter, please read Genesis 10–11.

When Did the Event at Babel Occur?

Renowned chronologist Archbishop James Ussher[1] placed the time of Babel at 106 years after the Flood, when Peleg was born.[2]

> To Eber were born two sons: the name of one *was* Peleg, for in his days the earth was divided; and his brother's name *was* Joktan (Genesis 10:25).

Although this may not be the exact date, it is in range because Peleg was in the fourth generation after the Flood.

---

1. James Ussher, *The Annals of the World,* trans. Larry and Marion Pierce (Green Forest, AR: Master Books, 2003), p. 22.
2. The use of Ussher's dates are not an across-the-board endorsement of his work. We recognize that any human work contains errors; however, Ussher meticulously researched biblical and ancient history, and we are comfortable with using many of the dates he proposed.

Some have suggested that this division refers to a geophysical splitting of the continents; however, this is associated with the flood of Noah's time — not the events at Babel. The massive amounts of water and the crustal breakup indicated in Genesis 7:11 (the fountains of the great deep burst forth) were substantial enough to cause catastrophic movements of plates. Continental collision formations, such as high mountains, were already in place prior to Peleg's day. For example, we know the mountains of Ararat had formed by the end of the Flood because the ark landed there. These mountains are caused by a collision with the Arabian plate and the Eurasian plate. So these would have already moved by the time the Flood had ended.

Continental splitting during the day of Peleg would have caused another global flood! Instead, the division mentioned here refers to the linguistic division that happened when God confused the language at Babel. Even the Jewish historian Josephus (who lived near the time of Christ) stated:

> He was called Peleg, because he was born at the dispersion of the nations to their various countries. . . .[3]

Prominent modern theologians such as John Whitcomb reaffirm this as well.[4] According to Archbishop Ussher, the date of Babel would have been near 2242 B.C.[5] See table 1 for a comparison to other events according to Ussher.

Table 1. Major Dates According to Ussher

Major event	Date (According to Ussher)
Creation	4004 B.C.
Global Flood	2348 B.C.
Tower of Babel	2242 B.C.
Call of Abraham	1921 B.C.
Time of the Judges (Moses was first)	1491 B.C. (God appeared to Moses in the burning bush)
Time of the Kings (Saul was the first)	1095 B.C.
Split Kingdom	975 B.C.
Christ Was Born	5 B.C.

3. William Whiston, *The Works of Josephus Complete and Unabridged* (Peabody, MA: Hendrickson Publishers, 1987), p. 37.
4. John Whitcomb, "Babel," *Creation*, June 2002, p. 31–33, online at www.answersingenesis.org/creation/v24/i3/babel.asp.
5. Ussher, *The Annals of the World*, p. 22.

It was during the days of Peleg that the family groups left the plain of Shinar and traveled to different parts of the world, taking with them their own language that other families couldn't understand. Not long after this, Babylon (2234 B.C.), Egypt (2188 B.C.), and Greece (2089 B.C.) began.[6] Civilizations that were closer to Babel (e.g., those in the Middle East) were established prior to civilizations farther from Babel (e.g., those in Australia or the Americas).

Even more fascinating is that as people went around the world, they left evidence of this event! Let's take a look.

Ziggurats throughout the World

The Tower of Babel has traditionally been depicted as a type of ziggurat, although the Bible doesn't give specific dimensions. The Hebrew word for *tower* used in Genesis 11, referring to the Tower of Babel, is *migdal*: a tower; by analogy, a rostrum; figuratively, a (pyramidal) bed of flowers.

Interestingly, this word means *tower* but figuratively reflects a flowerbed that yields a *pyramidal* shape. This gives a little support to the idea that the Tower of Babel may have been pyramidal or ziggurat shaped.

In what is now Iraq, Robert Koldewey excavated a structure some think to be the foundation of the original Tower of Babel. It underlays a later ziggurat that was thought to be built by Hammurabi in the 19th century B.C.[7]

When people were scattered from the Tower of Babel in the time of Peleg, they likely took this building concept with them to places all over the world. It makes sense that

6. Larry Pierce, "In the Days of Peleg," *Creation*, December 1999, p. 46–49.
7. David Down, "Ziggurats in the News," *Archaeological Diggings*, March–April 2007, p. 3–7.

many of the families that were scattered from Babel took varying ideas of the tower to their new lands and began building projects of their own.

Ziggurats, pyramids, mounds, and the like have been found in many parts of the world — from Mesopotamia to Egypt to South America. The ancient Chinese built pyramids and the Mississippian culture built mounds. Pyramids are classed slightly differently from ziggurats, as are mounds, but the similarities are striking.

Why did the people at Shinar build a tower? Some suspect that they were afraid of another flood, similar to the one that Noah and his sons had informed them about. However, Dr. John Gill casts doubt on this idea.

> It is generally thought what led them to it was to secure them from another flood, they might be in fear of; but this seems not likely, since they had the covenant and oath of God, that the earth should never be destroyed by water any more; and besides, had this been the thing in view, they would not have chosen a plain to build on, a plain that lay between two of the greatest rivers, Tigris, and Euphrates, but rather one of the highest mountains and hills they could have found: nor could a building of brick be a sufficient defense against such a force of water, as the waters of the flood were; and besides, but few at most could be preserved at the top of the tower, to which, in such a case, they would have betook themselves.[8]

The Bible records that the people said among themselves:

> Come, let us build ourselves a city, and a tower whose top is in the heavens; let us make a name for ourselves, lest we be scattered abroad over the face of the whole earth. (Genesis 11:4)

It seems that the tower was to be a special place to keep people together, rather than filling the earth as God had commanded them to (Genesis 9:1). It is possible that the tower was built under the guise that it was a place for sacrifice unto God. This would have prevented people from going too far since they would have to come back to offer sacrifices at Babel.

A recurring theme in Scripture is that people seek to do things they think will honor God but end up disobeying God. One example is when Saul offered a sacrifice when he wasn't supposed to (1 Samuel 13:8–13). It is better to obey

---

8. Note on Genesis 11:4 in: John Gill, D.D., *An Exposition of the Old and New Testament; The Whole Illustrated with Notes, Taken from the Most Ancient Jewish Writings* (London: printed for Mathews and Leigh, 18 Strand, by W. Clowes, Northumberland-Court, 1809). Edited, revised, and updated by Larry Pierce, 1994–1995 for The Word CD-ROM.

than sacrifice. In fact, many ziggurats and pyramids around the world were used for sacrifice or other sacred religious events, such as burying people (e.g., pharaohs of Egypt). Perhaps the concept of sacred sacrifice and religious festivities with ziggurats was a carryover from Babel.

Regardless, ziggurats and pyramids all over the world are an excellent confirmation of the original recorded in God's Word — the Tower of Babel.

Noah in Royal Genealogies of Europe

The Bible in Genesis 10 gives an outline of family groups that left Babel (see table 2).

These people moved throughout the world and populated virtually every continent. (Was Antarctica ever settled in the past? At this point I am unaware.) Historians have commented on genealogical records in the past and other ancient documents on the origins of various peoples.[9]

These genealogies seem to connect prominent modern houses and royal lines with the Table of Nations listed in the Bible. In these genealogies, Noah is found on the top of the lists on many of these documents, some of which feature variant spellings such as *Noe*, *Noa*, and *Noah*.

One historian discovered a relationship between the ancient name of *Sceaf* (*Seskef*, *Scef*) and the biblical *Japheth*.[10] This seems reasonable, as Japheth has

---

9. Nennius, *Historia Brittonium*, edited in the 10th century by Mark the Hermit, with English version by the Rev. W. Gunn, rector of Irstead, Norfolk, printed in London, 1819; Flavius Josephus, *The Complete Works of Flavius Josephus the Jewish Historian* (~100 A.D.), translated by William Whiston (~1850 A.D.) (Green Forest, AR: Master Books, 2008).
10. Bill Cooper, *After the Flood* (Chichester, England: New Wine Press, 1995), p. 92–96.

traditionally been seen as the ancestor of the European nations. Most of the European genealogies researched have a variant of *Sceaf* with the exception of

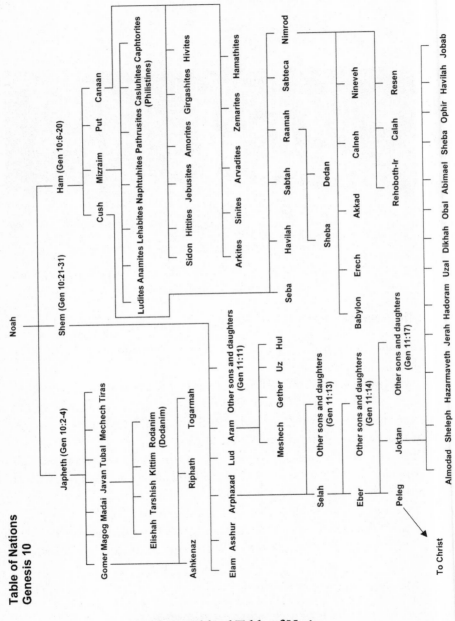

Table of Nations
Genesis 10

Table 2. Biblical Table of Nations

Irish genealogies, which still used the name *Japheth*. The Irish genealogical chart is reprinted in table 3.[11]

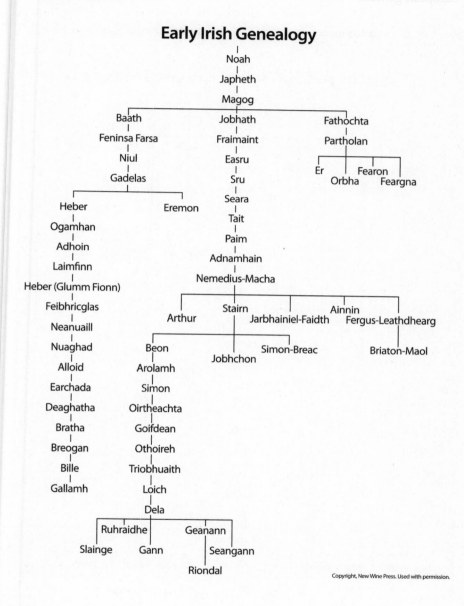

Table 3. Irish Genealogies

Permission for use granted by New Wine Press

11. Ibid., p. 108.

Anglo-Saxon chronologies feature six royal houses.[12] An eighth century Roman historian, Nennius, developed a table of nations of the lineages of many of the European people groups from Noah's son Japheth: Gauls, Goths, Bavarians, Saxons, and Romans. Nennius's table of nations is reproduced in table 4.[13]

Nennius and the Table of European Nations

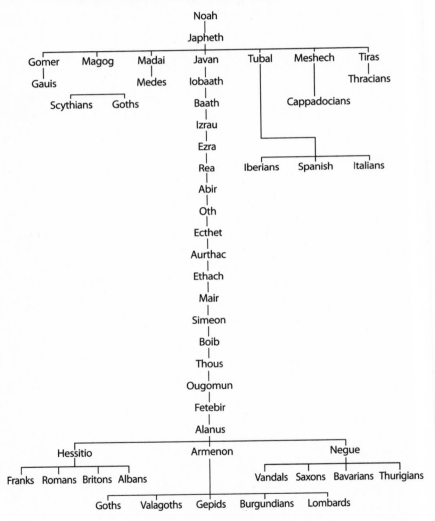

Table 4. Nennius's Table of Nations

Permission for use granted by New Wine Press

12. Ibid., p. 84–86.
13. Ibid., p. 49.

Though it repeats the Goths in two different areas, Nennius's chart bears strong similarities to the history that Josephus recorded,[14] as well as the Bible's Table of Nations. However, there are clearly enough differences to show that it was neither a copy from the biblical text nor from the Jewish historian Josephus.[15]

Chinese records also describe *Nuah* with three sons, *Lo Han, Lo Shen,* and *Jahphu,* according to the Miautso people of China.[16] Although original documents of ancient sources sometimes no longer exist and one has to rely on quotes from other ancient books, it is interesting how in many places we find similarities to the Table of Nations given in the Bible.

Noah's Grandsons' Names Are Everywhere!

History abounds with names that are reused. Names of places become names of people; names of people become names of places. After the Flood, several of Noah's descendants were named for places prior to the Flood. See table 5 for a list.

Table 5. A Few Pre-Flood and Post-Flood References

Name	Bible Reference Pre-Flood	Bible Reference Post-Flood	Person
Havilah	Genesis 2:11	Genesis 10:7, Genesis 10:29	Noah's grandson through Ham; Noah's great, great, great, great grandson through Shem.
Cush	Genesis 2:13	Genesis 10:6	Noah's grandson through Ham
Asshur	Genesis 2:14	Genesis 10:22	Noah's grandson through Shem

Names may vary throughout history. For example, Pennsylvania was named for William Penn; St. Petersburg in Russia was named for Peter the Great, who was ultimately named for Peter who penned two books of the Bible. Names can undergo many changes such as variations in spelling, differences in symbols, and alterations in pronunciation.

---

14. Whiston, *The Works of Josephus Complete and Unabridged*, p. 36–37.
15. Cooper, *After the Flood*, chapter 3.
16. Edgar Traux, "Genesis According to the Miao People," *Impact*, April 1991, online at www. icr.org/article/341/.

Despite any changes, however, the names of post-Flood regions, cities, rivers, or languages should bear similarity to the names of those leaving Babel. One would be surprised how often these names appear. Table 6 lists some of these.

Table 6. Noah's Descendants' Names Reflected Around the World[17]

Name	Descendant of Noah	What Is It?
Aramaic	Aram	Language that came out of Babel and still survives, likely with changes down the ages. Some short parts of the Bible are written in Aramaic. Jesus spoke it on the cross when He said: "ELOI, ELOI, LAMA SABACHTHANI?" (Mark 15:34).
Cush	Cush	Ancient name of Ethiopia. In fact, people of Ethiopia still call themselves Cushites.
Medes	Madai	People group often associated with the Persians.
Ashkenaz	Ashkenaz	Still the Hebrew name for Germany. The French name for Germany has similarities to this too: Allemagne.
Galacia, Gaul, and Galicia	Gomer	These regions are the old names for an area in modern Turkey, France ,and Northwestern Spain, respectively, where Gomer was said to have lived. His family lines continued to spread across southern Europe. The Book of Galatians by Paul was written to the church at Galatia.
Gomeraeg	Gomer	This is the old name for the Welsh language on the British Isles from their ancestor, Gomer, whose ancestors began to populate the Isle from the mainland.

17. Information in this table comes from the following sources: Whiston, *The Works of Josephus Complete and Unabridged*, p. 36–37; Cooper, *After the Flood*, p. 170–208.

Javan	Javan	This is still the Hebrew name for Greece. His sons, Elishah, Tarshish, Kittim (Chittim), and Dodanim still have reference to places in Greece. For example, Paul, the author who penned much of the New Testament, was from the region of Tarshish (Acts 21:39) and a city called Tarsus. Jeremiah mentions Kittim in Jeremiah 2:10 and is modern-day Cyprus (and other nearby ancient regions that now had varied names such as Cethim, Citius, Cethima Cilicia). The Greeks worshiped Jupiter Dodanaeus from Japheth/Dodanim. The Elysians, were ancient Greek people.
Meshech/ Moscow	Mechech	Mechech is the old name for Moscow, Russia, and one region called the Mechech Lowland still holds the original name today.
Canaan	Canaan	The region of Palestine that God removed from the Canaanites for their sin and gave as an inheritance to the Israelites beginning with the conquest of Joshua. It is often termed the Holy Land and is where modern-day Israel resides.
Elamites	Elam	This was the old name for the Persians prior to Cyrus.
Assyria	Asshur	Asshur is still the Hebrew name for Assyria.
Hebrew	Eber	This people group and language was named for Eber. Abraham was a Hebrew, and the bulk of the Old Testament is written in Hebrew.
Taurus/ Toros	Tarshish	A mountain range in Turkey.
Tanais	Tarshish	The old name of the Don River flowing into the Black Sea.
Mizraim	Mizraim	This is still the Hebrew name for Egypt.

We Don't Speak the Same Language Anymore!

The Tower of Babel explains why everyone doesn't speak the same language today.

There are over 6,900 spoken languages in the world today.[18] Yet the number of languages emerging from Babel at the time of the dispersion would have been much less than this — likely less than 100 different original language families.

So where did all these languages come from? Linguists recognize that most languages have similarities to other languages. Related languages belong to what are called *language families*. These original language families (probably less than 100) resulted from God's confusion of the language at Babel. Since that time, the original language families have grown and changed into the abundant number of languages today.

Noah's great-great-grandson Eber fathered Peleg when the events at Babel took place. The modern language of Hebrew is named after Eber. Noah's grandson Aram was the progenitor of Aramaic. The Bible lists Noah's grandsons, great-grandsons, great-great-grandsons, and great-great-great-grandsons who received a language at Babel in Genesis 10. Eber and Aram were but two!

From Japheth (Genesis 10:2–5) came at least 14 language families; from Ham (Genesis 10:6–20), 39; from Shem (Genesis 10:22–31), at least 25 (excluding Peleg and other children who may have just been born). The total number of languages that may have come out of Babel according to Genesis 10 may have been at least 78, assuming Noah, Ham, Shem, Japheth, and Peleg didn't receive a new language. This excludes some descendants of Shem who are given slight mention in Genesis 11:11–17; they may have also received a language.

Both *Vistawide World Languages and Cultures*[19] and *Ethnologue*,[20] companies that provide statistics on language, agree that only 94 languages *families* have been so far ascertained. With further study in years to come, this may change, but this figure is well within the range of families that dispersed from Babel (Genesis 10).

Is it feasible for 7,000 languages to develop from less than 100 in 4,000 years? The languages that came out of the confusion at Babel were "root languages" or language families. Over time, those root languages have varied by borrowing from other languages, developing new terms and phrases, and losing previous words and phrases.

18. Vistawide, "World Language Families," www.vistawide.com/languages/language_families_statistics1.htm.
19. Ibid.
20. Ethnologue, "Statistical Summaries," www.ethnologue.com/ethno_docs/distribution.asp?by=family.

Let's look at changes in the English language, as an example. English has changed so much over the course of 1,000 years that early speakers would hardly recognize it today. Table 7 provides a look at the changes in Matthew 6:9.

Table 7[21]

Beginning of Matthew 6:9	Date
Our Father who art in heaven and/or Our Father who is in heaven	Late Modern English (1700s)
Our father which art in heauen	Early Modern English (1500–1700) (KJV 1611)
Oure fader that art in heuenis	Middle English (1100–1500)
Fæder ure þu þe eart on heofonum	Old English (c. A.D. 1000)

Just as English has changed significantly over the past 1,000 years, it becomes easy to see how the original languages at Babel could have rapidly changed in the 4,000 years since that time, whether spoken or written.

In conclusion, there exist a great many confirmations of the Bible's account of the Tower of Babel and what happened as a result. Even stories about a tower and sudden language changes appear in ancient histories from Sumerian, Grecian, Polynesian, Mexican, and Native American sources.[22] This is what we would expect since the Tower of Babel was a real event. Language changes, ziggurats, names of Noah found throughout the world, and tower legends are excellent confirmations of the events at Babel.

21. Comparison of Matthew 6:9, Mansfield University, www.faculty.mansfield.edu/bholtman/ holtman/101/GmcVaterunser.pdf.
22. Pam Sheppard, "Tongue-Twisting Tales," *Answers*, April–June 2008, p.56–57.

29

When Does Life Begin?

DR. TOMMY MITCHELL

When does human life begin? This question has confounded individuals and divided our society. Opinions have come from the right and the left, from prolife advocates and those in favor of abortion on demand, from physicians and lawyers, from the pulpit and the courtroom.

When did I begin to be me? Is this a scientific question or a theological one?[1] Would this question be best left to scientists or to preachers and philosophers? Information and viewpoints from secular scientific sources and from theologians will be examined in this chapter, but the ultimate answer can have no authority unless that answer is based squarely on the Word of God. The Bible, because it is true, will not disagree with genuine science. Furthermore, the Bible is the only valid and consistent basis for making moral judgments, since it comes from the Creator of the whole world and all people in it. Any other basis for judgment would be a useless clamor of divergent, man-made opinions.

Who Is More Human?

Life is a continuum. From the season of growing in the womb to being born, from playing as a child to growing older, each stage of life seems to blend gracefully (or not so gracefully in my case) into the next. Life progresses

---

1. The answer to the question "What is life?" is beyond the scope of this article. There are several excellent resources dealing with this topic: see James Stambaugh, " 'Life' According to the Bible, and the Scientific Evidence," *TJ* 6, no. 2 (1992): 98–121, online at www.answersingenesis.org/tj/v6/i2/life.asp.

and time passes, culminating in death. Death, a very visible end point, is more easily defined than the point at which the continuum of human life begins.

Where is the starting point? If life is indeed a continual process, can we not just work backward to its beginning? There are a variety of opinions about life's beginnings. Many say life begins at conception. Others argue strongly that life does not start until implantation in the womb. Still others say that human life begins only when the umbilical cord is cut, making the newborn child an independent agent. How is fact separated from opinion?

Perhaps another way to ask the question is, when do we become human? Certainly a child sitting on grandpa's knee or a fully grown adult would be considered human. Is the adult *more* human than the child? Of course not. No reasonable person would consider the child to be less human. At what point along the journey did this child become human? Was it at conception, somewhere during his development, or at birth?

The Process

The initial event along the road of human development is fertilization. Twenty-three chromosomes from the mother and 23 chromosomes from the father are combined at the time of fertilization. At this point, the genetic makeup of the individual is determined. At this time, a unique individual, known as a *zygote*, begins to exist. But is this zygote human?

This zygote then divides again and again. Some cells develop into the placenta and are essential for implantation. Other cells develop into the anatomical parts of the baby.[2] The number of cells increases rapidly, and the name changes as the number increases. By the time this rapidly dividing ball of cells arrives in the uterus, it is called a *blastocyst*. Implantation in the uterine wall normally occurs about six days after fertilization.[3]

For reasons unclear to medical science, the mass of cells sometimes splits to produce identical twins. These twins are called identical because their sets of chromosomes are identical. Depending upon the stage of development when the split occurs, the twins may share certain placental parts, but the twins produced are distinct individuals. If the split occurs between the 13th and 15th days, the twins will actually share body parts, a condition known as *conjoined*

2. This process, called *differentiation,* is the process by which the dividing cells gradually become different from one another.
3. The name of the rapidly diving ball of cells continues to change as size and shape changes, with the name *embryo* being assigned at about three weeks after fertilization. The term *fetus* is used from about the eighth week of development.

twins, commonly called *Siamese twins*. (After that time, development and differentiation are too far along to allow successful splitting.)

Even though the names arbitrarily change throughout this process and certain milestones in development are evident, the process set in motion at the moment of conception is a continuous chain of events. In this sequence, groups of cells multiply and develop into specific body parts with amazing precision and a remarkably low rate of error, considering the complexity of changes that must occur. However, at no time in this process is there a scientific point at which the developing individual clearly "becomes a person," any more than a baby becomes more human when it walks, talks, or is weaned. These milestones in zygote, blastocyst, embryonic, and fetal development are simply descriptions of anatomy, not hurdles met in the test of humanness. From a scientific point of view, the words are arbitrary and purely descriptive.

Can Science Help?

Scientists have studied the marvelous process previously described for decades. The changes in the form of the embryo through each stage are well documented. The question still remains, at what point does human life begin? There are numerous positions on this. Some of these will be reviewed here.

A Genetic Position

The simplest view is based on genetics. Those who hold this position argue that since a genetically unique individual is created at the time of fertilization, each human life begins at fertilization. The zygote formed at fertilization is different from all others and, if it survives, will grow into a person with his or her own unique set of genes. In this view, the terms *fertilization* and *conception* are interchangeable. Thus, in this view, life would be said to begin at conception.

The phenomenon of twinning is sometimes used to argue against this position. Until about day 14, there is the possibility that the zygote will split, producing twins. Those who oppose a genetic view say that there is no uniqueness to the zygote, no humanness or personhood, until the potential for twinning has passed. They ask, if the zygote is an individual "person" at fertilization, then what is the nature of that "personhood" if the zygote should split into two individuals?

Another objection to this view is the fact the many fertilized eggs never successfully implant. An estimated 20–50 percent of fertilizations die or are spontaneously aborted.[4] Thus, those who raise this objection hold that, since

---

4. Christian Answers Net, "Does Life Begin Only When the Embryo Implants?" www.christiananswers.net/q-sum/q-life014.html.

there are such a large number of zygotes that never fully develop, those zygotes are not truly human.

However, neither of the objections can be so easily supported. The twinning objection falls short when one considers the problem presented by the existence of so-called Siamese twins. In these cases, the zygote does not completely split, and the children are born joined together, often sharing certain body organs. Nonetheless, both twins have distinct personalities and are distinct individuals. Here the "personhood" obviously could not be granted after twinning since the process was never completed.

The second objection, the high loss rate of zygotes, is also not logical. The occurrence of spontaneous abortions does not mean that the lost were not fully human, any more than the development of some deadly disease in a child makes the child suddenly nonhuman.

The Implantation View

An increasingly heard viewpoint today is related to the implantation of the blastocyst into the uterine lining. This implantation process begins on day six following fertilization and can continue until around day nine. Some now suggest that it is not until this time that the zygote can be called human life. However, achieving implantation does not make the individual more human; rather, implantation makes the individual more likely to survive.

Interestingly enough, the popularity of this view has led to some changes in how some define conception. Until recently, *conception* was synonymous with *fertilization*. In fact, in the 26th edition of *Stedman's Medical Dictionary*, conception was defined as the "act of conceiving, or becoming pregnant; fertilization of the oocyte (ovum) by a spermatozoon to form a viable zygote."[5] Conception was defined as the time of fertilization.

However, something interesting happened in the next five years. In the 27th edition of *Stedman's Medical Dictionary*, conception is defined as follows: "Act of conceiving; the implantation of the blastocyte in the endometrium."[6] Note here that *implantation* is now the defining point in conception. The scientific community arbitrarily, without any scientific justification, redefined the starting point of life.

According to the redefined view, a zygote less than nine or so days old, having not yet completed implantation, would not be considered alive. If it is not alive, it certainly cannot be human. This change was completely arbitrary,

5. *Stedman's Medical Dictionary*, 26th edition (Baltimore: Williams & Wilkins, 1995), p. 377.
6. *Stedman's Medical Dictionary*, 27th edition (Baltimore: Williams & Wilkins, 2000), p. 394.

for there was no basic change in the understanding of the developmental process that would make this redefinition necessary.

The new definition would, however, have great implications in the political, ethical, and moral arenas. Personal and governmental decision-making on such issues as embryonic stem cell research, cloning, and the so-called "morning after pill" directly depends on the validity of this definition. If preimplantation blastocysts were not really alive, they could be guiltlessly harvested or destroyed prior to the six-to-nine day mark because "conception" had not yet occurred.

The Embryological View

The embryological view holds that human life begins 12–14 days after fertilization, the time period after which identical twins would not occur. (*Embryo* can refer to the developing baby at two to three weeks after fertilization or more loosely to all the stages from zygote to fetus.) No individuality and therefore no humanness is considered to exist until it is not possible for twinning to happen. Here, the initial zygote is not human and possesses no aspect of "personhood." As stated previously, this line of reasoning fails because of the shortcoming of the twinning argument itself. Specifically, the fact that conjoined (Siamese) twins are distinct persons is undeniable; their humanity is not obviated by the fact that they share body parts.

The Neurologic View

In this view, human life begins when the brain of the fetus has developed enough to generate a recognizable pattern on an electroencephalogram (EEG). Here, it is proposed that humanness is attained when the brain has matured to the point that the appropriate neural pathways have developed.[7] This point is reached at about 26 weeks after fertilization. After this level of maturation has been achieved, the fetus is presumably able to engage in mental activity consistent with being human.

Others take a different view of neurological maturation and propose that human life begins at around 20 weeks gestation. This is the time when the thalamus, a portion of the brain that is centrally located, is formed. The thalamus is involved in processing information before the information reaches the cerebral cortex and also is a part of a complex system of neural connections that play a role in consciousness.

---

7. H.J. Morowitz and J.S. Trefil, *The Facts of Life: Science and the Abortion Controversy* (New York: Oxford University Press, 1992).

These distinctions are arbitrary. The developing brain does display some electrical activity before the 26-week mark. It could just as easily be argued that any brain activity would constitute humanness.

The Ecological View

Proponents of the ecological view hold that the fetus is human when it reaches a level of maturation when it can exist outside the mother's womb.[8] In other words, a fetus is human when it can live separated from its mother. Here the limiting factor is usually not neurological development, but rather the degree of maturation of the lungs.

This view of humanness presents a very interesting problem. The problem is that, over the last century, we have been becoming human earlier and earlier. Here the issue is not the actual stage of development of the fetus. The limiting factor rather is the current state of medical technology. For example, some 20 years ago the age of viability of a prematurely born fetus was about 28 weeks; today it is around 24 weeks. Thus, in this view, man himself, through his advances in technology, can grant humanness where it did not previously exist!

The Birthday View

Some hold the position that human life begins only at the point when the baby is born. Here the baby is human when the umbilical cord is cut, and the child survives based on the adequate functioning of its own lungs, circulatory system, etc.

The shortcoming of this reasoning is that even after birth, the child is not truly independent of its mother. Without care from someone, an infant would die very shortly after birth. This supposed "independence" is very much an arbitrary concept.

Other Views

There are still other points of view as to the question of when human life begins. Some suggest that a fetus is human when the mother can feel it move in the womb. Others say that humanness begins when the child takes its first breath on its own. Francis Crick, one of the co-discoverers of the structure of DNA, says that a child should not be declared "human" until three days after birth.[9]

---

8. Scott Gilbert, "When Does Human Life Begin?" Developmental Biology 8e Online, www.8e.devbio.com/article.php?ch=21&id=7.
9. Mark Blocher, *Vital Signs* (Chicago, IL: Moody Press, 1992), p. 91.

There are clearly significant differences in the way that the scientific community views the beginning of life. There is no obvious consensus among scientists about when human life begins. So, can science really help us answer this question? Perhaps science, by its nature, is not capable of dealing directly with this problem. Scott Gilbert, PhD, professor of biology at Swarthmore College, notes, "If one does not believe in a 'soul,' then one need not believe in a moment of ensoulment. The moments of fertilization, gastrulation, neurulation, and birth, are then milestones in the gradual acquisition of what it is to be human. While one may have a particular belief in when the embryo becomes human, it is difficult to justify such a belief solely by science."[10]

If Not Science, Then What?

If science cannot give us the answer, then is there another place we can turn? As Christians, we should turn to the Bible, God's Word, to see if there is a solution to this dilemma.

Psalm 139:13–16

Perhaps the most often quoted portion of Scripture on this subject is Psalm 139:13–16.

> For You formed my inward parts:
> You covered me in my mother's womb.
> I will praise You, for I am fearfully and wonderfully made;
> Marvelous are Your works,
> And that my soul knows very well.
> My frame was not hidden from You,
> When I was made in secret,
> And skillfully wrought in the lowest parts of the earth.
> Your eyes saw my substance, being yet unformed.
> And in Your book they all were written,
> The days fashioned for me,
> When as yet there were none of them.

Here we read about God knowing the Psalmist while he was "yet unformed," while he was being "made in secret," in a place invisible to human eyes. The uses of the personal pronouns in these verses indicate that there was, indeed, a person present before birth. R.C. Sproul notes, "Scripture does assume a continuity of life from before the time of birth to after the time of

---

10. Gilbert, "When Does Human Life Begin?"

birth. The same language and the same personal pronouns are used indiscriminately for both stages."[11]

Jeremiah 1:4–5

> Then the word of the LORD came to me, saying:
> "Before I formed you in the womb I knew you;
> Before you were born I sanctified you;
> I ordained you a prophet to the nations."

Here God tells Jeremiah that he was set apart before he was born. This would indicate that there was personhood present before Jeremiah's birth. The verse even indicates that God considered Jeremiah a person and that he was known before he was formed. Sproul indicates, "Even those who do not agree that life begins before birth grant that there is continuity between a child that is conceived and a child that is born. Every child has a past before birth. The issue is this: Was that past personal, or was it impersonal with personhood beginning only at birth?"[12]

Psalm 51:5

This verse is frequently used to make the case for human life beginning at conception. It reads:

> Behold, I was brought forth in iniquity,
> And in sin my mother conceived me.

The most often heard interpretation of this passage is that the author, David, sees that he was sinful even at the time he was conceived. If he was not a person, then it follows that he could not have a sinful human nature at that time. A prehuman mass of cells could not have any basis for morality. Only the "humanness" occurring at the time of conception would allow David to possess a sinful nature at that time.

Life before Birth

These Scriptures reveal that there is personhood before birth. The personal nature of the references in the Bible shows how God views the unborn child. Another text frequently used to prove the humanness of the fetus is found in the first chapter of Luke:

---

11. R.C. Sproul, *Abortion: A Rational Look at an Emotional Issue* (Colorado Springs, CO: NavPress, 1990), p. 53–54.
12. Ibid., p. 55.

Now Mary arose in those days and went into the hill country with haste, to a city of Judah, and entered the house of Zacharias and greeted Elizabeth. And it happened, when Elizabeth heard the greeting of Mary, that the babe leaped in her womb; and Elizabeth was filled with the Holy Spirit. Then she spoke out with a loud voice and said, "Blessed are you among women, and blessed is the fruit of your womb! But why is this granted to me, that the mother of my Lord should come to me? For indeed, as soon as the voice of your greeting sounded in my ears, the babe leaped in my womb for joy" (Luke 1:39-44).

We read in this passage of a meeting between Mary the mother of Jesus and Elizabeth, her cousin, the mother of John the Baptist. Here Elizabeth describes the life in her womb as "the babe." God's inspired Word reports Elizabeth's assessment that John "leaped" in the womb because of the presence of Jesus. Some try to discount this episode as a miracle, claiming it does not relate to the personhood of the unborn. Nonetheless, God's Word describes this unborn child as capable of exhibiting joy in the presence of his Savior.

Are the Unborn of Less Worth?

Exodus 21 has been put forth by some to suggest the God himself holds that the life of an unborn is less valuable than the life of an adult.

If men fight, and hurt a woman with child, so that she gives birth prematurely, yet no harm follows, he shall surely be punished accordingly as the woman's husband imposes on him; and he shall pay as the judges *determine*. But if *any* harm follows, then you shall give life for life, eye for eye, tooth for tooth, hand for hand, foot for foot . . . (Exodus 21:22–24).

This verse gives directions for dealing with a situation in which two men are fighting and they accidentally harm a pregnant woman. Two circumstances are noted here. The first situation is when the woman gives birth prematurely and "no harm follows." The common interpretation states that here the child is lost due to a premature birth, and the woman herself does not suffer a serious injury. Here the penalty is a fine of some type to compensate for the loss of the child.

The second circumstance is "if any harm follows." Here the common interpretation is that is the woman gives birth prematurely, the child dies, and the woman herself dies. Here the penalty is life for life. It is argued that since there is only a fine imposed in the first circumstance for the loss of only the premature child while the death penalty is imposed for the loss of the mother, the unborn is less valuable than an adult. Thus, the unborn need not be considered to have achieved full humanness before birth.

However, upon closer examination, this type of interpretation may not be valid. The "harm" indicated in these verses may refer to the child and not to the mother. In the first circumstance, the injured mother gives birth prematurely and no "harm" comes to the child. In other words, the premature child lives. Thus, a fine is levied for causing the premature birth and the potential danger involved. In the second situation, there is a premature birth and the "harm" that follows is the death of the child. Here the penalty is life for life. Therefore, the Bible does not hold that the life of the unborn is less valuable than the life of an adult.

John Frame, in the book *Medical Ethics,* says this, "There is *nothing* in Scripture that even remotely suggests that the unborn child is anything less *than a human person from the moment of conception*"[13] (emphasis his). Here, conception is meant to imply the time of fertilization.

So Where Are We?

A purely scientific examination of human development from the moment of fertilization until birth provides no experimental method that can gauge humanness. Stages of maturation have been described and cataloged. Chemical processes and changes in size and shape have been analyzed. Electrical activity has been monitored. However, even with this vast amount of knowledge, there is no consensus among scientists as to where along this marvelous chain of events an embryo (or zygote or fetus or baby, depending upon who is being asked) becomes human.

Science has, however, revealed the intricate developmental continuum from fertilization, through maturation, to the birth of the child. Each stage flows seamlessly into the next with a myriad of detailed embryological changes followed by organ growth and finely tuned development choreographed with precision. The more we learn about the process, the more amazingly complex we find it to be.

Life Begins at Conception

Although science has shown us the wonderful continuity of the development of life throughout all its stages, science has been unable to define the

13. John Frame, *Medical Ethics* (Phillipsburg, NJ: Presbyterian and Reformed Publishing Company, 1988), p. 95.

onset of humanness. However, there is ample information in Scripture for us to determine the answer to this problem.

The Bible contains numerous references to the unborn.[14] Each time the Bible speaks of the unborn, there is reference to an actual person, a living human being already in existence. These Scriptures, taken in context, all indicate that God considers the unborn to be people. The language of the text continually describes them in personal terms.

Since the Bible treats those persons yet unborn as real persons, and since the development of a person is a continuum with a definite beginning at the moment of fertilization, the logical point at which a person begins to be human is at that beginning. The answer is that life begins at conception (using the now older definition of the term, here to be synonymous with fertilization). Frankly, no other conclusion is possible from Scripture or science.

What are the implications of this conclusion? Why is this important? Quite simply, the status of the zygote/embryo/fetus is central to many issues facing our society. The most obvious issue in this regard is abortion. If the zygote is a human life, then abortion is murder. The same can be said of issues surrounding the embryonic stem cell debate. If the embryo is human, then destroying it is murder, no matter what supposedly altruistic reason is given as justification. The ethics of cloning require consideration of the concept of humanness and the timing of its onset. A person's acceptance or rejection of the controversial morning after pill is based upon the determination of when human life begins.[15]

Complex issues may not have simple solutions, but when examined objectively in light of God's Word, without biases introduced by other motivations, God's truth will reveal the correct answers. Science can give us better understanding of the world God created, and what we see in God's world will agree with the truth we read in God's Word. We dare not play word games with human life to justify personal agendas. Scripture provides no real loopholes or escape clauses to excuse us from the principle that God created human beings in His own image, designed them to reproduce after their kind, and sent Jesus Christ into the world as a human being to die for us all, thus demonstrating the inestimable love our Creator has for each human life.

---

14. See also Genesis 25:21–23; Isaiah 45.
15. David Menton, "Plan B: Over-the-Counter Abortion?" Answers in Genesis, www.answersingenesis.org/articles/am/v2/n1/plan-b.

30

Do Creationists Believe in "Weird" Physics like Relativity, Quantum Mechanics, and String Theory?

DR. DANNY FAULKNER

Science is the study of the natural world using the five senses. Because people use their senses every day, people have always done some sort of science. However, good science requires a systematic approach. While ancient Greek science did rely upon some empirical evidence, it was heavily dominated by deductive reasoning. Science as we know it began in the 17th century. The father of the scientific method is Sir Francis Bacon (1561–1626), who clearly defined the scientific method in his *Novum Organum* (1620). Bacon also introduced inductive reasoning, which is the foundation of the scientific method.

The first step in the scientific method is to define clearly a problem or question about how some aspect of the natural world operates. Some preliminary investigation of the problem can lead one to form a *hypothesis*. A hypothesis is an educated guess about an underlying principle that will explain the phenomenon that we are trying to explain. A good hypothesis can be tested. That is, a hypothesis ought to make predictions about certain observable phenomena, and we can devise an experiment or observation to test those predictions. If we conduct the experiment or observation and find that the predictions match the results, then we say that we have confirmed our hypothesis, and we have some confidence that our hypothesis is correct. On the other hand, if our predictions are not borne out, then we say that our hypothesis is disproved, and we can either alter our hypothesis or develop a new one and repeat the process of testing. After repeated testing with positive results, we say that the hypothesis is confirmed, and we have confidence that our hypothesis is correct.

Notice that we did not "prove" the hypothesis, but that we merely confirmed it. This is a big difference between deductive and inductive reasoning. If we have a true premise, then properly applied deductive reasoning will lead to a true conclusion. However, properly applied inductive reasoning does not necessarily lead to a true conclusion. How can this be? Our hypothesis may be one of several different hypotheses that produce the same experimental or observational results. It is very easy to assume that our hypothesis, when confirmed, is the end of the matter. However, our hypothesis may make other predictions that future, different tests may not confirm. If this happens, then we must further modify or abandon our hypothesis to explain the new data. The history of science is filled with examples of this process, and we ought to expect that this will continue.

This puts the scientist in a peculiar position. While we can definitely disprove a number of propositions, we can never be entirely sure that what we believe to be true is indeed true. Thus, science is a very changing thing. History shows that scientific "truth" changes over time. The uncertainty is the reason why continued testing of our ideas is so important in science. Once we test a hypothesis many times, we gain enough confidence that it is correct, and we eventually begin to call our hypothesis a *theory*. So a theory is a grown-up, well-developed hypothesis.

At one time, scientists conferred the title of *law* to well-established theories. This use of the word "law" probably stemmed from the idea that God had imposed some order (law) onto the universe, and our description of how the world operates is a statement of this fact. However, with a less Christian understanding of the world, scientists have departed from using the word *law*. Scientists continue to refer to older ideas, such as Newton's law of gravity or laws of motion as law, but no one has termed any new ideas in science as law for a very long time.

In 1687, Sir Isaac Newton (1643–1727) published his *Principia*, which detailed work that he had done about two decades earlier. In the *Principia*, Newton presented his law of gravity and laws of motion, which are the foundation of the branch of physics known as mechanics. Because he required a mathematical framework to present his ideas, Newton invented calculus. His great breakthrough was to hypothesize that the force that held us to the earth was the same force that kept the moon orbiting around the earth each month. From knowledge of the moon's distance from the earth and orbital period, Newton used his laws of motion to conclude that the moon is accelerated toward the earth 1/3600 of the measured acceleration of gravity at the surface of the earth. The fact that we on the earth's surface are 60 times closer to the earth's center than the moon allowed Newton to devise his inverse square law for gravity ($60^2 = 3,600$).

This unity of gravity on the earth and the force between the earth and moon was a good hypothesis, but could Newton test it? Yes. When Newton applied his laws of gravity and motion to the then-known planets orbiting the sun (Mercury, Venus, Earth, Mars, Jupiter, and Saturn), he was able to predict several things:

Isaac Newton (1643–1727)

1. The planets orbit the sun in elliptical orbits with the sun at one focus of the ellipses.

2. The line between the sun and a planet sweeps out equal areas in equal intervals of time.

3. The square of a planet's orbital period is proportional to the third power of the planet's mean distance from the sun.

These three statements are known as Kepler's three laws of planetary motion, because the German mathematician Johannes Kepler (1571–1630) had found them in a slightly different form several decades before Newton. Kepler empirically found his three laws by studying data on planetary motions taken by the Danish astronomer Tycho Brahe (1546–1601) over a period of 20 years in the latter part of the 16th century. Kepler arrived at his result by laborious trial and error for over two decades, but he had no explanation of why the planets behaved the way that they did. Newton easily showed (or predicted) that the planets must follow Kepler's law as a consequence of his law of gravity.

Johannes Kepler (1571–1630)

Many other predictions of Newton's new physics followed. Besides Earth, Jupiter and Saturn had satellites that obeyed Newton's formulation of Kepler's three laws. Newton's good friend who privately funded the publication of the *Principia*, Sir Edmond Halley (1656–1742), applied Newton's work to the observed motions of comets. He found that comets also followed the laws, but that their orbits were much more elliptical and inclined than the orbits of planets. In his study, Halley noticed that one comet that he observed had an orbit identical to one seen about 75 years before and that both comets had a 75-year orbital period. Of course, when the comet returned once again, Halley was long dead, but this comet bears his name.

In 1704, Newton first published his other seminal work in physics, *Optics*. In this book, he presented his theory of the wave nature of light. Together, his *Principia* and *Optics* laid the foundation of physics as we know it. Over the next two centuries, scientists applied Newtonian physics to all sorts of situations, and in each case the predictions of the theory were borne out by experiment and observation. For instance, William Herschel stumbled upon the planet Uranus in 1781, and its orbit followed Kepler's three laws as well. However, by 1840, astronomers found that there were slight discrepancies between the predicted and observed motion of Uranus. Two mathematicians independently hypothesized that there was an additional planet beyond Uranus whose gravity was tugging on Uranus. This led to the discovery of Neptune in 1846. These successes gave scientists a tremendous confidence in Newtonian physics, and thus Newtonian physics is one of the most well-established theories in history. However, by the end of the 19th century, experimental results began to conflict with Newtonian physics.

Quantum Mechanics

Near the end of the 19th century, physicists turned their attention to how hot objects radiate, with one practical application being the improvement of efficiency of the filament of the recently invented light bulb. Noting that at low temperatures good absorbers and emitters of radiation appear black, they dubbed a perfect absorber and emitter of radiation a *black body*. Physicists experimentally determined that a black body of a certain temperature emitted the greatest amount of energy at a certain frequency and that the amount of energy that it radiated diminished toward zero at higher and lower frequencies. Attempts to explain this behavior with classical, or Newtonian, physics worked very well at most frequencies but failed miserably at higher frequencies. In fact, at very high frequencies, classical physics required that the energy emitted increase toward infinity.

In 1901, the German physicist Max Planck (1858–1947) proposed a solution. He suggested that the energy radiated from a black body was not exactly in waves as Newton had shown, but was instead carried away by tiny particles (later called photons). The energy of each photon was proportional to its frequency. This was a radical departure from classical physics, but this new theory did exactly explain the spectra of black bodies.

In 1905, the German-born physicist Albert Einstein (1879–1955) used Planck's theory to explain the photoelectric effect. What is the photoelectric effect? A few years earlier, physicists had discovered that when light shone on a metal to which an electric potential was applied, electrons were emitted. Attempts to explain the details of this phenomenon with classical physics had failed, but Einstein's application of Planck's theory explained it very well.

Max Planck (1858–1947)

Other problems with classical physics had mounted. Physicists found that excited gas in a discharge tube emitted energy at certain discrete wavelengths or frequencies. The exact wavelengths of emission depended upon the composition of the gas, with hydrogen gas having the simplest spectrum. Several physicists investigated the problem, with the Swedish scientist Johannes Rydberg (1854–1919) offering the most general description of the hydrogen spectrum in 1888. However, Ryberg did not offer a physical explanation. Indeed, there was no classical physics explanation for the spectral behavior of hydrogen gas until 1913, when the Danish physicist Niels Bohr (1885–1962) published his model of the hydrogen atom that did explain hydrogen's spectrum.

In the Bohr model, the electron orbits the proton only at certain discrete distances from the proton, whereas in classical physics the electron can orbit at any distance from the proton. In classical physics the electron must continually emit radiation as it orbits, but in Bohr's model the electron emits energy only when it leaps from one possible orbit to another. Bohr's explanation of the hydrogen atom worked so well that scientists assumed that it must work for other atoms as well. The hydrogen atom is very simple, because it consists of only two particles, a proton and an electron. Other atoms have increasing numbers of particles (more electrons orbiting the nucleus, which contains more protons as well as neutrons) which makes their solutions much more difficult, but the Bohr model worked for them as well. The Bohr model is essentially the model that most of us learned in school.

While Bohr's model was obviously successful, it seemed to pull some new principles out of the air, and those principles contradicted principles of classical physics. Physicists began to search for a set of underlying unifying principles to explain the model and other aspects of the emerging new physics. We will omit the details, but by the mid-1920s, those new principles were in place. The basis of this new physics is that in very small systems, as within atoms, energy can exist in only certain small, discrete amounts with gaps between adjacent values. This is radically different from classical physics, where energy can assume any value. We say that energy is quantized because it can have only certain discrete values, or quanta. The mathematical theory that explains the energies of small systems is called quantum mechanics.

Quantum mechanics is a very successful theory. Since its introduction in the 1920s, physicists have used it to correctly predict the behavior and characteristics of elementary particles, nuclei of atoms, atoms, and molecules. Many facets of modern electronics are best understood in terms of quantum mechanics. Physicists have developed many details and applications of the theory, and they have built other theories upon it.

Quantum mechanics is a very successful theory, yet a few people do not accept it. Why? There are several reasons. One reason for rejection is that the postulates of quantum mechanics just do not feel right. They violate our everyday understanding of how the physical world works. However, the problem is that very small particles, such as electrons, do not behave the same way that everyday objects do. We invented quantum mechanics to explain small things such as electrons because our everyday understanding of the world fails to explain them. The peculiarities of quantum mechanics disappear as we apply quantum mechanics to larger systems. As we increase the size and scope of small systems, we find that the oddities of quantum mechanics tend to smear out and assume properties more like our common-sense perceptions. That is, the peculiarities of quantum mechanics disappear in larger, macroscopic systems.

Another problem that people have with quantum mechanics is certain interpretations applied to quantum mechanics. For instance, one of the important postulates of quantum mechanics is the Schrödinger wave equation. When we apply the Schrödinger equation to a particle such as an electron, we get a mathematical wave as a description of the particle. What does this wave mean? Early on, physicists realized that the wave represented a probability distribution. Where the wave had a large value, the probability was large of finding the particle in that location, but where the wave had low value, there was little probability of finding the particle there. This is strange. Newtonian physics had led to determinism — the absolute knowledge of where a particle was at a particular time from the forces and other information involved. Yet, the probability function does accurately predict the behavior of small particles such as electrons. Even Albert Einstein, whose early work led to much of quantum mechanics, never liked this probability. He once famously remarked, "God does not play dice with the universe." Erwin Schrödinger (1887–1961), who had formulated his famous Schrödinger equation stated in 1926, "If we are going to stick to this ****** quantum-jumping, then I regret that I ever had anything to do with quantum theory."

Note that with the probability distribution we cannot know precisely where a particle is located. A statement of this is the Heisenberg Uncertainty Principle (named for Werner Heisenberg, 1901–1976). We explain this by acknowledging that particles such as electrons have a wave nature as well as a particle nature. For that matter, we also believe that waves (such as light and sound) also have a particle nature. This wave-particle duality is a bit strange to us, because we do not sense it in everyday experience, but it is borne out by numerous experimental results.

For instance, let us consider a double slit experiment. If we send a wave toward an obstruction with two slits in it, the wave will pass through both slits and produce a distinctive interference pattern behind the slits. This is because the wave passes through both slits. If we send a large number of electrons toward a similar apparatus, the electrons will also produce an interference pattern behind the slits, suggesting that the electrons (or their wave functions) went through both slits. However, if we send one electron at a time toward the slits and look for the emergence of each electron behind the slits, we will find that each electron will emerge through one slit or the other, but not both. How can this be? Indeed, this is perplexing. The most common resolution is the Copenhagen interpretation, named for the city where it was developed. This interpretation posits that an individual electron does not go through either slit, but instead exists in some sort of meta-stable state between the two states until we observe (detect) the electrons. At the point of observation, the electron's wave equation collapses, allowing the electron to assume one state or the other. Now, this is weird, but most alternate explanations are even weirder, so you might understand why some people may have a problem with quantum mechanics.

Is there a way out of this dilemma? Yes. Why do we need an interpretation to quantum mechanics? No one demanded any such interpretation of Newtonian physics. No one asked, "What does it mean?" There is no meaning, other than the fact that Newtonian physics does a good job of describing what we see in the macroscopic world. The same ought to be true for quantum mechanics. It does a good job of describing the microscopic world. Whereas classical physics introduced determinism, quantum mechanics introduced indeterminism. This indeterminism is fundamental in the sense that uncertainty in outcome will still exist even if we have all knowledge of the relevant input parameters. Newtonian determinism fit well with the concept of God's sovereignty, but the fundamental uncertainty of quantum mechanics appears to rob God of that attribute. However, this assumes that quantum mechanics is a complete theory, that is, that quantum mechanics is an ultimate theory. There are limits to the applications of quantum mechanics, such as the fact that there is no theory of quantum gravity. If the history of science is any teacher, we can expect that quantum mechanics will one day be replaced by some other theory. This other theory probably will include quantum mechanics as a special case of the better theory. That theory may clear up the uncertainty question.

As an aside, we perhaps ought to mention that the determinism derived from Newtonian physics also produces a conclusion unpalatable to many Christians. If determinism is true, then all future events are predetermined from the initial conditions of the universe. Just as the Copenhagen interpretation of quantum mechanics led to even God not being able to know the outcome of an experiment, many people applying determinism concluded that God was unable to alter the outcome of an experiment. That is, God was bound by the physics that rules the universe. This quickly led to deism. Most, if not all, people today who reject quantum mechanics refuse to accept this extreme interpretation of Newtonian physics. They ought to recognize that just as determinism is a perversion of Newtonian physics, the Copenhagen interpretation is a perversion of quantum mechanics.

The important point is that just as classical mechanics does a good job in describing the macroscopic world, quantum mechanics does a good job in describing the microscopic world. We ought not expect any more of a theory. Consequently, most physicists who believe the biblical account of creation have no problem with quantum mechanics.

Relativity

There are two theories of relativity, the special and general theories. We will briefly describe the special theory of relativity first. Even before Newton, Galileo (1564–1642) had conducted experiments with moving bodies. He realized that if we move toward or away from a moving object, the relative speed that we measure for that object depends upon that object's motion and our motion. This Galilean relativity is a part of Newtonian mechanics. The same behavior is true for the speed of waves. For instance, if we ride in a boat moving through water with waves, the speed of the waves that we measure will depend upon our motion and on the motion of the waves. In 1881, Albert A. Michelson (1852–1931) conducted a famous experiment that he refined and repeated in 1887 with Edward W. Morley (1838–1923). In this experiment, they measured the speed of light parallel and perpendicular to our annual motion around the sun. Much to their surprise, they found that the speed of light was the same regardless of the direction they measured it. This null result baffled physicists, for if taken at face value, it suggested that the earth did not orbit the sun, while there is other evidence that the earth does indeed orbit the sun.

In 1905, Albert Einstein took the invariance of the speed of light as a postulate and worked out its consequences. He made three predictions concerning an object as its speed approaches the speed of light:

1. The length of the object as it passes will appear to shorten toward zero.

2. The object's mass will increase without bound.

3. The passage of time as measured by the object will approach zero.

These behaviors are strange and do not conform to what we might expect from everyday experience, but keep in mind that in everyday experience we do not encounter objects moving at any speed close to that of light.

Eventually, these predictions were confirmed in experiments. For instance, particle accelerators accelerate small particles to very high speeds. We can measure the masses of the particles as we accelerate them, and their masses increase in the manner predicted by the theory. In other experiments, very fast-moving, short-lived particles exist longer than they do when moving very slowly. The rate of time dilation is consistent with the predictions of the theory. Length contraction is a little more difficult to directly test, but we have tested it as well.

Einstein's theory of special relativity applies to particles moving at a constant rate but does not address their acceleration. Einstein addressed that problem with his general theory in 1916, but he also treated the acceleration due to gravity. In general relativity, space and time are physical things that have a structure in some ways similar to a fabric. Einstein treated time as a fourth dimension in addition to the normal three dimensions of space. We sometimes call this four-dimensional entity *space-time* or simply *space*. The presence of a large amount of matter or energy (Einstein previously had shown their equivalence) alters space. Mathematically, the alteration of space is like a curvature, so we say that matter or energy bends space. The curvature of space telegraphs the presence of matter and energy to other matter and energy in space, and this more deeply

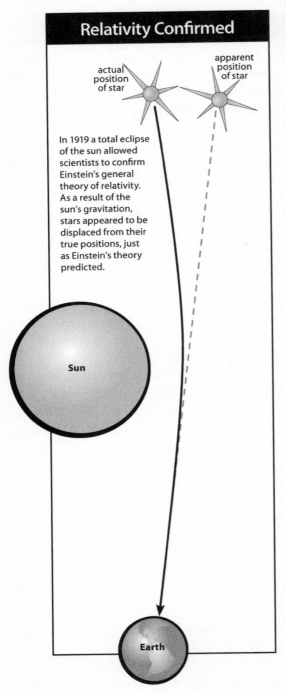

Relativity Confirmed

actual position of star

apparent position of star

In 1919 a total eclipse of the sun allowed scientists to confirm Einstein's general theory of relativity. As a result of the sun's gravitation, stars appeared to be displaced from their true positions, just as Einstein's theory predicted.

Sun

Earth

answered a question about gravity. Newton had hypothesized that gravity operated through empty space, but his theory could not explain at all how the information about an object's mass and distance was transmitted through space. In general relativity, an object must move through a straight line in space-time, but the curvature of space-time induced by nearby mass causes that straight-line motion to appear to us as acceleration.

Einstein's new theory made several predictions. The first opportunity to test the theory happened during a total solar eclipse in 1919. During the eclipse, astronomers were able to photograph stars around the edge of the sun. The light from those stars had to pass very close to the sun to get to the earth. As the stars' light passed near the sun, the sun attracted the light via the curvature of space-time. This caused the stars to appear closer to the sun than they would have otherwise. Newtonian gravity also predicts a deflection of starlight toward the sun, but the deflection is less than with general relativity. The observed amount of deflection was consistent with the predictions of general relativity. Astronomers have repeated the experiment many times since 1919 with ever-improving accuracy.

For many years, radio astronomers have measured with great precision the locations of distant-point radio sources as the sun passed by, and those results beautifully agree with the predictions. Another early confirmation was the explanation of a small anomaly in the orbit of the planet Mercury that Newtonian gravity could not explain. Many other experiments of various types have repeatedly confirmed general relativity. Some experiments today even allow us to test for slight variations of Einstein's theory.

We can apply general relativity to the universe as a whole. Indeed, when we do this, we discover that it predicts that the universe is either expanding or contracting; it is a matter of observation to determine which the universe actually is doing. In 1928, Edwin Hubble (1889–1953) showed that the universe is expanding. Most people today think that the expansion began with the big bang, the supposed sudden appearance of the universe 13.7 billion years ago. However, there are many other possibilities. For instance, the creation physicist Russell Humphreys proposed his *white hole cosmology*, assuming that general relativity is the correct theory of gravity (see his book *Starlight and Time*[1]). It is interesting to note that universal expansion is consistent with certain Old Testament passages (e.g., Psalm 104:2) that mention the stretching of the heavens.

Seeing that there is so much evidence to support Einstein's theory of general relativity, why do some creationists oppose the theory? There are at least three reasons. One reason is that, as with quantum mechanics, modern relativity theory appears to violate certain common-sense views of the way that the world works. For instance, in everyday experience, we don't see mass change and time appear to slow. Indeed, general relativity forces us to abandon the concept of simultaneity of time. *Simultaneity* means that time progresses at the same rate for all observers, regardless of where they are. As we previously stated, in special relativity, time slows with greater speed. However, with general relativity, the rate at which time passes depends not only upon speed but also on one's location in a gravitational field. The deeper one is in a gravitational field, the slower that time passes. For example, a clock at sea level will record the passage of time more slowly than a clock at mile-high Denver. Admittedly, this is weird. However, the discrepancy between the clocks at these two locations is so miniscule as to not appear on most clocks, save the most accurate atomic clocks. This sort of thing has been measured several times, and the discrepancies between the clocks involved always are the same as those predicted by theory. Thus, while our perception is that time flows uniformly everywhere, the reality is that the passage

---

1. D. Russell Humhreys, *Starlight and Time* (Green Forest, AR: Master Books, 1994).

of time does depend upon one's location, but the differences are so small in the situations encountered on the earth that we cannot perceive them. That is, the predictions of general relativity on earth are consistent with our ability to perceive time. However, there are conditions beyond the earth that the loss of simultaneity would be very obvious if we could experience them.

A second reason why some creationists oppose modern relativity theory is the misappropriation of modern relativity theory to support moral relativism. Unfortunately, modern relativity theory arose at precisely the time that moral relativism became popular. Moral relativists proclaim that "all things are equal," and they were very eager to snatch some of the triumph of relativity theory to support their cause. There are at least two problems with this misappropriation. First, it does not follow that a principle that works in the natural world automatically operates in the world of morality. The physical world is material, but the world of morality is immaterial. Second, the moral relativists either did not understand relativity or they intentionally misused it. Despite the common misconception, modern relativity theory does not tell us that everything is relative. There are absolutes in modern theory of relativity. The speed of light is a constant. While the passage of time may vary, general relativity provides an absolute way in which to compare the passage of time in two reference frames. The modern theory of relativity in no way supports moral relativism.

The third reason why some creationists reject modern relativity theory is that they think that general relativity inevitably leads to the big-bang model. However, the big-bang model is just one possible origin scenario for the universe; there are many other possibilities. We have already mentioned Russ Humphreys's white hole cosmology, and there are other possible recent creation models based upon general relativity. True — if general relativity is not correct, then the big-bang model would be in trouble. However, if general relativity is correct, then the shortcut attempt to undermine the big-bang model will doom us from ever finding the correct cosmology.

String Theory

With the establishment of quantum mechanics in the 1920s, the development of the science of particle physics soon followed. At first, only a few particles were known: the electron, proton, and neutron. These particles all had mass and were thought at the time to be the fundamental building blocks of matter. Quantum mechanics introduced the concept that material particles could be described by waves, and conversely that waves could be described by particles. That led to the concept of particles that had no mass, such as photons, the particles that make up light. Eventually, physicists saw the need for other particles, such as neutrinos and antiparticles. Evidence for these odd particles soon followed. Experimental results suggested the existence of other particles, such as the meson, muon, and tau particles, as well as their antiparticles. Many of these new particles were very short-lived, but they were particles nevertheless.

Physicists began to see patterns in the growing zoo of particles. They could group particles according to certain properties. For instance, elementary particles possess angular momentum, a property normally associated with spinning objects, so physicists say that elementary particles have "spin." Imagining elementary particles as small spinning spheres is useful, but modern theories view this as a bit naive. Spin comes in a quantum amount. Some particles have whole integer values of quantum spin. That is, they have integer multiples ($0, \pm1, \pm2$, etc.) of the basic unit of spin. Physicists call these particles Bosons. Other particles have half integer ($\pm1/2, \pm3/2$, etc.) amounts of spin, and are known as fermions. Bosons and fermions have very different properties. Physicists also noticed that elementary particles tended to have certain mathematical relationships between one another. Physicists eventually began to use group theory, a concept from abstract algebra, to classify and study elementary particles.

By the 1960s, physicists began to suspect that many elementary particles, such as protons and neutrons, were not so elementary after all, but consisted of even more elementary particles. Physicists called these more elementary particles *quarks*, after an enigmatic word in a James Joyce poem. According to the theory, there are six types of quarks. Many particles, such as protons and neutrons, consist of the combination of two quarks. The different combinations of quarks lead to different particles. Some of those combinations of quarks ought to produce particles that no one had yet seen, so these combinations amounted to predictions of new particles. Particles physicists were able to create these particles in experiments in particle accelerators, so the successful search for those predicted particles was confirmation of the underlying theory. Therefore, quark theory now is well established.

In recent years, particle physicists have in similar fashion developed string theory. Physicists have noticed that certain patterns among elementary particles can be explained easily if particles behave as tiny vibrating strings. These strings would require the existence of at least six additional dimensions of space. We already know that the universe has three normal spatial dimensions as well as the dimension of time, so these six extra dimensions bring the total number of dimensions to ten. The reason why we do not normally see the other six dimensions is that they are tightly curled up and hidden within the tiny particles themselves. At extremely high energies, the extra dimensions ought to manifest themselves. Therefore, particle physicists can predict what kind of behavior

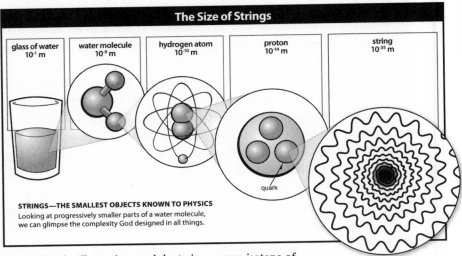

The Size of Strings

| glass of water 10^{-1} m | water molecule 10^{-9} m | hydrogen atom 10^{-10} m | proton 10^{-14} m | string 10^{-35} m |

quark

STRINGS—THE SMALLEST OBJECTS KNOWN TO PHYSICS
Looking at progressively smaller parts of a water molecule, we can glimpse the complexity God designed in all things.

We realize the illustration used deuterium, a rare isotope of hydrogen, to help convey the point.

strings ought to exhibit when they accelerate particles to extremely high energies. The problem is that current particle accelerators are not nearly powerful enough to produce these effects. As theoretical physicists refine their theories and we build new, powerful particle accelerators, physicists expect that one day we can test whether string theory is true, but for now there is no experimental evidence for string theory.

Currently, most physicists think that string theory is a very promising idea. Assuming that string theory is true, there still remains the question as to which particular version of string theory is the correct one. You see, string theory is not a single theory but instead is a broad outline of a number of possible theories. Once we confirm string theory, we can constrain which version properly describes our world. If true, string theory could lead to new technologies. Furthermore, a proper view of elementary particles is important in many cosmological models, such as the big bang. This is because in the big-bang model, the early universe was hot enough to reveal the effects of string theory.

Conclusion

Modern physics is a product of the 20th century and relies upon twin pillars: quantum mechanics and general relativity. Both theories have tremendous experimental support. Christians ought not to view these theories with such great suspicion. True, some people have perverted or hijacked these theories to support some nonbiblical principles, but some wicked people have even perverted Scripture to support nonbiblical things. We ought to recognize that modern physics is a very robust, powerful theory that explains much. At the same time, the theory is very incomplete in some respects. In time, we ought to expect that some new theories will come along that will better explain the world than these theories do. However, we know that God's Word does not change.

String theory has emerged in the 21st century as the next great idea in physics. Time will tell if string theory will live up to our expectations. What ought to be the reaction of Christians to this? We must be vigilant to investigate the amount of nonbiblical influences that may have crept into modern thinking, particularly in the interpretation of string theory (as with modern physics). However, we must be careful not to throw out the baby with the bath water. That is, can we reject the anti-Christian thinking that many have brought to the discussion? The answer is certainly yes. As with the question of origins, we must strive to interpret these things on our terms, guided by the Bible. Do the new theories adequately describe the world? Can we see the hand of the Creator in our new physics? Can we find meaning in our studies that brings glory to God? If we can answer yes to each of these questions, then these new theories ought not to be a problem for the Christian.

31

Doesn't the Order of Fossils in the Rock Record Favor Long Ages?

DR. ANDREW A. SNELLING

ossils are the remains, traces, or imprints of plants or animals that have been preserved in the earth's near-surface rock layers at some time in the past.[1] In other words, fossils are the remains of *dead* animals and plants that were buried in sedimentary layers that later hardened to rock strata. So the fossil record is hardly "the record of life in the geologic past" that so many scientists incorrectly espouse,[2] assuming a long prehistory for the earth and life on it. Instead, it is a record of the *deaths* of countless billions of animals and plants.

The Fossil Record

For many people, the fossil record is still believed to be "exhibit A" for evolution. Why? Because most geologists insist the sedimentary rock layers were deposited gradually over vast eons of time during which animals lived, died, and then were occasionally buried and fossilized. So when these fossilized animals (and plants) are found in the earth's rock sequences in a particular order

---

1. K.K.E. Neuendorf, J.P. Mehl Jr., and J.A. Jackson, eds., *Glossary of Geology* (Alexandria, VA: American Geological Institute, 2005), p. 251.
2. Ibid.

of first appearance, such as animals without backbones (invertebrates) in lower layers followed progressively upward by fish, then amphibians, reptiles, birds, and finally mammals (e.g., in the Colorado Plateau region of the United States), it is concluded, and thus almost universally taught, that this must have been the order in which these animals evolved during those vast eons of time.

However, in reality, it can only be dogmatically asserted that the fossil record is the record of the order in which animals and plants were buried and fossilized. Furthermore, the vast eons of time are unproven and unproveable, being based on assumptions about how quickly sedimentary rock layers were deposited in the unobserved past. Instead, there is overwhelming evidence that most of the sedimentary rock layers were deposited rapidly. Indeed, the impeccable state of preservation of most fossils requires the animals and plants to have been very rapidly buried, virtually alive, by vast amounts of sediments before decay could destroy delicate details of their appearance and anatomy. Thus, if most sedimentary rock layers were deposited rapidly over a radically short period of time, say in a catastrophic global flood, then the animals and plants buried and fossilized in those rock layers may well have all lived at about the same time and then have been rapidly buried progressively and sequentially.

Furthermore, the one thing we can be absolutely certain of is that when we find animals and plants fossilized together, they didn't necessarily live together in the same environment or even die together, but they certainly were buried together, because that's how we observe them today! This observational certainty is crucial to our understanding of the many claimed mass extinction events in the fossil record. Nevertheless, there is also evidence in some instances that the fossils found buried together may represent animals and plants that did once live together (see later).

Mass Extinctions

In the present world, when all remaining living members of a particular type of animal die, that animal (or plant) is said to have become extinct. Most scientists (incorrectly) regard the fossil record as a record of life in the geologic past. So, when in the upward progression of strata the fossils of a particular type of animal or plant stop occurring in the record and there are no more fossils of that animal or plant in the strata above, or any living representatives of that animal or plant, most scientists say that this particular creature went extinct many years ago. Sadly, there are many animals and plants that are extinct, and we only know they once existed because of their fossilized remains in the geologic record. Perhaps the most obvious and famous example is the dinosaurs.

There are distinctive levels in the fossil record where vast numbers of animals (and plants) are believed to have become extinct. Evolutionists claim that all these animals (and plants) must have died, been buried, and become extinct all at the same time. Since this pattern is seen in the geologic record all around the globe, they call these distinctive levels in the fossil record mass extinctions. Furthermore, because something must have happened globally to wipe out all those animals (and plants), the formation of these distinctive levels in the fossil record are called mass extinction events. However, in the context of catastrophic deposition of the strata containing these fossils, this pattern would be a preserved consequence of the Flood.

Now geologists have divided the geologic record into time periods, according to their belief in billions of years of elapsed time during which the sedimentary strata were deposited. Thus, those sedimentary strata that were supposedly deposited during a particular time period are so grouped and named accordingly. This is the origin of names such as Cambrian, Ordovician, Silurian, Devonian, Carboniferous, Permian, Triassic, Jurassic, Cretaceous, and more.

There are some 17 mass extinction events in the fossil record recognized by geologists, from in the late Precambrian up until the late Neogene, "just before the dawn of written human history." However, only eight of those are classed as major mass extinction events — end-Ordovician, late-Devonian, end-Permian, end-Triassic, early-Jurassic, end-Jurassic, middle-Cretaceous, and end-Cretaceous. Most people have probably heard about the end-Cretaceous mass extinction event, because that's when the dinosaurs are supposed to have been wiped out, along with about a quarter of all the known families of animals. However, the end-Permian mass extinction event was even more catastrophic, because 75 percent of amphibian families and 80 percent of reptile families were supposedly wiped out then, along with 75 to 90 percent of all pre-existing species in the oceans.

Asteroid Impacts and Volcanic Eruptions

So what caused these mass extinction events? Evolutionary geologists are still debating the answer. The popularized explanation for the end-Cretaceous mass extinction event is that an asteroid hit the earth, generating choking dust clouds and giant tsunamis (so-called tidal waves) that decimated the globe and its climate, supposedly for a few million years. A layer of clay containing a chemical signature of an asteroid is pointed to in several places around the globe as one piece of evidence, and the 124-mile (200 km) wide Chicxulub impact crater in Mexico is regarded as "the scene of the crime."

However, at the same level in the geologic record are the massive remains of catastrophic outpourings of staggering quantities of volcanic lavas over much of India, totally unlike any volcanic eruptions experienced in recent human history. The Pinatubo eruption in the Philippines in 1991 blasted enough dust into the atmosphere to circle the globe and cool the following summer by 1–2°C, as well as gases which caused acid rain. Yet that eruption was only a tiny firecracker compared to the massive, catastrophic Indian eruption. Furthermore, volcanic dust has a similar chemical signature to that of an asteroid. Interestingly, even more enormous quantities of volcanic lavas are found in Siberia and coincide with the end-Permian mass extinction event.

The Biblical Perspective

What then should Bible-believing Christians make of these interpretations of the fossil and geologic evidence? Of course, we first need to recognize that both creationists and evolutionists start with presupposed assumptions, which they then use to interpret the presently observed evidence. So this difference of interpretations cannot be "religion vs. science," as it is so often portrayed.

Furthermore, it needs to be noted that in the geologic record there are very thick sequences of rock layers, found below the main strata record containing prolific fossils, which are either totally devoid of fossils or only contain very rare fossils of microorganisms and minor invertebrates. In the biblical framework of earth history, these strata would be classified as creation week and pre-Flood. Also, a few fossils may also have been formed since the Flood due to localized, residual catastrophic depositional events, so Flood geologists do not claim all fossils were formed during the Flood.

As already noted, the only dogmatic claim which can be made is that the geologic strata record the order in which animals and plants were buried and fossilized. However, it is clear from Genesis 1–3, Romans 5:12, 8:20–22, and 1 Corinthians 15:21–22 that God created a good world which was severely marred by death as a result of Adam's sin. Because the animals were created as vegetarians (Genesis 1:29–30) and the whole creation was subsequently impacted with corruption and death due to the Fall, there could have been no animal fossils in Eden's rocks. Indeed, fossilization under present-day conditions is exceedingly rare, so evolutionary geologists applying "the present is the key to the past" have a real problem in explaining how the vast numbers of fossils in the geologic record could have formed. Thus, the global destruction of all the pre-Flood animals and plants by the year-long Flood cataclysm alone makes sense of this fossil and geologic evidence (though as noted above, a small percent of the geological and fossil evidence is from post-Flood residual catastrophism).

Indeed, not only did the animals and plants have to be buried rapidly by huge masses of water-transported sediments to be fossilized, but the general vertical order of burial is also consistent with the biblical flood. The first fossils in the record are of marine animals exclusively, and it is only higher in the strata that fossils of land animals are found, because the Flood began in the ocean basins ("the fountains of the great deep burst open") and the ocean waters then flooded over the continents. How else would there be marine fossils in sedimentary layers stretching over large areas of the continents? Added to this, "the floodgates of heaven" were simultaneously opened, and both volcanism and earth movements accompanied these upheavals.

In a global watery cataclysm, therefore, there would be simultaneous wholesale destruction of animals and plants across the globe. The tearing apart of the earth's crust would release stupendous outpourings of volcanic lavas on the continental scale found in the geologic record. The resultant "waves" of destruction are thus easily misinterpreted as mass extinction events, when these were just stages of the single, year-long, catastrophic global flood.

It is also significant that some fossilized animals and plants once thought to be extinct have in fact been found still alive, thus demonstrating the total unreliability of the evolutionary time scale. The last fossilized coelacanth (a fish) is supposedly 65 million years old, but coelacanths are still here, so where did they "hide" for 65 million years? The Wollemi pine's last fossil is supposedly 150 million years old, but identical living trees were found in 1994. The recent burial and fossilization of these animals and plants, and the extinction of many other animals and plants, during the single biblical flood thus makes better sense of all the fossil and geologic evidence.

Accounting for the Order of Fossils in the Rock Record

Even though the order of strata and the fossils contained in them (sometimes extrapolated and interpolated) has been made the basis of the accepted millions-of-years system of geochronology and historical geology, the physical reality of the strata order and the contained fossils is generally not in dispute. Details of local strata sequences have been carefully compiled by physical observations during field work and via drill-holes. Careful correlations of strata of the same rock types have then been made between local areas and from region to region, often by physical means, so that the robustness of the overall fossil order and strata sequence of the geologic record has been clearly established.

Indeed, it is now well recognized that there are at least six thick sequences of fossil-bearing sedimentary strata, known as megasequences, which can be traced right across the North American continent and beyond to other continents.[3] Such global-scale deposition of sediment layers (e.g., chalk and coal beds) is, of course, totally inexplicable to uniformitarian (long-ages) geologists by the application of only today's slow-and-gradual geologic processes that only operate over local to regional scales. But it is powerful evidence of catastrophic deposition during the global Genesis flood. Thus, it is not the recognized order of the strata in the geologic record that is in dispute, but rather the millions-of-years interpretation for the deposition of the sedimentary strata and their contained fossils.

It is true that the complete geologic record is hardly ever, if at all, found in any one place on the earth's surface. Usually several or many of the strata in local sequences are missing compared to the overall geologic record, but usually over a given region there is more complete preservation of the record via correlation and integration. However, quite commonly there is little or no physical or physiographic evidence of the intervening period of erosion or non-deposition of the missing strata systems, suggesting that at such localities neither erosion nor deposition ever occurred there. Yet this is exactly what would be expected based on the biblical account of the Genesis flood and its implications. In some areas one sequence of sedimentary strata with their contained fossil assemblages would be deposited, and in other areas entirely different strata sequences would be deposited, depending on the source areas and directions of the water currents transporting the sediments. Some strata units would have been deposited over wider areas than others, with erosion in some areas but continuous deposition in others, even when intervening strata units were deposited elsewhere. Thus, as a result of the complex interplay of currents, waves, and transported sediments with their entombed organisms, a variety of different types of sedimentary rocks and strata sequences would have been laid down directly on the pre-Flood strata sequences and the crystalline basement that probably dates back to the creation week itself. Thus the pattern of deposition of the strata sequences and their contained fossils is entirely consistent with the strata record the Flood might be expected to have produced. In contrast, by using the present to interpret the past, evolutionary geologists have no more true scientific certainty of their version of the unobservable, unique historic events which they claim produced the geologic record.

Nevertheless, if the general order of the strata and their contained fossil assemblages is not generally in dispute, then that order in the strata sequences still must reflect the geological processes and their timing responsible for the formation of the strata and their order. If, as is assiduously maintained here, the

3. L.L. Sloss, "Sequences in the cratonic interior of North America," *Geological Society of America Bulletin* 74 (1963): 93–114.

order in the fossil record does not represent the sequence of the evolutionary development of life, then the fossil record must be explainable within the context of the tempo of geologic processes burying these organisms in the sediment layers during the global flood cataclysm. Indeed, both the order of the strata and their contained fossils could well provide us with information about the pre-Flood world, and evidence of the progress of different geological processes during the Flood event. There are a number of factors that have been suggested to explain the order in the fossil record in terms of the Flood processes, rather than over the claimed long ages.

Pre-Flood Biogeography

If we look at today's living biology, we find that across mountains such as the Sierra Nevada of California, or in a trip from the South Rim of the Grand Canyon down to the Colorado River, there are distinct plant and animal communities in different life or ecology zones that are characteristic of the climates at different elevations. Thus, we observe cacti growing in desert zones and pines growing in alpine zones rather than growing together. Therefore, just as these life/ecology zones today can be correlated globally (all deserts around the world have similar plants and animals), so too some fossil zones and fossil communities may be correlated globally within the geologic record of the Flood.

Thus it has been suggested that there could well have been distinct biological communities and ecological zones in the pre-Flood world that were spatially and geographically separated from one another and that that were then sequentially inundated, swept away, and buried as the Flood waters rose. This ecological zonation model for the order of fossils in the geologic record[4] would argue that the lower fossiliferous layers in the strata record must therefore represent the fossilization of biological communities at lower elevations and warmer climates, while higher layers in the geologic record must represent fossilization of biological communities that lived at higher elevations and thus cooler temperatures.

Based on the vertical and horizontal distribution of certain fossil assemblages in the strata record, it has been concluded that the pre-Flood biogeography consisted of distinct and unique ecosystems which were destroyed by the Flood and did not recover to become re-established in the post-Flood world of today. These include a floating-forest ecosystem consisting of unique trees called lycopods of various sizes that contained large, hollow cavities in their trunks and branches and hollow root-like rhizomes, with associated similar plants. It also includes some unique animals, mainly amphibians, that lived in these forests

---

4. H. Clark, *The New Diluvialism* (Angwin, CA: Science Publications, 1946).

that floated on the surface of the pre-Flood ocean.[5] Spatially and geographically separated and isolated from this floating-forest ecosystem were stromatolite reefs adjacent to hydrothermal springs in the shallow waters of continental shelves making up a hydrothermal-stromatolite reef ecosystem.[6]

In the warmer climates of the lowland areas of the pre-Flood land surfaces, dinosaurs lived where gymnosperm vegetation (naked seed plants) was abundant, while at high elevations inland in the hills and mountains where the climate was cooler, mammals and humans lived among vegetation dominated by angiosperms (flowering plants).[7] Thus these gymnosperm-dinosaur and angiosperm-mammal-man ecosystems (or biomes) were spatially and geographically separated from one another on the pre-Flood land surfaces. In Genesis chapter 2, the river coming out of the Garden of Eden is described as dividing into four rivers, which may imply the Garden of Eden (with its fruit trees and other angiosperms, mammals, and man) was at a high point geographically, the rivers flowing downhill to the lowland swampy plains bordering the shorelines where the gymnosperms grew and the dinosaurs lived. This would explain why we don't find human and dinosaur fossil remains together in the geologic record, dinosaurs and gymnosperms only fossilized together, and angiosperms only fossilized with mammals and man higher in the record separate from the dinosaurs and gymnosperms.

It can therefore be argued that in a very general way the order of fossil "succession" in the geologic record would reflect the successive burial of these pre-Flood biological communities as the Flood waters rose up onto the continents. The Flood began with the breaking up of the fountains of the great deep (the breaking up of the pre-Flood ocean floor), so there would have been a sudden surge of strong ocean currents and tsunamis picking up sediments from the ocean floor and moving landward that would first of all have overwhelmed the stromatolite reefs in the shallow seas fringing the shorelines. This destruction of the protected lagoons between the stromatolite reefs and the shorelines by these severe storms would have then caused the strange animals that probably were unique to these stromatolite reefs to be buried and thus preserved in the lower-most Flood strata directly overlaying the burial of the stromatolites.

5. K.P. Wise, "The Pre-Flood Floating Forest: A Study in Paleontological Pattern Recognition," in *Proceedings of the Fifth International Conference on Creationism*, ed. Robert L. Ivey, Jr., (Pittsburgh, PA: Creation Science Fellowship, 2003), p. 371–381.

6. K.P. Wise, "The Hydrothermal Biome: A Pre-Flood Environment," in *Proceedings of the Fifth International Conference on Creationism*, ed. Robert L. Ivey Jr. (Pittsburgh, PA: Creation Science Fellowship, 2003), p. 359–370.

7. K.P. Wise, *Faith, Form, and Time* (Nashville, TN: Broadman & Holman, 2002), p. 170–175.

Increasing storms, tidal surges, and tsunamis generated by earth movements, earthquakes, and volcanism on the ocean floor would have resulted in the progressive breaking up of the floating-forest ecosystem on the ocean surface, and thus huge rafts of vegetation would have been swept landward to be beached with the sediment load on the land surfaces being inundated. Thus, the floating-forest vegetation would have been buried higher in the strata record of the Flood, well above the stromatolites and the strange animals that lived with them. Only later, in the first 150 days of the Flood, as the waters rose higher across the land surface, would the gymnosperm-dinosaurs ecosystem be first swept away and buried, followed later by the angiosperm-mammal-man ecosystem that lived at higher elevations. People would have continued to move to the highest ground to escape the rising Flood waters, and so would not necessarily have been buried with the angiosperms and mammals. Thus the existence of these geographically separated distinct ecosystems in the pre-Flood world could well explain this spatial separation and order of fossilization in the geologic record of the Flood.

Early Burial of Marine Creatures

The vast majority by number of fossils preserved in the strata record of the Flood are the remains of shallow-water marine invertebrates (brachiopods, bivalves, gastropods, corals, graptolites, echinoderms, crustaceans, etc.).[8] In the lowermost fossiliferous strata (Cambrian, Ordovician, Silurian, and Devonian), the contained fossils are almost exclusively shallow-water marine invertebrates, with fish and amphibian fossils only appearing in progressively greater numbers in the higher strata.[9] The first fish fossils are found in Ordovician strata, and in Devonian strata are found amphibians and the first evidence of continental-type flora. It is not until the Carboniferous (Mississippian and Pennsylvanian) and Permian strata higher in the geologic record that the first traces of land animals are encountered.

Because the Flood began in the ocean basins with the breaking up of the fountains of the great deep, strong and destructive ocean currents were generated by the upheavals and moved swiftly landward, scouring the sediments on the ocean floor and carrying them and the organisms living in, on, and near them. These currents and sediments reached the shallower continental shelves, where the shallow-water marine invertebrates lived in all their prolific diversity.

8. K.P. Wise, quoted in J.D. Morris, *The Young Earth* (Green Forest, AR: Master Books, 1994), p. 70.
9. S.M. Stanley, *Earth and Life Through Time*, second edition (New York: W.H. Freeman and Company, 1989); R. Cowen, *History of Life*, third edition (Oxford, England: Blackwell Scientific Publications, 2000).

Unable to escape, these organisms would have been swept away and buried in the sediment layers as they were dumped where the waters crashed onto the land surfaces being progressively inundated farther inland. As well as burying these shallow-water marine invertebrates, the sediments washed shoreward from the ocean basins would have progressively buried fish, then amphibians and reptiles living in lowland, swampy habitats, before eventually sweeping away the dinosaurs and burying them next, and finally at the highest elevations destroying and burying birds, mammals, and angiosperms.

Hydrodynamic Selectivity of Moving Water

Moving water hydrodynamically selects and sorts particles of similar sizes and shapes. Together with the effect of the specific gravities of the respective organisms, this would have ensured deposition of the supposedly simple marine invertebrates in the first-deposited strata that are now deep in the geologic record of the Flood. The well-established "impact law" states that the settling velocity of large particles is independent of fluid viscosity, being directly proportional to the square root of particle diameter, directly proportional to particle sphericity, and directly proportional to the difference between particle and fluid density divided by fluid density.[10] Moving water, or moving particles in still water, exerts "drag" forces on immersed bodies which depend on the above factors. Particles in motion will tend to settle out in proportion mainly to their specific gravity (or density) and sphericity.

It is significant that the marine organisms fossilized in the earliest Flood strata, such as the trilobites, brachiopods, etc., are very "streamlined" and quite dense. The shells of these and most other marine invertebrates are largely composed of calcium carbonate, calcium phosphate, and similar minerals which are quite heavy (heavier than quartz, for example, the most common constituent of many sands and gravels). This factor alone would have exerted a highly selective sorting action, not only tending to deposit the simpler (that is, the most spherical and undifferentiated) organisms first in the sediments as they were being deposited, but also tending to segregate particles of similar sizes and shapes. These could have thus formed distinct faunal "stratigraphic horizons," with the complexity of structure of deposited organisms, even of similar kinds, increasing progressively upward in the accumulating sediments.

It is quite possible that this could have been a major process responsible for giving the fossil assemblages within the strata sequences a superficial appearance

10. W.C. Krumbein, and L.L. Sloss, *Stratigraphy and Sedimentation*, second edition (San Francisco, CA: W.H. Freeman and Company, 1963), p. 198.

of "evolution" of similar organisms in the progressive succession upward in the geologic record. Generally, the sorting action of flowing water is quite efficient, and would definitely have separated the shells and other fossils in just the fashion in which they are found, with certain fossils predominant in certain stratigraphic horizons, and the supposed complexity of such distinctive, so-called "index" fossils increasing in at least a general way in a progressive sequence upward through the strata of the geologic record of the Flood.

Of course, these very pronounced "sorting" powers of hydraulic action are really only valid generally, rather than universally. Furthermore, local variations and peculiarities of turbulence, environment, sediment composition, etc., would be expected to cause local variations in the fossil assemblages, with even occasional heterogeneous combinations of sediments and fossils of a wide variety of shapes and sizes, just as we find in the complex geological record.

In any case, it needs to be emphasized that the so-called "transitional" fossil forms that are true "intermediates" in the strata sequences between supposed ancestors and supposed descendants according to the evolutionary model are exceedingly rare, and are not found at all among the groups with the best fossil records (shallow-marine invertebrates like mollusks and brachiopods).[11] Indeed, even evolutionary researchers have found that the successive fossil assemblages in the strata record invariably only show trivial differences between fossil organisms, the different fossil groups with their distinctive body plans appearing abruptly in the record, and then essentially staying the same (stasis) in the record.[12]

Behavior and Higher Mobility of the Vertebrates

There is another reason why it is totally reasonable to expect that vertebrates would be found fossilized higher in the geologic record than the first invertebrates. Indeed, if vertebrates were to be ranked according to their likelihood of being buried early in the fossil record, then we would expect oceanic fish to be buried first, since they live at the lowest elevation.[13] However, in the ocean, the fish live in the water column and have great mobility, unlike the

11. Wise, *Faith, Form, and Time*, p. 197–199.
12. N. Eldridge and S.J. Gould, "Punctuated Equilibria: An Alternative to Phyletic Gradualism," in *Mammals in Paleobiology*, ed. T.J.M. Schopf (San Francisco, CA: Freeman, Cooper and Company, 1972), p. 82–115; S.J. Gould and N. Eldridge, "Punctuated Equilibria: The Tempo and Mode of Evolution Reconsidered," *Paleobiology* 3 (2007): 115–151; S.J. Gould and N. Eldridge, "Punctuated Equilibrium Comes of Age," *Nature* 366 (1993): 223–227.
13. L. Brand, *Faith, Reason, and Earth History* (Berrien Springs, MI: Andrews University Press, 1997), p. 282–283.

invertebrates that live on the ocean floor and have more restricted mobility, or are even attached to a substrate. Therefore, we would expect the fish to only be buried and fossilized subsequent to the first marine invertebrates.

Of course, fish would have inhabited water at all different elevations in the pre-Flood world, even up in mountain streams, as well as the lowland, swampy habitats, but their ranking is based on where the first representatives of fish are likely to be buried. Thus it is hardly surprising to find that the first vertebrates to be found in the fossil record, and then only sparingly, are in Ordovician strata. Subsequently, fish fossils are found in profusion higher up in the Devonian strata, often in great "fossil graveyards," indicating their violent burial.

A second factor in the ranking of the likelihood of vertebrates being buried is how animals would react to the Flood. The behavior of some animals is very rigid and stereotyped, so they prefer to stay where they are used to living, and thus would have had little chance of escape. Adaptable animals would have recognized something was wrong, and thus made an effort to escape. Fish are the least adaptable in their behavior, while amphibians come next, and then are followed by reptiles, birds, and lastly, the mammals.

The third factor to be considered is the mobility of land vertebrates. Once they become aware of the need to escape, how capable would they then have been of running, swimming, flying, or even riding on floating debris? Amphibians would have been the least mobile, with reptiles performing somewhat better, but not being equal to the mammals' mobility, due largely to their low metabolic rates. However, birds, with their ability to fly, would have had the best expected mobility, even being able to find temporary refuge on floating debris.

These three factors would tend to support each other. If they had worked against each other, then the order of vertebrates in the fossil record would be more difficult to explain. However, since they all do work together, it is realistic to suggest that the combination of these factors could have contributed significantly to producing the general sequence we now observe in the fossil record.

In general, therefore, the land animals and plants would be expected to have been caught somewhat later in the period of rising Flood waters and buried in the sediments in much the same order as that found in the geologic record, as conventionally depicted in the standard geologic column. Thus, generally speaking, sediment beds burying marine vertebrates would be overlain by beds containing fossilized amphibians, then beds with reptile fossils, and, finally, beds containing fossils of birds and mammals. This is essentially in the order:

1. Increasing mobility, and therefore increasing ability to postpone inundation and burial;

2. Decreasing density and other hydrodynamic factors, which would tend to promote later burial; and

3. Increasing elevation of habitat and therefore time required for the Flood waters to rise and advance to overtake them.

This order is essentially consistent with the implications of the biblical account of the Flood, and therefore it provides further circumstantial evidence of the veracity of that account. Of course, there would have been many exceptions to this expected general order, both in terms of omissions and inversions, as the water currents waxed and waned, and their directions changed due to obstacles and obstructions as the land became increasingly submerged and more and more amphibians, reptiles, and mammals were overtaken by the waters.

Other factors must have been significant in influencing the time when many groups of organisms met their demise. As the catastrophic destruction progressed, there would have been changes in the chemistry of seas and lakes from the mixing of fresh and salt water, and from contamination by leaching of other chemicals. Each species of aquatic organism would have had its own physiological tolerance to these changes. Thus, there would have been a sequence of mass mortalities of different groups as the water quality changed. Changes in the turbidity of the waters, pollution of the air by volcanic ash, and/or changes in air temperatures, would likely have had similar effects. So whereas ecological zonation of the pre-Flood world is a useful concept in explaining how the catastrophic processes during the Flood would have produced the order of fossils now seen in the geologic record, the reality was undoubtedly much more complex, due to many other factors.

Conclusions

In no sense is it necessary to capitulate to the vociferous claim that the order in the fossil record is evidence of the progressive organic evolution to today's plants and animals through various transitional intermediary stages over millions of years from common ancestors. While there are underlying thick strata sequences which are devoid of fossils and were therefore formed during creation week and the pre-Flood era, most of the fossil record is a record of death and burial of animals and plants during the Flood, as described in the biblical account, rather than being the order of a living succession that suffered the occasional mass extinction.

Asteroid impacts and volcanic eruptions accompanied other geological processes that catastrophically destroyed plants, animals, and people, and reshaped the earth's surface during the Flood event. Rather than requiring long ages, the order of fossils in the rock record can be accounted for by the year-long Flood, as a result of the pre-Flood biogeography and ecological zonation, the early burial of marine creatures, the hydrodynamic selectivity of moving water, and the behavior and higher mobility of the vertebrates. Thus, the order of the fossils in the rock record doesn't favor long ages, but is consistent with the global, catastrophic, year-long Genesis flood cataclysm, followed by localized residual catastrophism.

CONCLUSION

The Biggest Question
of All

DR. DAVID R. CRANDALL

Hopelessness Abroad

My body trembled as I watched a young student from the University of Rome take a suicide plunge from the top of the Roman Coliseum. I was only 19 years old and visiting my first foreign country. I witnessed firsthand the hopelessness of a world without the Lord Jesus Christ. That young man had asked the question "Is life worth living?" Obviously, his answer was no.

That experience changed my life. I stood on Via Cavour in Rome, Italy, and promised God that I would spend my life telling others the truth about the loving Creator God so that people all over the world could have hope. For the last 40 years I have ministered on every habitable continent and have preached in 86 countries. But to this day, the image of the student in Rome still motivates me to be involved in spreading the good news of the gospel that gives people a reason for living and a plan for life and eternity.

The Biggest Question of All

Late in His life and ministry, Jesus wanted His disciples to articulate in His presence their beliefs about Him. So He asked them the biggest question of all time: "Who do you say that I am?" (Matthew 16:15).

In this book, you have read answers to many questions. As important as these questions are, they pale in significance compared to Jesus' question. You can be wrong about your answers to many questions in this book, but you dare not be wrong about your answer to this question. You see, your answer to Jesus' question will determine your eternal fate; it will determine where you will be living 200 years from now.

A Divine Answer

The disciples were a bit stunned by the question, and only the apostle Peter attempted an answer. His answer needs to be your answer: "You are the Christ, the Son of the living God" (Matthew 16:16).

The amazing thing about this answer is that Peter did not come up with it on his own. It had come from the Heavenly Father (Matthew 16:17). God himself helped Peter mold the correct answer to this all-important question. So, when you read this answer, realize that it is a divinely given response! "You are the Christ, the Son of the living God."

Three Views of Christ

"Who do you say that I am?" Former atheist-turned-Christian C.S. Lewis tackled this question by coming up with three possible responses: Jesus Christ is the Lord (God); Jesus was a liar; or Jesus was a lunatic. As we look at the historical Jesus, we find His uniqueness in His birth (conceived by the Holy Spirit, miraculously born of a virgin), His death upon the cross, and His resurrection from the grave.

John Duncan, quoted in *Colloquia Peripatetica* (1870), put it best: "Christ either deceived mankind by conscious fraud, or He was Himself deluded and self-deceived, or He was Divine." Who do you believe Jesus Christ is?

Your Answer

This chapter is the last chapter in this book, but someday you will face the last chapter of your life. Are you prepared for "The End"? About 6,000 years ago, a young couple by the name of Adam and Eve lived in a beautiful garden that their Creator had made especially for them. They were told by the Creator that they could enjoy this home fully with one exception: they were not to eat from the tree of the knowledge of good and evil, otherwise they would die (Genesis 2:17).

Sadly, they disobeyed God, and sin and death came into the world. As a result, everyone is born in sin, and we all are under a death sentence because we sin, too (Romans 5:12). But God is a God of grace and mercy and He did the unthinkable. He took that punishment upon himself due to His love for each one of us. Jesus Christ came to earth and paid the penalty for sin. He offers himself to us as Savior (1 Corinthians 15:22).

The Bible is clear on the subject of salvation: "Whoever believes in Him [Jesus] should not perish but have eternal life" (John 3:15). As you consider the world's most important question, consider taking these action steps:

- Admit that you are a sinner (Romans 3:23; 1 John 1:8; Galatians 5:19–21).

- Repent of your sins before a Holy God and turn away from them (Mark 1:15; 2 Corinthians 7:10; Acts 20:21).

- Receive Jesus Christ as Lord of your life (John 1:12).

- Realize that eternal life is a gift from God (Romans 6:23).

- Receive God's gift by faith — by taking God at His Word (Romans 10:8–11).

- Read and believe what the Bible says: "For by grace you have been saved through faith, and that not of yourselves; it is the gift of God, not of works, lest anyone should boast" (Ephesians 2:8–9).

- Express this to God in prayer. Although there is no one prayer that should be prayed, you may want to say something like: "Dear God, thank you for sending Your Son, the Lord Jesus Christ, to pay for my sins on the cross. Thank you that He died for me. I acknowledge that I am a sinner and that I cannot save myself. I repent of my sins and I receive Your gift of salvation by faith. Thank you for loving me enough to save me. In Jesus' name, amen."

It's a Sure Thing

The Bible says "that if you confess with your mouth the Lord Jesus and believe in your heart that God has raised Him from the dead, you will be saved" (Romans 10:9).

How do you know that you are saved? The Bible says you can know! "These things I have written to you who believe in the name of the Son of God, that you may know that you have eternal life" (1 John 5:13).

Saved from Death

During the 2000 Olympic games, I had the joy of taking 65 Americans to Sydney, Australia, for personal evangelism. Because of their grandeur and beauty, the Blue Mountains outside Sydney became a magnet for the tourists. Teams from our group were sent to the mountains to talk to visitors about the Lord. Among those visitors was an Aussie from Melbourne named Paul. One of our team members engaged Paul in conversation for over 45 minutes, explaining about the God of the Bible and His love for Paul.

Paul responded with enthusiasm and prayed to receive Christ as his personal Savior. When he was asked where he was going from there, Paul shared that he had no place to go. He told us a story of family rejection and bad decisions on his part. We stood speechless as he told us that he had come to the Blue Mountains that day to commit suicide "Because no one in this world cares about me."

Once again, like in Rome, my body trembled; but this time it trembled with delight. Paul had found hope for what appeared to be a hopeless life. Paul had found love, forgiveness, and acceptance from God. Paul had found friendship from a bunch of Americans who lived halfway around the world.

Three months after his salvation on the Blue Mountains, Paul suffered insulin shock and died. But we know that Paul is in heaven with his Lord! That, my friend, is real *hope*!

The Christian's Global Assignment

If you have trusted Christ as your personal Savior from sin, God has given you a new mandate. It is called the Great Commission: "'Go therefore and make disciples of all the nations, baptizing them in the name of the Father and of the Son and of the Holy Spirit, teaching them to observe all things that I have commanded you; and lo, I am with you always, even to the end of the age.' Amen." (Matthew 28:19–20). The word translated *nations* in verse 19 in Greek is *ethnos*, which speaks to us of *all the ethnic groups* in the world. Our Lord wants us to reach all the ethnic groups in the world. He did not give us this assignment knowing it would be impossible for us to reach; rather, He gave us this assignment expecting us to fulfill it.

Reaching the World, Closing the Knowledge Gap

Answers in Genesis is called to proclaim the life-changing message of the gospel, beginning in the Book of Genesis. One of the most thrilling developments in recent years is a method of evangelism called "creation evangelism," in which the Bible is taught chronologically. People hear about a loving Creator God who made them in His image and is the Creator of the universe. This God sent His Son, Jesus, to die on a cross in Jerusalem to pay the penalty of our sins. This form of evangelism answers modern mankind's most searching questions and gives every reason for hope.

Because of our mission, AiG WorldWide is translating a massive amount of creation literature, DVDs, radio programs, and web articles into the languages of the world. After the translation teams have completed a project, we will print and distribute the material, preferably without cost, to mission field leaders all over the globe. Here are three ways we plan to carry out our vision:

- AiG libraries will provide literature for Christian Bible schools and mission organizations to give answers to the next generation of Christian leaders.

- Christian pastors and leaders will be brought to AiG for training on how they can become creation spokesmen in their own countries.

- New and innovative programs will be initiated to help provide answers for believers and hope for the lost. We want to create a massive creation movement worldwide.

To Every People Group

As I travel globally, I still tremble with raw "Roman emotion" when I see the masses of unsaved people without hope. I have watched them light incense, bow before statues, chant memorized prayers, beat themselves, and worship multitudes of gods. And with the world's population edging closer to seven billion people, I see greater opportunities for missions today than ever before. Jesus commands us to get the Word out. So we prayerfully invite you to join us! Together we can dispel the hopelessness abroad with the hope of the glorious gospel of Jesus Christ.

Contributors

Dr. David Crandall

David has been involved in full-time ministry for nearly 40 years. For the last 12 years he has served as international director of Gospel Literature Services. He led this ministry to publish and translate Christian literature into 117 different languages, and he has ministered cross-culturally in 68 different countries. In 2006, he joined Answers in Genesis as the director of AiG World-Wide. Dr. Crandall currently serves on the executive board of the Association of Baptists for World Evangelism.

Brian H. Edwards

Brian was pastor of an evangelical church in a southwest London suburb for 29 years, and then president of the Fellowship of Independent Evangelical Churches from 1995–1998. He is the author of 16 books, and continues a ministry of writing and itinerant preaching and lecturing. His wife, Barbara, died in 1998; he has two sons and three granddaughters.

Dr. Danny R. Faulkner

Danny has a BS (math), MS (physics), MA and PhD (astronomy, Indiana University). He is full professor at the University of South Carolina–Lancaster, where he teaches physics and astronomy. He has published about two dozen papers in various astronomy and astrophysics journals.

Ken Ham

Ken is the president and CEO of Answers in Genesis (USA). He has authored several books, including the best-seller *The Lie: Evolution*. He is one of the most in-demand speakers in the United States and has a daily radio program called *Answers . . . with Ken Ham,* which is heard on over 850 stations in the United States and over 1,000 worldwide.

Ken has a BS in applied science (with an emphasis in environmental biology) from Queensland Institute of Technology in Australia. He also holds a diploma of education from the University of Queensland (a graduate qualification for sci nce teachers in the public schools in Australia). Ken has been awarded two honorary doctorates: a Doctor of Divinity (1997) from Temple Baptist College in Cincinnati, Ohio, and a Doctor of Literature (2004) from Liberty University in Lynchburg, Virginia.

Bodie Hodge

Bodie earned a BS and MS in mechanical engineering at Southern Illinois University at Carbondale in 1996 and 1998, respectively. His specialty was in materials science, working with advanced ceramic powder processing. He developed a new method of production of submicron titanium diboride.

Bodie accepted a teaching position as visiting instructor at Southern Illinois in 1998 and taught for two years. After this, he took a job working as a test engineer at Caterpillar's Peoria Proving Ground. Bodie currently works at Answers in Genesis (USA) as a speaker, writer, and researcher after working for three years in the Answers Correspondence Department.

Carl Kerby

Carl, who is one of AiG's most dynamic lecturers on the Book of Genesis, is a founding board member of AiG. In addition to being AiG's vice president for ministry relations, Carl conducts a number of faith-building AiG meetings each year. His passion is to proclaim the authority and accuracy of the Bible, and Carl does so in a highly effective way for all audiences. He is much in demand as a speaker among both young people and adults. A former air traffic controller at Chicago's busy O'Hare International Airport, Carl's thrilling testimony has been shared in churches throughout America.

Carl has several DVDs, including *Genesis: The Bottom Strip of the Christian Faith; Genesis — Today's Answer to Racism;* and *What Is the Best Evidence that God Created?*

Dr. Jason Lisle

Dr. Lisle received his PhD in astrophysics from the University of Colorado at Boulder. He specializes in solar astrophysics and has interests in the physics of relativity and biblical models of cosmology. Dr. Lisle has published a number of books, including *Taking Back Astronomy* and *The Ultimate Proof of Creation*, plus articles in both secular and creationist literature. He is a speaker, researcher, and writer for Answers in Genesis–USA.

Stacia McKeever

Stacia worked for Answers in Genesis for 12 years until leaving full-time work to raise her son She is currently involved in the Answers in Genesis VBS programs and other writing projects. She coauthored the "Answers for Kids" section in *Creation* magazine for several years and has written or coauthored a number of articles for *Creation* and the AiG website. She has a BS in biology and a BA in psychology from Clearwater Christian College.

Stacia has conducted hands-on workshops for young children around the United States for several years and has written curricula (*Beginnings, The Seven C's of History*) and workbooks for elementary-aged children and adults. Stacia has written for *The Godly Business Woman* and *Evangelizing Today's Child* and has researched and written copy for several Bible-themed calendars.

Dr. David Menton

Dr. Menton was an associate professor of anatomy at Washington University School of Medicine from 1966 to 2000 and has since become associate professor emeritus. He was a consulting editor in histology for *Stedman's Medical Dictionary*, a standard medical reference work.

David earned his PhD from Brown University in cell biology. He is a popular speaker and lecturer with Answers in Genesis (USA), showing complex design in anatomy with popular DVDs such as *The Hearing Ear and Seeing Eye* and *Fearfully and Wonderfully Made*. He also has an interest in the famous Scopes trial, which was a big turning point in the creation/evolution controversy in the USA in 1925.

Dr. Elizabeth Mitchell

Elizabeth earned her MD from Vanderbilt University School of Medicine and practiced medicine for seven years until she retired to be a stay-at-home mom. Her interest in ancient history strengthened when she began to homeschool her daughters. She desires to make history come alive and to correlate it with biblical history.

Dr. Tommy Mitchell

Tommy graduated with a BA with highest honors from the University of Tennessee–Knoxville in 1980 with a major in cell biology and a minor in biochemistry. He subsequently attended Vanderbilt University School of Medicine in Nashville, where he was granted an MD in 1984.

Dr. Mitchell's residency was completed at Vanderbilt University Affiliated Hospitals in 1987. He was board certified in internal medicine, with a medical practice in Gallatin, Tennessee (the city of his birth). In 1991, he was elected a Fellow of the American College of Physicians (FACP). Tommy became a full-time speaker, researcher, and writer with Answers in Genesis (USA) in 2006.

Dr. Terry Mortenson

Terry earned a BA in math at the University of Minnesota in 1975 and later went on to earn an MDiv in systematic theology at Trinity Evangelical Divinity School in 1992. His studies took him to the United Kingdom, where he earned a PhD in the history of geology at Coventry University.

Terry has done extensive research regarding the beliefs of the 19th century scriptural geologists. An accumulation of this research can be found in his book *The Great Turning Point*. Terry is currently working at Answer in Genesis (USA) as a speaker, writer, and researcher.

Larry Pierce

Larry is a retired programmer from Canada who did his undergraduate and graduate work at the University of Waterloo in mathematics. He greatly enjoys ancient history. This passion led him to spend five years translating *The Annals of the World* from Latin into English. He is also the creator of a sophisticated and powerful Bible program, The Online Bible.

Dr. Georgia Purdom

Georgia received her PhD in molecular genetics from Ohio State University in 2000. As an associate professor of biology, she completed five years of teaching and research at Mt. Vernon Nazarene University in Ohio before joining the staff at Answers in Genesis (USA).

Dr. Purdom has published papers in the *Journal of Neuroscience,* the *Journal of Bone and Mineral Research*, and the *Journal of Leukocyte Biology*. She is also a member of the Creation Research Society, American Society for Microbiology, and American Society for Cell Biology.

She is a peer reviewer for *Creation Research Society Quarterly*. Georgia has a keen interest in and keeps a close eye on the Intelligent Design movement.

Dr. Ron Rhodes

Ron has a ThM and ThD in systematic theology from Dallas Theological Seminary and is the president of Reasoning from the Scriptures Ministries. He has authored 35 books and is a popular conference speaker across the United States. During his schedule, he finds time to teach cult apologetics at several well-known seminaries.

Mike Riddle

As a former captain in the Marines, Mike earned a BS in mathematics and an MS in education. He has been involved in creation apologetics for many years and has been an adjunct lecturer with the Institute for Creation Research. Mike has a passion for teaching and he exhibits a great ability to bring topics down to a lay-audience level in his lectures.

Before becoming a Marine, Mike became a U.S. national champion in the track-and-field version of the pentathlon (in 1976). His best events were the 400 meters, javelin, long jump, and 1,500 meters. In his professional life, Mike worked for many years in the computer field with Microsoft (yes, he has met Bill Gates).

Dr. Andrew A. Snelling

Dr. Andrew Snelling received his PhD (geology) from the University of Sydney (Australia). After research experience in the mineral exploration industry, he was founding editor of the *Creation Ex Nihilo Technical Journal* (Australia). He also served as a professor of geology at the Institute for Creation Research. In 2007 he joined Answers in Genesis–USA as director of research. A member of several professional geological societies, Dr. Snelling has written numerous technical papers in geological journals and creationist publications.

Paul F. Taylor

Paul F. Taylor is the senior speaker for Answers in Genesis (UK/Europe). He holds a BSc in chemistry from Nottingham University and a masters in science education from Cardiff University. He is the author of several books, including *Cain and Abel, In the Beginning*, and *The Six Days of Genesis*. Paul and his wife, Geri, have five children between them.

Dr. A.J. Monty White

Formerly the chief executive of Answers in Genesis (UK/Europe), Dr. Monty White joined AiG after leaving the University of Wales in Cardiff where he had been a senior administrator for 28 years. He is a graduate of the University of Wales, obtaining his BS in chemistry in 1967 and his PhD for research in the field of gas kinetics in 1970. Monty spent two years investigating the optical and electrical properties of organic semiconductors before moving to Cardiff, where he joined the administration at the university there.

Monty is well known for his views on creation, having written numerous articles and pamphlets, as well as a number of books dealing with various aspects of creation, evolution, science, and the Bible. Monty has appeared on British television programs and has been interviewed on local and national radio about creation.

Dr. John Whitmore

John received a BS in geology from Kent State University, an MS in geology from the Institute for Creation Research, and a PhD in biology with paleontology emphasis from Loma Linda University. Currently an associate professor of geology, he is active in teaching and research at Cedarville University. Dr. Whitmore serves on the board of Creation Research Science Education Foundation located in Columbus, Ohio, and he is also a member of the Creation Research Society and the Geological Society of America.

Index

Josephus, 58, 171–172, 256–257, 260, 296, 300, 307
Judaism, 171, 173
Jurassic, 10, 343
knucklewalkers, 91
lament, 271
laud, 45
lefthanded, 67–68, 70–71
legend, 224
leukocyte, 364
liberal, 31, 116–117, 279, 281
limestone, 91, 240–241
limit, 16, 163–164
limitation, 164
linguistic, 93, 300
Linnaeus, 145
lithification, 230–232
lithium, 107
longevity, 165–166
Lucifer, 185, 265–267, 272
Lucy, 83, 90–91
luminaries, 267
lunar, 254
LXX, 44, 60, 221, 297
lycopods, 347
Maccabees, 221
magnetic, 50, 99, 106, 146–147
magnetism, 200, 362
magnitude, 114, 236
mammalian, 136
mandible, 90
manuscript, 58, 112, 286
Masoretic, 42, 44–45
materialism, 195–197, 205–206
mathematical, 71, 199, 256, 326, 330, 337
Maxwell, James Clerk, 146
Mayans, 45, 255
Mayr, Ernst, 119, 210
measurements, 30, 85, 125, 253, 271
mechanism, 73, 136, 162, 164, 184
mechanistic, 70

Mediterranean, 239
Mentuhotep, 256–257
Mercury, 327, 335
Mesopotamia, 302
Messiah, 160, 188, 224–225
meteorites, 50
meteors, 267
methodology, 93
Methuselah, 44, 61, 159–160, 167
Metzger, Bruce, 178
Miautso, 307
microbes, 140, 231, 237
microbiology, 364
microorganisms, 136, 344
mineralogy, 112
minerals, 350
Mississippian, 302, 349
Missoula, 235–237
mistranslated, 288
mistranslation, 291
Mizraim, 255, 262
modification, 120
molecules, 65–66, 68, 126, 205, 210–211, 330
mollusks, 242, 351
monopole, 106–107
mountain, 132, 229, 270, 352
mudflow, 234–235
mudstones, 233
Muratorian, 174
mutated, 76, 81, 164
Nabopolassar, 254
naturalism, 135, 138
naturalistic, 47, 69, 71–72, 137, 204, 210–212, 229
Neandertals, 91–93
neanderthalensis, 91
Neferhotep, 258, 263
Nefrubity, 260
Nennius, 45, 306–307
neocatastrophist, 118
Neogene, 343

The New Answers Book 1

KEN HAM, GENERAL EDITOR

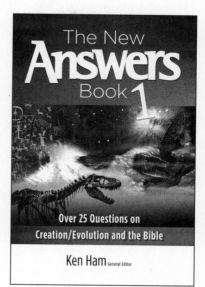

In today's world, Christians find challenges to their faith every day. This new resource from Answers in Genesis gives answers for some of the most difficult questions that modern Christians face. An impressive list of reputable creation scientists join author Ken Ham to answer the top 25 questions on creation/evolution scientifically, biblically, and logically. Christians of all ages face challenges to their faith from those who emphasize evolution and millions-of-years thinking. This resource will provide you with a ready answer!

- Is there really a God?
- Did God really take six days to create everything?
- What about evolution?
- Does archaeology support the Bible?
- What about ETs and UFOs?
- Was there really an ice age?
- Where did the races come from?

6 x 9 • paperback • 384 pages • $14.99
ISBN: 978-0-89051-509-9

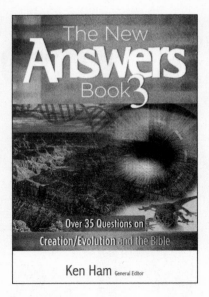

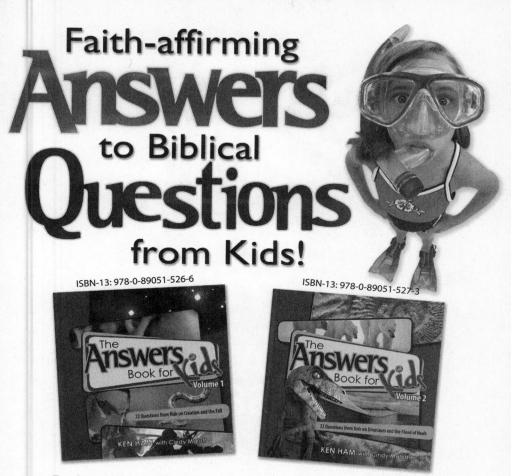
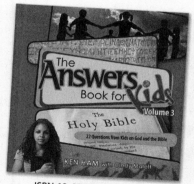

CREATION MUSEUM
Prepare to believe.

The Creation Museum presents a fully engaging "walk through history." Designed by a former Universal Studios exhibit director, this state-of-the-art 70,000 square foot museum brings the pages of the Bible to life with realistic murals and scenery, computer-generated visual effects, dozens of exotic animals and life-sized people, and dinosaur animatronics. Our special-effects theater, complete with misty sea breezes and rumbling seats, adds adventure to family-sized fun, right from the beginning!

For ticket and exhibit information, please visit us at
creationmuseum.org.

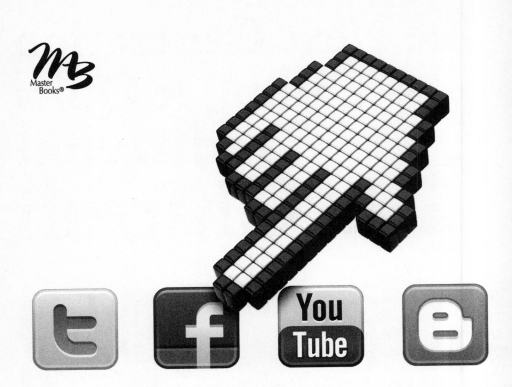

Connect with Master Books®

masterbooks.net   An imprint of New Leaf Publishing Group

facebook.com/**masterbooks**

twitter.com/**masterbooks4u**

youtube.com/**nlpgvideo**

nlpgblogs.com
nlpgvideos.com

join us at **Creation**Conversations.com